D0088268

LIBERALISM AND THE
ECONOMIC ORDER

LIBERALISM AND THE ECONOMIC ORDER

Edited by

**Ellen Frankel Paul, Fred D. Miller, Jr.,
and Jeffrey Paul**

CAMBRIDGE
UNIVERSITY PRESS

Published by the Press Syndicate of the University of Cambridge
The Pitt Building, Trumpington Street, Cambridge CB2 1RP, England
40 West 20th Street, New York, NY 10011, USA
10 Stamford Road, Oakleigh, Melbourne, Victoria 3166, Australia

Copyright © 1993 Social Philosophy and Policy Foundation

First published 1993

Printed in the United States of America

Library of Congress Cataloging-in-Publication Data

Liberalism and the economic order / edited by Ellen Frankel Paul,
Fred D. Miller, Jr., and Jeffrey Paul.   p.   cm.
Includes bibliographical references and index.
ISBN 0-521-45724-6 (pbk.)
1. Europe, Eastern — Economic policy — 1989- .   2. Former Soviet
republics — Economic policy.   3. Post-communism — Europe, Eastern.
4. Post-communism — Former Soviet republics.
I. Paul, Ellen Frankel.   II. Miller, Fred Dycus, 1944–
III. Paul, Jeffrey.
HC244.L468   1993
338.947–dc20   93-3509
CIP

ISBN 0-521-45724-6 paperback

The essays in this book have also been published,
without introduction and index, in the semiannual journal
Social Philosophy & Policy, Volume 10, Number 2,
which is available by subscription.

CONTENTS

INTRODUCTION

The fall of Communism, and the economic devastation that system bequeathed, leave the people of Eastern Europe and the former Soviet Union facing an uncertain economic future. The collapse of the totalitarian order means that many countries of the region must deal with political instability as well. The breakdown of order has aroused old enmities and has given rein to ethnic conflicts of the sort currently raging in Bosnia and in many of the former Soviet republics.

The antidote widely prescribed for the ills of the region is liberalism, conceived as democratic politics and free-market economics. It is assumed that the East should solve its problems by emulating the West. Yet the West is not monolithic; there are a number of models available to reformers in the East. It may be that no single political-economic system can succeed in bringing stability and prosperity to all the formerly Communist countries. As reformers in each country pursue their own solutions, they must take into account their people's distinctive history and cultural traditions.

To understand the process of transition as it unfolds, we must answer a number of questions. What are the attitudes of Easterners toward capitalism, and how can these be modified? What institutional obstacles exist to reform, and which of the institutional remnants of the old order must be changed or discarded if reform is to proceed? What new institutions must be introduced? More broadly, what model should reformers follow in making the transition to new political and economic systems? Is democratic capitalism the system they should embrace, or does that system have its own flaws and inconsistencies? The essays in this volume address these questions, offering a variety of perspectives on the transition process.

Three economic systems—other than the purely free market—are commonly offered as models for the newly liberated countries of Eastern Europe to adopt: market socialism, the Swedish system, and the German social market economy. In the opening essay of this collection, "The Social Market Economy," Norman Barry examines these models, focusing on the last. Theorists of the social market economy, he notes, endorse the market's primary role in the allocation of resources, but they reject laissez-faire capitalism. They argue that, without some central control of the economy, a free market will lead to monopolies and cartels which ultimately destroy the exchange system, and that without some public welfare arrangements the market will lack moral authority. Barry takes a historical look at the social market economy as it was implemented in

Germany and argues that only some of its features are appropriate for the countries of Eastern Europe. He maintains that these countries would do well to adopt the social market economy's system of property rights, its sound currency policy, and its civil and commercial law. At the same time, he argues that they should forgo the welfare schemes associated with it — schemes which tend to overburden the market and which the fragile economies of the region cannot afford to implement. Barry concludes with an assessment of the prospects for successful liberalization of the post-Communist economies, suggesting that the results are likely to vary. He predicts that those countries with the closest ties to the European liberal tradition — former East Germany, Poland, Czechoslovakia, and Hungary — will probably be able to implement the social market economy, though they will need to be wary of political pressures from special interests that could undermine the market. Other countries, especially those of the former Soviet Union, will need to establish stable political orders before undertaking any experiments in economic design.

John Gray agrees that some of the post-Communist countries may succeed in adopting a version of the social market economy, but argues that many others are unlikely to import Western economic or political institutions. In "From Post-Communism to Civil Society: The Reemergence of History and the Decline of the Western Model," Gray contends that the downfall of Communism heralds a return to traditional ethnic and religious conflicts — a "reemergence" of Europe's history after a totalitarian interlude. The task that faces the people of Eastern Europe and the former Soviet Union is the establishment of the institutions of civil society: a stable legal order and a system of private property and freedom of contract. The renewal of traditional conflicts in the region makes this task especially difficult; it means that stable institutions are not likely to emerge spontaneously, as they did in some Western countries, but may have to be imposed by fiat. The model most relevant to the countries of the former Soviet bloc may be that of the East Asian market economies, where modernization and the shift to free markets took place under authoritarian political regimes — regimes which intervened strategically in economic affairs in order to protect and nurture fledgling industries. In any case, Gray concludes, each country is likely to follow its own path, drawing on its own pre-Communist traditions as it struggles to establish order and pursue economic growth.

Gray examines the issue of ethnic strife as an obstacle facing those countries currently in transition; the next three essays in this volume deal with other obstacles. In "Asymmetrical Reciprocity in Market Exchange: Implications for Economies in Transition," James M. Buchanan explores the extent to which certain negative attitudes toward trade can inhibit change. Buchanan notes that Westerners understand, at least implicitly, that there are gains to be made from trade, and that in a free market both parties to an exchange share in these gains. In the East, however, this understanding is missing. Decades under Communist rule have shaped people's thinking about trade, and the differences in attitudes and behavior between East and West can, Buchanan suggests, be explained in terms of economic theory. In the West, the buyer is typically at an advantage: he offers money to the seller in exchange for goods or services, and money is more generally desired than other goods. The result is that sellers of goods adopt a deferential attitude toward buyers; they tend to treat potential buyers with courtesy and to advertise in order to attract their business. In the East, this deferential attitude is wholly absent. Under a centrally controlled economy, where goods are rationed, buyers lack any advantage. They still have money to exchange for goods, but money is not enough; in order to complete a transaction, they must also pay some nonmoney price—for example, obtaining bureaucratic approval or waiting in long lines. Chronic shortages of goods, and the absence of any profit motive, mean that sellers have no incentives to cater to the needs of potential buyers—there will always be plenty of others eager to buy. With this kind of background, Buchanan contends, it is no wonder that the countries of Eastern Europe and the former Soviet Union are experiencing a difficult transition. The absence of a tradition of entrepreneurship, moreover, presents a further difficulty, as those who once focused their energies on obtaining bureaucratic favors must now turn their attention to discovering and exploiting opportunities for production.

Like Buchanan, Svetozar Pejovich believes that changes brought about by Communism will make a transition to free markets extremely difficult. In "Institutions, Nationalism, and the Transition Process in Eastern Europe," Pejovich explores three factors which are likely to obstruct institutional change. First, the Communist dictatorships of the region subverted the rule of law to the will of the ruling elite, seriously eroding the people's confidence in their institutions and leaving them with little hope of being treated justly. Second, Communist rule strengthened the old ethos, with its emphasis on national pride and distrust of outsiders—an ethos which served as a refuge from the harsh conditions brought on by years of failed central planning. Finally, the intellectual tradition of the region, which prizes family and community above the individual, lacks an understanding of classical-liberal philosophy or economics. This means that the people of the region will need to come to grips with the theory of the free market, even as they attempt to implement it in practice. At the same time, they must guard against the dangerous and divisive influence of nationalism. Pejovich concludes that the transition from centrally planned economies to markets will depend on the ability of new leaders to create conditions under which capitalist institutions can evolve spontaneously, become incorporated into the old ethos, and be voluntarily accepted (rather than imposed by fiat).

While Buchanan and Pejovich examine background conditions which are likely to inhibit the transition process, William H. Riker and David

L. Weimer look at problems that may arise out of the process itself. In "The Economic and Political Liberalization of Socialism: The Fundamental Problem of Property Rights," Riker and Weimer focus on the central task of liberalization: the establishment of secure private property rights as a necessary condition for growth. They sketch the historical and cultural factors that must be overcome: ancient ethnic hostilities and the long experience of collective ownership of land and other resources. These factors, together with political instability, are likely to lead to a climate of uncertainty—a climate that will tend to discourage many forms of needed investment. The resulting poor economic performance during the period of transition may lead to demands for redistribution or for more gradual reforms. This, in turn, may lead to the undermining of property rights, and to further poor economic performance. The net result may be an overall lessening of support for the transition, as various interest groups voice their objections and attempt to manipulate the process. The problem facing the countries pursuing reform, then, is to maintain a liberal political scene—one open to dissent and debate—while at the same time pushing through economic changes which are likely to be painful, at least in the short run. In the end, Riker and Weimer conclude, social science offers little guidance about the course the transition will, or should, follow; the transition does, however, offer social science a unique "natural experiment" for studying the growth and evolution of institutions.

An underlying theme of Riker and Weimer's essay is the relationship between economic liberalism and political liberalism, and the next four essays in this collection deal with that same relationship, each from a different perspective. In "Democracy, Markets, and the Legal Order: Notes on the Nature of Politics in a Radically Liberal Society," Don Lavoie argues that the demise of one radical ideology—socialism—makes room for the development of another—radical liberalism. Lavoie notes that liberalism, in its classical sense, stood for two ideals: democracy and markets. Yet these ideals have never meshed well in the experience of Western democratic capitalism. There has always been a perceived tension: if more decisions are made democratically, less will be left to the market; if more decisions are left to the market, there will be less need for political discourse. This apparent tension seems to mean that a radical liberalism would have to sacrifice one of its ideals; they cannot both be taken to their logical extremes. Lavoie contends that those who hold this view are mistaken, because they fail to understand the nature of democracy. He sketches a conception of democracy as openness—the kind of openness that was crushed under Communism and that began to reappear with *glasnost*. He conceives of a democratic society not in terms of the kinds of elections it holds, but in terms of the manner in which the give and take of public discourse is allowed to shape social institutions. On this view, markets and democratic processes are not opposed but related. Both are characterized by a complex web of voluntary interpersonal relationships that can lead to benefits for all who take part in them. The project of advancing a radical liberalism turns out to be potentially viable after all, and Lavoie concludes by looking at debate among some modern libertarians over how far that project can be taken.

Russell Hardin's essay, "Liberalism: Political and Economic," continues the exploration, begun by Lavoie, of the compatibility of the two strands of liberalism. Hardin takes as his starting point the development of the two strands, contrasting a consciously designed political liberalism with a spontaneously evolved economic liberalism. Political liberalism, he notes, had its origins in the efforts of eighteenth-century political theorists to find ways of easing religious conflict and promoting tolerance. Economic liberalism, on the other hand, developed slowly through the workings of custom and the common law, culminating in a system of property rights and rules of contract. Hardin accounts for these differences in origin in terms of the kinds of problems the two liberalisms serve to address: issues of tolerance addressed by political liberalism are collective in nature, while the interactions regulated by economic liberalism typically involve pairs of trading partners or small groups engaged in joint ventures. The joining of the two strands of liberalism in Western democratic-capitalist states results in a complex whole that may not, in the end, be consistent and coherent. Yet the two strands do seem to be united in their justification, as conditions necessary for the promotion of well-being. Some early theorists, such as Hobbes and Locke, separated the two liberalisms conceptually, according to the kind of well-being they promoted: economic liberalism was thought strictly to promote material well-being, while political liberalism was thought to promote nonmaterial or spiritual well-being. But Hardin argues that the dividing line between material and nonmaterial well-being is difficult to draw, especially in modern societies, where individuals often turn to the marketplace for the satisfaction of at least some of their important spiritual needs. It may be that liberalism — political and economic — is a conceptually coherent theory after all.

Both Lavoie and Hardin propose that free markets are the proper economic complement to democratic politics, but some theorists have argued that socialism is more consistent with democracy. In "Socialism as the Extension of Democracy," Richard J. Arneson evaluates the view that, in modern societies, the strict application of democratic principles entails a commitment to a socialist reconstruction of society. Arneson opposes this view, on normative and interpretive grounds: he argues that democratic procedures are not a suitable moral basis for fundamental social criticism, and that forcing socialist critiques and proposals into the mold of democratic theory distorts their character. The key value underlying socialism, Arneson suggests, is not democracy but a principled opposition to exploitation; and a central aim of his project is to clarify exploitation's nature. To oppose exploitation, he says, is to view as undesirable the fact that some people take advantage of undeserved assets in ways that improve their position relative to others. On this interpretation, socialism is a means for achieving a radical egalitarian brand of distributive justice — and not, as on the democratic view, a means for promoting collective self-determination. Arneson concludes by noting that the Communist regimes of the former Soviet bloc did not embody either view of socialism, and that the collapse of those regimes should not be taken as discrediting socialist theory.

Daniel M. Hausman agrees that the downfall of Communism does not necessarily herald the failure of socialism, and he suggests that reformers in the countries of Eastern Europe and the former Soviet Union should be cautious about embracing free-market economic systems. His contribution to this collection, "Liberalism, Welfare Economics, and Freedom," is an attempt to illuminate some problems facing reformers by exploring the foundations of political liberalism and its relation to economic theory. The case for free markets and limited government rests largely on contemporary economic theory, which assumes that people are rational and self-interested, and that they act to increase their own welfare. But Hausman argues that concerns with equality and autonomy are more central to liberalism than are concerns with welfare, and consequently that contemporary welfare economics is not particularly liberal. Nevertheless, liberals can support market reforms for a number of reasons, not all of which have to do with welfare. Hausman sketches three sorts of arguments that could support such reforms: the liberal can support markets because they make people better off, because they enhance individual independence and freedom, and because they shore up political liberty by limiting the power of government. Hausman maintains, however, that the central concerns of liberalism provide justification for government regulation and intervention in markets. Reformers should recognize the role of government in mitigating the inequalities in wealth and power that markets tend to cause — inequalities which can undermine individual autonomy.

Hausman's essay touches on a central question facing citizens of the countries currently undergoing liberalization, the question of the proper role of the state. The final four essays in this collection deal with various aspects of this question, theorizing about what sorts of policies and institutions best promote freedom and justice. Peter C. Ordeshook looks specifically at the constitutional arrangements appropriate to a democratic state. In "Some Rules of Constitutional Design," Ordeshook notes that political scientists have been able to give little practical guidance in the construction of stable democratic institutions. The reason for this shortcoming, he suggests, is that they have failed to understand how constitutions can become self-enforcing documents. Political scientists have generally assumed that constitutions function as social contracts, in which people agree to surrender certain powers to their government, in return for guarantees of security. But this view gives no account of how social contracts are enforced. Ordeshook suggests an alternative view of constitutions as coordinating devices that allow societies to achieve stable outcomes when making collective decisions about controversial issues. He sets out a number of guidelines for the drafting of constitutions, showing how a state can achieve stability by, for example, instituting a separation of powers; avoiding lists of utopian policy goals (universal employment, guaranteed health care, and so on); and establishing fundamental rights (to free expression and freedom of religion, among others) which serve to remove certain issues from the arena of political debate. He emphasizes the importance of limiting the functions of the state so as to reduce the potential for the abuse of state power – a prospect which is especially ominous in Eastern Europe and the former Soviet republics, where ethnic majorities are likely to attempt to use such power to exercise control over minorities.

The functions of the state, and its responsibilities toward ethnic minorities, are also the focus of "The Morality of Inclusion," Allen Buchanan's contribution to this volume. Buchanan considers whether there are principles reformers must follow when they deliberate about redrawing political boundaries on the basis of nationality or economic advantage. He asks whether there are any general moral obligations to include others in political arrangements, obligations which would place limits on groups wishing to form a new state or secede from an old one. To answer the question, he sketches two opposing conceptions of the function of the state and of the scope and nature of justice. The first conception views the state as a mechanism for enforcing rules of interaction among those who choose, on the grounds of self-interest, to take part in a cooperative scheme. The second conception views the state as a device for enforcing basic rights or principles of justice which apply to all individuals, independently of their capacity to be net contributors in this or that cooperative scheme. According to the first conception, there are no obligations of inclusion; according to the second, there are at least some such obligations. Buchanan goes on to make a case for the second conception, arguing that those who advocate reform must take into account their obligations toward those at risk of being excluded from political arrangements – arrangements which, in the context of the current upheaval in much of the former Soviet bloc, could be essential to securing the future of the people of the region.

Two other important issues facing reformers are the institution of tax policies and the formulation of regulatory measures designed to protect the interests of workers and the public. In "A New Contractarian View of Tax and Regulatory Policy in the Emerging Market Economies," Robert H. Frank proposes a way of thinking about these issues that departs from standard Western assumptions and practices. He begins by noting that scholars in the contractarian tradition have attempted to explain laws and a variety of other institutions by asking what constraints rational, self-interested actors might deliberately impose upon themselves. While this approach explains many of our laws and institutions, it cannot, Frank argues, explain them all. A more general version of contractarianism is needed, based on a characterization of preferences that differs from the self-interest model and that is theoretically and empirically more plausible. The key feature of Frank's version of contractarianism is that it takes into account positional preferences—the desire of individuals for a better relative position in the distribution of wealth and other advantages throughout society. In an unregulated market, such preferences can lead to undesirable effects; for example, they can cause workers to choose jobs that pay high wages but entail higher than average safety risks. Workers may choose such jobs in hopes of improving their economic position relative to others, but as more and more workers make similar choices, their overall positions relative to one another do not change. In terms of position, they are no better off than they were before; yet in terms of safety risks, they are much worse off. To deal with such problems, Western governments have resorted to cumbersome workplace safety regulations, but Frank suggests that a tax on positional consumption—consumption designed to improve one's position relative to others—would be simpler and more effective. He concludes with further discussion of how tax policy can replace direct regulation as a means of achieving desired outcomes, illustrating his position with a description of a scheme for taxing pollution.

The final essay in this volume deals again with the regulatory functions of the state, and with institutional arrangements for carrying out those functions. In "Associations and Democracy," Joshua Cohen and Joel Rogers look at the role that associations can play in helping to devise and implement regulations and to achieve compliance with them. The associations discussed in the essay—trade unions, employer associations, citizen lobbies, and other private groups—are generally thought to be capable of either retarding or advancing progress toward egalitarian political reform. Cohen and Rogers argue that the activities of such groups can be directed in positive ways, and they recommend specific changes in government policy which would affect the status and powers of associations, allowing them to take over certain regulatory functions. Associations could provide the state with information, aiding in the definition of problems to be addressed by governmental action. They could assist in enforcement of regulations and, in so doing, could help remove a constraint on political debate by countering the common reservation that certain policies, while desirable, are unenforceable. On the other hand, there are serious objections that can be raised against the idea of giving associations governmental power. Associations might represent the special interests of their leaders, rather than the interests of their members. They might abuse their powers to enhance their own status and entrench their position. Moreover, in the absence of clear guidelines, the powers delegated to associations are bound to be vague, and their exercise danger-ously open to discretion. Cohen and Rogers address each of these concerns, maintaining that a well-designed system of institutions could harness the energies of associations while avoiding the pitfalls that often accompany the delegation of governmental authority.

The countries of Eastern Europe and the former Soviet Union face a double challenge: to establish political order and to institute free markets. By exploring the nature of liberalism and the various strategies for liberal reform, the thirteen essays in this volume offer insights into how these challenges can be met.

ACKNOWLEDGMENTS

This volume could not have been produced without the help of a number of individuals at the Social Philosophy and Policy Center, Bowling Green State University. Among them are Mary Dilsaver, Terrie Weaver, and Maureen Kelley.

The editors would like to extend special thanks to Executive Manager Kory Swanson, for offering invaluable administrative support; to Publication Specialist Tamara Sharp, for attending to innumerable day-to-day details of the book's preparation; and to Managing Editor Harry Dolan, for providing dedicated assistance throughout the editorial and production process.

CONTRIBUTORS

Norman Barry is Professor of Politics at the University of Buckingham in the United Kingdom. In 1989–90, he was a Visiting Scholar at the Social Philosophy and Policy Center in Bowling Green, Ohio. His books include *Hayek's Social and Economic Philosophy* (1979), *An Introduction to Modern Political Theory* (1981, 1989), *The New Right* (1987), *Welfare* (1990), and *The Morality of Business Enterprise* (1991). His research interests include political philosophy, political economy, and business ethics.

John Gray was educated at Exeter College, Oxford University, where he received his B.A., M.A., and D.Phil. degrees. Since 1976 he has been a Fellow of Jesus College, Oxford. His books include *Mill on Liberty: A Defence* (1983), *Hayek on Liberty* (1984, 1986), *Liberalism* (1986), *Liberalisms: Essays in Political Philosophy* (1989), and *Post-Liberalism: Studies in Political Thought* (1993). He has been Visiting Professor in Government at Harvard University; Visiting Distinguished Professor in Political Economy at the Murphy Institute, Tulane University; and Visiting Professor in Philosophy at Bowling Green State University. Much of his research over the past several years has been conducted during periods of residence as Stranahan Distinguished Research Fellow at the Social Philosophy and Policy Center, Bowling Green State University. He is currently working on a history of political thought.

James M. Buchanan is Advisory General Director of the Center for Study of Public Choice, and Harris University Professor at George Mason University in Fairfax, Virginia. He is the holder of the Nobel Prize in Economic Sciences, 1986. He received his B.A. from Middle Tennessee State College in 1940, his M.S. from the University of Tennessee in 1941, and his Ph.D. from the University of Chicago in 1948. His major works include *Explorations into Constitutional Economics* (1989), *Economics: Between Predictive Science and Moral Philosophy* (1987), *The Reason of Rules* (with Geoffrey Brennan, 1985), *Freedom in Constitutional Contract* (1978), *The Limits of Liberty* (1975), and *The Calculus of Consent* (with Gordon Tullock, 1962).

Svetozar Pejovich is Rex B. Grey Professor of Economics at Texas A&M University. He is the author of *The Economics of Property Rights: Towards a Theory of Comparative Economic Systems* (1990), and the editor of *Economic and Philosophical Foundations of Capitalism* (1982) and *Socialism: Institutional, Philosophical, and Economic Issues* (1987).

CONTRIBUTORS

William H. Riker is Wilson Professor of Political Science, Emeritus, at the University of Rochester. He is the author of several works on positive political theory, including *The Theory of Political Coalitions* (1963), *Liberalism against Populism: The Confrontation between the Theory of Democracy and the Theory of Social Choice* (1983), and *The Art of Political Manipulation* (1986), as well as a number of essays on the theory of property rights.

David L. Weimer is Professor of Political Science and Public Policy at the University of Rochester. From 1985 to 1989, he was editor of the *Journal of Policy Analysis and Management*. His recent books include *Policy Analysis and Economics* (1991), *Policy Analysis: Concepts and Practice* (with Aidan Vining, 1989, 1992), and *Responding to International Oil Crises* (with George Horwich, 1988).

Don Lavoie is Associate Professor of Economics at the Center for the Study of Market Processes, George Mason University. He is author of *Rivalry and Central Planning: The Socialist Calculation Debate Reconsidered* and *National Economic Planning: What is Left?*, which are critiques of Marxian and market-socialist theories of central planning; and he is editor of *Economics and Hermeneutics*, a collection of essays on the philosophy of science.

Russell Hardin is Mellon Foundation Professor of Political Science and Philosophy at the University of Chicago. He is currently working on issues in ethics and public life and on the foundations of rational choice and social order. He is author of *Morality within the Limits of Reason* (1988) and *Collective Action* (1982), and past editor of *Ethics: An International Journal of Social, Political, and Legal Philosophy*. During the 1992–93 academic year, he was a Visiting Scholar at the Russell Sage Foundation in New York.

Richard J. Arneson is Professor and Chair of the Department of Philosophy at the University of California, San Diego. He has been an associate editor of the journal *Ethics* since 1986. His recent work has explored contemporary theories of justice and the ethics of socialism. He was educated at Brown University and the University of California, Berkeley.

Daniel M. Hausman is Professor of Philosophy at the University of Wisconsin–Madison. He is co-editor of the journal *Economics and Philosophy* and editor of the anthology *The Philosophy of Economics* (1984). He is the author of *Capital, Profits, and Prices: An Essay in the Philosophy of Economics* (1981), *The Inexact and Separate Science of Economics* (1992), and *Essays on Philosophy and Economic Methodology* (1992).

Peter C. Ordeshook is Professor of Political Science at the California Institute of Technology. He received his B.S. degree from the Massachusetts

Institute of Technology in 1964 and his Ph.D. from the University of Rochester in 1969. A member of the American Academy of Arts and Sciences, he is the editor of *Game Theory and Political Science* (1978), and the author of *An Introduction to Positive Political Theory* (with W. H. Riker, 1973), *Game Theory and Political Theory: An Introduction* (1986), *The Balance of Power: Stability in International Systems* (with E. M. S. Niou and G. F. Rose, 1989), and *A Political Theory Primer* (1992). In addition, he has published extensively on models of election systems, on the application of game theory to political science, on the analysis of balance-of-power and collective-security systems in international politics, and on the general character of cooperation in political systems.

Allen Buchanan is Professor of Philosophy at the University of Arizona. He has written numerous articles in ethics, epistemology, political philosophy, bioethics, and other areas of applied ethics, and is the author of *Marx and Justice: The Radical Critique of Liberalism* (1982), *Ethics, Efficiency, and the Market* (1985), *Deciding for Others* (with Dan W. Brock, 1989), and *Secession: The Morality of Political Divorce from Fort Sumter to Lithuania and Quebec* (1991).

Robert H. Frank currently holds a joint appointment as Professor of Economics in Cornell University's Johnson Graduate School of Management and as Goldwin Smith Professor of Economics, Ethics, and Public Policy in Cornell's College of Arts and Sciences, where he has taught since 1972. He received his B.S. in mathematics from Georgia Tech in 1966, his M.A. in statistics from the University of California at Berkeley in 1971, and his Ph.D. in economics in 1972, also from U.C. Berkeley. He has published on a variety of subjects, including price and wage discrimination, public-utility pricing, the measurement of unemployment spell lengths, and the distributional consequences of direct foreign investment. For the past several years, his research has focused on rivalry and cooperation in economic and social behavior. His recent books include *Choosing the Right Pond: Human Behavior and the Quest for Status* (1985), *Passions within Reason: The Strategic Role of the Emotions* (1988), and *Microeconomics and Behavior* (1991).

Joshua Cohen is Professor of Philosophy and Political Science at the Massachusetts Institute of Technology. He is co-author (with Joel Rogers) of *On Democracy* (1983), *Inequity and Intervention* (1986), and *Rules of the Game* (1986).

Joel Rogers is Professor of Law, Political Science, and Sociology at the University of Wisconsin–Madison. He is co-author (with Joshua Cohen) of articles on political theory and American politics published in *The Canadian Journal of Philosophy*, *New Left Review*, *The Nation*, *Boston Review*, *Monthly Review*, *Socialist Register*, and Japan's *Economist* magazine.

THE SOCIAL MARKET ECONOMY

By Norman Barry

Introduction

The collapse of Communism in the regimes in Eastern Europe and the former Soviet Union has brought forth a plethora of alternative political and economic models for the reorganization of those societies. The vacuum that has been left could be regarded as an ideal laboratory for the testing of competing theories, and the temptations to experiment with the more benign forms of constructivist rationalism[1] are likely to prove irresistible. If liberal capitalism is to be successfully created, it will clearly not have the same biography as it has had in the Western European and Anglo-American countries, where its emergence was the result of slow evolution: often its appearance and survival were due to a quite fortuitous combination of circumstances. In those countries it was not the result of any deliberate democratic choice but the outcome of a happy confluence of traditional rules and customary practices, and the participants in them had little idea of the form of the system that they were creating. Indeed, ideological sanctification was almost an afterthought, and democratic approval was belated and in most cases not enthusiastic.[2] Britain was a liberal capitalist society, and possessed the necessary body of private law, some time before the franchise was significantly democratized (which did not occur until 1867). It is, of course, recent theoretical and empirical research which has revealed that the political choice mechanisms that developed haphazardly after the success of the market are a potential threat to it.[3]

[1] "Constructivist rationalism" designates that style of thinking which supposes that it is possible to impose on a social system a pattern of social and economic organization which is derived from a notion of human reason uninformed by experience and the lessons of tradition. It is most clearly exemplified in systems of centralized economic planning which dispense with the price signals provided by spontaneous markets. Constructivist rationalism presupposes that a single mind or institution is capable of organizing the necessarily dispersed knowledge in society. Its most articulate critic is F. A. Hayek, who does not limit his critique to rationalistic economic planning but includes refutations of attempts to design whole legal systems from *a priori* principles. See his *Rules and Order*, vol. 1 of *Law, Legislation, and Liberty* (London: Routledge and Kegan Paul, 1973).

[2] Though, of course, the U.S. has been, with the exception of slavery, a liberal democracy since 1789.

[3] James Buchanan's innovative works are especially relevant here. See his *The Limits of Liberty* (Chicago: University of Chicago Press, 1975), and *Fiscal Theory and Political Economy* (Chapel Hill: University of North Carolina Press, 1960); James Buchanan and Gordon Tullock, *The Calculus of Consent* (Ann Arbor: University of Michigan Press, 1962); and James

© 1993 Social Philosophy and Policy Foundation. Printed in the USA.

The former Communist countries are not the lucky beneficiaries of a spontaneous order but the penniless inheritors of a past experiment in constructivism. A number—for example, Poland, Czechoslovakia, and Hungary—can attempt to recapture an order of either incipient or developed market capitalism that was shattered by Communism, and another, the former East Germany, can live for a while almost parasitically off the economic and intellectual capital of its partner in a natural but unexpected political marriage. But the immediate task for them all must be to create, almost in a "bootstraps pulling" manner, not merely new economic arrangements but also the set of intermediary or auxiliary social institutions of civil society which are essential for the maintenance and reproduction of economic order. Given the variety of cultural traditions on which Communism was imposed, there can be no one universal panacea for the problems it has bequeathed, though there are permanent constraints within which all must operate.

One must assume that the "market versus the state" debate is over. The immense calculational (and ultimately epistemic) problems involved in a socialist order which treats the economy as one giant firm have been demonstrated many times as a matter of theory[4] and these theories were corroborated with grisly repetition in reality. One must also dismiss the once fashionable convergence thesis,[5] i.e., the claim that fundamental similarities in the production problems that confront market capitalist and centrally planned economies will generate some economic hybrid that embodies the virtues of each. But there was no such convergence, rather the gradual admission from socialists that their fundamentally different planning method failed dismally in comparison to the market in the solution of the same problems that confront all economies. Of these, the most important are scarcity and the efficient allocation of resources. Without an internal price mechanism to indicate scarcities, planning authorities were compelled to rely on the international market to provide the necessary economic information. In any case, resources were not primarily allocated to satisfy consumer preferences but simply to fulfill the arbitrary dictates of political rulers. Shortages of basic goods were therefore an endemic feature of life under planned systems.

The absence of entrepreneurship in planned economies, and the inadequacy of all the surrogates (such as the replacement of profit-seeking

---

Buchanan and Richard Wagner, *Democracy in Deficit* (New York: Academic Press, 1977). See also Gordon Tullock, *The Vote Motive* (London: Institute of Economic Affairs, 1976).

[4] Ludwig von Mises, "Economic Calculation in the Socialist Commonwealth," in *Collectivist Economic Planning*, ed. Friedrich von Hayek (London: Routledge and Kegan Paul, 1935), pp. 87–130; Hayek, "Socialist Calculation," in Hayek, *Individualism and Economic Order* (London: Routledge and Kegan Paul, 1948), pp. 119–208; Don Lavoie, *Rivalry and Central Planning: The Socialist Calculation Debate Reconsidered* (Cambridge: Cambridge University Press, 1985).

[5] See John Kenneth Galbraith, *The New Industrial State* (Boston: Houghton Mifflin, 1978).

private agents by paid managers) for this essential mechanism of coordination that were tried, revealed that the market and the plan are radically different types of economic organization. Furthermore, there is no evidence that the collectively owned industrial systems overcame that "alienation" between the worker and his product that was alleged to be a feature of private enterprise.

Yet the triumph of the market over the state is not an automatic endorsement of all the market systems now prevailing in the Anglo-American portions of the West, nor an intellectual license for their immediate transplantation to former Communist regimes, leaving aside the cultural factors that may inhibit the success of any proposed transplantation. It is not assumed by the inhabitants of these regions that the ideal of liberty is best illustrated by the Anglo-American conception or that the form of property which is most desirable for them is that which emerges from self-interested action in anonymous markets subject only to abstract rules. Above all, it cannot be assumed that notions of individuality and community which detach agents from all but the minimum of social bonds are likely to be attractive to populations which have little or no experience of the subtlety of these abstract rules. It would be the high point of naiveté to suppose that an economic order bounded by contract, tort, and the intricacies of corporate law can be grafted onto communities which have little experience of capitalist legality. This is especially true of Russia, whose nascent (but potentially successful) commercial order was swept away by the Revolution of 1917 and its aftermath.

Indeed, the vacuum created by the collapse of Communism is likely to feature pockets of anarchy in which the entrepreneurial spirit, subject to no legal restraint, and operating in the absence of specified property rights, is certain to function in a malign manner. Indeed, it would appear that this is already happening.[6]

It takes some persuasive art to convince inhabitants of communities which are still pervaded by the most primitive notions of social justice that there is both an economic rationale to pure entrepreneurial profit (i.e., profit that accrues not to a factor of production, labor, but to mental alertness to wealth-creating opportunities) and a moral justification for it.[7] This is especially so when those most alert are likely to be former officials of the Communist regime. Under Communism, individuals were alienated from the system because to them it appeared to be a mechanism for enhancing the interests of the Communist Party, whose members masqueraded as representatives of the public. For this reason it was accorded little legitimacy. However, this alienation is likely to be reproduced even if an inchoate capitalist legal system were to replace anarchy,

---

[6] See reports in *Express and Chronicle*, Moscow, March 3–10, 1992.
[7] Israel Kirzner, *Discovery, Capitalism, and Distributive Justice* (Oxford: Blackwell, 1989).

since the immediate beneficiaries of it will most probably be those who acquire their assets by force.

In capitalist regimes the discovery of a profitable opportunity by a creative economic agent is regarded as legitimate if, and only if, existing legal forms and established private-property rights are respected. However, under post-Communism, entrepreneurial activity is almost certain to involve the seizure of hitherto commonly held assets by the *nomenklatura*. At the moment there are simply no rules of just acquisition, so a perverse form of privatization is taking place. This will, of course, prevent the legitimization of capitalist processes.

Within the range of possible market alternatives to Communism, the Anglo-American model (I refer to it simply as a model so that the very serious depredations to it that have occurred in this century can be conveniently ignored) is not the only one. It is rivaled by market socialism, the Scandinavian welfare state, and the original German doctrine of the social market economy. All three have been offered to former Communist regimes, although it is surely obvious that each depends upon the prior establishment of a predictable and stable constitutional and legal order. (However, it should not be thought that legal and economic orders are theoretically separate, that a neutral political order can be constructed which can accommodate any economic system.) There is a fourth alternative, South East Asian capitalism, but I have limited this inquiry to Anglo-American and West European models, since it is these that are being offered to former Communist regimes. This is probably because some of these countries, but by no means all, have histories and social structures which are, or were at one time, close to the mainstream European experience.

The first of these alternatives, market socialism,[8] is deeply flawed in theory, and has proved to be quite inadequate in practice. The only serious examples of its implementation are Yugoslavia and the voluntary system in Mondragon in Northern Spain.[9] Both are characterized by lower productivity than capitalist orders operating with similar natural resources. In Yugoslavia the power quickly shifted from workers to managers. The idea that there can be collective ownership and direction of resources alongside an individualistic market signaling system for labor and consumer goods is no more than an attempt to "square the circle."[10] In its efforts to simulate the perfectly competitive equilibrium model of resource allocation, market socialism enervates those human faculties that enable

---

[8] The most recent argument for market socialism is contained in David Miller, *Market, State, and Community: Theoretical Foundations of Market Socialism* (Oxford: Clarendon Press, 1989).

[9] See Brian Chiplin, John Coyne, and Ljubo Sirc, *Can Workers Manage?* (London: Institute of Economic Affairs, 1977).

[10] Antony de Jasay, *Market Socialism: A Scrutiny* (London: Institute of Economic Affairs, 1991), p. 22.

actual markets to work toward equilibrium. Again, entrepreneurship is the vital ingredient, for without the possibility of profits (as distinct from payments to a factor according to its marginal productivity) to lure actors, the necessary coordination will not take place and economizing opportunities will be missed. If capital is to be allocated by the state, how are its officials to *know* where the best investments are? Almost certainly, entrepreneurship (a fundamental category of human action) will reappear in a less benign form, i.e., in the search for the profits that accrue from political activity.

If workers are to be forbidden from owning individually any of the share capital of the enterprise, then rationality dictates that surpluses will be consumed in the form of wages, with the consequent lowering of investment. This is especially so if consumption and investment decisions are "democratized." Yet if workers are permitted to own resources, and these are marketable, then a version of orthodox capitalism will quickly emerge, and with it the familiar inequalities that market socialism is supposed to eliminate.

The two other models, the Scandinavian welfare state and the German social market economy, are often confused—largely, I think, because the actual practice of the West German economy began to resemble the Swedish experience, from at least the 1960s, in significant ways. But they are theoretically different. The Swedish system originally involved the imposition of heavy welfare responsibilities on a more or less unhindered market system. It was a market system characterized by almost exclusively private ownership in the means of production. It was and is, in effect, a "transfer" state in which political intervention took the form of the establishment of extraordinarily costly welfare services.[11]

If a measure of personal liberty is the amount of income left in the hands of individuals, then by the 1980s Sweden had become a not particularly free society. In many areas, including health, pensions, education, and aspects of family life, personal responsibility for action had been removed.[12] Furthermore, the Swedish system had no comprehensive theory of the social welfare state, a theory that would connect social, legal, political, and economic life in both its explanatory and normative aspects. It was reasonably effective when central government left the economy alone and pursued its own welfare policies, preserving a rather unlikely division of labor. However, the encroachment of the state into

---

[11] Eric Brodin, "Collapse of the Swedish Myth," *Economic Affairs*, February 1992, pp. 14–22.

[12] Swedish socialist thinkers (including Gunnar and Alva Myrdal) regarded the bourgeois family as an obstacle to the full realization of the welfare state. Hence, a whole range of family services, including home allowances, child care, and home care for the ill and elderly, are provided by the state. In addition to zero-priced medical care, everyone on sick leave gets 90 percent of their wage without a doctor's certification. Furthermore, incentives exist for unmarried motherhood, the right of parental discipline is severely restricted by law, and social workers have extensive powers to interfere with family life.

more and more areas of social life has made the terms of the contract economically disadvantageous.[13] Although large-scale nationalization has
been eschewed, the state has taken significant stakes in industry, notably pharmaceuticals and steel.

Marginal income tax rates have been as high as 92 percent, and they are
rarely less than 70 percent. Furthermore, the burden of company taxation
has increased: until the mid-1970s it was exceptionally low, but since then
successive Social Democratic governments introduced taxation on "surplus" profits (although this, at 20 percent, is at least an improvement on
the original intention of confiscating all profits above a certain level). Also,
there was a scheme to return the tax on surplus profits to the trade unions to invest in the shares of listed companies. This would, if implemented in full, lead eventually to the nationalization of Swedish industry.
A modified version was introduced in 1982, but it was not successful.
Nevertheless, it is a constant threat to private enterprise and has led to
a massive increase in overseas investment by Swedish firms.[14]

The combination of high labor costs, a bloated public sector, and a very
expensive welfare state has produced a marked decline in the Swedish
growth rate. In the century 1870 to 1970, only Japan grew faster than
Sweden, but in the 1980s, the rate had fallen to about 2 percent per annum.
The conservative coalition government which was returned in 1991, after
a long period of almost uninterrupted Social Democratic rule, specifically
rejected the Swedish model as a "third way" between socialism and capitalism. It is in the process of dismantling parts of the welfare state and
selling off state holdings in private industry.

I. Origins of the Social Market Economy

A much more plausible model for former Communist regimes to follow
is that provided by the German social market economy — or at least the
model as it was described by its most prominent theorists. Although there
are crucially important differences between the position of postwar Germany and former Communist regimes today, there are enough similarities
to make some meaningful comparisons. Both areas experienced ruinous
central planning and wrecked monetary systems. More important is the
fact that the theory of the social market economy included significant
modifications of pure laissez faire: variations which might make capitalism more palatable to societies struggling to end central planning. As I
shall indicate below, in many respects some of the former Communist regimes are in such a perilous state that mere survival is their most immediate problem. But in some countries, notably Czechoslovakia, Poland,

---

[13] See Gabriel Stein, "The Death of the Swedish Model," *Policy*, vol. 7, no. 1 (1991),
pp. 2–5.
[14] *Ibid.*, p. 4.

and Hungary, some version of the social market economy appears to be appropriate.

In the original German *Soziale Marktwirtschaft* (social market economy), there was no attempt to locate some middle ground between the extremes of collectivism and the market economy. Ludwig Erhard, the economic architect of the regime and accomplished theoretician of it, specifically precluded the Scandinavian model.[15] He argued that it was too statist and that not only would its implementation be very costly in the circumstances of postwar Germany, but it would have a deleterious long-term effect on personal responsibility. It was not that Germans were unused to extensive social welfare; they had had it since Bismarck's day. The point was that for the theorists of the social market economy there were interrelations between economy and society, feedbacks from social institutions to personal action, which required explanation: society and economy, in other words, are not hermetically sealed entities. The theorists of the social market economy sought an account of the *Wirtschaftsordnungspolitik*, or the order of economic society. Such a comprehensive theory would explain economy, polity, and society and account for their interrelationships.

The social market economy is in principle the doctrine that private property and the price system are the best means of exploiting scarce resources for the maximization of human well-being. It enjoins a limited state with the primary responsibility of securing law and order and a stable monetary system. That state is in theory precluded from the use of Keynesian fiscal policies to cure unemployment, since the theorists argued that this is primarily a microeconomic problem caused by rigidities in the labor market, normally trade-union power. However, the social market economy differs, as we shall see, from classical liberalism in that its theorists were skeptical of the claim that a market system is always self-correcting, especially in relation to the emergence of monopoly power. The legal system would have to be designed so that freedom is preserved, and not threatened, as these theorists claimed it would be, by untrammeled markets.

They also believed that the state had certain welfare responsibilities for the innocent victims of necessary economic change. But in the theory of the social market economy, if not in the practice of West German policy making, the state should not take a role in those areas of welfare which most individuals can handle for themselves, e.g., in pensions and other forms of social insurance. The postwar West German government inherited a range of state welfare functions which continued, even though the purists were later to object to their extension. They thought that this would have feedback effects, not only on productivity but also on indi-

[15] Quoted in Hans-Joachim Braum, *The German Economy in the Twentieth Century* (London: Routledge, 1990), p. 178.

vidual autonomy. Thus, the "order" of economic society could only be maintained by a judicious mixture of carefully designed welfare measures and regulatory devices which are required to modify and correct laissez-faire economics.

The obvious success of postwar Germany has led many people to think that the theorists got it right, that the rigors of the free market were softened by socially oriented institutions and policies without those arrangements weakening at the same time the productivity of the exchange system or undermining the autonomy of its inhabitants. It is not then surprising that the social market economy has been recommended for former Communist regimes. This was explicitly so in the debate leading up to German reunification and in the case of Hungary's attempts to slough off the remnants of Communism. No doubt the phrase was used rhetorically, as an anodyne slogan designed to induce into markets populations which were alienated by Communism yet fearful of an unknown capitalist future.

The theory originated during the prewar and war periods. In Germany a remarkable group of social and economic thinkers had been working out a blueprint or rational plan for the post-Nazi and postwar reconstruction of the country. Although they are collectively known as the "Ordo" group (Ordo Kreis) there were two differing, if not distinct, strands: a group of economists, of whom the leading figures were Walter Eucken, Franz Böhm, and Fritz Meyer, based at Freiburg; and a number of more socially oriented thinkers, the "exiles" Wilhelm Röpke, Alfred Müller-Armack (who coined the phrase "social market economy"), and Alexander Rüstow.[16] It should be noted, however, that none of the latter, with the possible exception of Müller-Armack, had a doctrine that bore much resemblance to Scandinavian welfarism. Of great significance is the fact that West Germany's first Economics Minister, Erhard, was closely associated with Ordo.

Before examining in detail the economic and political thought of the social market economy, it might be helpful to look briefly at the circumstances in which it arose.[17] From 1936 to 1948, during both the Hitler and the Allied Occupation periods, the German economy was subject to rigid

---

[16] Most of the major works of the Ordo group are now available in English. See *Standard Texts on the Social Market Economy* (New York: Ludwig Erhard Institute, 1982). Especially important individual works are: Walter Eucken, *The Foundations of Economics* (Edinburgh: William Hodge, 1951), and *This Unsuccessful Age* (Edinburgh: William Hodge, 1951); Wilhelm Röpke, *The Social Crisis of Our Time* (Edinburgh: William Hodge, 1950), and *A Humane Economy* (London: Wolf, 1960).

See also Konrad Zweig, *The Origins of the German Social Market Economy* (London: Adam Smith Institute, 1980); *Germany's Social Market Economy: Origins and Evolution*, ed. Alan Peacock and Hans Willgerodt (London: Macmillan, 1989); and *German Neo-Liberals and the Social Market Economy*, ed. Alan Peacock and Hans Willgerodt (London: Macmillan, 1989).

[17] For a historical account, see Gustav Stolper, *The German Economy: 1870 to the Present*, new edition, revised by Karl Hauser and Knut Borchadt (London: Weidenfeld and Nicholson, 1967), pp. 219–72.

controls. But price fixing, rationing, and a hopelessly inefficient monetary system (the reichsmark was worthless) had produced ruinous economic results: output plummeted, the black market flourished, and barter had replaced normal monetary exchange. Full employment was maintained, but only by a system which produced goods that nobody wanted. The Allied Occupation powers, engaged in the process of denazification, were determined that West Germany should not have a liberal market economy. In fact, the economic advisers at the time were Keynesian and broadly sympathetic to economic planning. However, it was realized that currency reform was essential, and Ludwig Erhard (chief official of the Administration for Economic Affairs for the British and American Occupation Zones), used the occasion of the establishment of the new deutschemark to secure (by the use of not a little chicanery)[18] the immediate lifting of a whole range of price and other controls. Erhard simply let the market operate freely in the new regime of monetary stability. He specifically did not use an expansionary budget to mop up the unemployment that inevitably appeared as an immediate consequence of the removal of controls.

This was greeted with skepticism by the Allied economists. None other than John Kenneth Galbraith was economic adviser to the American Military Government, and he made the following comment on the liberalization program: "There has never been the slightest possibility of getting German recovery by this wholesale repeal [of price controls], and it is quite possible that its reiteration has delayed Germany's recovery. The question is not whether there must be planning . . . but whether that planning has been forthright and effective."[19] Yet the subsequent events showed Galbraith, and almost all conventional economic observers at the time, to be spectacularly wrong.

As the liberalization of the hitherto controlled economy proceeded throughout the late 1940s and early 1950s, West Germany quickly recovered. From 1953 to 1963, GNP grew at an annual average rate of 6.7 percent, compared with 4.7 percent in France and 2.7 percent in Britain.[20] Alongside that of Britain, West Germany's performance in industrial output and exports was phenomenal, and by the 1960s the country was on top of the European economic league. Although factors other than the social market economy were important, such as a surplus of labor from Eastern Europe which reduced pressure on wages and ensured (relative)

[18] The three military governments had little idea what to do about the West German economy but probably favored the continuation of the controls. Erhard simply went ahead with the liberalization without asking their permission. He gambled that the success of the measures would make them irreversible. See Hans Willgerodt, "Planning in West Germany: The Social Market Economy," in *The Politics of Planning*, ed. A. Lawrence Chickering (San Francisco: Institute for Contemporary Studies, 1976), pp. 61–82.

[19] Quoted in *ibid.*, p. 64.

[20] See A. Gruchy, *Comparative Economic Systems* (Boston: Houghton Mifflin, 1977), ch. 5.

trade-union docility, the application of that particular economic philosophy was instrumental in securing this remarkable transformation.

There was no *Wirtschaftswunder* (economic "miracle") but merely the result of the pursuit of well-tried economic orthodoxies (although at the time they were almost radical). Some credit must be given to Erhard, as senior Economics Minister in the Adenauer government, for sticking to free-market principles against many pressures, ideological as well as political. Nevertheless, there was no "pure" market economy in postwar West Germany. There were many state interventions, of which perhaps the most significant was the deliberate use of fiscal policy to encourage personal savings.[21]

It is a significant fact that the social market economy was imposed on the German people. Most commentators doubt that it had much support from the major political groups, including the Christian Democrats, who were wedded to a kind of Christian socialism; and but for the ruinous situation at the time, it might never have been given a hearing. It is also pertinent to note that Germany's defeat had effectively destroyed all those special-interest groups that had succeeded in undermining the market system in Britain.[22] However, once the success of the social market economy became manifest, the doctrine came to be embraced by all the political parties, although the Social Democrats did not formally abandon Marxism until 1959.

Despite the devastation of war, there were some features peculiar to Germany which made it propitious for the establishment of a market economy. Although productive capacity was badly damaged by war, the effect should not be overestimated.[23] What was left was still serviceable in comparison to the vast tracts of more or less unusable heavy industry bequeathed by Communism. Although the Nazis had operated a command economy, it had functioned through a system of private ownership (heavily cartelized though it was) and private law (heavily compromised though that had become). Most important of all, there still existed significant social and intellectual capital invested in market arrangements, even though it required considerable replenishing. In comparison, most former Communist regimes will have to be marketized *ab initio*.

Nevertheless, there is one startling similarity. Former Communist regimes, if they are to introduce successfully a free-market economy, are likely to do so in a nondemocratic context. This is not to say that market arrangements, in principle, are unpopular, but rather than in the immediate short-term it is likely that a coalition, consisting of those who benefit from the status quo, could form against particular market proposals if they were put to an immediate vote. The market system is itself a pub-

---

[21] Tax incentives were offered to encourage investment, especially for house-building. There were also subsidies to agriculture and selected industries.

[22] Mancur Olson, Jr., *The Rise and Decline of Nations* (New Haven: Yale University Press, 1982), pp. 129–33.

[23] Braum, *German Economy in the Twentieth Century* (see n. 15 above), ch. 8.

lic good, the benefits of which go to unknown people and, in the case of former Communist regimes especially, at unknown dates. We are already seeing evidence of this in Poland, where there has been a significant retreat from earlier economic reforms. This is largely the result of the recent election (1991), which led to the downfall of the market-oriented government. The Polish parliament is now splintered into a myriad of factions, out of which it will be difficult to form a coalition favorable to radical reform. This is why large swaths of unproductive industry have remained immune from change. Similar phenomena are visible in the republics of the former Soviet Union, whose legislatures still consist largely of unreconstructed Communists.

The Germans were advantaged in having their first postwar general election in late 1949, *after* the reintroduction of the market and when its benefits were just showing. But it took some time to secure overwhelming support (not the least of the opposition came from the Christian socialist wing of Erhard's own party, the Christian Democratic Union).

I have no doubt that some version of the same lesson will apply to the former Communist regimes. The benefits of marketization will be too slow in coming for there to be an automatic endorsement of the new arrangements. Those governments that introduce them are likely to suffer electoral retribution. In West Germany, however, the introduction of the deutschemark and the rapid removal of price controls produced only a short-lived inflation, since there was already in place productive capacity to respond to the new demand in a manner sufficient to endear the population to the new regime (albeit precariously at first). The transition to the new monetary system involved some injustice because of the way in which the vast amount of money in the form of the reichsmark was taken out of circulation. Put simply, each citizen could only exchange sixty reichsmarks for sixty deutschemarks on a one-to-one basis. Above this, a citizen's credit balance was convertible at a ratio of ten reichsmarks to one deutschemark. This disadvantaged those who had held their assets in cash in comparison to those who owned property (which was automatically revalued in terms of the deutschemark). This injustice was to some extent remedied in later legislation, which imposed special levies on the holders of property and other assets that had not been devalued by the monetary reform.[24] There are certain to be similar, if not greater, injustices in monetary transformations in former Communist regimes.

II. THE DOCTRINE

The doctrine of the social market economy, if it is to have any plausible exportability, must be seen in two aspects. First, it must be seen as a

---

[24] This was achieved by the Equalization of Burdens Act passed in 1952. For a description of the currency reform, see Dennis L. Bark and David R. Gress, *A History of West Germany: Vol. I, From Shadow to Substance* (Oxford: Blackwell, 1989), pp. 198–209.

normative account of an economic "constitution," i.e., a system of social relationships that describes not merely the private property, free exchange system, but also those moral, legal, and political rules without which it is not sustainable. They are in some significant ways different from those that feature in Anglo-American classical liberalism. Second, the doctrine must be seen as the set of welfare and redistributive measures that happened to emerge in the later development of the West German economy. Although both these aspects feature in Ordo writings (which, in fact, cover a range of opinion within a broad liberal framework), the latter measures were treated with considerably more caution by the authors than they were by the politicians, and many writers argued that certain measures, for example, the introduction of unfunded state pensions and other high-cost social-security policies, were incompatible with the original doctrine.

It was probably a number of perversions of the original idea that led to classical-liberal skepticism of the theory. Indeed, a prominent second-generation Ordo theorist, Hans Lenel, was to pose in 1971 the question: "Do we still have a social market economy?"[25] In Hayek's view,[26] the addition of the word "social" to the noun "market" was either an adjectival frill (all market relationships are necessarily social) or the illegitimate imposition of some arbitrary redistributive purpose on an otherwise self-developing and self-correcting spontaneous order.

Undoubtedly, it is the second aspect of the social market economy that has proved *politically* attractive, but Hayek's criticism has been a constant source of confusion. Historically, the success of the West German system was achieved by the implementation of more or less free-market measures between 1948 and 1952,[27] and though collectively they had a "purpose," it did not at that time have much to do with social justice or any other of the rationalistic end-states that have since been proposed. Of the social market economy thinkers only Müller-Armack[28] envisaged a "Second Phase" of the social market in explicitly redistributivist terms. In his view, the state must, in effect, "tame" the market in order to achieve what he called an "irenical" (balanced and harmonious) order. I think it is fair to say that other Ordo theorists, such as Eucken, Böhm, and Röpke, believed that a properly organized market and legal order would necessarily narrow the ambit of the state.

---

[25] Hans Lenel, "Does Germany Still Have a Social Market Economy?" in *Germany's Social Market Economy* (see n. 16 above), ch. 17.

[26] See Friedrich Hayek, "What is Social? What Does it Mean?" in Hayek, *Studies in Philosophy, Politics, and Economics* (London: Routledge and Kegan Paul, 1967), pp. 237–44.

[27] Hans Lenel, "Evolution of the Social Market Economy," in *German Neo-Liberals* (see n. 16 above), ch. 2.

[28] Alfred Müller-Armack, "The Principles of the Social Market Economy," *German Economic Review*, vol. 3, no. 1 (1965), p. 94. See also his "Economic Systems from a Social Point of View," in *Economy and Development*, ed. J. Thesing (Mainz: Konrad Adenauer-Stiftung, 1979), pp. 95–122.

The reason why controversy arose over the precise meaning of the so-cial market economy (and its connection with capitalism) is that theorists such as Eucken, Böhm, and Röpke (all of whom had serious doubts about welfare and redistribution, at least in the form that those are customar-ily achieved) were as critical of laissez faire as they were of any overt redistributivist doctrine. Röpke wrote that: "Like pure democracy, undi-luted capitalism is intolerable";[29] Erhard was "unwilling to accept with-out reservation and in every phase of development the orthodox rules of a market economy according to which only demand and supply deter-mine price";[30] and Eucken argued that "experience of *laissez-faire* goes to prove . . . that the economic system cannot be left to organize itself. So there is no question of any return to *laissez-faire*."[31] Still, although these theorists and practical men did not believe that the "just" wage equaled marginal productivity, they did not therefore endorse a Scandinavian-style welfare state.

They did not mean that the market was ethically deficient because it did not meet some explicit redistributive goal, but rather that its survival was imperiled if it were not underpinned by a complex set of moral and legal rules and if it showed no concern for its potential victims. Thus, it is not sufficient to demonstrate the utility-maximizing virtues of markets; the German theorists were concerned equally to stress the importance of those institutional arrangements which make exchange feasible (primarily an autonomous legal order that is, to an extent, independent of the state). The realization that the market would not secure a wide social legitimacy if it were not made compatible with some degree of state-decreed welfare led Eucken, Röpke, Böhm, et al. to accept those social-security arrange-ments that had long been a feature of German life. There is, indeed, evidence of the lingering influence of Christian socialism in some social market economy thinking.

It is this version of the social market economy which is of direct rele-vance to the former Communist regimes, whose transition to liberal cap-italism will be hazardous, and their experience of it short-lived, if it is seen as a mere exchange system. Thus, if fair property rules that are to govern both acquisition and transfer are not established, the system will lack legitimacy; if there is no system of private law, disputes between individuals will be irresolvable and anarchy will probably ensue; if there is unlimited democracy, the state will become prey to pressure groups; and if no concern is shown toward those harmed by markets, capitalism will have an insecure ethical foundation. The last point indicates that the former Communist regimes will have to maintain elements of the old wel-

---

[29] Röpke, *Social Crisis of Our Time* (see n. 16 above), p. 119.

[30] Ludwig Erhard, *Prosperity Through Competition* (London: Thames and Hudson, 1958), p. 102.

[31] Eucken, *This Unsuccessful Age* (see n. 16 above), p. 93.

fare system, no matter how inefficient it is, since a successful transition to capitalism will inevitably involve hardship as old and useless industries are liquidated.

Thus, the real debate between classical liberalism and Ordo liberalism was not just about redistribution but about the latter's denial of the extreme version of the spontaneity thesis, i.e., the belief that a total social system requires very little in the way of guidance and control. Neither the free-exchange system nor its legal concomitant could be left to themselves, the Ordo theorists argued. Unlimited freedom of contract would lead, it was claimed, to the undermining of liberty, because contractors would contract into cartels, monopolies, and so on, which would lead to the closure of the market.[32] Without careful design, government would dispose favors to pressure groups, especially protectionist measures. The limited state of laissez-faire theory, operating through uncorrected private law, would be unable to maintain order, justice, predictability, and, ultimately, the market system itself. In Röpke's work especially, it was further argued that moral relativism, so characteristic of much of classical-liberal thought, would generate nihilism. He was, in fact, a proponent of objective natural law.[33]

There is no doubt that this skepticism about the self-correcting features of the market under a simple version of private law was influenced by a feature of twentieth-century German economic history: this was cartelization, the gradual closure of the market. This had proceeded apace in the first thirty years of the twentieth century: the Hitlerian command economy was run through monopolies and cartels which had long been invulnerable to competition. According to Rüstow, it was the state's "lamentable weakness"[34] that was the problem, and this weakness, in combination with an unregulated market, made totalitarianism possible. This looks, superficially, as if it is the reverse of the classical-liberal claim, i.e., that a diminution of the range of state authority, outside its public-good functions, necessarily increases individual liberty. Does the doctrine of the social market economy have then the startling implication that the former Communist countries need a strong state?

This is, of course, misleading and only appears to be the case because some writers (primarily Rüstow) in the Ordo tradition used an idealized, or sanitized, neo-Hegelian conception of the state; they saw it as an impartial body that exists to regulate the conflicts within civil society while itself remaining resistant to the overweening demands of any subset of that society. The possibility of such an institution permanently operating this way has been thoroughly undermined by public-choice theory.

---

[32] *Ibid.*, pp. 31–33.

[33] Röpke, *Social Crisis of Our Time*, p. 4.

[34] Quoted in C. J. Friedrich, "Political Thought of Neo-Liberalism," *American Political Science Review*, vol. 49, no. 4 (1955), pp. 509–25.

A more sustainable version of the Ordo doctrine posits a distinction between state and economic society, with both being regulated by law[35] — the ideal of the *Rechtsstaat* (rule-of-law state), in fact. One of the most pressing tasks of the former Communist countries, then, if they are to follow Ordo, is to put all public authorities under the rule of law. For example, it was the impossibility of suing the state under Communism that made the pollution problem strictly speaking intractable, for there were no methods by which social pressure could be translated into corrective action.

III. ECONOMIC CONSTITUTIONS

Thus, the first priority for Eastern European and former Soviet regimes is to establish an "economic constitution" on the lines suggested by Eucken.[36] This comprises constitutive and regulatory principles. Briefly, constitutive principles govern money, private property, freedom of contract, open markets, and personal liberty for action. But following these *alone* could lead to the self-destruction of the market, and they have to be supplemented by regulatory principles (which actually dilute the classical liberalism contained in the constitutive principles) if freedom is to be preserved. These regulatory principles cover, for example, the regulation of the money supply to prevent inflation and deflation (though not for contra-cyclical policy) and the abolition (not merely control) of monopolies. The state and the constitution cannot be "neutral" but must protect an *order of liberty*, not just individual choice. And this can only be done by taking certain things out of the realm of politics. Thus, if there is a coherent end-state in the theory of the social market economy, it is not social justice but ordered liberty, as distinct from negative liberty.

Leaving aside the question of the original designation of property titles, the above might seem to be a reasonable set of recommendations for a newly established liberal market society: one that must unavoidably, in Eastern Europe, come about by design. Still, it is worth analyzing the extent to which the regulatory principles *should* dilute the constitutive principles. Do the newly emerging economies require that type of regulation of competition approved by all Ordo writers? As those writers recognized, the problem of monopoly is better dealt with by private rather than public law, by litigation rather than hands-on regulation. Monopolies, and certainly cartels, can indeed arise in open economies, but two points are relevant here. First, they are precarious and vulnerable to competition if the market is kept open. Second, monopoly profits can be a reward for genuine entrepreneurship, acts of discovery in the market which create

---

[35] See Franz Böhm, "The Rule of Law," in *Germany's Social Market Economy* (see n. 16 above), ch. 4.
[36] Eucken, *Foundations of Economics* (see n. 16 above), pp. 80–121.

new value.[37] In economies freeing themselves from central control, a state-directed competition policy, derived from abstract theories of perfect competition, may well impede economic progress, just as anti-trust law in the U.S. and monopoly policy in the U.K. have obstructed processes of benign industrial integration. These processes are vulnerable to public law because they look as if they are anti-competitive.

What is needed is not cumbersome public law, which may well be counterproductive and itself subject to pressure-group influence, but private law which is protective of individual rights to compete in the market. The cartel problem in Germany arose out of a highly controversial *Reichtsgericht* (Supreme Court) decision in 1897 which upheld a contract that was blatantly in restraint of trade.[38] It is quite consistent with orthodox liberal theory to maintain that competition is a public good which the courts, through private law, should protect.

It will be easier for a newly emerging economy to develop without anti-competitive monopolies if the law enforces international free trade, since this always poses a threat to any market-closing agreement which might be smuggled in under private law. There is a distinction between a conspiracy against the public good of open competition (which the 1897 case involved) and the emergence of apparent concentrations of ownership. The latter are not necessarily harmful. As long as the state maintains the market order, such concentrations will always be vulnerable to competition. Still, as the Ordo theorists appreciated, there is the danger that concentrations of wealth may generate inequalities of political power.

There is some disagreement among observers as to whether cartelization, even in the extreme form it took in Germany, was a threat to market efficiency. In fact, what probably motivated the Ordo group was not so much the economic argument but a more important political consideration, i.e., the fact that the cartelization of German industry, and the growing concentration of ownership, made the rise of a totalitarian command economy possible.

Thus, anti-cartelization and pro-competitive interventionist policies were pursued vigorously in the postwar years—but with, apparently, varied success. Some Ordo thinkers maintained that the original anti-cartelization law (1957) allowed too many exemptions for certain industries.[39] However, there is a curious irony here, for some of the success of the social market economy may be due to the absence of the strict form of anti-trust

---

[37] See Israel Kirzner, *Competition and Entrepreneurship* (Chicago: University of Chicago Press, 1973).

[38] For a brilliant analysis of this issue, see Jan Tumlir, "Franz Böhm and the Development of Economic-Constitutional Analysis," in *German Neo-Liberals* (see n. 16 above), ch. 6.

[39] See Werner Möschel, "Competition Policy from an Ordo Point of View," in *German Neo-Liberals*, ch. 7. For the argument that cartelization was not a serious problem for the German economy, see H. C. Wallich, *Mainsprings of the German Revival* (New Haven: Yale University Press, 1955), p. 139.

legislation that prevails in the United States. What is also important here is the relatively "closely held" nature of German corporations, in which banks and other institutional shareholders play an important supervisory role. Some observers say that such corporations are relatively invulnerable to takeovers and hence able to plan for the long term without having to worry too much about short-term share-price fluctuations.[40] Such a development is consistent with the theory of spontaneous order.

Two other important social implications follow from these observations — implications which may have relevance for former Communist regimes. First, German industrial enterprises display a "social conscience"[41] which inhibits their managements from indulging in the wholesale plant restructuring and relocation that characterizes industrial change in Anglo-American liberal capitalist economies. Corporate raiders are regarded with a certain amount of social disdain (as they are in the U.S.). However, what is probably more decisive here is the fact that the structure of ownership in German industry allows for close monitoring of management by shareholders. In the "loosely held" corporation of the United States and Britain, the takeover threat is the only mechanism that shareholders have for disciplining management. Also, in Germany, trade unions have a role in management, including representation on the boards of public companies. These features make for a more intimate style of economic relationship in Germany, which contrasts with the aggressive, "arm's length" attitudes of American industrialists and financiers. The former may be more appropriate for regimes trying to come to terms with capitalism.

Secondly, it is undoubtedly the case that, rightly or wrongly, entrepreneurial profits (especially those of financial intermediaries) earned in American industrial reorganization offend popular notions of social justice (primitive though these may be). Of course, apologists for liberal capitalism have coherent explanations for these profits, but an understanding of them requires some sophistication and indeed considerable experience of the sometimes arcane workings of capitalism. It is probably true that all of the original theorists of the social market economy would have been disturbed by the apparently bizarre distributions of incomes thrown up by financial markets in Anglo-American capitalist systems. No one could accuse Eucken and other social market theorists of lacking economic sophistication.

These are speculative thoughts which may be disproved by events. Already the takeover mentality may be influencing industrial organization in Germany (and the rest of continental Europe). Nevertheless, they do suggest that some features of Anglo-American capitalism, especially the anonymity of the forces that drive it and the indifference to its outcomes

---

[40] Eric Owen Smith, *The West German Economy* (London: Croom Helm, 1963), ch. 7.
[41] *Ibid.*, p. 213.

that its major spokesmen proclaim, are not easily exportable. They belong, perhaps exclusively, to communities whose inhabitants are prepared to accept the discipline of abstract rules and to conduct their lives according to the constraints of (an often costly) formal law rather than compromise their individuality by the informal enforcement of more extensive social obligations. This attitude is not to be dismissed. Indeed, it represents a considerable human achievement and one which has generated immense prosperity. However, as the Ordo group was anxious to stress, in ruinous situations, its apparent moral relativism and its toleration of a certain kind of gratification may not be conducive to social order.

IV. POLITICS AND THE DEGENERATION OF THE SOCIAL MARKET ECONOMY

Yet there is clearly some confusion in the original theory of the social market economy between the effectiveness of moral restraints on egoism and a reliance on fortified institutional arrangements to generate stability. It could be argued that what is lacking in Eucken's "economic morphology"[42] is a set of prescriptions for those political rules that should form a *written* economic constitution. In a sense the demand for competition from the Ordo group did not go far enough: it did not extend to the political arena. No mention is made of the possibility that the *Wirtschaftsordnungspolitik* (the order of economic society) might best be preserved by competition between political institutions: giving polities (and individuals) the "exit" option in fact. In most existing federal systems (including Germany's), the predominant feature is not competition between component units for the delivery of a range of public services but, rather, the allocation of these services to the various units (fiscal federalism). This is certainly true of America, whose original genuine federalism has ceased to exist. The states are little more than administrative units of a centralized state.[43]

It is argued by some sympathetic critics of the social market economy that it was the lack of adequate constitutional arrangements embodying political competition that led to the degeneration of the original ideal: as evidenced by the inexorable rise in government spending (now around 44 percent of GDP) since the 1950s, the emergence of budget deficits, the imposition of heavy nonwage labor costs on employers, and the persistence of subsidies to agriculture and industry.[44]

[42] This is Eucken's instructive phrase; see his *Foundations of Economics*, pp. 85–90.

[43] Federalism seems to exist in the U.S. only in a "representational" form; i.e., the states are represented in Congress but lack the original constitutional protection of their authority. This seems to have been confirmed in a U.S. Supreme Court decision in 1985 (*Garcia v. San Antonio Transit Authority*). See Thomas R. Dye, *American Federalism: Competition Among Governments* (Lexington: D. C. Heath, 1990), ch. 1.

[44] See Walter Hamm, "The Welfare State at Its Limit," in *Germany's Social Market Economy*, ch. 12. For a philosophical critique of the welfare state, see Röpke, *Humane Economy* (see n. 16 above), pp. 156–80.

The real exception is the survival of the principle of a sound currency; one feels that this has been as much due to a "taboo" against inflation as it has to the strict rules that obligate the Bundesbank (formally established in 1957). It is a taboo the origins of which can be traced to Germany's disastrous experience of hyperinflation in the 1920s. All German opinion leaders are very much aware of the political as well as the economic consequences of inflation. But there was a shift to neo-Keynesian contracyclical macroeconomic policies in the late 1960s and the emergence of a kind of "planning." All this was even given a name—the enlightened market economy.[45]

There was, however, a principle in the original theory of the social market economy to govern government intervention. It was known as *marktkonform*.[46] A policy is *marktkonform* if it aids the market system (even if it is redistributive) rather than impedes it. Thus, aid (cash) to the homeless is *marktkonform*, rent control is not; a negative income tax for the poor is, fixing a minimum wage is not; most forms of protectionism are not *marktkonform*. It is a superficially attractive principle, combining as it does the criterion of efficiency and the imperative of compassion.

It is, however, a deceptive principle, since it is obvious that any redistributive policy must have some effect on the market. This calls for another principle to determine just how many market impediments are acceptable. It is not inconceivable that massive redistributive measures could be validated under the rubric of *marktkonform*. In any case, the typical interventionist measures associated with the later development of the social market economy could by no stretch of the imagination be made consistent with the original ideas of Ordo liberalism.

The history of the development of counterproductive welfare measures in postwar West Germany reflects similar processes that were taking place in other Western democracies. The reproduction of conventional democratic procedures in the Basic Law of the Federal Republic led to a gradual increase in the power of pressure groups—the absence of which had been so significant in the rejuvenation of the economy from its almost ruined state in 1948. Röpke et al. were certainly aware of the debilitating effect of some forms of group action on an economic and political order. None was more so than Eucken, who was keenly aware (in a nonformal way) of the public-good features of the total system of economic and political arrangements. As he observed: "Many men are genuine experts in their own economic environment, but they are unable to weigh up dispassionately the wider interrelationships."[47] What he had in mind were those groups that sought exemption from the rule of law and protection

---

[45] See Norbert Kloten, "The Role of the Public Sector in the Social Market Economy," in *German Neo-Liberals* (see n. 16 above), ch. 4.

[46] Röpke, *Social Crisis of Our Time* (see n. 16 above), pp. 160–62. For a critique of *marktkonform*, see Gerard Radnitzky, "The Social Market and the Constitution of Liberty," in *Britain's Constitutional Future*, ed. Frank Vibert (London: Institute of Economics, 1991), pp. 6–8.

[47] Eucken, *Foundations of Economics*, p. 29.

from economic competition. What was required, then, was not merely a constructivist act in the creation of an order but attention to the need for its repair in the context of more or less universal human motivations. Müller-Armack's hope that the social market economy would generate a personality that belonged neither to laissez faire nor to socialism was an illusion.

V. The Social Market Economy and Post-Communism

It is unfortunate that the social market economy being offered to former Communist regimes is the one regarded as degenerate by admirers of the original theory. It is said to be so, not because the original version excludes a type of welfare (although most theorists argued that increased prosperity brought about by the market would reduce the need for collective provision), but because it has proved to be costly and because it developed in an ad hoc way. Also, it was said to undermine personal responsibility and individual autonomy—the ethical principles of the original social market economy. The *Wirtschaftsordnungspolitik* was flawed in its direct constitutional manifestation. In the end, politics triumphed over the market.

What prevents an easy application of the original principles of the social market economy to Eastern Europe and the former Soviet Union is the absence there of crucial features, notably stable money, a system of private law, and a structure of property rights. Of equal importance is the fact that in the former Soviet Union there is little understanding of the *meaning* of market relationships; more specifically, the idea that two-person exchange is mutually beneficial is only reluctantly accepted, if it is accepted at all. Furthermore, decades of central planning have deprived citizens of knowledge of rational banking and accounting practices.[48] The only advantage they have is that there is much more outside intellectual support for their transformation into European-style market economies than there was for the similar venture in postwar Germany.

The tasks that are involved in the rational construction of civil order are obvious enough, but how to meet them is mind-numbing in its complexity. Of course, the construction of an economic constitution cannot be identical for all the emerging market systems, since no order can be designed in isolation from particular cultural traditions. In terms of immediate economic problem solving, the former East Germany is at an obvious advantage compared to the ex-Soviet republics, and its absorption into an already successful market system makes it almost a special case. In other European former Communist countries, the task is one of recovering a

---

[48] See Ronald McKinnon, *The Order of Economic Liberalization* (Baltimore: Johns Hopkins University Press, 1991).

lost tradition of law and commerce; in Russia and other similarly located regions, the change involves a step into the unknown. What is required of them all, however, is the establishment of an overarching system of rules which protects the civil society of private law, a private economy, and voluntary associations: a predictable order in which politics has an assigned role, not an all-embracing one.

The most immediate necessity is the construction of a system in which economic value is determined by the subjective opinions of market trans-actors rather than by the arbitrary dictates of political authorities. How-ever, a market economy cannot perform this task without a system of property rights which are protected by private law. Israel Kirzner's theory of entrepreneurship is unhelpful in a context in which property entitle-ments are unknown; the market signals that will indicate scarcities in a regime of decontrolled prices will be ineffective if there are no private arrangements through which potential producers can respond to the lure of profit; and all will be in vain if there is no efficient productive system which can turn black markets (the only "economies" that worked under Communism) into white markets. West Germany was to some extent freed from those problems in 1948, but because of their all-pervading presence in the former command economies of today, the scope for con-scious direction and control is, superficially at least, wider. It is impera-tive, however, that political control should be limited to the construction of the rules of economic order and not extended to guiding that order in any particular direction. That was, indeed, the agenda of the theory of the German social market economy.

Privatization is a case in point. At the moment it is assumed by most Western observers that the vast industrial tracts of much of Eastern Europe and the former Soviet Union are pretty much worthless. But nobody can know this until a market has been formed, and this cannot be effective without property rights. Yet if the industries are disposed of by state agencies it is almost inevitable that the sale will be influenced by politi-cal factors. The government will not want to be seen as selling off national assets too "cheaply," especially in the context of newly established dem-ocratic electoral politics. Yet, given the extraordinarily high risks attached to most purchases, potential buyers will be looking for high returns. It is certain that the fear of unemployment and the disruptive reallocation of resources which is predicted to follow necessary and rapid disposals will inhibit the politicians from allowing the market to operate properly. Furthermore, the likelihood that foreign investors will be the only ones capable of taking the high risks (in return for high rewards) will inflame nationalist sentiments. Already in the former East Germany it is appar-ent that the *Treuhandanstalt*[49] (the state selling agency) is putting onerous

---

[49] See Amity Shlaes, "Germany's Treuhand—A Too Visible Hand," *Wall Street Journal Europe*, January 3, 1992.

conditions, derived from the degenerate social market economy, on potential purchasers; they include the preservation of existing industries and of employment levels.

Privatization is the most obvious solution, but privatization in Eastern Europe is vastly different from experiments in the West, especially Britain's. Here selected state industries were successfully sold off to the public through a sophisticated merchant banking system and in the context of a functioning market economy which was already supplying some information about the values of the assets to be disposed. In former Communist regimes there is very little information precisely because markets have been suppressed for decades.

In these circumstances the best solution is probably that being tried in Czechoslovakia (1992): the method of popular share distribution devised by Vaclav Klaus.[50] Under the plan most of the country's eleven million adults purchased books of vouchers at a very low cost (thirty-six dollars per book). The vouchers entitled the owners to make bids for shares in two thousand of the country's enterprises, covering an enormous range of activities (which were given an original notional value). Once distributed, the shares can be bought and sold and the true values of the enterprises will then emerge through the normal process of supply and demand. To prevent atomization of share ownership, most of the stock is being owned through mutual funds, although the Czech parliament limited mutual-fund ownership to 40 percent of every enterprise. No doubt this limitation will be evaded. But it is difficult to see why that should necessarily be harmful, since in the early stages of privatization some concentration of ownership will be extremely useful in order to monitor managements.

It is, of course, far too early to evaluate the scheme. One problem is that individuals may wish to dispose of their assets quickly for cash. This would cause a massive fall in the price of shares, enabling foreign investors to buy up vast tracts of Czech industry very cheaply. Still, the government itself had already sold off some valuable assets to foreigners before the privatization process. At least under the latter scheme the people will be aware of the fact that it is *they* who have sold off the nation's assets. This should deflect criticism from the government. Furthermore, given the perilous state of the Czech economy, the population should welcome any inflow of foreign capital.

One must assume that the Czech-style transformation into capitalism will only be possible in certain parts of the former Communist world: Eastern Europe and possibly the Baltic states. In those areas that completely lack a commercial tradition, the former republics of the Soviet

[50] See Peter Passell, "A Capitalist Free-for-All in Czechoslovakia," *New York Times*, April 12, 1992.

Union, history will have to be "concertina-ed." Europe's evolutionary process of capitalist development will have to be compressed into a short period—or not emulated at all, for the recent freedom experienced may well reveal to some peoples that the forced industrialization of the twentieth century, brought about by a "modernistic" Communism, was a catastrophic error. The opening of international trade might show that Russia's comparative advantage lies in agricultural production. This, of course, means that collectivized agriculture will have to end and that a proper system of individual property rights will have to be restored to land ownership. Whatever industry does remain will have to be justified economically and not retained for purposes of national pride or for the pointless maintenance of full employment at any price.

The real reason why the problems of liberalization are especially difficult for the republics of the former Soviet Union is that civil order has apparently broken down. Experiments in economic reform of any kind will have to be postponed until some semblance of order is restored to fractious and ethnically divided regions. This was not a problem faced by postwar Germans, who could rebuild the market economy in a homogeneous population whose territory (though divided) was secure. Thus, the kind of regulation of economic life permitted by the theory of the social market economy was predicated upon the prior establishment of cultural and political integrity. Only in Poland, Hungary, and the Czech part of Czechoslovakia[51] does that exist. Elsewhere, the existing political circumstances indicate that Thomas Hobbes rather than Adam Smith provides better insights into the conditions necessary for social survival.

The relationship *between* the states of former Communist regimes will be crucial, and here the lessons of the social market economy are relevant. As a competitive order, the system is, in theory, one that stresses diversity and genuine decentralization. This of course derives from the epistemological doctrine of the dispersed nature of social knowledge. All the early theorists had firsthand experience of central planning and had analyzed its errors. However, they were writing about particular economies rather than the relationships between national economies. But their notion of freedom theoretically includes the idea that competition between national economies is an essential ingredient in economic progress. This notion of freedom involves not merely free trade in goods and services but competition between nations in the offering of different laws and institutions, and of course the right of free movement of labor and capital.

In international terms this implies that any grouping of states should

---

[51] At the time of writing, it is apparent that the Czechoslovak republic is about to break up into Czech and Slovak entities. The future Slovak republic is almost certain to be less market-oriented and more nationalistic than its erstwhile partner.

be loose and confederal, with few compulsory transnational laws and regulations. The ultimate threat of exit from such a grouping is the only mechanism that can ensure the preservation of competition. Thus, the way that the European Community is developing should not constitute the model for any international association of former Communist states. Ludwig Erhard had fears that the (then) European Economic Community would develop into a protectionist bloc, and he was skeptical of the imposition of uniform industrial and welfare standards.[52] In this he was, of course, remarkably prescient. This is already happening with the "social chapter," which purports to impose common regulatory norms across member states and will ultimately reduce the competitive advantage, in crucial areas, that the poorer members now have. The intention is that they will be compensated by the richer ones through significant interregional transfers. All this is of course anti-competitive and hence productive of "Eurosclerosis." The policy of "harmonization" of industrial practices currently pursued by the Commission of the European Community would be fatal if it were applied to any grouping of former Communist states, given the variety of economic conditions prevailing among them. And behind all this stands the economically crass but politically immovable Common Agricultural Policy.

The original social market economy was deficient in not extending the ideal of competition into the political arena. The former Communist regimes, which consist in many cases of fragile political units, could remedy this defect by forming associations, the members of which could compete with each other in the supply of economic constitutions. Even forms of market socialism and co-determination,[53] which might have some favorable cultural antecedents in special areas, would not be excluded in an international competitive context.

CONCLUSION

Thus, only some features of the social market economy outlined above are feasible for the former Communist regimes. The decisive factor is not just that these countries are simply incapable of meeting the demands set by what I have called the degenerate version of the system: the equally important point is that this mutation included the partial abandonment of those competitive arrangements that are the prerequisites of economic and social stability. There is a variety of differing (if not competing) strains within the theory of the social market economy: the temptation for for-

---

[52] See Bark and Gress, *History of West Germany* (see n. 24 above), p. 385.

[53] Co-determination, i.e., the involvement of workers' representatives in the management of companies, was an early innovation in the West German economy. However, the power of final decision on key issues is left with the owners. See *ibid.*, pp. 269–70.

mer Communist regimes to choose the most politically attractive rather than the most economically feasible might be irresistible.

Whatever economic arrangements are proposed, they are dependent upon a prior stable political order, a point constantly emphasized by Ordo liberals. The theory of the spontaneous development of social institutions is likely to be tested as never before in former Communist regimes, lacking as they do so many of the cultural conditions that were present in the earlier developments of markets and private-law systems.

Politics, University of Buckingham

FROM POST-COMMUNISM TO CIVIL SOCIETY: THE REEMERGENCE OF HISTORY AND THE DECLINE OF THE WESTERN MODEL

By John Gray

Introduction

For virtually all the major schools of Western opinion, the collapse of the Communist regimes in Eastern Europe and in the Soviet Union, between 1989 and 1991, represents a triumph of Western values, ideas, and institutions. If, for triumphal conservatives, the events of late 1989 encompassed an endorsement of "democratic capitalism" that augured "the end of history,"[1] for liberal and social democrats they could be understood as the repudiation by the peoples of the former Soviet bloc of Marxism-Leninism in all its varieties, and the reemergence of a humanist socialism that was free of Bolshevik deformation. The structure of political and economic institutions appropriate to the transition from post-Communism in the Soviet bloc to genuine civil society was, accordingly, modeled on Western exemplars — the example of Anglo-American democratic capitalism, of Swedish social democracy, or of the German social market economy — or on various modish Western academic conceptions, long abandoned in the Soviet and post-Soviet worlds, such as market socialism. No prominent school of thought in the West doubted that the dissolution of Communist power was part of a process of Westernization in which contemporary Western ideas and institutions could and would successfully be exported to the former Communist societies. None questioned the idea that, somewhere in the repertoire of Western theory and practice, there was a model for conducting the transition from the bankrupt institutions of socialist central planning, incorporated into the structure of a totalitarian state, to market institutions and a liberal democratic state. Least of all did anyone question the desirability, or the possibility, of reconstituting economic and political institutions on Western models, in most parts of the former Soviet bloc.

The uncritical assumption that the collapse of Communist regimes should, and would, result in the swift adoption of Western institutions, has left Western opinion wholly unprepared for the real course of events, as it has unfolded over the past year or so (from mid-1991 to mid-1992), and as it seems likely to develop over the coming decades. In parts of the

---

[1] See Francis Fukuyama, "The End of History," in *National Interest*, Summer 1989.

 © 1993 Social Philosophy and Policy Foundation. Printed in the USA.

former Soviet bloc, it is true, rapid integration into Western institutions is both feasible and, in terms of the historical traditions of the peoples concerned, desirable. The Czechs and the Hungarians, along with the Lithuanians and the Slovenians, are likely to be in the first wave of post-Communist associate member states of a European Community that (because of its recent agreement with the European Free Trade Association, concluded in 1991 and set to become operational in 1993) will very soon constitute the largest single market in the world. If there is little doubt as to the Western destinies of these people, the case of Poland remains more doubtful, as do even those of Latvia and Estonia, with their large Russian minorities. If Poland is integrated into the political and economic institutions of a reunified Europe, it will be partly in virtue of the fact that it lacks the destabilizing ethnic minorities possessed by many other post-Communist states. This is only an instance of an evident truth that has thus far eluded the dominant schools of Western opinion: that in throwing off the universalist institutions that supposedly nurtured *Homo Sovieticus*, the post-Soviet peoples have *not* thereby adopted the Western liberal self-image of universal rights-bearers, or buyers and sellers in a global market. Instead, they have returned to their pre-Soviet particularisms, ethnic and religious — to specific cultural traditions that, except in Bohemia, are hardly those of Western liberal democracy. This return has spelled ruin for the transnational Communist states constructed in the Caucasus in the twenties and in Yugoslavia after the Second World War, and it currently threatens the *rebalkanization* of South Eastern Europe. What has already occurred in parts of Eastern Europe, and is unfolding in many parts of the former Soviet Union and in the Russian Federation itself, is not, manifestly, an ending of history, but rather its resumption on decidedly traditional lines — of ethnic and religious conflicts, irredentist claims, strategic calculations, and secret diplomacies. This return to the historic realities of European political life will remain incomprehensible, so long as those realities are viewed through the spectacles of ephemeral Enlightenment ideologies. We will not, for example, understand current developments in Poland if our model for them is the transitory nightmare of Marxian Communism; we will gain insight into them if we grasp them as further variations on historical themes — such as the relations of Poland with Russia and Germany, and the place of the Roman Catholic Church in Polish government and society — that are millennial.

This is not to say that the current transitional situation does not contain developments that are radically novel. One of them is, indeed, the confounding of Western rationalist expectations of universal convergence on a secular civilization. Even where the phenomenon has not been fundamentalist, the cultural and spiritual renaissance of traditional religiosity, and the resurgence of ancient ethnic identities, are near-universal in the post-Communist societies. From one point of view, indeed, this is only to be expected, since what failed in the Communist world was not any traditional faith or set of institutions, but instead a secular humanist *Weltanschauung* (philosophy of life) that was wholly *Western* in origin and inspiration. The Marxist world-view that governed Russia and the other subject nations of the Soviet state for much of this century was conceived by a German philosopher, heavily influenced by Hegel, Feuerbach, Proudhon, and other major Western European thinkers: it did not originate in a Russian monastery. Western failure to anticipate, and even to perceive, the return to pre-Soviet cultural traditions in former Communist countries, reflects the fact that the Western origin of Communist regimes goes unperceived or denied, with their universal repressive features being blamed upon the distinctive, but in fact highly diverse cultural traditions of their subject peoples, rather than upon the totalitarian institutions and obscurantist ideology that characterizes all of them.

There is another respect in which the present transitional situation in the post-Communist societies is novel, and for that matter unique. This is found in the fact that we have no historical example of a command economy on anything resembling the scale of the post-Soviet states being transformed into a market economy, without either an accompanying dictatorship, as in Chile, or the destruction of its supportive totalitarian polity in war, as in National Socialist Germany. It is worth noting that in neither of these cases had totalitarian control of economic life proceeded as far as it did in all of the Communist regimes. The central thesis of this essay is that there is, in the end, no historical model for transition from post-Communism to civil society, since the regimes that have at length collapsed in the Communist world are entirely unprecedented in human history. Except in a few countries, where European traditions in economic, political, and legal institutions have survived somewhat intact through the Communist period, policies of privatization on a Western model of the assets of the collapsed command economy are likely to fail. They will fail most dramatically where, as in most of the post-Communist states but above all in Russia, they are sponsored by, and controlled by, elements in the corrupt and exploitative *nomenklatura* inherited from the Communist regime, which is in turn protected by the networks of organized crime, or mafia, in collusion with command structures inherited from the former KGB, that have effectively replaced the Party and its organs as the only organized structures in economic life in Russia. It will be one of my principal theses that such spontaneous or wild privatization is likely under democratic institutions to be politically unstable because it lacks popular legitimacy.

My argument has another aspect, or implication. If, as I maintain, it is neither feasible nor, in many cases, desirable that the institutions of Western democratic capitalism be transplanted to the post-Communist states, aside from a few of them that retain European cultural and political traditions that are vital and adaptable, then the post-Communist states—

especially Russia and, in due course, when it sheds finally its Marxist incubus, China—will have no alternative to reviving their earlier, pre-Communist traditions. It is, indeed, in such a revival—of traditions of political authoritarianism rooted in Orthodoxy in Russia and in Neo-Confucianism in China—that the best prospect of peaceful development for these peoples probably lies. It is most unlikely that, having been desolated by a barbarizing Western ideology, the political cultures of Russia and China would benefit from a further infusion of Western ideology—in this case, that of messianic liberalism. They will be well-advised, instead, to refrain from emulating Western institutions in either the political or the economic spheres, and to seek their own, novel paths, arising from their own pre-Communist inheritances. At the same time, if my argument is not mistaken, they will be compelled to adopt the constitutive institutions of civil society—the institutions of the market and of private property—if they are to renew themselves as modern civilizations. The challenge they face, accordingly, is that of reinventing their pre-Communist traditions and thereby asserting their cultural identities against the tendency to further Westernization, while at the same time resisting tendencies to nativism and xenophobia that would threaten the undoing of the emergent forces of civil society. It is a task of extraordinary difficulty and delicacy.

It is further evident that a Hobbesian peace is a necessary condition of a successful transition from the post-Communist anarchy of many of the former Soviet states to genuine civil societies. I mean by a Hobbesian peace a condition in which civil order is maintained under a rule of law, such that the business of ordinary life can go on without the threat of violence, and the powers of coercion are restricted to government. This entails, in turn, that the sources of extra-legal violence—the mafias and irregular armies—be repressed or co-opted by government, and that economic life come within the compass of the rule of law. In some cases, where ethnic conflicts are otherwise intractable, that law may well have to be martial law. A Hobbesian peace, imposed by a government which represents no totalitarian ideology and which is prepared to act decisively to mediate or suppress the conflicts of warring ethnicities, is an indispensable precondition of a stable civil society throughout the post-Communist world. My understanding of civil society here is meant to encompass civil societies in all their varieties. In dialectical contrast with Marxian totalitarianism or Islamic (or other) fundamentalism, civil societies have three defining features. First, their political institutions are not those of a Weltanschauung-state, embodying a totalistic world-view, but instead permit a diversity of perspectives and values to coexist in peace. Second, by contrast with traditional despotisms, civil societies are governed by a rule of law—though this may take a variety of forms, and be sometimes honored in the breach. Third, in all civil societies, the bulk of economic life is conducted in autonomous institutions, themselves defined and protected by law — in voluntary associations, intermediary institutions, and markets, operating under institutions of private property and contractual liberty. Note that the variety of civil societies is such that Western democratic capitalism is only one, perhaps short-lived, instance of them. Civil societies may be, as most historically have been, sheltered by an authoritarian political regime, in which civil liberties may have legal protection, but in which democratic participatory liberties are lacking. Examples are the state of Prussia under Frederick the Great, Tsarist Russia during its last six decades, and, in our own time, Singapore and Hong Kong. They may contain forms of private property, and of contractual liberty, that are not those of Western corporate capitalism. And they may be animated by forms of moral culture that are very different from the liberal individualism that pervades Western civil society.

It is not to be expected that any one form of civil society — say, that of Western democratic capitalism or East Asian authoritarian market institutions — will be appropriate for all the post-Communist states, with their vastly divergent cultural inheritances. Indeed, the model of Anglo-American capitalism will be successfully exported to few, if any, of the post-Communist states. The argument of this essay, nevertheless, is that civil society, with its economic base in market institutions, is the reproduction mechanism of any modern civilization — the essential precondition for the renewal over time of an industrial society. (Saudi Arabia is a possible exception to this generalization, though I have doubts as to its long-term stability.) For the post-Communist states, there is no option but to construct the institutions of civil society that were destroyed or damaged, if they ever fully existed, by Communist totalitarianism. I argue further, however, that no post-Communist state has yet fully effected the transition to civil society. All, in very varying degrees, are in a no-man's land of Hobbesian anarchy, without property rights or any rule of law. A Hobbesian peace is thus the most vital precondition of the next stage of the transition process.

If there is a model for such a transition, it is certainly not that of Anglo-American democratic capitalism, nor yet that of Swedish social democracy or even the German social market economy. If any historical exemplar exists at all, it may be found in the East Asian economies, which were modernized against a background of political authoritarianism, and by a policy of strategic governmental intervention in the economy, *not* of laissez faire. One of the many paradoxes of the current situation may be that it is to China, where market reform is proceeding under the remnants of a Communist gerontocracy, rather than to any Western country, that many of the post-Soviet states, but especially Russia, may turn for lessons in how to cope with their unique historical dilemma.

In order to demonstrate the irrelevance of Western models to the post-Communist transition process, especially in Russia, it is necessary briefly to characterize the present situation of the post-Communist societies. It is then appropriate to examine consecutively the several Western models that have been advanced, here and in the former Soviet bloc, for the transition period. I conclude by considering speculatively whether there are non-Western models for the transition and, if so, whether these are realistically applicable to the post-Soviet states.

I. Post-Communism

Whereas the post-Communist regimes differ widely in their present circumstances and prospects, and have returned to their divergent cultural traditions, all bear the burden of the historical inheritance of Communist institutions and practices whose common features are far more prominent than their differences. Inasmuch as post-Communism is the negation of the institutions and practices of the Communist period, it is useful to specify what were the constitutive, defining features of "actually existing socialism" during that period. Six of these stand out as being centrally important. First, despite ubiquitous cynicism and contempt, all the Communist regimes were animated by an ideology that aspired to be hegemonic in the societies it sought to remold. This ideology, as we all know, was Marxism-Leninism—an Enlightenment political religion fused with a technology of power. Secondly, all of the Communist regimes were characterized by a totalitarian fusion of the economy with the polity: economic and political power were, to a considerable extent, one and the same—an inexorable result of the socialist command economy.[2] Thirdly, all of the Communist regimes were dominated by a privileged class of *nomenklaturists*, which arrogated to itself such goods as access to good housing and health care, education, and the opportunities and perquisites of travel abroad, and which in many countries succeeded in becoming a cross-generational exploitative caste. Fourthly, all of the Communist regimes, but above all Russia, possessed a massive military-strategic economy, far greater in magnitude than that of any Western state, which was to a large extent insulated from the inefficiency and waste of the ordinary consumer economy. This strategic sector of the economy may in the Russian case amount to around 50 percent of the economy as a whole; in every Communist regime it was large—it preempted resources from the consumer economy and achieved a level of technological innovation superior in many areas to that of the Western military-industrial complexes.[3] Fifthly, all Communist regimes were what have been called *counter-*

[2] On this, see my article "Totalitarianism, Reform, and Civil Society," in *Totalitarianism at the Crossroads*, ed. Ellen Frankel Paul (New Brunswick and London: Transaction Publishers, 1990), pp. 97–142.

[3] For further evidence on this, see my monograph *The Strange Death of Perestroika: Causes and Consequences of the Soviet Coup* (London: Institute for European Defence and Strategic Studies, European Security Study 13, 1990).

intelligence states:[4] that is to say, states whose relations with their subject populations, and with non-Communist states, were mediated through a colossal apparatus of surveillance and espionage, itself further preempting resources from the rest of society to a degree unknown in any non-Communist regime. Sixthly, and lastly, all Communist states have depended for their capacity to reproduce themselves as industrial economies, and so perhaps for their very survival, on recurrent, and almost continuous, injections of Western aid—in the form of food, technology, expertise, and credit. Importantly, though governmental guarantees by Western states of such aid have sometimes been significant, at other times the major part of Western assistance to Communist states has been in the form of unsecured loans and direct investment by Western commercial banks and corporations.[5] In technological and industrial terms, the Soviet Union (for example) was to a large extent an artifact of Western capitalist wealth and technology. It is therefore the case, not only that the Communist states were products of a Western ideology, but also that their capacity for renewal depended crucially on a virtually uninterrupted stream of Western economic aid.

How have these six constitutive features of the Communist regimes fared—altered or mutated—in the post-Communist period? The hegemonic ideology, to begin with, has everywhere suffered a comprehensive collapse. Long derided and despised in private, never accepted by the bulk of the workers, reproduced only in the work of a small class of abjectly servile academic *nomenklaturists*, Marxism-Leninism, like Marxism itself, survives only in the form of a few vestigial habits of thought and practice. Among the *nomenklaturists*, Leninism survives as a technique of political manipulation, of mass mobilization, of deception and disinformation, and of contempt and cynicism about democracy. It is dead, even among the *nomenklaturists*, as a world-view, and as an expansionist political movement. Among ordinary people, it survives as the common belief that market exchange is typically a zero-sum transaction—a belief well corroborated by the exploitative parallel economies of the Communist period and by their *nomenklaturist*-dominated successors. The remnants of the Communist institutions are therefore thoroughly delegitimated (if legitimacy they ever had). The *nomenklatura* itself is thoroughly demoralized. The result of *glasnost* has been to reveal in all their stark horror the results of decades of socialist planning: a bankrupt industrial economy, most of which (outside the strategic sector) lags behind the West by a generation or more; levels of health in the population, especially in Russia, which are comparable only with Third World countries, and are falling; levels of pollution and of environmental degradation which are every-

---

[4] I owe the term "counter-intelligence state" to John J. Dziak, who uses it in his book *Chekisty: A History of the KGB* (Lexington: Lexington Books, D. C. Heath and Co., 1988).

[5] Evidence on this is given in my monograph *The Strange Death of Perestroika*.

where worse than in any Western state and which in some areas — such as the former Soviet Central Asia — amount to almost apocalyptic ecological catastrophes; an epidemic of crime; and levels of income which are fractions of those of comparable groups in the West, and even in many developing countries. Aside from confirming the suspicion of ordinary people that decades of privation have been in vain, the revelations of *glasnost* have illuminated to the *nomenklaturists* the sad fact that, notwithstanding their status as members of a corrupt exploitative caste, their standard of living, even on the higher rungs of the *nomenklatura*, compares unfavorably with that of a primary school teacher in most Western countries.

If the ideology is dead and the *nomenklatura* in disarray, what of the other four elements that characterized the Communist regimes? The totalitarian fusion of the economy and the polity has broken down with the collapse of the state planning institutions. It has nowhere yet been replaced by the institutions of civil society and a market economy. In all the Communist states, but again above all in Russia, the collapse of central planning has been accompanied by a process of "wild," "spontaneous," or "Hayekian" privatization — a process of privatization bizarrely akin to the unplanned emergence of market institutions postulated in F. A. Hayek's theorizings, but which, because of its extensive penetration and control by criminal elements, lacks many of the classical attributes of private property and voluntary exchange. This process has been largely controlled by the *nomenklatura* and often inaugurated by the secret police; it is a privatization in which assets which were formerly parts of the planning apparatus have been appropriated by their former managers and elements in the Party hierarchy. The degree of success of this defensive *nomenklaturist* strategy varies widely, from country to country, with some (such as Czechoslovakia) trying to resist it entirely, and with others (such as Russia) finding the rule of the Party and the *nomenklatura* being replaced by the "anarcho-capitalism" of the mafia, itself in a symbiotic relationship with the KGB and its successor services. None of the post-Communist states yet possesses the institutional infrastructure of a civil society: a law of property and contract, a fully independent judiciary, and so on. In none of them, accordingly, has the transition, so often talked about, yet occurred. In other words, Gorbachev's reformist project for the socialist command economy has failed, as it was bound to do; a revolutionary collapse has occurred instead.[6] The former Soviet bloc is now irreversibly

---

[6] In the *Times Literary Supplement* of July 27, 1989, I wrote: "Whatever the immediate outcome of current negotiations, it is safe to assert that neither the division of Germany in its present form, nor West Germany's current relationship with NATO, can be sustained for long. As it stands, the political and military posture of West Germany disregards both the realities of history and legitimate German aspirations for unification; and the pressures for a separate settlement between West Germany and the Soviet Union are probably irresistible. . . . The darker side of the dissolution of the post-war settlement is in the prospect

post-totalitarian; but nowhere has a civil society yet been stably installed. The central question that arises is: Will the radical project of supplanting the socialist command economy with market institutions not also fail, if for other reasons?

Whatever the answer to that question, it is worth noting the current condition of the military-industrial complex in the post-Soviet states, and of their security services. On these issues hard information is difficult to come by, and any conjecture one may make is bound to be largely speculative in character. A few aspects of the current situation can be discerned however. At present, the Russian military-industrial complex is not being dismantled and may even be expanding; further, except for warheads that are no longer serviceable but remain dangerous, there is little prospect that it will be dismantled or reduced significantly in the near future, if only because of the further economic dislocation that would entail. Civilianization of the strategic sector of the economy remains a hope, not an ongoing project—a fact worth recalling in the context of the massive program of unilateral Western disarmament now underway. On the other hand, demoralization and despair are rampant in the regular armed forces, such that the prospect of their being used either for external aggression or for domestic repression is remote. What, then, of the special forces—the troops of the Ministry of the Interior's army, the *spetznaz* teams, and the former KGB units, amounting to perhaps nearly a million men? It seems likely that, with the command structure of the Red Army splintering, particularly as between Russia and the Ukraine, an analogous fracturing is occurring in the special forces and in the KGB proper. It is plausible to suppose, in any case, that Yeltsin's emergence from the abortive "coup" of August 1991 was made possible only in virtue of support he had received from powerful elements in the former KGB. This is to say that the KGB's successor services remain powerful,[7] but they have been subject to fragmentation and cannot mount a systematic repression in the former Soviet Union nor act as its organizational spine. If this is true, then any attempt to retard or reverse the disintegrative process of the past five years within the former Soviet Union, whether by the regular armed

---

of . . . West Germany prised loose from NATO only to inherit the rusting industries and indigent pensioners of the GDR." I wrote in *The Financial Times*, London, September 13, 1989: "The danger is that the decay of the totalitarian system built up by Stalin and Lenin will result not in the reconstitution of a stable civil society, but in mounting chaos and economic collapse. . . . If this is so, then what we are witnessing in the Soviet Union is not the middle of a reform, but the beginning of a revolution, whose course no-one can foretell." In October 1989 in *Totalitarianism at the Crossroads*, p. 134, I wrote: ". . . classical Communist totalitarianism is already showing signs of weakness (as in Bulgaria) and even Romania may not prove immune to change or collapse. . . . The model for such a prospect . . . may be contemporary Yugoslavia, with its intractable ethnic conflicts, profound economic problems, weak populist governments, and chronic tendencies toward political disintegration." These warnings were widely dismissed as alarmist.

[7] They remain powerful partly in virtue of their collusion with organized crime in Russia.

forces or by special forces, if it occurs at all, is most unlikely to succeed or to succeed for long.

The situation in the Russian Federation itself may well be different. Such anecdotal evidence as is currently available suggests that, because it is the only part of the Russian economy whose products can compete in global markets, the military-industrial complex continues to expand, especially in its high-technology sectors. Reforms in the former KGB, and related services, appear to have been substantially ones in nomenclature and, to a lesser extent, organization. In the case of the Russian Federation, in all likelihood, an apparatus of repression remains intact which could impose a military dictatorship, perhaps for a protracted period. Should the present wave of economic reform founder, as my argument implies, it is more than likely that nascent democratic institutions will be swept away and an authoritarian regime installed. It will be the thrust of my argument that, provided such an authoritarian regime was committed to the construction of a civil society in Russia and avoided the worst excesses of atavistic nativism, it could well prove a better guarantor of peaceful development than political institutions modeled on Western exemplars that, for the most part, are themselves in evident decadence and decline.

One final common factor in both Communist and post-Communist regimes is the flow of Western aid. The Gorbachev regime did not receive economic aid in the amounts it demanded, partly because the resources for such governmental aid no longer existed, particularly in the United States, and partly because there is now a general perception in the West that the funds transferred as part of a Grand Bargain or a new Marshall Plan would most likely simply vanish. Future aid is likely to be extended in the context of the post-Soviet states becoming members of Western financial institutions, such as the World Bank and the International Monetary Fund, even as they join Western security organizations, such as NATO. It is evident that the present policy of the post-Soviet regime in Russia is to seek integration with Western institutions, so that its fate and the interests of the Western powers are further entwined. If the prospects for the transition to civil society in most of the post-Communist states are as poor as I shall argue, the wisdom of the Western powers in promoting such integration is questionable. There is a real danger that the already fragile global economic balance — threatened as it is by the emergence of trade blocs and the subversion of the General Agreement on Tariffs and Trade by protectionism, by unsustainable governmental debt in the United States, and by a decline of asset values in Japan that endangers the world banking system — will be shattered by economic collapse and military upheaval in Russia, with the possibility of an ensuing thirties-style Great Depression engulfing the world. Can this be prevented by the successful export of Western institutions to the post-Communist states?

Or is the best hope of stability, in Russia and China at least, to be found in the development of market institutions and civil societies under the auspices of authoritarian regimes sustained by indigenous Russian and Chinese cultural traditions rather than by imported Western ideologies? Let us first consider, one by one, the various Western models that have been advanced for the post-Communist regimes.

II. Western Models for the Post-Communist States

By far the most influential model for the post-Communist regimes, especially in Eastern Europe, is the German social market economy.[8] This is so for a number of straightforward reasons having to do with the history and current circumstances of the relations between Germany and Eastern Europe. In the first place, much of the institutional and cultural inheritance of the Eastern European peoples is German in origin. The legal and educational systems of Czechoslovakia and Hungary, even in some measure that of Poland, bear the mark of their German exemplars. Except where the influence of France has been important, as it has to a degree in Romania and to some extent in Poland, Germanic culture has enjoyed hegemony in Eastern Europe for centuries, and everything suggests that, after the aberrant Nazi and Communist periods, it is set to reclaim this hegemony again. The hegemony will be economic as well as cultural. For Eastern Europeans, it is self-evident that Germany has become the dominant economic power in Europe, and it is likely that this dominance will be increased, rather than diminished, over the coming decades. That this perception is not groundless is suggested by the composition of Western investment in Eastern Europe and in the post-Soviet states: it is overwhelmingly German in origin. Nor are the real economic costs and problems of German unification perceived in Eastern Europe as threats to the German economic miracle: rather, the difficulties of unification are seen as a necessary prelude to the next phase of German policy, which will be the economic colonization of the East. The German model, then, is perceived in Eastern Europe, and even in Russia, as the real success story of the postwar period. By contrast, Anglo-American capitalism is perceived to be in steep and inexorable decline—its banks and governments broke and its culture in disrepute and disarray; nothing is expected of it in terms of a contribution to the transition process, and it is nowhere adopted as a model.

What are the principal characteristics of the German social market economy, and how far is it relevant to the post-Communist states? In historical terms, this question can be readily answered, since the original exemplar of the German model is the deregulation of the postwar Ger-

---

[8] I have discussed the German social market economy at length in my monograph *The Moral Foundations of Market Institutions* (London: Institute for Economic Affairs, 1992).

man economy, without the consent and against the wishes of the occupying Allied powers, and the spectacular economic recovery that ensued. The planning and price controls installed by the Allies were removed along with the remnants of the Nazi command economy, and a full-scale liberalization of the German economy was enforced. Beyond this historical specification, any characterization of the German social market economy becomes controversial, since it encompassed a variety of schools and perspectives, ranging from Catholic communitarians, through latter-day classical liberals of a somewhat Hayekian orientation, to virtual social democrats. Because of its internal complexity, both theoretical and (after its initial golden period) historical, it may seem impossible to specify its central, defining ideas.

This appearance is deceptive, however, since all of the theorists of the social market economy accepted three key ideas that distinguish them from other theorists of market institutions, including most thinkers in the English-speaking world. First, they roundly rejected the proposition that market institutions are, or should be, the unplanned upshot of cultural or institutional evolution. For all of the social market theorists, the institutions of the market were *not* forms of spontaneous order, given to us by history, but instead artifacts created, and reformed, by constructivist legal and political intervention.[9] On this view, market freedoms are not guaranteed by a policy of nonintervention, or laissez faire; they are created and protected by a competition policy that requires the constant monitoring, and recurrent reform, of the legal framework within which market exchange occurs. Second, and as an implication of this first point, all the social market theorists rejected the conception of economic freedom, owing its inspiration to Locke, and regarded as axiomatic in the United States, in which it is constituted by a structure of individual rights. For them, market institutions are justified not by their embodiment of any supposed structure of fundamental rights, but by their contribution to individual and collective well-being. They are therefore perpetually open to revision and reform by reference to this undergirding purpose. Third, market institutions must on this view, shared by all the social market theorists, be complemented by other institutions, which confer on market participants forms of security possessed by them as citizens.[10] Market institutions are not free-standing, but come embedded in other institutions, including those in which government acts to protect citizens from forms of insecurity that market institutions by themselves may create, or are powerless to prevent—a task of government that is, in any case, enshrined in the Basic Law of the German constitution. These three ideas, interpreted in fashions more or less liberal, more or less corporatist, are the common currency of the German social market model, and

[9] See *ibid.*, p. 83.
[10] *Ibid.*, p. 98.

have animated thought and policy in Germany to the present day, to a very considerable extent, in all the major political parties.

The advantages of this German model for Eastern Europe and for the post-Soviet states are clear enough. As against the generalization of the English historical experience of the emergence of market freedoms through the development of common law, which Hayek advances as a form of institutional or cultural Darwinism,[11] the German social market theorists perceived that, in most historical contexts and certainly in theirs, market institutions were not, and could not be, the results of "spontaneous" social processes: they could only be—what they have always been in most societies—products of institutional design and legislative fiat. The relevance of this insight to the predicament of the post-Communist societies stands in little need of clarification. Because they lack the legal and institutional infrastructure of market competition, the post-Communist states will be fatally misled if they expect market institutions to come about by a process of spontaneous emergence. If they adopt such a view, they will in effect preside over a Hobbesian state of nature, in which productive assets are captured by alliances of *nomenklaturists* and mafiosi, and in which market competition occurs through corruption and intimidation. This is not a recipe for prosperity, for the popular and political legitimacy of market institutions, or for a civil society of any sort. What is required in the post-Communist states, if a civil society and a genuine market economy are to be created, is not a policy of political quietism, but rather an active engagement by government in constructivist institution-building—a fact acknowledged, virtually alone among Western theorists of transition, in the writing of James Buchanan.[12]

The constructivist orientation of the German social market economy has crucial relevance to the current situation of the post-Communist states, especially in the former Soviet Union, in illuminating the utterly delusive character of Western hopes that liberal regimes will prevail—as if there were a natural process whereby this could reasonably be expected—through a jurisdictional competition among the post-Communist states. The idea is that, if even one of them adopts a liberal constitution and implements policies of economic liberty, then by a "demonstration effect," others will emulate it. Or, if this benign process of emulation fails to occur, investment capital will migrate to the liberal polity and economy, and so assure its survival and success. It is hard to see how this scenario can have credibility with anyone with the slightest grasp of European (or other) history. As the collapse of the Romanov dynasty in 1917 and of the Hapsburgs after World War One shows, the collapse of em-

---

[11] See F. A. Hayek, *The Constitution of Liberty* (Chicago: Henry Regnery, 1960), ch. 11, for this erroneous generalization.

[12] I refer in particular to Buchanan's "Tacit Presuppositions of Political Economy: Implications for Societies in Transition" (George Mason University, Fairfax, VA: Center for Study of Public Choice, 1991), mimeograph.

pires typically issues in the emergence of nation-states which are protectionist and which interdict the mobility of capital and labor. Even if one of the post-Communist states were to adopt an ideally liberal constitution, and this proved internally stable, historical experience suggests that others would inhibit emulation, or the migration of capital, by coercive means. Indeed, if history is any guide, emulation would be thwarted by sheer enmity, as old rivalries assumed traditional military forms. The classical-liberal idea that jurisdictional competition among sovereign states, in the post-Communist world and elsewhere, assures or enhances the prospects of liberal regimes, expresses the absurd delusion that market processes are natural phenomena, rather than creatures of political power, governed in the end by the exigencies of strategy and mortal conflict in war. It is a signal advantage of the theory that underlies the German model that, correctly understood, it dispels this fantastic mirage of classical liberalism.

The German social market model has another clear implication for the post-Communist states. This is that the democratic legitimacy of market institutions depends on their being complemented by other institutions, particularly those protecting citizens from insecurity. In the Eastern European post-Communist states, though it will be extraordinarily difficult to implement, this implication holds good, in that it is difficult to see how market institutions can gain or keep legitimacy in a context of democratic government, if their early stages of development impose large and uncompensated losses, and attendant insecurity, on many people.

There are three large difficulties confronting the application of the German model (in itself probably the least inappropriate of the Western models) to the post-Communist states. The first is that, whereas postwar Germany was fortunate in that its Nazi *nomenklatura* had been substantially destroyed or dispersed, all of the post-Communist states are burdened by a resourcefully exploitative *nomenklaturist* caste that has, and will, distort the reform process to its own advantage (by, for example, milking newly privatized enterprises of value, and thereby compromising their success). The post-Communist states are, paradoxically, less fortunate than post-Nazi Germany in that in them there has been a less comprehensive destruction of the totalitarian regime, so that it is much harder, if not altogether impossible, to start with a political or economic clean slate. The second difficulty is almost the obverse of the first. Whereas the Nazi regime and its functionaries were destroyed by defeat in war, the Nazi regime had destroyed far less of the institutional infrastructure of civil society in Germany. Doubtless largely because of its relative brevity, National Socialism had not comprehensively destroyed, though it had grievously damaged, the legal matrix of civil society—the law of property and contract, private and commercial law, corporate and banking law, and so on. The legal matrix of civil society did not, for this reason, have to be created *de novo* in postwar Germany. Taking these two difficulties together, we may say that the post-Communist states are in a circumstance in which they must reinvent the institutions of civil society from scratch, while being burdened by a vast *nomenklatura* which (unless it succeeds in co-opting the reform process) stands to lose heavily from a successful transition — which is a combination that counts against the successful adoption of any Western model, not only the German, and that hinders the development of market institutions in any of their varieties. The third difficulty arises from a central feature of the German model specifically, namely its correct acknowledgment that the democratic legitimacy of market institutions depends upon their being supplemented or complemented by security-promoting welfare institutions. The difficulty facing the post-Communist states is that their poverty prevents the adoption of this aspect of the German model — an aspect essential to its success. They cannot, for the most part, afford a welfare state on German lines — not even the smaller welfare state with which it started, prior to its evolution into its current neo-corporatist form. In the cases of Hungary and Czechoslovakia (and particularly Bohemia), a version of the German model is likely to be adopted, and even to achieve a measure of success. Elsewhere, and especially in Russia, it stands no chance of successful implementation.

What, then, of the other, recently fashionable model, that of Sweden? We may at once dismiss the notion of Swedish egalitarian social democracy as a viable third way between liberal capitalism and totalitarian socialism. For, firstly, as we shall soon see in greater detail, this piece of academic folklore betrays a profound ignorance of the actual history of Sweden, and, secondly, the Swedish model, so conceived, has now suffered a self-avowed economic and political collapse. Let us look first, though, at the real historical development of the Swedish model, which is very different from that projected by the academic conventional wisdom. There can be no doubt that, measured by the standard of economic growth, Sweden has until the past decade or so been an extraordinary success story. Between 1870 and 1970, Sweden transformed itself from an underdeveloped country to one of the richest in the world, with a per-capita growth rate during that period second only to Japan's.[13] But how was this achieved? From 1870 to 1930, Sweden was ruled by a small, ultraliberal limited government whose interventions in the economy were largely restricted to modest agricultural and industrial protectionism. Governmental welfare provision was initiated on a national scale in 1913, with the creation of universal old-age pensions, but remained limited until well after the Social Democrats came to power in 1932. Universal suffrage, importantly, was not implemented until the early twenties. In short, the first and decisive period of economic development occurred un-

---

[13] I owe these data to an excellent paper by Peter Stein, "Sweden: From Capitalist Success to Welfare-State Sclerosis," *Policy Analysis*, no. 160 (September 10, 1991).

der a limited government of a classical-liberal type, with correspondingly limited democracy. "Furthermore," as Peter Stein observes, "the Swedish population remained ethnically and culturally homogeneous, which may have created an atmosphere of cooperation and avoided tensions."[14] The benefits of neutrality in two global wars are also significant.

However, it should not be supposed that, when the Social Democrats came to power in Sweden, they at once imposed the sort of highly regulated, radically redistributionist policies that are associated with the Swedish model by the historically illiterate in the Western academies. Indeed, until the collapse of the Social Democrats in 1991, regulation in Sweden was less restrictive than in most other Western countries, including the United States; capital gains taxation was slight or nonexistent; and little of industry—far less than in the United Kingdom, even after a decade of privatization—was in state ownership. Indeed, in 1960, government spending was 31 percent of GNP in Sweden, just three points higher than in the United States; and in the same year tax levels were about the same in the two countries. The seeds of destruction were planted in the Swedish model only in the seventies, when the proportion of GNP appropriated by government rose to 60 percent, and redistributionist and welfarist policies began to be applied more radically. When the Swedish model collapsed, it did so because the tax and transfer system that had been superimposed on a highly capitalistic productive system had become simply too top-heavy against the background of a sort of chronic stagflation in the economy. Even at its most interventionist, Sweden was never as corporatist as the UK in the seventies; and for most of its recent history it has been more thoroughly capitalist in its productive institutions than most other Western countries.

If the Swedish model has any relevance to the post-Communist states, it is clearly its earlier, rather than its later phase that is salient. None of the post-Communist states can afford the welfare state that Sweden developed from the sixties onwards: they are, and will remain for several generations, far too poor. Again, it is not insignificant that the early phase of the Swedish model was conducted under limited democratic institutions, whereas most of the post-Communist states have opted for unlimited democracy. Will the fragile democracies of the post-Communist states survive the economic dislocations—including massive unemployment, and a weak or nonexistent safety net—of the transition period? It may well be that limited democratic institutions—of the sort under which the Industrial Revolution occurred in England—are the ideally appropriate ones for the post-Communist states; but, as I shall argue later, the proposal that the post-Communist states adopt the minimal governments of the eighteenth and nineteenth centuries, which has been advanced by lat-

[14] *Ibid.*, p. 7.

ter-day classical liberals, is an exercise in anachronism and utopianism. As far as the Swedish model is concerned, the crucial point is that the costs of redistributionist taxation and of an overextended welfare state, which in the end brought to its knees even the rich Social Democratic regime, will be ruinous in the post-Communist states, which start from a base of underdevelopment and poverty.

If the Swedish model is to be rejected, what of the model of Anglo-American capitalism? The first point to be made is that, because (unlike the German social market economy) Anglo-American capitalism is the result of a long, unplanned evolutionary development in which the common law played a large part, it is not readily exportable—especially to countries with very different cultural, legal, and political traditions. It was transplanted successfully to Australasia, but not, for example, to Africa or India. The second point to be made is that, far from being the paradigm case of the development of market institutions, as Hayek supposes, the unplanned emergence of capitalism in England was, if anything, an exceptional and limiting case. As Alan Macfarlane has shown, undermining the sociological and historical myth of the Great Transformation,[15] industrial capitalism emerged in England against a background of centuries of agrarian capitalism and possessive individualism. This was otherwise in Scotland, which developed a commercial economy on the basis, not of common law, but of Roman law, which was imposed by fiat. Again, in the American case, English institutions were transplanted to the New World by people whose cultural traditions were also, in large part, English. It is very difficult to see how such a transplantation could be effected in any of the post-Communist states.

The Anglo-American model is inappropriate for other reasons. It is far from clear whether the Western capitalist corporation is the proper vehicle for market competition in the post-Communist states, particularly in Russia, where (as Buchanan has perceptively observed)[16] a *radical decon-centration* of economic activity to municipal and cooperative levels may be a better alternative in many areas. Private property in most productive assets, contractual liberty, and market competition are essential elements in any civil society; but market institutions come in many varieties, of which Anglo-American capitalism is only one. The fact that it is widely perceived as being in steep and probably irreversible decline, by comparison with both German-style neo-corporatism and the East Asian economies, suggests that it is not on the historical agenda for any of the post-Communist states.

Nor, finally, is it clear that market institutions on the Anglo-American model are compatible with the democratic political institutions that the

---

[15] See Alan Macfarlane, *The Origins of English Individualism* (Cambridge: Cambridge University Press, 1978).

[16] Buchanan, "Tacit Presuppositions of Political Economy."

post-Communist states are urged to adopt by the West. After all, industrialization on the capitalist model occurred in England under conditions of very limited government and a tiny franchise: would it, or could it, have happened under conditions of unlimited democracy, when its human costs would have been given full political expression? This is *not* to say that limited government along classical-liberal lines is an option for any of the post-Communist states. In all of them, conceptions of political legitimacy framed on the lines of popular government (but not necessarily, or usually, of liberal democracy) are strong, and traditions of limited government are weak or nonexistent. More to the point, attempts to shackle government by constitutional rules, which in the United States, by far the most favorable case, have plainly failed, are most unlikely to work in the political cultures and historical circumstances of the post-Communist states. Most likely, any such limited government would simply be swept away by popular revolution and subsequent dictatorship. It is well to remember that the only nondemocratic limited government in recent times has been a colonial government—Hong Kong. In an age of ethnicity and populism, reversion to the political models of the English-speaking world a century or more ago is an anachronistic and utopian project that is not on any forseeable historical agenda. This is a result derivable, in any case, from the manifest failures of the experiments in the United States, the United Kingdom, and New Zealand to restrict the scope and activity of government. If such projects have failed in the English-speaking countries that are the home of the Anglo-American model, what chance have they in the post-Communist states, where the costs of transition are far greater and political traditions vastly different?

Having considered the three main variants of the Western model, we need not detain ourselves long over others that have been advanced. The Latin American model of privatization by "big bang," as advocated by Jeffrey Sachs, for example, neglects the fact that most economic life in Bolivia, say, already occurred in private (albeit parallel) economies, and there was not a vast command economy, dominated by state-owned industries, to be dismantled. The Chilean model of capitalist development under authoritarian dictatorship has been, and continues to be, discussed in several post-Communist states, including Poland and Russia, and an attempt to emulate it, in one or more of these states, is highly likely. Once again, however, even the Chilean model stands a chance of working in economic terms, only if the legal infrastructure of market institutions is in place—and that is true of few, if any, of the post-Communist states at present. Our conclusion remains: except for a few fortunate cases, Western models are unworkable, in the forseeable future, in the post-Communist states. It follows that, except in the few cases I have specified, policies of privatization and democratization on Western lines will fail, even as *perestroika* failed before them.

III. Non-Western Models

Stated in its most general terms, my argument has been, first, that the human and social costs of transition to a market economy are for most of the post-Communist states so great that it is foolish to suppose that the transition can be conducted under liberal democratic institutions. Or, to put the same point in other terms, the preconditions of a market order in most of the post-Communist states are incompatible with those of liberal democracy. Further, I have argued that, so far, the legal infrastructure of civil society — a rule of law, laws of property and contract — is still largely lacking in most of the post-Communist states. The result is that they are all to some degree stuck in a no-man's land between totalitarianism and civil society: indeed, post-Communism is that very no-man's land.

Can anything useful be learned from the non-Western models with which we are familiar? It is worth stressing certain features of these models, held in common by them all, which distinguish them from Western models of economic development, and which undermine many conventional Western theories of economic life. In the first place, the East Asian economies, with their Confucian ethic, show that the connection between flourishing market institutions and a culture of individualism, taken (with considerable anxiety) by the early Scottish theorists of commercial society to be necessary and universal, is a historical accident. Successful market institutions no more require an individualist moral culture than they require English common law. (It is noteworthy, also, that the East Asian economies have achieved their spectacular success without accepting any of the Western liberal shibboleths of constitutionalism, individualism, cultural pluralism, universalism, fundamental rights, the idea of progress, and other relics of the Enlightenment.) Indeed, if, as seems increasingly plausible, J. A. Schumpeter was on the right track when he speculated[17] that individualist cultures devour their own moral capital and slide into debt-ridden stagnation as individualism corrodes family life and long-term planning and investment, then the nonindividualist market economies are likely to achieve an ever greater comparative advantage over the declining individualist cultures over the coming decades.

A second feature of industrialization and economic development in the East Asian economies is that, except in Hong Kong, they have been accompanied everywhere by strategic governmental intervention in the economy. In South Korea, the banks have long been virtual instruments of governmental policy; in Taiwan, tariffs and subsidies have been used to sponsor and protect new industrial developments; in Singapore and Malaysia, governmental guidance of the economy is pervasive; and in Japan, where industrialization began in the Meiji period under the aegis of cartels and interlocking firms whose structure was inherited from the

---

[17] J. A. Schumpeter, *Capitalism, Socialism, and Democracy* (New York: Harper, 1942).

feudal period,[18] the MITI — the Ministry of Trade and Industry — exercises a decisive influence over research and development in the medium to long term, even as in the short term it acts to spur competition. In short, in all of the East Asian examples other than Hong Kong, the role of government in the economy has been activist and interventionist. This is a fact, easily documented, that is denied by those (such as the laissez-faire economists) whose view of the world is structured by *a priori* theories; but it is one of direct relevance to some at least of the post-Communist states.

It is not plausible to suppose that the East Asian model, any more than the Western model, can be transplanted wholesale to any of the post-Communist states, which manifestly lack the solidaristic cultural traditions (and, in general, the ethnic homogeneity) of most of the Asian examples. A number of points of striking affinity or relevance can still be discerned. The East Asian models bear many intriguing resemblances to the pattern of economic development during the last half-century of Tsarist Russia. Let us recall that, in 1909, Russia was the world's fourth industrial power, and the world's largest wheat exporter. By 1915, over two thirds of all military conscripts were literate. From the late 1880s until 1913, economic growth was faster in Russia than in any other country. Contrary to the academic folklore, also, Tsarist Russia was far from being among the most repressive regimes existing at that time in Europe; indeed, if it were compared with late twentieth century states, it would probably rank among the thirty or so least repressive.[19] The extraordinarily rapid economic growth achieved in Russia during these decades was associated, not with policies of laissez faire, but with large-scale infrastructural investment by the state, the active encouragement of foreign investment, cartelization of industry and legal entrenchment of labor unions, and, toward the end of the Tsarist period, legislative intervention by the brilliant and ill-fated Stolypin to create agrarian capitalism in Russia. Market institutions flourished during this period in Russia in a context, in other words, not of nonintervention but of *dirigisme*. The implication for policy in post-Communist Russia is that successful market institutions will be of necessity artifacts of authoritarian intervention, created and protected by governmental power.

The model of China in its present phase of authoritarian reform may also be relevant to Russia, since the Chinese economic reform began in agriculture. Given that much of Russia's nonstrategic industrial sector will in the end have to be liquidated, not privatized, it would seem sensible to begin the next phase of economic reform in Russia with an attempt at renewing agriculture through privatization or cooperativization. This will

---

[18] On this, see Barrington Moore, *Social Origins of Dictatorship and Democracy: Lord and Peasant in the Making of the Modern World* (London: Penguin Books, 1966), ch. 5.

[19] I owe these data to M. Heller and A. Nekrich, from their magnificent study *Utopia in Power: A History of the USSR from 1917 to the Present* (London: Hutchinson, 1986), ch. 1.

be not at all easy, since, by contrast with China, the Communist regime in Russia may have come close to success in its project of exterminating the peasantry as a class and a cultural tradition. At the same time, as Aleksandr Solzhenitsyn has recently emphasized,[20] agricultural renewal is a vital precondition of any viable reform in Russia: if it fails, or is not seriously attempted, every other reform is endangered. It will be a nice irony if one of the few models to have any relevance to the post-Communist situation in Russia turns out to be that of China, where agrarian capitalism is being promoted under the auspices of a Communist oligarchy.

It may well be that the prospects of a successful transition to a market economy are brighter in China than in Russia. By contrast with Russia, China has fewer ethnic divisions and an unbroken peasant culture; it is at a disadvantage with Russia only in virtue of its not yet having thrown off the atavistic Westernizing ideology of Marxism-Leninism. In both Russia and China, authoritarian political institutions, buttressed by indigenous cultural traditions, seem to offer the best matrix for the emergent civil society. Both stand to gain by throwing off the incubus of Western ideology. In both, market institutions are most likely to be stable and successful if they do *not* replicate those of the West, but are instead molded so as to reflect the distinctive values and surviving traditions of their native cultures. China is fortunate in having as a historical exemplar the Neo-Confucian authoritarian states, immensely successful both in economic terms and in terms of social order, of Singapore, Taiwan, and South Korea. There is no such model for Russia. It seems likely that successful transition in Russia will be effected only if the remnants of the dynamic civilization of late Tsarism can be salvaged. This, in turn, will be feasible only if Russians can overcome the cultural inferiority complex instilled in them by decades of Western and Leninist propaganda focusing on the lack in Russia of the formative Western experiences of the Renaissance, the Reformation, and the Enlightenment. The task of reasserting indigenous Russian traditions against this Westernizing project, while building up a civil society in Russia, is a most subtle and daunting one, if only because in present circumstances it involves the construction, for the first time in history, of a Russian nation-state. If the alternative is anarchy and the prospect of a nuclear Yugoslavia, however, the Western powers may yet be persuaded that it is in this prospect, rather than the bankrupt Enlightenment projects of Gorbachevism, that hope for Russia is to be found. It is in helping Russia to achieve a *via media* between its European and its Asiatic inheritances, which it has never before historically sustained, that the West may be of assistance—if at all.

No reform of any of the post-Communist economies can be undertaken consistently or successfully in the absence of civil peace. Throughout most of the former Soviet Union, including most of the Russian Federa-

---

[20] See Aleksandr Solzhenitsyn, *Rebuilding Russia* (London: Harvill, 1991), pp. 29–33.

tion, civil peace is at risk from resurgent ethnicities and religious enmities. If civil society is to have any chance in these conditions, a civil peace
must be imposed of a Hobbesian character. Here another, so far neglected
non-Western example may have some relevance — that of Attaturkist Turkey. It will be recalled that there (during the decades after the First World
War when Turkey was under the rule of Kemal Attaturk), as will be the
case in most of the post-Communist lands, civil society did not result
from a process of evolutionary emergence; it was imposed by authoritarian fiat — by a secularized army and by the adoption of the Swiss civil
code, which in effect created the legal individual in Turkey, and so inaugurated a civil society there. (The example of Attaturkist Turkey has a
direct and immediate relevance to the nations of post-Soviet Central Asia,
where perhaps fifty or sixty million are currently rediscovering, and reasserting, their Turkic cultural identity.) If, as is overwhelmingly likely,
the transition to a market economy can be conducted in Russia only under the aegis of political authoritarianism, it is to be hoped that the form
of authoritarian regime that Russia acquires resembles that of Attaturk,
and therefore that of those reforming Tsars who sought to strengthen an
emergent civil society in Russia, rather than the xenophobic authoritarianism currently advocated by the neo-fascist demagogues of *Pamyat* and
similar organizations (all of which have proven links with elements in the
former KGB). Like all the other post-Communist peoples, Russians have
no alternative but to salvage from their ruined traditions whatever is serviceable in the current transition. If they are to achieve the transition to
civil society that was the aim of the reformist Tsars, they must confront
the daunting task of imposing a civil order on their society that is Hobbesian in that it seeks only for peace and (though it would be bound to rely
on traditions of Russian Orthodoxy) not the triumph of any ideology or
ethnicity.

Conclusion

Several truths have been taken for granted in this essay. It has been
taken for granted that the institutions of civil society, and therefore of the
market, are indispensable preconditions for the reproduction of any modern civilization. It has further been taken for granted, however, that civil
societies come in many shapes and forms, as do their component market
institutions of private property and contractual liberty, so that no one variant of civil society is likely to be appropriate for all the post-Communist
states, with their greatly differing circumstances. What has been argued,
rather than merely taken for granted, is that specifically Western models
of civil society and of market institutions have little relevance to most of
the post-Communist states, while some non-Western models may possess a measure of relevance. The implication of this argument is that each
of the post-Communist states will be forced to improvise its institutions,

with this improvisation taking the form of a return to pre-Communist traditions, together with eclectic borrowings from other societies and polities. The truism that has been asserted is that civil society will be created
nowhere in the post-Communist world in the absence of civil peace. In
some parts of the former Soviet Union, where ethnic conflicts are intractable in the absence of imperial power, it follows that the prospects for
civil society are small, or negligible.

The larger theme of the argument is that Western models stand little
chance of successful adoption in most of the Communist world, with
the partial exception of the German model, which a few of the post-
Communist states with intact European political and cultural traditions
may be able partly to emulate. Underlying this larger thesis is a yet larger
historical conjecture. The disintegration of the Soviet order has plainly
ended the postwar division of Europe, and promises to unravel the central institutions of the postwar settlement, such as NATO. Its deeper
significance is that it spells the end, not only of the spurious socialist
humanity of the Soviet system, but also of the liberal universalism of
the Western settlement of 1919.[21] Europe is returning to the nationalisms
and ethnicities of the pre-1914 era, with the universalist illusions of Marxism and classical liberalism vanishing like the ephemeral mirages they
always were. This is no less true in Western Europe than in Eastern Europe. In Western Europe, the universalist ideals that animated the founders of the European Community are foundering, and traditional national
rivalries are reemerging, so that it is a very safe bet that there will be no
single European currency, no political union, and no European Army—
none, at any rate, to which all EC states belong—in short, no federal European super-state. The prospect for Europe, rather, is, at best, a *Europe
de patries*, on classical Gaullist lines.

Yet larger world-historical shifts will make even harder the transition
process in the post-Communist lands. The population of the former Soviet Union will soon be predominantly Muslim, and that of the world as
a whole will contain over a billion Muslims. In Europe, Muslim immigration from the Maghreb—currently estimated at between twenty and forty
million people over the next decade—will pose a major issue. The boundaries between Europe and Asia are likely to be, once again, as in medi-
eval times, defined in religious terms. (This is not to rule out the
possibility of new Islamic states being founded on the European continent
for the first time in centuries—as, perhaps, in that part of former Yugoslavia presently called Bosnia-Herzegovina—if it is not absorbed by Serbia.) The difference is that, as the Muslim people of the former Soviet
Union renew their links with their coreligionists in the Middle East and
elsewhere, they will also acquire access to the ever cheaper technologies
of mass destruction that are proliferating there.

---

[21] I develop this point further in *The Strange Death of Perestroika*, p. 32 *et seq.*

The deepest implication of the disintegration of Communist power is that it heralds the end of Western global hegemony. The postwar world order is undone by the same forces that destroyed Soviet power, as the failure of GATT (the General Agreement on Tariffs and Trade) speeds the end of global free trade and accelerates the formation of trade blocs, and the economic and (soon) military decoupling of Europe from the United States signals the passing away of the postwar global security structures. The decomposition of postwar security structures presages a tilting of the balance of nuclear deterrence from the North to the advantage of the anarchic South — a shift in the global strategic environment that is compounded by the growing availability and inexpensiveness of chemical and biological weaponry and by the ever-increasing lethality of conventional armaments. The American retreat from globalism — signaled to all the world by the inconclusive, disastrous, and farcical Gulf War — creates a power vacuum throughout the Third World that no other state is likely to be willing, or able, to fill. The project cherished by the Pentagon of imposing a *Pax Americana* on the world through the new military technologies at its disposal is likely to run aground on the reefs of American indebtedness and isolationism. The result of an implosion of American power will not, however, be the benign polycentric world order envisaged by *bien-pensant* Western opinion, but instead a global power vacuum, with no hegemonic power willing or capable of shoring up global free trade, or preventing predation. If, in the medium term of a few decades, new aspirant hegemonic powers arise, they are likely not to be Occidental, but rather East Asian, in their cultural traditions. This is a prospect that Western opinion is, as yet, very ill-prepared for.

In the Asia-Pacific region, the inevitable consequence of American decline, early next century, is the reemergence of Japan as a military power in its own right — probably by then the second greatest in the world after Russia, given that it may already be the third in terms of overall military expenditure and that, unlike the Western powers, it is not currently engaged in a policy of military self-emasculation. (It may well be that the event occurring in our century that has the most significance for the coming one is the destruction of the Russian navy by Japan in 1905; but this is a point I cannot here elaborate upon.) The continuing and rapid acquisition of new weaponry by China, including sophisticated naval technology, is also a portent for the future. The impact of these changes on the United States cannot be other than profound; taken by Francis Fukuyama to be the paradigm case of the post-historical society, it will be ravaged more than most countries by the resumption of history on classical lines, as its loss of economic preeminence is followed, inexorably, by its demise as a military superpower. The coming decades are, indeed, likely to be particularly harsh ones for the United States, as the liberal illusion that modern states shelter post-military societies is rudely dispelled by events, and the United States comes to be at risk from weapons technologies it is itself presently disposing of. In the most general terms, however, the likely metamorphosis, over the next decade or so, of the United States from a global hegemonic power to a weak regional power, protectionist and isolationist in policy and tending toward increasing ungovernability and race-war in its domestic affairs, is significant chiefly as the most dramatic evidence of the evanescence of the postwar liberal world order.

The geopolitical circumstances in which the post-Communist states struggle toward civil society and the market economy are not propitious. If present trends are any guide, the coming century augurs, not the end of history, but a tragic epoch in which history is resumed on traditional lines, but on a yet vaster scale — an epoch of Malthusian wars and religious convulsions, of ecological catastrophes and mass deaths of a magnitude far greater even than those of our century, an epoch in which the Occidental supremacy of the past few hundred years is at length eclipsed. The challenge facing the post-Communist states is that of effecting a transition to civil society that presupposes a Hobbesian peace at a time when in most of them ancient enmities augur civil disorder and war, and when on the global scale the passing of the postwar settlement has issued not in a new world order but in a chaos of nations.[22]

Politics, Jesus College, Oxford University

---

[22] I owe the expression "chaos of nations" to Pierre Lellouche's superb book *Le nouveau monde de l'ordre de Yalta au chaos des nations* (Paris: Gasset, 1992). Lellouche is foreign policy adviser to J. Chirac, leader of the Gaullist Opposition in France.

ASYMMETRICAL RECIPROCITY IN MARKET EXCHANGE: IMPLICATIONS FOR ECONOMIES IN TRANSITION*

By James M. Buchanan

I. Introduction

Western visitors to those parts of the world that before 1991 were politically organized as the Soviet Union have been impressed by the attitudes of persons toward behavior in ordinary exchanges, attitudes that seem to be so different from those in Western economies. The essential elements of an "exchange culture" seem to be missing, and this absence, in itself, may be central to the effective functioning of market economies.[1] Individual participants in ordinary exchange relationships in Western economies act as if they understand the simplest of all economic principles, namely, that there are mutual gains from trade, that the benefits are reciprocal, that exchange is a positive-sum game. This "as if" understanding, which remains perhaps below our level of consciousness in the West, is largely missing from the public attitudes of citizens of the former Soviet Union, who behave as if the gains from trade do not exist, or at least are one-sided rather than mutual.

There is a familiar story that illustrates the thesis: "In the Soviet Union, both parties to an exchange lose; one party loses the goods; the other party loses the money." This statement may offer a concise, if exaggerated, summary of the general attitude toward exchange that seems to describe the behavior of many (of course, not all) persons in the republics that were formerly parts of the Soviet Union.

In this essay, I propose to offer an *economic* explanation for some of the differences in behavioral attitudes that we observe, as between Western economies and those of the Eurasian republics. In the West, with developed market systems, economists concentrate initial attention on the mutuality of trading gains and on the *reciprocity* in any exchange relationship. And a recognition of this reciprocity seems to inform public participation in markets. What is often overlooked is the asymmetry in the reciprocal relationship between buyer and seller in developed money

---

* I am indebted to my colleague Roger Congleton for helpful discussions.

[1] See James M. Buchanan, "Tacit Presuppositions of Political Economy: Implications for Societies in Transition" (George Mason University, Fairfax, VA: Center for Study of Public Choice, 1991), mimeograph. The present essay builds on, extends, and modifies the arguments of this earlier paper.

© 1993 Social Philosophy and Policy Foundation. Printed in the USA.

economies. The buyer of goods and/or services who offers, or "sells," money in exchange possesses a bargaining advantage that is often over-looked. The central-command economy reverses the direction of advantage, even when exchange dealings are permitted. The differences in the incentives that confront participants in the two organizational settings generate predictable differences in observed behavior and in behavioral attitudes.

I should stress at the outset that my focus is exclusively on the economic, as opposed to the ideological sources of explanation of observed behavior in the exchange process. The ideological denigration of market exchange, as a general system of organizing economic relationships, may have exerted influences on individual behavior over and beyond those analyzed here. And, of course, at some higher system level where organizational-institutional decisions on structure were made, ideological motivation may explain why persons were confronted with the circumstances that contain divergent economic incentives.

In Section II, I introduce the formal analysis by reference to the workings of an idealized model of a barter economy in the absence of transactions costs. This model is introduced solely for the purpose of comparison with the workings of a money economy, still idealized, but as made minimally necessary by the presence of transactions costs. This second model is examined in Section III. In Section IV, I identify the asymmetry in the reciprocal exchange relationship, even in the idealized money economy, and I indicate observable features of Western economies that do not falsify the hypothesis that such an asymmetry exists. Section V takes the obvious next step and extends the analysis to the command economy that does not allow full scope for the operation of the institutions of market exchange. The results suggest that the behavioral roles of participants in such economies may become quite different from those in market cultures. In Section VI, I discuss some of the implications of the analysis for problems of transition from a command to a market structure.

II. IDEALIZED EXCHANGE – A PURE BARTER ECONOMY

Consider a setting in which the exchange process operates ideally, in the analytical-conceptual sense and beyond any feasibility limits imposed by the limits to human capacities. Persons enter into exchange dealings, one with another, in the full knowledge of all potential trading opportunities. Further, the exchange network, the economy, is sufficiently large such that, for each and every buyer or seller in the market for each and every good or service, input or output, there exist large numbers of sellers or buyers, among whom any single buyer or seller may choose. Finally, there are no costs incurred by any buyer or seller in shifting custom from one alternative to another.

Note that, in such an idealized, zero-transactions-cost setting, no person, whether buyer or seller, in any exchange relationship secures any differential gain from exchanging with the single seller or buyer with whom a particular exchange is effectuated. Neither party's action, in making the particular cross market transfer, generates benefits for the other, for the simple reason that alternative buyers or sellers, to whom trade may be shifted, are available at no cost. Gain emerges, of course, to any person, whether buyer or seller, from the availability of or access to "the market," without which grossly inefficient self-production would be necessary.

For my purpose, the noteworthy feature of this idealized model is the implied behavioral indifference that each participant in the exchange network will exhibit toward those with whom exchanges are made. In such a setting, nothing that might be called an "exchange culture" would have meaning. Each participant may, if he or she chooses, behave as if he or she exists in total independence of others, despite the complete interdependence among all persons who participate in the inclusive network. No buyer need invest any effort in persuading, cajoling, or convincing any seller to offer goods and services, and no seller, similarly, will find it rational to try to persuade any buyer to take his wares off the shelf. The reason is straightforward: there exists a sufficiently large number of alternative sellers or buyers to insure that, if one person does not trade, a replacement immediately appears to whom trade can be shifted and at no differential cost.

III. Idealized Exchange with Money

I now propose to modify the idealized exchange model described in Section II in only one respect. Assume, as before, that there are no costs of making exchanges, and that all participants have full knowledge about the qualities of goods. Further, assume, again as before, that the economy is large, and that there are many sellers and many buyers in the market for each good and service. Assume now, however, that there are limits to the knowledge that any participant has about the location of those persons in the economy who seek to purchase precisely the same good he or she seeks to sell, and vice versa. That is to say, direct barter is costly in the sense that each participant in a potential trade must undergo some search effort in locating the desired matching trading partner.

Recognition of the costs of search that make direct barter inefficient provides an economic explanation for the emergence of money, either in the form of some good that comes to be widely accepted as a medium of general exchange through some process of cultural evolution, or in the form of some good or some symbolic representation, the value of which is guaranteed by the collective body that protects private property, that is,

by the state. The existence of money allows sellers to eliminate costly
searches for other persons who are themselves sellers of goods that are
desired in exchange. Similarly, money allows buyers to purchase goods
that they desire without the necessity of searching for persons who seek
to buy precisely that which they offer in exchange as sellers. The familiar metaphor that refers to money as the lubricant of the exchange system is helpfully explanatory.

Under the severely restrictive conditions assumed to exist, however,
the behaviorally relevant conclusions reached above with reference to the
idealized exchange economy seem to continue to hold. Since there are
many buyers and many sellers in the markets for any good or service, any
input or output, the individual participant need not be at all concerned
about the person with whom an exchange is effectuated. The seller of red
shoes need not invest in efforts to convince potential buyers to purchase
his stocks since, by definition, there exist alternative buyers who will purchase the stocks and with no cost to the seller. Similarly, the buyer of
red apples need not invest in attempts to persuade any single apple seller
to offer his wares, since, again by definition, there exist many alternative
apple sellers to whom the apple buyer may turn and without cost. There
is no economic basis for the emergence of any attitude other than behavioral indifference toward specifically identified cross-exchange partners.

IV. ASYMMETRICAL RECIPROCITY

The summary analysis of the preceding paragraph is, I submit, incor-
rect at worst and misleading at best. The introduction of money, even under idealized settings for the operation of an exchange economy, modifies
the presumed anonymity, and consequent symmetry, in the pairwise
buyer-seller relationship; and this modification has important behavioral
implications.

Consider, again, the working properties of an idealized money economy. Figure 1 reproduces the familiar "wheel of income" diagram from
introductory textbooks in economics. The individual at A, who either possesses or produces a good or service (perhaps an input into some process)
that is not desired for his own or internal use, enters one market as a
seller of that good or service, which we may call X. If we ignore sequencing here, we can say that this individual simultaneously enters another
market as a buyer of that good or service (or bundle of goods and services) that is desired for final end use; say this good or service is Y. The
individual in question is a supplier of X and a demander of Y, in the two
separated markets.

A person cannot, however, enter unilaterally in any market. The reciprocity relationship requires that each participant in an exchange enter
simultaneously as buyer and seller. The individual identified above as the
seller-supplier of X and the buyer-demander of Y enters the market for

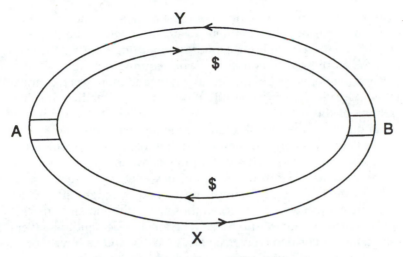

FIGURE 1. Wheel of income.

X and the market for Y in the necessary reciprocal positions as a buyer-demander of money ($\$$) in the X market, and a seller-supplier of money in the Y market. The generalized or fully fungible good, money, becomes the intermediate instrument of value that allows the individual entry into the two markets of his ultimate interest.

The asymmetry enters when we recognize that the money side of any exchange has an inherent "transactions costs" advantage, which in turn improves the "bargaining" power of the person who takes such a role. Consider, once again, a pure barter economy without money, but with some limits on knowledge. Clearly, the person who possesses or produces a good that is, relatively, more generally desired than others will find it less costly to effectuate exchanges for whatever good he ultimately desires. Money becomes the limiting case of a good that is generally desired by all participants in the exchange network, even if not intrinsically but instrumentally. The trader who accepts money for units of any nonmoney good or service secures a nonspecific medium of value that facilitates reentry into any market. The ideal fungibility of money gives the supplier-seller of money an asymmetrical claim to the gains from exchange. By the very definition of what money is, the possessor, and hence potential supplier, of money faces lower transactions costs in completing any exchange than the possessor, and potential supplier, of any nonmoney good or service. The fungibility of money provides the possessor with enhanced power to "walk away" from any exchange for goods and services, a power that the possessor of any nonmoney good or service simply does not have.

The basic asymmetry in the money-goods exchange is obscured by the proclivity of economic theorists to "define away" the features of the exchange process that are sometimes of most interest. As noted, if transactions costs were, literally, defined away, there would be no need for money at all; the pure barter economy would operate with ideal efficiency. When the rigorous assumptions required for the working of a pure barter economy are modified, however, and money is recognized to be an efficiency-enhancing institution, attempts are made to idealize the operations of the money economy by postulating that each and every buyer and seller, whether of goods or money, faces a sufficiently large number of cross-exchange options to guarantee that no person has market or exchange power, in the differential sense instanced above. Once transactions costs are introduced at all, however, there seems to be no plausibly acceptable logic for refusing to acknowledge differentials in "bargaining" advantages as between those persons who enter markets as suppliers-sellers of money and those who enter as demanders-buyers. To put the same proposition conversely, it is the demanders-buyers of goods and services that have an asymmetrical advantage over the suppliers-sellers, and in all markets.

As we move away from the abstracted models for the working of a production-exchange economy and toward a more descriptively satisfying appreciation of the economy as it actually seems to function, the basic asymmetry identified here may become painfully obvious, and my whole discussion may be taken to represent trituration. I suggest, however, that the money-goods asymmetry assists in an understanding of much of the behavior that we observe in developed economies, both historically and currently. The institutions of market exchange, as we know them, incorporate a recognition of this asymmetry, even to the extent that their familiarity breeds analytical oversight.

In markets as we know them, sellers of goods and services peddle their wares, advertise, create attractive displays, adopt attitudes of deferential demeanor toward potential buyers, and behave, generally, as if their customers' interests are their own. "We aim to please"—this slogan describes the attitudes of those traders on the goods-and-services side of the goods-money exchanges, rather than vice versa. And we should find ourselves surprised if this behavior were absent. We do not observe buyers of goods and services setting up their own market stalls with signs that read "we buy apples," except in unusual circumstances. In product markets, we see some, but not much, buyer advertising. Potential buyers of goods and services apparently feel under no compulsion to act as if the interests of a seller are of relevance. Such buyers remain behaviorally indifferent toward the interests of any identified seller.[2]

[2] Labor markets may seem to offer an exception to the generalizations suggested here. Sellers of labor (a service) sometimes advertise their availability, but more often it is buyers of labor (employers) who advertise to attract sellers. The absence of homogeneity among separate units demanded (that is, the variation in skills and qualifications among potential employees) may offset, or even reverse, the direction of effect emphasized here generally.

The distinction between the two sides of the money-goods exchange stressed here does not depend on the pricing institutions that are in place. In developed economies, sellers tend to offer their wares to potential buyers at quasi-fixed prices, and the latter remain free to purchase varying quantities. In many developing economies, by contrast, sellers do not fix prices in advance, save as some preliminary move in what becomes a complex bargaining game with buyers. In both sets of pricing arrangements, however, we observe sellers-suppliers in the active roles of seekers for potential buyers and investors in efforts at persuasion, rather than the opposite.

The asymmetry stressed here is, of course, implicitly recognized in the usage of the term "consumers' sovereignty" to describe the exchange economy. This term, which might be better replaced by "buyers' sovereignty," suggests that sellers of goods and services, or suppliers, are and must be responsive to the interests of buyers, and, hence, that the latter are the ultimate sources of evaluation. Conventional discussion of the consumers'-sovereignty feature of market economies does not, however, take much note of the relevant behavioral implications.

An alternative way of discussing the asymmetry in the money-goods exchange relationship is to introduce the differential specificity of valued assets, as held by each party prior to exchange. Whether we analyze a pure exchange economy, in which persons commence with determinate endowments of goods, or a production-exchange economy, in which persons commence with endowments of talents that may be organized to produce goods, the potential supplier in any exchange for money is, by definition, locked in, relatively, by the specificity of the valued asset in possession, pre-exchange, and, for this reason, is more vulnerable to terms-of-trade manipulation than the potential cross-exchange demander, whose pre-exchange valued asset takes the form of money.[3]

V. Asymmetry Inversion in Command Economies

How would it be possible to remove or even to reverse the asymmetry in the basic exchange relationship in an economy? Reversion to a system of barter through some prohibition of a generalized money medium could remove the asymmetry here, but only at the expense of gross inefficiencies occasioned by the costs of search. In such an economy — one without

---

[3] The relationship between differential asset specificity as between parties to contract, and the vulnerability to opportunistic behavior, has been discussed by Armen Alchian and Susan Woodward, "Reflections on the Theory of the Firm," *Journal of Institutional Theoretical Economics* (*Z. Ges. Staatswiss*), vol. 143, no. 1 (1987), pp. 110–37.

More generally, economists have analyzed the effects of asymmetric information in the operation of exchange. The pioneer in these efforts was George Akerlof, "The Market for 'Lemons': Quality Uncertainty and the Market Mechanism," *Quarterly Journal of Economics*, vol. 84 (August 1970), pp. 488–500.

money but with transactions costs — each market participant is both a buyer and a seller of goods (services), and there is no generalized advantage to either side of an exchange. As noted earlier, there would be a particularized advantage to either the buyer or seller of the goods that are in relatively wider usage in the economy.

Let us consider, now, an economy in which money has been introduced, but where money is not, in itself, a sufficient medium to insure the effectuation of an exchange. Such an economy would be described by money prices for goods, but accompanied by some set of complementary nonmonetary "prices," or arrangements, that would be required to complete a transaction. The nominal money prices for goods and services would be politically established — and at a level below those prices that would clear markets, that would equate demand and supply. Straightforward public-choice analysis of the incentives of persons in bureaucratic authority to set money prices suggests that such prices will remain always below market-clearing levels.[4] Bureaucrats lose any rationing authority if prices are set at market-clearing levels, and such authority is desired both for its own sake and as a source for the extraction of favors (rents). There will tend to exist excess demands for the supplies of goods brought forth in all markets. Each seller will tend to face more demanders for his product than can possibly be satisfied.

In such a setting, any reason that a seller-supplier might have for acting as if he is motivated by the interests of buyers is absent. Sellers will be behaviorally indifferent toward each and all potential buyers; they will have no incentive to please particular buyers, not even to the extent of providing quality merchandise, since there will always be buyers ready and willing to purchase whatever is made available to them.

Consider, by contrast, the behavioral stance of the participant who enters the exchange relationship as a potential buyer, who possesses a stock of money in the hope of securing goods and services. Each person in such a role will face the frustration experienced in an inability to get the goods in the quantities desired, and of the quality standards wanted. Buyers, with money, become the residual claimants to the gains from exchange, a role that is directly contrary to that which buyers occupy in the well-functioning money economy, as analyzed earlier. "Buyers' sovereignty," which was mentioned earlier as a shorthand description of the central feature of the exchange economy, is replaced by "sellers' sovereignty," provided we are careful to include within the "sellers" category those persons who hold bureaucratic authority to establish arrangements for nonprice rationing among demanders of goods and services.

In the command economy, as sketched out in capsule here, buyers of goods and services become the supplicants, who must curry favor with the sellers and their agents, who must, somehow, "aim to please," over

---

[4] David Levy, "The Bias in Centrally Planned Prices," *Public Choice*, vol. 67, no. 3 (December 1990), pp. 213–26.

and beyond some mere offer of generalized purchasing power in the form of money. Sellers remain indifferent to the pleas of buyers, and not only because of the excess number of demanders. Sellers also realize that if they exchange goods for money, they, too, must return to other markets, as buyers, who must, in turn, expect to encounter the frustrations of buyers throughout the system.

The chronic "shortage" of goods that describes the workings of the command economy stems directly from the imposed politicization of money prices, as does the generalized supplication of buyers toward sellers-suppliers, including the relevant members of the bureaucratic apparatus. The institution of money, as such, is not allowed to serve its standard efficiency-enhancing function. The nonprice rationing arrangements, which emerge as supplementary to money prices, become analogous, in their economic effects, to the search costs that barter involves in the absence of money.

The command economy, with politicized money prices, along with supplementary rationing arrangements, will be characterized by a "money overhang," that is, by a supply of money that is in excess of that which is needed in exchange transactions, at the politically set money prices. Indeed, without such "money overhang" the authority that is exercised by the whole price central regime loses its "bite." Unless potential consumers-buyers are provided with more money (through wage payments) than they can spend on products, at the controlled prices, the authority of bureaucrats to ration scarce supplies becomes unnecessary. This excess money supply, in its turn, sets up additional incentives for the emergence of exchange transactions that are outside the boundaries of legitimacy in some formal sense. Black, shadow, or underground markets will emerge more readily when persons are unable to satisfy their demands for goods through standard exchange channels and when they have available, at the same time, unused and unusable stocks of money. As this shadow sector increases in size over time, as measured either by the volume of transactions or by the number of participants, the behavioral norms that describe the operation of the whole legal order must be undermined.

The fact that money is not allowed fully to perform its efficiency-enhancing role in the economy must also set in motion evolutionary pressures toward the emergence of some good that will secure general acceptability as "real money," quite distinct from the money issued by the state monopoly. In Russia, and in other former socialist economies, the currency of developed nations (dollars, marks, Swiss francs) has emerged to fill this role, at least in part. And, in the shadow exchanges between these monies and goods, the asymmetry observed in Western economies is partially restored. Sellers of goods do, indeed, seek out and court potential buyers who are thought to possess hard currencies.

This transitional stage aside, however, the point to be emphasized is that, in the command economy, as it traditionally functions, the whole economic culture is dramatically different from that which we observe in Western market economies. The near-total absence of seller-supplier efforts to attract custom and to please potential buyers shocks Western observers who visit the territories of the former Soviet Union. The paucity of billboards in the Moscow of 1990 was not primarily attributable to regulatory prohibition. This result emerged directly from the fact that no seller-supplier of any good or service felt any economic pressure to respond to customer interests or to expand the demands for products. The sales clerk at the kiosk, as a selling agent, behaved very differently from her Western counterpart, but not because of ethnic origins; she behaved differently because in the Russian mindset that permeates the citizenry generally, the seller-purveyor of goods need not be concerned about customers.

The Russian visitor to the United States is equally surprised when the behavior of sellers-suppliers is observed, both directly and indirectly. Such a visitor is overwhelmed by the neon blazes, the multicolored billboards, the slick magazine pages, and the TV commercials, as well as behaviorally by the stance of those persons who act as agents for suppliers for almost all goods and services. Coming out of an economic culture where buyers are the universal supplicants, the Russian visitor stands aghast at the supplication of sellers and their agents. Neither this Russian visitor nor his American counterpart in Moscow understands that the dramatic differences in the two cultures can be explained, at least in large part, by variations in the incentive structures. The American setting allows the asymmetry in the money-goods exchange relationship to be played out fully in the development and operation of its market institutions. The Soviet Union, by contrast, attempted, throughout its existence, to counter this asymmetry by the politicization of money prices, with an acknowledged major increase in the costs of making transactions, but also with the unrecognized impetus given to the emergence and operation of an economic culture that must be subversive in any effort to move toward the market structure.

VI. Implications for the Transition from a Command to a Market Economy

This essay is not presented as a contribution to the explanation of how economies operate—either exchange (market) economies or command (socialized) economies. My emphasis is on and my interest is in the behavioral differences that the separate systems tend to motivate and to accentuate, differences that are readily observable, and on the implications of these differences for the problems of transition from a command to a market economy—the transition that the countries of Central and Eastern Europe now face.

In an earlier essay (see footnote 1), I concentrated attention on the apparent failure of participants in the socialist economy to recognize the reciprocal nature of the exchange relationship and the presence of mutuality of gain to all parties. I did not, of course, suggest that participants in the developed market economies of the West explicitly understand even this most elementary principle of economics and that a comparable understanding was missing in the command economies. I did suggest, however, that the basic principle of reciprocal exchange had come to inform the consciousness of many persons in Western economies, even if there seems to be little or no articulation of such a principle within the range of ordinary competence.

In that essay, which was advanced only in an exploratory fashion, as is this one, I attributed the absence of such an "exchange mentality" or mindset to the conjectural history that persons accept as descriptive of their social development. I suggested that in Western societies, and especially in the United States, the central notion of gains-from-trade emerges naturally from a historical imagination that traces economic and social development from family independence and self-sufficiency (the frontier homestead) through stages of increasing interdependence as specialization proceeds, always accompanied by increasing standards of living. In this imagined history, however, the exit option, the potential for withdrawal into independence, remains at the back edge of understanding and interpretation, thereby insuring that the expansion of trade and exchange must enhance well-being for all members of the society.

I suggested that participants in the former Soviet economy carried with them no such historical imagination of economic development, and that there was no comparable conjectural history of self-sufficient independence from which the economy emerged. Instead, cooperation was always imagined, not as achievement of mutual gains through exchange, but as taking place within a collective-community enterprise. Individual cooperative behavior, even as idealized, was modeled exclusively as the fulfilling of tasks assigned in a collective endeavor, assigned by some command authority. When I sketched the elements of my analysis to a Russian intellectual, he aptly described, and accepted, the thesis as, "the Russians are natural slaves; the Yankees are natural traders."

I see no reason to back off from or to withdraw the arguments made in my earlier essay; I remain convinced that the analysis contributes to an understanding of some of the difficulties in making the transition from a command to a market economy. I now think, however, that the arguments advanced in this essay supplement and extend those of the earlier essay usefully, and allow me to offer an economic explanation of some of the apparent differences in mindsets that need not be so critically dependent on a presumed divergence in historical imaginations. The importance of historical imagination may have been exerted at a more fundamental level than that discussed in the earlier essay. An imagination that is grounded on the liberty and independence of individual families might have proved a formidable barrier against collectivization of the economy. A "socialized United States" may never have been within the realm of the possible. History, and the historical imagination that it shapes, matters. And different national experiences may affect the feasibility of adaptation to different organizational structures. In the view of many observers, Poland's role in the revolution against the Communist regime was due, in part, to the historical position of the Catholic Church.

The possible oversight of the earlier treatment lay in my failure to appreciate that the "exchange mentality" that I took to be descriptive of Western attitudes toward markets generally, is manifested largely, even if not exclusively, in the observed activities of those who find themselves in roles as sellers-suppliers (or their agents) of goods and services, and that their behavior finds its origins, at least in part, in the asymmetry of the goods-money exchange. Conversely, I generalized the behavioral indifference of sellers or selling agents in the former Soviet Union to the whole culture, without noting that the structure within which exchanges take place removes incentives for sellers to behave in ways comparable to their Western counterparts.

Entrepreneurial or leadership roles in implementing exchanges-transfers of valued goods among persons and units in the command-control economies have been taken by those persons who possess differential access to nonmoney means of influencing choices, through personalized relationships, through extra-market barter arrangements, through sublegal bribes, payoffs, and kickbacks. In other words, the entrepreneurial talents that have been rewarded in the command economy, as it operated, were those of the "fixers" rather than those which might have represented some differential ability to recognize latent demand in nonexisting goods and to design and organize the production of such goods in response to such demand. In other words, there was little or no supply-side entrepreneurship, as such—in dramatic contrast with Western-style capitalist economies, where, at least in principle, such entrepreneurship should remain a dominant feature.

The entrepreneurship manifested in the activities of the "fixers" is not, of course, absent from Western economies, especially as these economies have developed to include large and rapidly growing socialized or public sectors. As governments have grown, in all dimensions, over the course of the century, there has been the developing recognition that private profits may be located in the exploitation of public as well as private opportunities.[5] Entrepreneurs who seek to capture the rents created by the artificially contrived scarcities stemming from politicized economic regulation, sometimes called "rent-seekers," are behaviorally similar to

---

[5] For a generalized discussion, see James M. Buchanan, Robert D. Tollison, and Gordon Tullock, eds., *Toward a Theory of the Rent-Seeking Society* (College Station: Texas A&M University Press, 1980), and especially my introductory paper, "Rent Seeking and Profit Seeking," pp. 3–15.

those that emerge in the more pervasive regulatory structure of command economies. We need only point to the thousands of lawyer-lobbyists whose activity consists exclusively in exploiting loopholes in the complexities of tax law and in seeking the creation of still further loopholes through new legislative changes.

The unanswered empirical question is whether or not the scarce set of entrepreneurial talents are generalizable over the two quite distinct roles. And the answer here will be critical for the problems of transition. Is a successful rent-seeker, who has demonstrated an adeptness at implementing value transfers in a regulated-politicized setting, likely to be equally successful when, as, and if the incentive structure shifts and success requires that attention be paid to organizing production to meet demands of consumers? Or do the distinct entrepreneurial roles require quite divergent talents? These questions stand as a challenge to my economist peers who place their primary reliance on direct empirical results.

My own intuition-interpretation suggests that the experience of the command economy, in which there has been little or no differential reward offered for supply-side creativity, will exert relatively long-lasting effects, and that the transition to a market economy will be made more difficult because of this absence of an entrepreneurial tradition. Those persons who have been skillful in responding to the disequilibria of the command structure may find the switch to the new role beyond their limits.

Entrepreneurs are, of course, emerging in the transition economies. Both those who were and might have been the "fixers" and those who held positions of bureaucratic authority are moving to take advantage of the opportunities opened up by institutional changes. The question is not so much whether entrepreneurship will emerge as whether that which does emerge will prove sufficiently creative to stimulate the impoverished and sluggish economies in ways that may prove necessary to insure that the revolution's ultimate result will be positive.

A useful distinction may be made at this point between the Kirznerian and the Schumpeterian definitions of entrepreneurship, a distinction that has been the source of longstanding debates within the subdiscipline of Austrian economics. Israel Kirzner, who has long stressed the importance of the entrepreneurial function in an economy, models the entrepreneur as responding to disequilibria, essentially as an arbitrageur, who locates and exploits disparities in potential exchange values as among separate locations, persons, and production opportunities.[6] In this conceptualization of the entrepreneurial role, there should be relatively little difficulty encountered in transforming the "fixer" of the command economy into the equilibrating supply-side organizer of production and distribution in

---

[6] Israel Kirzner, *Competition and Entrepreneurship* (Chicago: University of Chicago Press, 1973).

the operative market economy. By contrast, Joseph Schumpeter models the entrepreneur as a disequilibrating force, as a creator of destruction to established ways of doing things, as a disrupter of existing and predicted channels of exchange.[7] In this conceptualization, the supply-side entrepreneur acts quite differently from the arbitrageur, even if the latter is defined in the broadest possible terms. The entrepreneur creates that which does not exist independently of his or her action. To the extent that the ongoing market or capitalist economy is understood to be progressively created by Schumpeterian entrepreneurs, there can be no easy transition from the command system, quite independently from the institutional reforms that may be put in place.

Both types of entrepreneur can coexist as highly productive contributors to the successful transition toward market economies and to the growth of such economies, once established. In my own view, the supply-side or Schumpeterian entrepreneur is unlikely to become dominant in the economies that are now in transition. And, indeed, such entrepreneurs may have almost disappeared in Western economies. In this perspective, while successful transition to a market economy is possible for the former command systems, there will be no *Wirtschaftswunder* (economic miracle) in the near term, East or West.

Economics, Center for Study of Public Choice, George Mason University

---

[7] Joseph A. Schumpeter, *Theorie der wirtschaftlichen Entwicklung* (Leipzig, 1912); English translation, *Theory of Economic Development* (Cambridge: Harvard University Press, 1934).

INSTITUTIONS, NATIONALISM, AND THE TRANSITION PROCESS IN EASTERN EUROPE*

By Svetozar Pejovich

I. Introduction

In the late 1980s, the actual accomplishments of capitalism finally made a convincing case against socialism. After several decades of experimentation with human beings, socialism in the former Soviet Union and Eastern European countries (hereafter, Eastern Europe) died an inglorious death. To an economist, the present value of the expected future benefits from socialism fell relative to their current production costs. And Marx was finally dead and, hopefully, buried.

Short of risking a social breakdown, new leaders in Eastern Europe could not and did not immediately put an end to all the institutions and legacies of socialism. Instead, they were confronted with two critical issues: (1) how to choose new institutions, and (2) at what rate the new rules of the game should replace the old ones. Evidence shows a significant disparity among Eastern European countries in dealing with those two issues. It has become quite clear that, in a heterogeneous region like Eastern Europe, the transition paths and the rate of institutional change have to differ. Whenever we get impatient with the rate of transformation to capitalism in Eastern Europe, we should remind ourselves that, notwithstanding our free-market institutions, political freedoms, and stock of human capital, the transition to capitalism has not been completed in the West either.

The end of totalitarian socialist rule in Eastern Europe has indeed opened a highway to liberty along which there are many incentives to take detours. The detours are set by the ideas and perceptions that Eastern Europeans have of the Western world. They have also been created by the ideas that the West has about what the East ought to do. In fact, the transition process in the East has been a gift from heaven for social engineers from the West. They have responded to this gift by flooding the economic and political markets with all sorts of models, proposals, and schemes for the development of new institutional arrangements in the

* An earlier version of this essay was presented at the Einaudi Foundation seminar in Rome on June 25, 1992. I would like to thank the Earhart Foundation and the Lynde and Harry Bradley Foundation for support of my research on the economics of property rights in Eastern Europe. I also wish to thank professors E. Colombatto, H. Kliemt, A. Petroni, and especially E. Paul for many useful suggestions.

© 1993 Social Philosophy and Policy Foundation. Printed in the USA.

region. The problem with most of those models is that they are not likely to be implemented spontaneously; that is, they would have to be introduced by fiat.

The purpose of this essay is to discuss the causes of the resurgence of nationalism in the multi-ethnic states of Eastern Europe and the effects of nationalism on the direction and rate of institutional change in the region.

II. Some Evidence of Rising Nationalism in Eastern Europe

Nationalism is not a monopoly of Eastern Europe. We observe a strong dose of nationalism in Ireland, Canada, Israel, Palestine, Italy, Germany, and many other countries. "In the historical perspective, nationalism is neither returning, rising nor reappearing. It never left Eastern Europe. Marxism-Leninism was supposed to make it irrelevant, and the Soviet power was calculated to suppress it. But it was always more durable than either."[1] An important characteristic of nationalism in the multi-ethnic states of Eastern Europe lies in the effect it has on the transition path in those countries.

Nationalism could become a serious problem in Bulgaria and Romania. It is a serious problem in Czechoslovakia. Serious fighting has already occurred in Georgia, Armenia, Moldova, and Azerbaijan. It is clear that numerous national groups within Russia are getting restless. And nationalism has taken the most violent turn in Croatia, Bosnia, and Serbia.

The main minority ethnic groups in Bulgaria are the Turks and the Macedonians. They account for 8.5 percent and 2.5 percent, respectively, of the population in that country. After five centuries of Ottoman rule, the Turks are not the Bulgarians' favorite people. The last Communist ruler of Bulgaria, Todor Zhivkov, even hoped to save the regime by actively "encouraging" the Turks to leave the country. The new (non-Communist) government of Bulgaria has abandoned Zhivkov's anti-Turk policies. However, the Bulgarian people have not. Clashes between Turks and Bulgarians, some of them serious, are happening often enough to be noticed. As for Macedonia, Bulgaria and Serbia fought a short but bitter war over Macedonia in 1913. Bulgaria has yet to recognize the Macedonians as a national group.

In June 1991, Romania asked for Bessarabia and Bukovina to be returned to Romania, because the majority of people in that region are Romanians. The government of Ukraine responded by saying that parts of the area are ancient Ukrainian lands which Romanians acquired by force after the October Revolution of 1917. Of course, the problem with

[1] J. Brown, "The Resurgence of Nationalism," *Report on Eastern Europe*, no. 2 (June 1991), p. 35.

"historical" rights in Eastern Europe is that they are quite confusing. In this case, Romania was never a sovereign state until the end of World War I. Thus, Bessarabia and Bukovina were part of the state of Romania only from 1918 until 1939. In 1939, the Molotov-Ribbentrop Treaty gave this area to the USSR, and part of it ended up in Ukraine. The issue between Romania and Ukraine is the same as that between Serbia and Croatia: the former favor ethnic borders, while the latter argue for current administrative borders.

After several centuries of Hapsburg rule, Czechoslovakia became a sovereign state in 1918. The country quickly became a showcase of political democracy, civil liberties, and economic progress. Today, Czechoslovakia is a major testing ground for the transition from socialism to capitalism. Unfortunately, the country's political stability is threatened by a conflict between the two major national groups: the Czechs and the Slovaks. These groups account for 63 percent and 32 percent, respectively, of the population in Czechoslovakia. While the Czechs seem indifferent to ethnic issues, the Slovaks are not. Slowly but ceaselessly, former Communists in Slovakia have turned to nationalism as a vehicle to retain some of their old power. Under their influence, the Slovaks have come to believe that the economic reform taking place is anti-Slovak, that privatization is proceeding too fast, and that the role of the state in the economy has been reduced too much. In June 1992, the Czechs elected Vaclav Klaus, a strong anti-Communist, whose major interest seems to lie in returning the country as quickly as possible to its pre-Communist prosperity. The Slovaks elected Vladimir Meciar, a former member of the Communist Party, and a "born-again" nationalist. As of this writing, Meciar and his cohorts have taken Czechoslovakia dangerously close to a breakup into two sovereign states (and as I revise this essay for publication, in the fall of 1992, they have just about taken the country apart).

The former Soviet Union has over one hundred national groups within its borders. These groups have their own languages, traditions, customs, and cultures. They also have ethnic problems with each other. The Armenians are fighting for their ethnic independence; the Islamic Renaissance Party is fighting against the perceived Slavic influence in former Soviet Asia; Moldova, Georgia, and the three Baltic states (Latvia, Lithuania, and Estonia) seem to be as interested in settling their accounts with Russia as with the former USSR. Within the Slavic family (75 percent of the population in the former USSR), the Ukrainians have historically felt threatened by the Russian state. In Russia proper, nationalism is becoming a major political and social force and is creating a powerful coalition which includes a variety of political groups, ranging from the Communist left to the "holy" Russian right. The sentiments the leaders of this coalition promote sound exactly like those we have been hearing from Franju Tudjman in Croatia and Slobodan Milosevic in Serbia: "Russian nationalism pure and simple. . . . Blame the communists, blame the democrats, blame the West. Blame everyone, in fact, apart from the great and long-suffering Russian people themselves."[2]

Alexis de Tocqueville once said that the most dangerous time for a bad government is when it starts to reform itself. His statement is certainly applicable to Milosevic's government in Serbia and Tudjman's in Croatia in the early 1990s.

Serbia became a sovereign state in the early twelfth century. Toward the end of the fourteenth century, the country was conquered by the Ottoman Empire. Independence was regained in 1878. Croatia was a sovereign state for only a brief period in the eleventh century and during World War II (1941–1945). Otherwise, it was a province of the Austro-Hungarian Empire. Bosnia is a region inhabited by three peoples who have lived together for centuries: Moslems (40 percent), Serbs (32 percent), and Croats (18 percent). Kosovo is a region in southern Serbia where the first Serbian state was formed. As late as the sixteenth century, the Serbs accounted for 97 percent of the total population in Kosovo. After many wars and several migrations — brought on, in part, by Turkish terror — Albanians now account for about 90 percent of the population in Kosovo. I believe that the Kosovo problem is likely to be potentially more explosive than those we have witnessed in Croatia and Bosnia. Finally, the Serbs account for about 14 percent of the population in Croatia, and are concentrated in a few areas that are ethnically Serbian. During World War II, the state of Croatia carried out a massacre of the Serbs. The Serbs took to the mountains, and a terrible civil war ensued. According to Dr. Drago Roksandic of the University of Zagreb, the number of Serbs from Croatia who died during the war was 131,000, or 22 percent of their total number in Croatia. The conflict between the Serbs and the Croats, which triggered an all-out war in 1991, was over borders: the Serbs wanted borders drawn on ethnic lines; the Croats preferred those drawn by Tito in 1945.

III. The Transition Process and Nationalism in Eastern Europe

There are three main causes of post-Communist nationalism in Eastern Europe: institutional instability, the region's philosophical heritage, and its nomenklatura. These factors are having profound effects on the transition paths taken by the multi-ethnic states in the region.

Post-socialist institutional instability

The end of totalitarian socialist rule in Eastern Europe has destabilized institutional arrangements that have been in place for nearly five decades. What we refer to as the transformation of former socialist states is, in effect, their search for a new set of institutions.

---

[2] "The Nationalist with a Dash of Paranoia," *The European*, May 28, 1992, p. 11.

Institutions are usually defined as the legal, regulatory, and customary arrangements for repeated human interactions — or, what comes to the same thing, as the rules of the game. They provide members of the community with some specific benefits and impose on them some specific costs. From an individual's standpoint, rules yield a flow of *benefits*: the predictability of other people's behavior. The *costs* borne by an individual are the satisfactions forgone due to his inability to engage in some specific activities. The flow of benefits from a set of rules depends on their stability. As time goes by, people learn how to adjust to the prevailing set of institutions, identify exchange opportunities, and exploit the most preferred ones.

Most human interactions have future value consequences (e.g., buying a car, getting married, joining a religious community, and even eating out). With uncertainty and incomplete information, any person's evaluation of the expected future consequences of his current decisions has to be subject to large errors. Yet these are decisions that we have to make each day. A stable set of rules reduces uncertainties involved in making all decisions, but especially in those that have long-term consequences. South Americans prefer the lower expected returns on their investments in the United States to the much higher rates that are often available in their homelands; an investor in Guatemala seeks a shorter payoff period than an investor in North Dakota; and a Croatian guest worker in Switzerland prefers a deposit in a Swiss bank at zero interest to a two-digit interest rate promised by a bank in Croatia.

Frequent changes or expectations of frequent changes in the rules of the game reduce the time horizon over which individuals make their decisions. Consequently, the most beneficial rules are those that are self-sustaining and produced spontaneously within the system itself. Such rules eliminate the time-horizon problem and create a sense of social stability, because they provide incentives for individuals in the community to maximize the extent of voluntary human interactions. The critical function of institutional arrangements is, then, to foster the predictability of behavior.

Socialist rule in Eastern Europe subverted the rule of law to the will of the ruling elite and seriously undermined the people's confidence in enforcement mechanisms. During the immediate post-Communist years, the prevailing socialist institutions themselves have been destabilized. Although most socialist institutions were not immediately jettisoned, it was clear that they were not going to last. Theory tells us that when the rules of the game are seriously compromised, the extent of exchange among individuals is reduced, and this is precisely what has happened.[3]

---

[3] The reason for this reduction in exchange has to do with the nature of interactions. Voluntary interactions among individuals are vehicles by which they seek to increase their well-being (utility). However, interactions are frequently not simultaneous (e.g., A pays B a sum of $1,000 for the right to use water from B's well over a period of five years), and most interactions have consequences that occur after the agreement is concluded (e.g., X mar-

Perceiving an institutional vacuum, Eastern Europeans needed a stable set of rules for carrying out transactions among themselves and with the rest of the world. In the multi-ethnic states, members of various groups began to fall back on their traditional, pre-Communist norms of behavior, the old ethos, which links them together through shared values, shared traditions, shared culture, shared language, and shared historical experiences. The predictability of behavior fostered by those rules is, however, limited to a group of people that share the same traditions and values. In Eastern Europe, those groups of people are usually members of the same ethnic groups. Interactions within any specific ethnic group are then subject to rules of behavior that do not necessarily hold in exchanges across ethnic lines. In fact, the general ethos in Eastern Europe is a repository of the old unsettled scores among the region's ethnic groups. It follows that the old ethos creates incentives for members of each ethnic group to interact primarily with other group members and to be cautious in dealing with "aliens."

The post-Communist era has given the dark hand of the past an opportunity to influence the present. Unfortunately, the old ethos has not been adaptable enough to prevent old feuds from being translated into the rise of nationalism throughout the region and the proliferation of ethnic wars in Croatia, Serbia, Bosnia, and a growing number of former Soviet republics.

The region's philosophical heritage

The intellectual tradition of Eastern Europe has remained largely free of such Western European ideas as classical liberalism and methodological individualism.[4] Instead, the ethos in Eastern Europe has a strong bias toward communalism. The prevailing concept of the community in the region is not the classical-liberal one of a voluntary association of individuals who, in the pursuit of their private ends, join and leave the

---

ries Y believing that Y is a good person). The problem with these interactions is that their future consequences might and often do differ from those expected at the time of the agreement. Some of those unintended consequences are inevitable, but many are man-made (e.g., B could decide to build a fence around his well). A major purpose of the rules of the game is to protect interactions among individuals by alleviating risks and uncertainties associated with those problems.

[4] It is frequently said that there was more of a Western tradition in Czechoslovakia, Slovenia, and perhaps Hungary, than in other Eastern European countries. That is certainly true. However, classical liberalism, which is only a part of the Western tradition, does not have deep roots in the region. *Classical liberalism* usually is taken to mean individual liberty, openness to new ideas, tolerance of all views, and a government under law. The liberal community does not have a preordained set of outcomes: a common good. *Methodological individualism* is a method for understanding social phenomena. Its main postulate is that the individual is the only decision maker. That is, governments, universities, corporations, and other entities do not and cannot make decisions, only individuals can and do. To understand the behavior of any social, economic, or political entity, it is necessary to identify incentive structures under which individuals operate.

community by free choice. Instead, the community is seen as an organic whole to which individuals are expected to subordinate their private ends and in which all cooperate to pursue their common values. The communities in Eastern Europe have developed their customs and common values along ethnic lines. This has strengthened mutual understanding within each ethnic group, but it has done so at the cost of reducing their ability to communicate with outsiders. The Serbs in Croatia, the Albanians in Serbia, the Turks in Bulgaria, and the Hungarians in Romania are examples of this spontaneous cultural autonomy.

This tradition in Eastern Europe has survived more than four decades of Communist rule (more than seven in the former USSR). With its emphasis on ethnicity, the extended family (clan), and shared values, the old ethos was a powerful fortress behind whose walls most people were able to hide and learn to live with Communist institutions without ever accepting them. However, Communist rule had an unintended effect on the mentality of Eastern Europeans. It helped to reinforce the communalism of the old ethos, which is now responsible for much of the military, social, and political conflict in the multi-ethnic regions of Eastern Europe.[5] Even though the Communist ideal of the "new socialist man" died long before the system met its end, Eastern Europeans have yet to appreciate that the decision maker, the responsible agent, in all social systems is the individual, and that the individual always has pursued and always will pursue his self-interest.

Given their historical and cultural background, Eastern Europeans are predictably confused about capitalist institutions and their effects on the quality of life. In 1989, the prevailing mode of thinking about capitalism in Eastern Europe was to identify it with a life style based on bountiful supplies of goods and equally large incomes to buy those goods. The benefits of capitalism were somehow to be added to the prevailing socialist welfare programs. After a half-century of Marxist indoctrination, Eastern Europeans did not and could not see capitalism as *a way of life* based on (1) the constitutional guarantees of individual liberty, (2) the right of private ownership and contractual freedom, (3) the exchange culture in which each and every individual bears the value consequences of his decisions, and (4) the behavioral principles of self-interest, self-determination, and self-responsibility. The term "capitalism" was used by Marxists in a tone of ethical and social denigration. A much better term is Adam Smith's: the "natural system of economic liberty."

The ethos in Eastern Europe, the region's intellectual tradition, and the people's perceptions of capitalism explain why, in the search for new

---

[5] It is probably an oversimplification to blame Communist rule for the current turmoil in the multi-ethnic states. It is like blaming labor unions for inflation. Inflation happened before labor unions were organized, and ethnic wars happened before Marx was born. Former Communists trying to cling to their positions of power are only exploiting the opportunity provided by the old unsettled scores.

institutions, "fairness" and "justice" are emphasized over values more suitable to a free-market society. The concern ought to be in creating institutions that reward performance, cultivate tenacity for overcoming risk, promote the development of individual liberties, and place high value on the keeping of promises. The problem with fairness and justice is two-fold. First, they are at best a hazy vision of values that it would be nice for social institutions to promote: something for the intellectuals to shout about and the bureaucrats to shoot at. Second, they require an activist government, as a means of imposing and maintaining them. With their implications for the redistribution of wealth, the objectives of fairness and justice are particularly vulnerable to disagreements, conflicts, and divisions along ethnic lines.

In contrast, government in a free-market, private-property society is supposed to restrict itself to a passive role of monitoring and enforcing the rules of the game. The rules of the game in capitalism are developed to grant individuals a range of freedom to pursue their own ends, make their own decisions, and bear the consequences of those decisions.[6] If I love disco music or football, or prefer emulating Mother Theresa, the system allows me to pursue my own ends. Patterns of social behavior derive from these diverse motivations: driven by their self-interest, individuals seek the most valuable partners, reward those who are industrious and perform well, and give repeat business to those who keep promises. Abundant evidence confirms this proposition about the penalty/reward system in capitalism. For example, the median income of Asian-American households, whose culture instills a strong work ethic, exceeds the median income of white Americans.[7] Much of East Asia has prospered by encouraging these sorts of capitalist transactions and behavior, while Africa has languished under the rule of antithetical principles.[8]

Capitalist society — that is, a society of free and responsible individuals — would mute ethnic animosities in Eastern Europe's multi-ethnic

[6] The system also provides people with a right to give up some of their freedoms. For example, when a person joins a religious community, he or she freely chooses to give up the right to make decisions over a range of issues.

[7] "Two Measures of Household Income," *New York Times*, July 24, 1992, p. A10. Median household income for Asian Americans is $36,784 and for whites is $31,435.

[8] In a long and interesting article, Keith Richburg discusses the issue of why African development has lagged so far behind that of East Asia, which suffered from a similar set of obstacles: "Why has East Asia . . . become a model of economic success, while Africa, since independence, has seen increasing poverty and hunger . . . ?" Richburg offers several possible explanations for those differences in economic development. Two of them are related to my discussion in this essay: the economic choices and the ethos. First, after independence, most countries in Africa opted for government ownership of enterprises, due to a distrust of private-sector initiative and foreign investment. Asians chose a brand of capitalism. Second, the ethos in Africa turned out to be less adaptable (relative to the ethos in East Asia) to the requirements of efficiency in production and exchange. Keith Richburg, "Why is Black Africa Overwhelmed While East Asia Overcomes?" *International Herald Tribune*, July 14, 1992, pp. 1 and 6.

states by providing incentives for people to seek exchange opportunities across ethnic lines. Driven by their self-interest, people would, sooner or later, learn to judge others on merit and performance rather than on ethnic origin. Thus, the institutions that promote and strengthen a society of free and responsible individuals could spontaneously curb the rise of nationalism in Eastern Europe and reduce nationalism's menace to the transition process.

Nationalism and the regional nomenklatura

As Communist rule ended in Eastern Europe, the ruling elite had incentives to seek ways to preserve its power and privileges. In the face of significant opportunities for the economic advancement of private individuals, and thus their liberation from elite control, former leaders in the multi-ethnic regions of Eastern Europe realized that creating the perception of an external threat to their respective ethnic groups would give them their best chance to retain power and authority. Most former Communists quickly transformed themselves into virulent nationalists. It was an easy thing for them to do because nationalism and Communism have two important traits in common: (1) the collectivist mode of looking at the world, and (2) the recruitment of political leaders on the basis of their loyalty to the cause or group rather than merit. Thus, the transition of former "internationalists" into newly minted nationalists did not require much of a change of their normal habits. Indeed, most leaders in the multi-ethnic states of Eastern Europe are former Communists. Milosevic in Serbia, Tudjman in Croatia, Meciar in Slovakia, Kravchuk in Ukraine, and Yeltsin in Russia are only the most conspicuous examples. Their human capital — their skills and knowledge — qualify them only for seeking advantages for themselves in a bureaucratic environment; therefore, a free-market, private-property system is a threat to these former Communists' well-being. To preserve the value of their human capital, they have to create a state-centered system. A way of doing this is to convince their people that other ethnic groups are either threatening their political independence, or trying to steal their resources, or both. With many unsettled scores from centuries gone by, these arguments are not too difficult to sell. In the process, the former "internationalists" have become the most zealous defenders of the ethos of their ethnic groups.

The conversion of many former Communist leaders into present-day nationalists was the most efficient way for them to retain some power and influence. It also turned out to have two important implications for the transition paths in the multi-ethnic states. First, the old ethos, with its memories of unsettled scores, translates rather easily into ethnic conflicts, which necessarily result in economic losses. Second, the artificial creation of external threats has deterred the development of individual liberty and the growth of individual responsibility in the multi-ethnic states. Evidence for this is the difference in the transition paths between Eastern European countries that have been able to avoid ethnic conflicts and those that have not. The case of Czechoslovakia is quite important. As I pointed out earlier in the essay, former Communists in Slovakia have, in their quest to retain power and influence, adroitly exploited Slovak nationalism, bringing the country to the point of dissolution into two sovereign states. In contrast, the Czechs, with virtually no former Communists in positions of power, are treating ethnic issues as a nuisance that is interfering with getting the country on the road to economic recovery.

IV. In Lieu of a Conclusion: Big Bang Versus Gradual Changes

The basic premise of a free society is to let people make their own choices. Yet the end of totalitarian socialist rule in Eastern Europe has resulted in an avalanche of studies by Western scholars on what should be done in the region. Even some free-market-oriented individuals and groups have been advising new leaders in Eastern Europe on how to use the strong hand of the state—the method of institutional change that they consistently condemn at home—to build free-market, private-property economies.

The real problem is that we have scant evidence of what Eastern Europeans themselves want. Political parties that seek to implement free-market reforms have done better in some countries than in others, but their overall strength in the region is not too encouraging. There is even less evidence that ordinary people in Eastern Europe[9] are able to appreciate the consequences of alternative institutional arrangements. What is happening in Eastern European countries is that new institutions are being introduced by fiat[10] and that the direction and rate of institutional changes are largely controlled by their bureaucracies.

---

[9] There is a tendency among intellectuals, especially those inclined toward social engineering, to deprecate the ability of "ordinary" people to make their own survival choices (an economist would say "to maximize their utility"). One has to wonder how ordinary people—and there were only ordinary people around some million years ago—managed to survive against competition from other forms of life. They must have somehow managed to make some right choices. Survival of any species is based on its adaptive behavior rather than on someone's foresight. With uncertainty and incomplete information, people make choices which are, in effect, their best bets. It is from those behaviors that are actually tried that "success" is selected and copied by others. Some Eastern Europeans will eventually try new types of behavior, which others will copy if and when they decide that those behaviors have strong survival potentials. Ordinary people might then choose capitalism when the time is right for them to make that decision, *provided* they have freedom of choice.

[10] Legal changes can be of two sorts: adjustments in the rules to the new requirements of the game that social and economic developments have made possible; or changes in the rules that are imposed from above by those in political power. The term "fiat" in this essay means the latter.

It is a mistake to identify Eastern Europeans' success in throwing the Communists out of power with the median voter's preference for free-market economies. The forty years of socialism (seventy for the former USSR), the old ethos, and the intellectual heritage of the region are conducive to nationalism, hierarchy, and welfarism, but not to "instant" capitalism. Like a good medicine that could either save your life or kill you, depending on how you use it, economic reforms that promise to improve efficiency in production and exchange could cause more harm than good if implemented too hastily. Lifting price controls and privatization are two such problematic reforms.

In Russia, on January 2, 1992, the government decreed a comprehensive price liberalization which (supposedly) freed about 80 percent of wholesale and 90 percent of retail prices (basic food items remained under price controls).[11] Prices perform two functions in a world in which goods are scarce. In the short run, they allocate the goods and services that have already been produced to their highest-valued uses. In the long run, prices generate a flow of goods that conforms to consumers' preferences. Freeing prices in Eastern European countries *would not* accomplish the latter function. For that, Eastern European governments need to (1) guarantee free entry for all potential producers of goods and services, (2) provide incentives for those who determine the use of resources to respond to consumers' preferences, and (3) provide incentives to discover the value of resources in alternative uses. Guaranteeing the right of private ownership and contractual freedom would do the job specified by these three points quite well.

Privatization of state factories is bound to have a negative effect on the people's appreciation of the benefits and essentials of free enterprise.[12] Most factories in Eastern Europe were built without any regard for prices. Their technology is inferior, and the management skills that were prized under socialism have no comparative advantage in a free-market economy. The ability of those firms to survive in competitive markets is quite low. Yet it is very likely that Eastern Europeans will fail to attribute the

[11] The term "supposedly" is used to suggest a few doubts about the real extent of price liberalization. The distribution sector in Russia has a markup ceiling of 25 percent, which is a form of price control. Local governments are issuing regulations that often contradict or ignore price liberalization decrees issued by Moscow. Prices of basic foods are still controlled by the state.

[12] It appears, from time to time, that economists working for the International Monetary Fund (IMF) and the World Bank have a monopoly on economic nonsense. In one of the IMF's recent publications we read: "A mass privatization of the state enterprise sector is the centerpiece of the transition to a market economy" (J. Odling-Smee et al., "Russian Federation," *Economic Review*, IMF, April 1992, p. 35). Some people think that the freedom to choose the methods of organizing production is the centerpiece of a free society. Also, at the Hayek Symposium in Freiburg in June 1992, when Professor Jermakowicz, a leading "expert" on privatization, presented a paper on the aims and methods of privatization in Poland, V. Naishul, a free-market economist from Russia, remarked that the language the Polish bureaucrats use today is exactly the same as the language Soviet planners used yesterday.

dismal performance of these firms (layoffs, bankruptcies) to the decades of economic mismanagement under Communism. Instead, they are likely to "observe" that the free-market, private-property economy is not working either. For example, Zbigniew Janas, a leader of the market-oriented wing of the old Solidarity coalition in Poland has said: "The laissez-faire theory has not proven right. We have got to have state intervention. The question is how deep it should be."[13]

It seems important to identify two basic misunderstandings, one in the East and one in the West, about the transition process in Eastern Europe. The first is related to the image of capitalism among the ordinary people in Eastern Europe. When they voice their disappointments in capitalism, Eastern Europeans are merely revealing their own perceptions of the system. It will take time for them to understand that capitalism is not about getting rich — that the system is about individual liberty, self-responsibility, and self-determination in a world where the role of government is to enforce and maintain a stable set of rules. The second misunderstanding relates to the attitude of many free-market-oriented intellectuals in the West toward the transition to capitalism in Eastern Europe. They seem to ignore the importance of the region's "carriers of history." Western economists, especially neoclassical economists, are trained to think in terms of instantaneous adjustments to new equilibria. Thus, they tend to ignore the role of history and traditional values in shaping people's reactions to various social problems. It could easily turn out to be self-defeating to the cause of freedom in Eastern Europe to impose capitalism by fiat.

To attribute a slow rate of transition to capitalism in Eastern Europe solely to the resistance of socialist institutions and the "old roaders," as former Communists and bureaucrats are called, is a mistake. I believe that the major obstacle to the transition is the "hand of the past." Former Communists and bureaucrats are simply exploiting the old ethos to their advantage. The problem lies with this old ethos and with the philosophical heritage of the region; they are not well attuned to the exchange culture of capitalism and its emphasis on individual liberty. But Western "experts" are not taking this into account. For example, Jeffrey Sachs, a free-market-oriented Harvard professor of economics, has sold himself to a number of Eastern European (and Third World) countries as a transition expert. While Sachs's technical knowledge of economics is undoubtedly sound, his transition models make no allowances for cultural and historical differences between the countries and ethnic groups that he has been advising. The "big bang"[14] approach to the transition, promoted by Sachs and other Western scholars, envisions institutional changes that are

---

[13] Quoted in *Dallas Morning News*, August 4, 1991, p. 28.

[14] The term "big bang" means a quick change in the system. It is hard to find a better example of a big bang than the October Revolution of 1917. Yet it took Lenin and his cohorts quite a few years to implement changes — and they were willing to spill blood in order to get things done.

exogenous to the system.[15] Thus, these changes will confront the difficult task of overcoming beliefs and behaviors that are firmly embedded in the fabric of community life in the countries of Eastern Europe, with consequences unanticipated by any economist's models.

An alternative approach to the problem of the transition to capitalism in Eastern Europe is to let the preferences of the median voter play an important role in choosing both the direction and the rate of institutional change, and hope that capitalist institutions will win support through their performance in the marketplace. Instead of building capitalism by fiat, Eastern European governments could try to create a framework for competitive markets for institutions. That would require a credible guarantee of (1) equal legal protection of all property rights, (2) equal fiscal treatment of all sources of income, (3) efficient financial markets, (4) open entry and exit in all markets, and (5) free access to foreign goods and capital. Instead of imposing capitalist enterprise by fiat, Eastern European states should provide—admittedly by fiat—a legal environment that would allow people to choose among alternative institutional arrangements, including even socialist ones. The existing enterprises held over from the Communist era would then have to compete with newly emerging cooperative, corporate, joint stock, private, or other sorts of voluntarily formed enterprises.[16]

Points (1) through (5) are a normative alternative to what is now going on in most Eastern European states—save, perhaps, Hungary, where spontaneous changes seem to be playing a larger role than they are elsewhere. The implementation of this framework, and even more its en-

---

[15] An explanation of the difference between endogenous and exogenous change is in order. Suppose there is an event that creates new opportunities for individuals to interact. If the prevailing institutional structures are poorly attuned to those opportunities and fail to enforce new interactions, utility-seeking individuals will generate spontaneous pressure to modify the rules of the game to embrace the novelty. For example, technological developments made mass production of goods relatively cheap. However, exploiting new opportunities required a large initial investment in capital assets. But the rule of unlimited liability made contractual agreements for raising large sums of capital difficult. A new rule eventually emerged: limited liability. This was an *endogenous* change that adjusted the rules of the game to the new requirements of the game.

Instead of adapting the rules to the changing requirements of the game, *exogenous* changes force the game to adjust to the rules. For example, codetermination (labor participation in the management of business firms) in Germany was introduced by law. However, prior to this law there was no law in Germany that prohibited codetermination. Managers, workers, and the owners of resources were free to write any contract they chose. Indeed, we observe a large number of different types of business firms in the West, including Germany. All those firms have emerged voluntarily and survived competition from other types of firms. The fact that the German government had to *impose* codetermination by fiat is evidence that the value to the employees of their participation in management was less than the costs to the owners and managers of providing it. Most exogenous changes in institutional arrangements are brought about by ideologists, pressure groups, and bureaucrats in pursuit of their own private ends, while hiding behind the facade of the public interest.

[16] In order to give capitalist institutions enough time to tell their story, a stable social environment is a necessity. This means that the government might have to subsidize a number of large state enterprises over a limited number of years.

forcement, could be quite difficult, but that certainly should not be a reason to give up on it. It could be especially difficult for Eastern European governments to give credible constitutional guarantees within an environment in which the tradition of the rule of law and independent constitutional courts either was never established or was decimated by the Communists. However, the difficulty of implementing this kind of institutional framework is certainly not a good reason for accepting exogenous bureaucratic control of the transition path.

The existing institutions would then have to compete with new ones that people freely choose. Some new institutions will survive, while some old ones will also, but many more will expire. Even before legal guarantees, a large number of small private firms have emerged throughout Eastern Europe. These are mostly kiosks or miniature shops. Many of them will not last, but some have already passed the market test. Currently, these firms represent a small percentage of GNP in Eastern European countries, although their significance has grown in Poland. However, they represent something that is much more important than their current contribution to the aggregate output. These small firms are the breeding grounds for entrepreneurs, a work ethic, a capitalist exchange culture, and constructive attitudes toward individual liberty.

Endogenous institutional changes discussed in this section of the essay suggest neither a specific transition path in Eastern Europe nor the rate of institutional change. In fact, they cannot even guarantee that Eastern Europeans will choose the institutions of capitalism. However, if new governments in Eastern Europe were able and willing to limit the role of the state in the transition process to creating and enforcing the environment in which alternative forms of economic organization could compete with each other, I believe that the institutions of capitalism would eventually and spontaneously emerge, survive competition from other types of institutions, and become dominant in the region.

Economics, Texas A&M University

THE ECONOMIC AND POLITICAL LIBERALIZATION OF SOCIALISM: THE FUNDAMENTAL PROBLEM OF PROPERTY RIGHTS*

By William H. Riker and David L. Weimer

All our previous political experience, and especially, of course, the experience of Eastern Europe and Central Asia, offers little hope that democracy can coexist with the centralized allocation of economic resources.[1] Indeed, simple observation suggests that a market economy with private property rights is a necessary, although not sufficient, condition for the existence of a democratic political regime. And this accords fully with the political theory of liberalism, which emphasizes that private rights, both civil and economic, be protected and secure.[2] At the same time, our previous experience also indicates that market economies are more successful than centrally planned economies not only in producing, but also in distributing, both private and collective goods.[3] This economic experi-

* The authors thank Roger James, Brendan Kiernan, Nikolai Mikhailov, Ellen Frankel Paul, and the other contributors to this volume for helpful comments.

[1] Charles E. Lindblom, *Politics and Markets* (New York: Basic Books, 1977), ch. 12. The most extreme cases of centralized planning in democracies seem to be the wartime experiences of the United States and Great Britain. In the context of our discussion, it is worth noting that these episodes did not radically alter the existing system of property rights.

[2] We take voting as the central method and ideal of democracy. By "voting" we mean, of course, all of the institutional environment of elections, e.g., political parties, free speech, etc. The degree to which a political system is democratic depends on the practical effectiveness and political relevance of voting in terms of participation (the promotion of popular choice), liberty (the freedom to pursue one's goals), and equality (the facilitation of self-respect and self-realization). Liberalism emphasizes the role of voting in controlling officials (by expulsion, or threat of expulsion, from office) and the value of individual rights in protecting liberty against tyranny by the majority. In contrast to populism, it does not interpret majority opinion as necessarily right and therefore vests in it no special moral character. See William H. Riker, *Liberalism against Populism* (San Francisco: W. H. Freeman and Company, 1982).

[3] For example, in his score card comparing advanced capitalist and advanced socialist polities, Peter Rutland considers thirty-eight social values, finding the following: capitalism strongly superior (thirteen); capitalism weakly superior (six); no major difference (fifteen); socialism weakly superior (three — freedom from crime, wealth and income equality, housing for the poor); and socialism strongly superior (one — unemployment). Peter Rutland, "Capitalism and Socialism: How Can They Be Compared?" *Social Philosophy & Policy*, vol. 6, no. 1 (Autumn 1988), pp. 197–227. One might question the claimed superiority of socialist systems in terms of wealth and income equality in view of the common finding that higher levels of wealth seem to be positively correlated with greater equality. For an overview, see Michael Don Ward, *The Political Economy of Distribution* (New York: Elsevier, 1978). For an assessment of recent Soviet experience, see Richard E. Ericson, "Classical Soviet-Type Economy: Nature of the System and Implications for Reform," *Journal of Economic Perspectives*, vol. 5, no. 1 (Fall 1991), pp. 11–27; and Abram Bergson, "The USSR Before the Fall: How

© 1993 Social Philosophy and Policy Foundation. Printed in the USA.

ence is supported by neoclassical economic theory, which treats clearly defined and secure rights to private property as essential to a market economy.

Until recently, the former Soviet Union and the other political systems of Eastern Europe rejected private ownership of capital and, in some cases, of land and labor as well. Now, however, their desire for economic development and political liberalization forces the leaders of these countries to confront the issue of private property. Absent considerable movement toward the private ownership of the factors of production, the potential benefits of a decentralized market economy are unlikely to be realized; absent a well-functioning decentralized economy, democratization lacks a secure foundation and remains highly vulnerable to authoritarian resurgence. Thus, the extent and form of institutional, indeed constitutional, change from state to private ownership will be one of the fundamental determinants of the rate, degree, and stability of the political liberalization achieved by these socialist and formerly socialist countries.

For these countries, their previous economic experience, their political culture, and their politics pose fundamental problems for the establishment of private property and the other institutions essential for the operation of effective market economies. Furthermore, the particularistic features of these countries are likely to modify these essential institutions, possibly significantly and certainly uniquely, from country to country.

When it became apparent that the Soviet Union would allow challenges to the dominance of the Communist parties in the Warsaw Pact countries, the opportunity for radical change arose. As these countries were already undergoing economic and political change to varying degrees, moving generally toward liberalization, they now each confront the great opportunity with different levels of institutional development and democratic political experience. It is within these different contexts — historical, cultural, and political — that interests and alternative institutions will emerge and compete politically.

First, the previous economic experience of these countries has set the course of development of the institutions that now exist. Thus, for example, it is not only relevant that agricultural land still is, and has been, owned collectively, as in Hungary or Czechoslovakia, but also that previous owners who suffered expropriation nearly fifty years ago may still put forth claims to its ownership. In the former Soviet Union, there are probably no identifiable private owners, but members of the collective farms (the *kolkhozs*, if not the *sovkhozes*) surely have ownership claims of

Poor and Why," *Journal of Economic Perspectives*, vol. 5, no. 1 (Fall 1991), pp. 29–44. For the argument that Communism should be viewed as "vulgar capitalism" that is more subject to Marx's criticisms than the modern capitalism of the West, see John Clark and Aaron Wildavsky, "Why Communism Collapses: The Moral and Material Failures of Command Economies Are Intertwined," *Journal of Public Policy*, vol. 10, no. 4 (October 1990), pp. 361–90.

some sort. Speaking generally, we believe that historical institutional differences among the countries will lead to different paths of institutional development. In other words, we accept the notion of "path dependence" advanced by Douglass North as highly relevant to interpreting the transitions now underway.[4]

Second, political culture is important because it shapes perceptions about the relative desirability of various social outcomes and the legitimacy of political processes. If debate is cast in terms of a single-play zero-sum game (a one-time division of spoils), then it may be difficult for politicians to make the compromises that will undoubtedly be needed to create more effective institutions. An unwillingness to transcend particularistic interests and move "behind the veil of ignorance" may hinder the achievement of the constitutions that can moderate the inefficiencies that often result from distributional politics.

Third, at a fundamental level, the absence of a stable set of political rules, both formal and informal, opens the door for political disequilibrium.[5] A practical consequence of the political disequilibrium is instability in economic policy. This instability in turn creates uncertainty that discourages many important types of investment, especially investment in physical and institutional capital. The resulting low, or even negative, rate of economic growth draws attention to the immediacy of distributional concerns.

Indeed, in the extreme, a sort of vicious circle may operate: the ineffectiveness of economic institutions in creating wealth concentrates political attention on wealth distribution; and excessive focus on distribution leads, in turn, to even less effective economic institutions. What might reverse such a downward cycle? Perhaps an informal economy, beyond the easy reach of government control, will contribute a sufficient amount to wealth to permit, or even force, the strengthening of economic institutions. Perhaps the demands of external lenders or the market discipline of international trade will enable the political system to move beyond distributive issues. Or perhaps an authoritarian regime will emerge to suppress open political debate over distributive issues so that economic institutions can be strengthened.

Even if the countries in transition do not fall victim to such a vicious circle, they nevertheless face great obstacles in moving to liberal economic systems that will support liberal political systems. Many old institutions, both formal and informal, must be dismantled rather than reformed. The institutions that are needed to support effective liberal economic systems

---

[4] Douglass C. North, *Institutions, Institutional Change, and Economic Performance* (New York: Cambridge University Press, 1990), pp. 92–104.

[5] We use "disequilibrium" here in sense of the failure of a collective-decision rule to yield stable social choices even for a stable distribution of individual preferences. See William H. Riker, "Implications from the Disequilibrium of Majority Rule for the Study of Institutions," *American Political Science Review*, vol. 74, no. 2 (June 1980), pp. 432–46.

are highly interdependent, raising perplexing questions of priorities and sequencing.

While many Western economists have jumped on airplanes with transition plans in hand, economic science offers little guidance. Neoclassical economics generally takes a particular institutional framework as given, namely the regime of private and secure property rights, decentralized management of resources, and unfettered markets for trading the factors of production (labor, land, and capital) and the products of these factors.[6] Even when efforts are made to compare alternative institutions, the usual approach is to look at one equilibrium compared to another, with no attention to the paths reaching them. Such comparative statics do not seem to offer much to our understanding of the dynamics and consequences of radical institutional change.

In Section I, we briefly review what economics does tell us about the role of property rights in market economies. We then consider the notion of property rights as an economic institution in Section II, focusing on allocation, alienation, trespass, and credibility as important characteristics. In Section III, we turn to theories of the origin of property rights. In Section IV, we speculate about the transition from socialism to market economies and its implications for political liberalization. We conclude in Section V by noting that social science does not have much to offer in understanding the transitions underway, but that the transitions themselves offer a rare opportunity for social scientists.

I. The Role of Property Rights in Market Economies

Neoclassical economic theory begins with the assumption of private property: all factors of production and all consumption goods are owned by individuals who have a fully effective right of exclusive use. The owners can costlessly transfer their rights to use of factors and goods in competitive markets so as to maximize the utility they obtain from consumption. With only a few additional assumptions about the nature of factors and goods (each is homogeneous in quality and rivalrous in use), about the technology for converting factor inputs to goods (a marginal increase in the output of each good requires more than a proportional increase in the use of factor inputs), about the motivation behind the operation of the technology agents choose (factor inputs are chosen to maximize the excess of revenue over costs, taking market prices as given), and about the nature of individuals' utility (other things equal, consuming more of any good increases utility, but at a decreasing rate), one can show that a set of prices exists supporting a unique equilibrium such that no individual

---

[6] For an overview of the institutional assumptions of neoclassical economics, see Daniel W. Bromley, *Economic Interests and Institutions: The Conceptual Foundations of Public Policy* (New York: Basil Blackwell, 1989).

could increase his or her utility through market transactions.[7] Further, this competitive equilibrium is Pareto efficient in the sense that it would be impossible to find an alternative allocation that would give one or more individuals greater utility without reducing the utility of at least one other individual. Comparing equilibria under different assumptions about the initial distribution of factor inputs, utility, and technology is the fundamental approach of positive neoclassical economics; the notion of Pareto efficiency plays a central role in welfare theory, the normative side of neoclassical economics.

Two violations of the assumption of perfectly effective property rights enjoy prominent places in neoclassical theory as yielding competitive equilibria that are not Pareto efficient.[8] One violation occurs in situations of "open access" involving the absence of an effective right of exclusive use.[9] Certain species of whales until recently, the American bison in the nineteenth century, and some Third World forests today are examples of open-access goods consumed at economically inefficient rates. The other violation occurs in "externality" situations where production or consumption activities of one individual or firm affect the production or consumption activities of others. For example, one person's consumption of loud radio music in the park may be a positive externality for people with similar tastes who are in the mood to listen, but a negative externality for people who want to enjoy a quiet walk.

Within the neoclassical paradigm, each of these "market failures" can be corrected directly through the establishment of property rights. Ownership of the open-access resource can be given to someone; liability for externalities can be assigned. This simple approach, however, ignores the costs of making the rights effective. The very nature of an open-access resource, such as migrating fish, may make it costly for the owner, even backed by the coercive powers of government, to enforce the property right. In the case of negative externalities, Ronald Coase argues that any complete allocation of rights will be sufficient to yield economic efficiency, but only if bargaining and the enforcement of agreements are costless.[10]

---

[7] For a review of the development of this "general equilibrium theory," see E. Roy Weintraub, "On the Existence of a Competitive Equilibrium: 1930–1954," *Journal of Economic Literature*, vol. 21, no. 1 (March 1983), pp. 1–39.

[8] For an overview, see David L. Weimer and Aidan R. Vining, *Policy Analysis: Concepts and Practice* (Englewood Cliffs, NJ: Prentice Hall, 1989), ch. 3.

[9] Economists often use "open access" and "common property" interchangeably. We consider common property to be a special case of open access in which the good is open only to members of a clearly identified group. On the definition of property regimes, see Daniel W. Bromley, *Environment and Economy: Property Rights and Public Policy* (Cambridge, MA: Basil Blackwell, 1991), ch. 2. For an extensive treatment of institutions for governing the use of common property, see Elinor Ostrom, *Governing the Commons: The Evolution of Institutions for Collective Action* (New York: Cambridge University Press, 1990).

[10] Ronald H. Coase, "The Problem of Social Cost," *Journal of Law and Economics*, vol. 3, no. 1 (October 1960), pp. 1–44. Note that Coase's examples all involve externalities between producers. When considering externalities involving consumers, wealth effects may negate the economic neutrality of alternative allocations of rights.

When these activities are costly, economic efficiency may require that government go well beyond the designation of property rights to create legal and administrative institutions that make the rights effective.

The central importance of property rights becomes even more profound when the neoclassical framework is expanded to include multiple periods and uncertainty. Assuming secure property rights and complete contingent claims markets (insurance can be purchased against all risks), the competitive economy can be shown to be intertemporally Pareto efficient.[11] Yet if individuals cannot be persuaded that they will be allowed to realize future returns on current investments, they will not willingly defer a sufficient amount of current consumption to achieve efficient levels of capital accumulation.

The neoclassical framework becomes strained when the notion of information asymmetry, the unequal distribution of information between participants to a transaction, is introduced. Its manifestations as moral hazard and adverse selection, prevent the realization of the complete contingent claims market assumed in the extended competitive model.[12] Of more immediate concern to our understanding of economic behavior, it raises a whole range of questions about the efficient organization of economic activity. For example, agency theory provides a framework for considering the implications of the separation of ownership from management in firms: efficient contracts minimize the sum of the cost of contracting between owners and managers (bargaining, monitoring, and bonding) and the cost to owners of the residual loss due to inappropriate decisions on the part of managers.[13]

The general effort to take account of information asymmetry and other transactions costs, while preserving the assumption that individuals maximize utility, is coming to be called "neoinstitutional economics."[14] It incorporates and extends the earlier work on the economics of property rights found mainly in the law and economics tradition, taking systems of property rights as subjects of investigation rather than as assump-

---

[11] The extension of the competitive model involves distinguishing consumption by time period and contingency. See Kenneth J. Arrow and Gerard Debreu, "Existence of an Equilibrium for a Competitive Economy," *Econometrica*, vol. 22, no. 3 (July 1954), pp. 265–90.

[12] *Adverse selection* arises when individuals have more information about the risks they face than do insurers; if insurance is priced for the average risk of the group, then those with greater risks will find the insurance relatively most attractive, and they will be over-represented among policy holders. The equilibrium result will be a higher price that drives the best risks from the group. Adverse selection explains why individual health-insurance policies often cost several times as much as similar policies sold to inclusive groups such as the employees of a firm. *Moral hazard* refers to the reduced incentive that insurees have to prevent compensable losses. Policies often require co-payments by insurees to give them a stronger incentive to avoid losses.

[13] See, for example, Michael C. Jensen and William H. Meckling, "Theory of the Firm: Managerial Behavior, Agency Costs, and Ownership Structure," *Journal of Financial Economics*, vol. 3, no. 4 (October 1976), pp. 305–60.

[14] For an overview, see Thrainn Eggertsson, *Economic Behavior and Institutions* (New York: Cambridge University Press, 1990).

tions.[15] It views property rights as an important part of the relatively stable rules that define economic institutions.

II. Property Rights as Institutions

Four characteristics of property rights provide a focus for understanding and interpreting the institutions that support economic activity: allocation, alienation, trespass, and credibility. Yet these characteristics cannot be usefully viewed as independent of political and social institutions, especially in periods during which all major institutions are undergoing change. The stability of political institutions is especially important in determining credibility. The characteristics of the system of property rights influence, in turn, the stability of political institutions, by affecting the creation of wealth and the domain of economic policy making.

Every economic system allocates rights to the use of property such as land, capital, labor, and consumption goods. The rights may be assigned to individuals, as in private property, or to groups of persons, as in common property. The allocation may be legally explicit or result from de facto use. For example, the state may legally "own" a factory, while the managers exercise de facto rights over its use. A significant task facing the formerly socialist countries attempting to achieve well-functioning market economies is the difficulty of making a more explicit allocation of property rights to individuals so as to support decentralized economic decision making. This task is difficult not only because of its immense scale and complexity, but also because it often involves significant *reallocation* away from de facto users to new owners.[16]

The transfer of ownership from the state to individuals raises fundamental questions about the appropriate role of the public sector in a market economy. Even in capitalist economies the state often owns roads, the electromagnetic spectrum, wilderness areas, and other property. Economists often disagree about whether such state ownership contributes to economic efficiency, and policy makers often raise other values, such as distributional concerns, that might justify state ownership. Therefore, the appropriate boundary between state and private property is not clear. The problem is further complicated by the poor record of the state in manag-

---

[15] For reviews of the property rights literature, see Erik G. Furubotn and Svetozar Pejovich, "Property Rights and Economic Theory: A Survey of Recent Literature," *Journal of Economic Literature*, vol. 10, no. 4 (December 1972), pp. 1137–62; Louis De Alessi, "The Economics of Property Rights: A Review of the Evidence," *Research in Law and Economics*, vol. 2 (1980), pp. 1–47; and Yoram Barzel, *Economic Analysis of Property Rights* (New York: Cambridge University Press, 1989).

[16] In the case of Russia today, and previously in Poland and Hungary, a considerable amount of reallocation by de facto users to new owners or new de facto users seems to be underway. See Simon Johnson and Heidi Kroll, "Managerial Strategies for Spontaneous Privatization," *Soviet Economy*, vol. 7, no. 4 (October–December 1991), pp. 281–316.

ing property that would normally be publicly owned in capitalist economies. For example, the failure to pave rural roads in the former Soviet Union contributed to the wastage of farm products before they reached consumers. The general point is that, because some property is appropriately held by the state, bureaucrats who expect to lose their positions because of privatization have an opportunity to argue that the property managed by their bureau should remain under state ownership.

Demographic, technological, wealth, and taste changes alter the efficient allocation of economic resources. The less costly the alienation of property, the more effectively market forces can move resources to their most economically valued uses. The nominal legality of alienation is itself often an important determination of the costs of transferring property. A black market may work fairly well for simple trade goods whose quality can be determined by simple inspection. Yet more complex trade goods, or investment goods that maintain use value well beyond the time of exchange, may be very costly to transfer in black or gray markets where the parties must use their personal resources to enforce agreements. Even when transfer is legal, transfer costs depend on the system of contract law and its enforcement. The formerly socialist countries have neither well-developed bodies of contract law nor the tradition of an independent judiciary for fairly resolving contract disputes. Capital investment and the creation of intellectual property, both essential to economic growth, are likely to be greatly impeded by the underdeveloped institutions of contract. Transfer costs also depend on the availability of money with stable value and on such public policies as price controls and ownership restrictions that introduce important nonmonetary aspects to transactions. Here too, the formerly socialist countries have an unfortunate legacy that may hinder efforts to create property rights that support an efficient economy. For example, although most of these countries, especially Poland, Czechoslovakia, Hungary, and Russia, have made substantial progress in decontrolling prices, several have imposed restrictions on ownership of property by foreigners.[17]

The willingness of people to engage in productive, as opposed to defensive or predatory, economic activity depends on the vulnerability of resources to trespass.[18] When property is free from the risk of loss to unauthorized use, those who control it can use it in the way they think is

[17] As we write, Poland is restricting foreign ownership generally, perhaps as a way of precluding German investment in the formerly German territories. Russia and Czechoslovakia are restricting foreign participation in aspects of their privatization plans. Only Hungary seems to have fully embraced investment by foreigners. In any case, no Eastern European country yet has an active stock market on which capital can be freely exchanged.

[18] See William J. Baumol, "Entrepreneurship: Productive, Unproductive, and Destructive," *Journal of Political Economy*, vol. 98, no. 5, pt. 1 (October 1990), pp. 893–921. For a very explicit exposition of the consequences of ineffective property rights in Peru, see Hernando De Soto, *The Other Path: The Invisible Revolution in the Third World* (New York: Harper and Row, 1989).

most productive. When the legal system—especially criminal law, tort law, and the judicial resources to implement them with certainty, fairness, and swiftness—fails to guarantee freedom from trespass, those who control property may find that certain of its uses are not feasible because they expose property to easy trespass, and that other uses demand high investments in self-protection. The opportunity for profitable trespass may induce predatory behavior that hinders efficient use of property and diverts labor and entrepreneurial effort from socially productive activities. An extreme example is the formation of "mafia," organizations that threaten the use of force to extort or steal from businesses. As in the case of contracts, the formerly socialist countries face difficulty in creating freedom from trespass because an appropriate legal tradition and adequate judicial resources are lacking.[19]

The efficient use of economic resources requires not only that rights to property be currently effective (clearly allocated to individuals, alienable at low cost, and secure from trespass), but that those now exercising the rights believe that they will continue to enjoy their effectiveness in the future.[20] In other words, they must believe that they have a credible commitment from government to preserve the rights. The less credible the commitment, the less willing individuals will be to forgo current consumption to accumulate capital and preserve the economic value of natural resources, activities that contribute to future private and social wealth. A fear that one will not be able to enjoy the potential future gains from risky efforts to invent, adapt, and adopt new technologies, both in production and organization, slows the innovation that drives long-term economic growth.[21]

The formerly socialist countries face severe problems in establishing the credibility of their systems of property rights for several reasons.

---

[19] Some observers see the problem of establishing "economic legality" as fundamental to liberalization. See, for example, John M. Litwack, "Legality and Market Reform in Soviet-Type Economies," *Journal of Economic Perspectives*, vol. 5, no. 4 (Fall 1991), pp. 77–89.

[20] In the theory of rights offered by Wesley Hohfeld, the claims of right-holders and the respect of those claims by duty-bearers constitute the first-order relations defining rights. Second-order relations include the power to change, and immunity from changes in, the first-order relation between claims and duties, and thus encompass the notion of credibility. See Wesley Newcomb Hohfeld, *Fundamental Legal Conceptions* (New Haven, CT: Yale University Press, 1919). Most modern legal writers concentrate on the first-order relations, taking for granted immunity, perhaps because of the stability and continuity of our legal institutions—just as neoclassical economists assume an effective system of property rights.

[21] Obviously, the most urgent kind of innovation for the countries of Eastern Europe and the former Soviet Union is in the area of organization. Whereas more efficient physical processes for converting inputs to outputs can be relatively easily imported from abroad, organizational innovations, such as various forms of corporate ownership and credit systems, cannot as easily be replicated, because the prerequisite systems of property rights and economic law are not yet in place. See, for example, Robert D. Cooter, "Organization as Property: Economic Analysis of Property Law as Applied to Privatization," in Christopher Clague and Gordon C. Rausser, eds., *The Emergence of Market Economies in Eastern Europe* (Cambridge, MA: Basil Blackwell, 1992), pp. 77–97.

First, their governments have yet to achieve levels of stability that make policy at least somewhat predictable. Institutions and norms for the new political systems are just being created — constitution writers are operating in an environment in which almost all issues are subjects of debate and bargaining.[22] The central role of the state under socialism as owner, employer, and focus for opposition seems to provide a weak base for the emergence of political organizations that might play a stabilizing role by articulating interests and facilitating explicit and politically supported compromises over policy.[23] Until constitutions, written or unwritten, take hold to give structure to political processes, policy is likely to be unstable and therefore not credible.

Second, although there seems to be a general belief among the populations and elites of these countries that market economies offer the prospect for a better life, there does not seem to be a broad and deep understanding of the role of private property in market economies. For example, a recent national survey conducted in the Soviet Union found that only 7 percent of respondents favored the abolition of existing restrictions on entrepreneurship and almost 50 percent held beliefs that the state should not permit the existence of millionaires.[24] Thus, there may be significant disagreements about the social desirability of any particular system of property rights, giving maneuvering room to those who wish to preserve the de facto rights that they now enjoy. Consequently, even if there were well-developed political institutions, we might expect considerable uncertainty about the policies that are likely to be chosen.

Third, both the historical and current experience of these countries undermines credibility. Each country has some citizens who actually witnessed the expropriation of private property at the onset of socialism. In view of the great difficulty of the task these countries face in establishing

[22] Jon Elster, "Constitutionalism in Eastern Europe: An Introduction," *University of Chicago Law Review*, vol. 58, no. 2 (Spring 1991), p. 480.

[23] David Ost develops this point in the context of Poland. He argues that the absence of organized interests renders theories of democratic transition, which were motivated largely by the experiences of South America and Southern Europe, inapplicable to Eastern Europe. See David Ost, "Shaping a New Politics in Poland: Interests and Politics in Post-Communist East Europe," Program on Central and Eastern Europe Working Paper Series No. 8, Minda de Gunzburg Center for European Studies, Harvard University, March 1991.

[24] Seweryn Bialer, "Is Socialism Dead?" *Bulletin, The American Academy of Arts and Sciences*, vol. 44, no. 2 (November 1990), p. 25. A 1990 study based on random samples of New Yorkers and Muscovites, however, failed to find many significant differences in attitudes toward the fairness of allocation by price and income inequalities, and in their understanding of market processes. Robert J. Shiller, Maxim Boycko, and Vladimir Korobov, "Popular Attitudes Toward Free Markets: The Soviet Union and the United States Compared," *American Economic Review*, vol. 81, no. 3 (June 1991), pp. 385–400. One may not necessarily be reassured by the finding of little difference in attitudes between a U.S. city that embraces residential rent control and a Russian city that has been at the forefront of liberalization! Nevertheless, in the U.S. case the popular attitudes are only occasionally an impediment to market freedom, while in Russia such attitudes pose a risk to free institutions at the threshold.

effective property rights, it will not be surprising if any number of false starts occur. Correcting these false starts risks undermining the credibility of whatever system of property rights is created.

Our discussion so far has dealt with the problem that unstable political institutions pose for the establishment of effective and credible property rights. Let us turn briefly to consideration of what effective and credible property rights would contribute to the achievement and stability of liberal political institutions. We see three contributions as important.

First, by facilitating economic growth and the creation of wealth, effective and credible property rights facilitate political compromise. It becomes at least possible for the political system to adopt policies that improve the positions of all groups in society, thus facilitating compromise within democratic institutions.[25]

Second, from the perspective of social choice theory, credible property rights contribute to stability by reducing the number of dimensions of policy over which political systems must routinely make choices. If a right to property is given constitutional status, or at least enjoys immunity against simple majorities, it is less likely to be the subject of policy debate. In terms of spatial voting theory, we can think of credible property rights as fixing policy choices at specific points along certain dimensions, thus reducing the range over which cyclical majorities are likely to occur.[26] Thus, property rights can contribute to structure-induced equilibria that avoid the "chaos" that may result under unrestricted majority rule.[27]

[25] The notion that wealth as a general social resource contributes to stability by making society more resilient against shocks is developed by Aaron Wildavsky in *Searching for Safety* (New Brunswick, NJ: Transaction Publishers, 1988).

[26] Spatial voting theory represents the considerations for a political choice as dimensions in (usually) Euclidean space. Voters are assumed to have ideal points (most desired policy outcomes) that can be represented as points in the Euclidean space. For each voter, assume that, as between two alternatives, the voter prefers the alternative closer to her ideal point. And, of course, she is indifferent between any points of equal distance from her ideal point. Then an indifference curve, a set of points that give equal utility, can be drawn for each voter. By constructing indifference curves that include, for each voter, the status quo, it is possible to identify any alternatives that would win a majority of voters as points that lie inside the indifference curves of a majority of voters. Assuming a single dimension with an odd number of voters, the equilibrium—that is, the alternative that cannot be beaten in a head-to-head vote by any other alternative—is the median of the ideal points (the Median Voter Theorem). With two or more dimensions and three or more voters, with the exception of a few special cases, it is always possible to find an alternative preferred by a majority to the status quo. Thus, in the absence of restrictions on the introduction of alternatives, there is no equilibrium. For an excellent introduction to spatial voting theory, see Keith Krehbeil, "Spatial Models of Legislative Choice," *Legislative Studies Quarterly*, vol. 13, no. 3 (August 1988), pp. 259–319.

[27] On the fundamental problem of instability, see Kenneth Arrow, *Social Choice and Individual Values*, 2d ed. (New Haven, CT: Yale University Press, 1963); and Amartya K. Sen, *Collective Choice and Social Welfare* (San Francisco: Holden-Day, 1970). On instability under majority-rule voting, see Richard D. McKelvey, "Intransitivities in Multi-dimensional Voting Models and Some Implications for Agenda Control," *Journal of Economic Theory*, vol. 12, no. 3 (June 1976), pp. 472–82. On the notion of structure-induced equilibria, see Kenneth A. Shepsle, "Institutional Arrangements and Equilibrium in Multidimensional Voting Models," *American Journal of Political Science*, vol. 23, no. 1 (February 1979), pp. 27–59.

Third, the wealth creation facilitated by effective property rights provides a resource for political participation that can help prevent the concentration of political power in the state. Wealth gives individuals voice. It also makes it easier for organizations to operate without direct support from the state, so that these organizations are less susceptible to state control.

To summarize: Effective and credible property rights facilitate the creation of wealth; stable liberal political institutions facilitate the establishment of effective and credible property rights, which, in turn, help give stability to liberal political institutions. The profound problem facing the countries of Eastern Europe and the former Soviet Union is that they currently have neither stable liberal political institutions nor effective and credible property rights. Do theories of the evolution of rights offer any insight into how this profound problem might be resolved?

III. Theories of the Evolution of Property Rights

Most goods and resources are claimed by some persons. Of course, some resources are unclaimed in the sense that no one can physically exert control over them (e.g., deep oceans, perhaps, though their time may be coming), or in the sense that no one desires to control them (e.g., deserts), or in the sense that there are deep moral or legal prohibitions (e.g., slavery). But claims over most of the objects and creatures around us are nigh universal. And the claimants themselves are various: individual persons, nuclear families, extended families, tribes, villages, kings, conquerors, and corporate bodies (e.g., churches, firms, associations).

How are these claims and claimants sorted out and decided upon? What makes the decisions stick? Answers to these questions are crucial for the guidance of countries attempting to change from government or common ownership of some sort to private ownership by individuals or firms. The main issues have to do with the origins of private rights and with their maintenance.

Looking first at origins, there are two broad categories of descriptions.[28] On the one hand, some philosophers and economists have argued that it is the claimants themselves who originate private individual ownership. On the other hand, some lawyers and political scientists have argued that political authorities create private property. (This division parallels a rather consistent division today between economists' and political scientists' versions of causality in the world of affairs. Economists tend to see the men in the agora bribing and forcing the men on the acropolis to do the marketers' bidding, while political scientists tend to see men on the acropolis bribing and forcing the men in the agora to support the priest-soldier-rulers' control.)

---

[28] William H. Riker and Itai Sened, "A Political Theory of the Origin of Property Rights: Airport Slots," *American Journal of Political Science*, vol. 35, no. 4 (November 1991), pp. 951–69.

Among those who see the men in the agora as determinative, Locke stands out as the pristine voice: men in a state of nature mix their labor with resources (i.e., they invest) and then in mutual cooperation create government and rights of property in order to protect their investment. In the modern (often libertarian) versions of this theme, cooperation arises out of commercial interaction. The interacting traders reciprocally recognize and respect each other's rights in order to render their own rights secure.[29] In contrast, lawyers recite the history of English land ownership: its devolution from the monarch's temporary distribution of the realm (i.e., his estate) among military subordinates as payments for services to, then, the subsequent recognition of possession by the king's courts as inheritable and finally alienable estate. Clearly this whole process was initiated and sponsored by political authority. Private persons might petition for ownership, but it was the king and his courts that recognized and enforced it. One of us (Riker) in a recent examination of a brand new kind of ownership (landing time slots at busy airports) came to the same conclusion as the lawyers: the active agent generating ownership was indeed the government, and the motive of the rulers was indeed to solicit political support by providing efficient operation of what had been an exceedingly inefficiently operated common property.

As between these two approaches to the origin of private property, we subscribe generally to the political version.[30] The Lockean story seems to us simply a Platonic myth, and the contemporary economists' version is deficient because it is about trade practices, not about rights and ownership. It is certainly true, we concede, that traders who fail to reciprocate in their recognition of others' rights will probably not be traders for very long. But the banishment of the uncooperative is a feasible method of creating rights only when people frequently interact, which is why we call such matters "trade practices." Ownership, by contrast, is supposed to last over time, despite infrequent exchanges, and in the absence of personal acquaintanceship among the actors. It is instructive to survey the history of mining claims in California following the discovery of gold in 1849. Since the Mexican law on ownership of ores had been officially abrogated following the end of the conquest in 1848, and since the new owner of the mineral rights, the United States, had not yet established police authority, a Lockean state of nature appeared to exist. So mining villages adopted rules of ownership and provided rudimentary police au-

---

[29] Harold Demsetz, "Toward a Theory of Property Rights," *American Economic Review*, vol. 57, no. 2 (May 1967), pp. 347–59; and Gary D. Libecap, *Contracting for Property Rights* (New York: Cambridge University Press, 1989).

[30] Specifically, we accept the four necessary conditions for the emergence of a right identified by Riker and Sened: (1) scarcity — the content of a right is scarce, driving its value above enforcement costs; (2) right-holders desire the right — if they do not, then they will not seek the right; (3) rule makers (government) desire to recognize the right; and (4) duty-bearers must respect the right at the levels of enforcement made by the rule makers. See Riker and Sened, "A Political Theory of the Origin of Property Rights," p. 955.

thority in a quite Lockean way for a quite Lockean purpose.[31] This arrangement worked well enough as long as claims were small and villages intimate. Ownership was a matter of trade practice, not a general public right. It depended on person-to-person reciprocity, and certainly was not alienable to someone outside the village. But when mining became a large and stable industry, the United States established true property rights, grandfathered the possession of those who were essentially squatters, and created a whole new system of ownership: that is, a system of rights recognized over time and distance and alienable in world markets.[32] This is almost the exact opposite of the Lockean story. The initial possessors did possess in the small, but they could not create a state to protect their property in the large. Rather, the strong preexisting state granted protection—in return, presumably, for political support.

If, as we believe, the origin of private property lies thus in the actions of political authority, there must, we recognize, be a political motive. And there is: the rulers' conviction that private ownership works to the advantage of the rulers by rendering the economy efficient and trade profitable. It is not that rulers necessarily care about those economically pleasant outcomes for their own sake—indeed, rulers might reasonably prefer (and often have preferred) costly and unprofitable war and conquest to the material pleasures of peace—but rather that they care about the resultant popular approval of their tenure. But, of course, rulers can hardly create and enforce private rights if they do not share these convictions and if they do not believe that prosperity will redound to their credit. The immediate and inescapable question for countries abandoning socialism is, therefore, the legislators' and executives' perceptions of the effect of private property, decentralized trading, and market pricing on their personal political fortunes.

It is far from certain that Eastern European legislators and executives have the requisite perceptions. For example, they may be unwilling to put up with the high costs of transition from common to individual ownership. As is now vividly apparent, the costs of transition are immediate and high: inflation, disorganization, and significant decreases in productivity. The benefits of transition are, on the other hand, far from immediate, although they may eventually be far greater than the costs. Before the efficiencies of a market economy can be realized, traders must be convinced of the security of their ownership, not only of trade goods, but also of land and physical capital. Similarly, traders must have easy access to methods of enforcement of their rights, contracts, and physical possessions. Consequently, one prerequisite for efficient markets is effective property law. And such systems are hard to create *de novo*. The legisla-

---

[31] See John R. Umbeck, *A Theory of Property Rights with Application to the California Gold Rush* (Ames: Iowa State University Press, 1981).

[32] See Libecap, *Contracting for Property Rights*.

tors of some formerly socialist states recognize this, but not all do. Some seem willing to tolerate long delays while they work out equitable divisions of formerly common or state property. And achieving equity may well delay interminably the development of a new legal system. Thus, it may well be that, faced with immediate costs and distant benefits, legislators will temporize, keeping much of the old system simply because they cannot agree on anything else, and delaying thereby for far too long the development of the new system.

Moreover, it is far from certain that the legislators of the former Soviet empire believe that the credit they may obtain from capitalist prosperity will be as great as what they may obtain from ethnic warfare abroad and ethnic persecution at home. There is at least the possibility of interminable national and ethnic disputes—Armenia and Azerbaijan; Croatia, Bosnia, and Serbia; Hungary and Romania; Russians in Moldova, the Ukraine, the Baltic states, and the Crimea; Czechs and Slovaks—these are just the tip of the iceberg. Piling warfare and retribution on top of economic chaos can only mean that economic development will be delayed. Nor is it clear that legislators in the former Soviet empire believe that capitalist prosperity is worthwhile, given the inequities that they almost universally believe are associated with it. They are, of course, mistaken about the long-term effects of capitalism on equality, for the greater the national wealth, the greater the equality. But in the immediate short term, it is probably true that only successful traders prosper while the income of most others decreases. Furthermore, the successful traders are very likely to be exactly those persons who dominated in the old system, for they are the educated and the experienced deal makers. The enrichment of the *nomenklatura* is not likely to commend itself to anti-Communist legislators as a desirable outcome that will win them popular approval. This is all the more reason for them to go slowly in creating the necessary legal basis for a market economy.

A few brief sketches of privatization efforts in four countries illustrate the magnitude and complexity of the problems they face in moving toward market economies supported by private property. The situations of Hungary and Czechoslovakia seem quite promising; the situations in Poland and Russia seem much less so.

Hungary.[33] Beginning in 1988, even before the end of Communist rule, managers of large state enterprises began "spontaneous" privatization, creating new entities under private ownership at a fast rate. Public dissatisfaction with managers setting prices to facilitate transfers that protected their jobs, and with the stripping of profitable activities from state enterprises, led to the establishment of the State Property Agency (SPA) in March 1990. The SPA has made some progress in sorting out "owner-

---

[33] Our account is based primarily on Michael Marrese, "Hungary Emphasizes Foreign Partners," *RFE/RL Research Report*, vol. 1, no. 17 (April 24, 1992), pp. 25–33.

ship" of small enterprises by various government bureaus and councils, so that auctions for leases and sales to private parties have begun; little progress has been made in preparing cooperatives for privatization, however. Hungary has also had success in resolving claims by those who had property expropriated by the Communists. Compensation is being given in the form of certificates that can be used to purchase state property.

The SPA strategy for privatization of the approximately 20 percent of large enterprises it directly controls involves five steps: first, the clarification of state ownership by transfer to the SPA; second, conversion of enterprises to corporations; third, sale of a portion of stock to a foreign investor; fourth, restructuring of the enterprise in cooperation with the active foreign partner; fifth, sale of SPA stock, often with preferential purchase by employees and managers. With respect to the remaining large enterprises that it does not directly control, the SPA regulates stock sales worth more than $150,000.

Although the SPA processes have been criticized for moving too slowly and for attracting only a small amount of domestic private investment, they have quieted public outcry against the abuses of spontaneous privatization, and they have helped to make Hungary the most attractive Eastern European country for foreign investment. Overall, Hungary's privatization must be judged the most successful undertaken so far, helping to explain why Hungary is the only country under transformation that is predicted to show growth in gross domestic product in 1992.

Czechoslovakia.[34] Rather than following the sort of gradual privatization relying heavily on foreign investment now underway in Hungary, Czechoslovakia has adopted plans for the rapid transfer of state-owned enterprises to its citizens. Most small state enterprises have already been transferred through public auctions. Several thousand large state enterprises are to be transferred through an ambitious voucher plan that aims to distribute ownership widely.

Under the voucher plan, citizens can obtain coupons for bidding on shares in stock auctions by registering and paying administrative fees of 1,035 koruny (about $37).[35] (Over 8.5 million of a possible 11.5 million eligible citizens have registered so far.) Each share of the enterprises being offered will have the same book value. Specified enterprises will be offered in each of a series of waves. Each bidder has 1,000 points to bid per wave. Bids proceed in rounds. The opening price (in points) of each share is calculated as the book value of enterprises to be privatized in the wave divided by the total number of registrants. If the number of bids at

[34] Our discussion is based largely on Jiri Havel and Eugen Kukla, "Privatization and Investment Funds in Czechoslovakia," *RFE/RL Research Report*, vol. 1, no. 17 (April 24, 1992), pp. 37–41.

[35] We rely on Josef C. Brada, "The Mechanics of the Voucher Plan in Czechoslovakia," *RFE/RL Research Report*, vol. 1, no. 17 (April 24, 1992), pp. 42–45, for our sketch of the voucher plan.

the opening price for shares in an enterprise does not exceed the number of shares available, then the bidded shares are transferred and the remaining shares are offered at a lower price in the subsequent round. If the number of bids exceeds the number of shares available, then no transfers are made and the shares are offered again at a higher price in the next round. Over successive rounds, the outstanding points and shares decline. Remaining points cannot be carried over to the next wave of offerings.

Over four hundred investment funds have been formed to make bids and hold shares for registrants. Some funds have lent money to investors to pay their registration fees; others have guaranteed investors minimum returns. Many of the guarantees were made when participation rates were expected to be much lower and the book value of firms much higher. There is the danger, therefore, that the funds may be unable to abide by their guarantees, potentially undermining public support for the entire voucher plan.

Though issues concerning compensation for prior owners of state property and potential difficulties in implementing the voucher plan could substantially slow the rate of privatization actually achieved over the next few years, the most serious problem is likely to be the issue of separation between the Czech and Slovak Republics. Slovaks appear to hold attitudes much less supportive of economic reform than Czechs.[36] Preserving the federation might involve a compromise on economic policy that would slow reform. Separation would greatly complicate the privatization of assets held by the federal government and almost certainly result in slower economic reform in Slovakia.

Poland.[37] The successful decontrol of prices and the transfer of many state-owned shops, stores, and small firms to the private sector contrasts with the little progress made toward the overall privatization of state-owned property in Poland. So far, successive Polish governments have been unable to develop privatization plans that are both politically and economically feasible.

Spontaneous privatization began during the last months of Communist rule with the issuing of stock by state-owned enterprises. Many state and Party officials used their inside positions to gain shares in, and control over, newly created joint-stock companies. They were often able to use their positions to secure the most lucrative assets for the joint-stock companies, leaving the less desirable assets under state ownership. This "propertization of the *nomenklatura*" reduced state revenues and elicited

[36] See Michael Deis and Jill Chin, "Czech and Slovak Views on Economic Reform," *RFE/RL Research Report*, vol. 1, no. 23 (June 5, 1992), pp. 64–65.

[37] For an overview of privatization in Poland, see Ben Slay, "Poland: An Overview," *RFE/RL Research Report*, vol. 1, no. 17 (April 24, 1992), pp. 15–21.

an extremely negative public reaction undercutting support for privatization in general.

In August 1990, the Ministry of Ownership Transfer brought spontaneous privatization to a halt. Though the Mazowieki government remained committed to privatization, it made little progress in selling medium and large state enterprises. With the exception of a few sales to foreign firms and one sale of five large enterprises, most privatization was accomplished through the liquidation of assets by smaller state enterprises.

The Bielecki government launched a "privatization offensive," including a proposal to distribute shares among the Polish population to approximately ten investment funds that would be capitalized with about 60 percent of the stock in Poland's four hundred largest state enterprises. This "mass privatization" effort was stalled in 1991 by concerns about the state budget and problems encountered in restructuring state enterprises.

In December 1991, the Olszewski government further slowed the privatization process in an effort to gain greater control over it. A reprivatization fund is being established to settle claims for property expropriated by the Communists. The "mass privatization" effort seems to be going forward, but with registration fees to cover the administrative costs of general distribution of stock to the population. Under current plans, however, it may take as long as three years to form the investment funds. During this period, restructuring of enterprises in preparation for privatization will face continued opposition from interests within the enterprises themselves.[38] Management, workers' councils (previously established as proxy owners for the state by the Communist government), and trade-union officials often form alliances to preserve state ownership as long as possible because they fear the loss of their positions under privatization.

It thus appears that privatization in Poland will continue to be slow-paced. Indeed, political instability and poor economic performance could slow the pace even further.

Russia. Generations of Communist central planning, little previous experimentation with property and other market institutions, and the sheer scale and diversity of the Russian Federation pose great difficulties for economic reform. Nevertheless, Russia made considerable progress toward economic liberalization during the first half of 1992: a freeing of most prices beginning in January (though energy prices are a notable exception), the establishment of a bankruptcy law in June (though by presidential decree rather than parliamentary law), and further steps toward true convertibility of the ruble in July. Despite the strong commitment of President Yeltsin, however, privatization is progressing very slowly.

[38] Wojciech Bienkowski, "Poland's Bermuda Triangle," *RFE/RL Research Report*, vol. 1, no. 17 (April 24, 1992), pp. 22–24.

Problems of implementation aside, reaching political consensus on a privatization strategy has proven difficult. Enterprise managers remain an important elite, and over 40 percent of the deputies in the parliament are former Communist Party apparatchiks. Amidst staggering projections for 1992 of a decline of gross domestic product of as much as 20 percent and triple-digit inflation, popular dissatisfaction with the immediate consequences of reform provide its political opponents with a potentially large base of support. President Yeltsin's simultaneous appointment of Yegor Gaidar, a leading reformer, as prime minister and three managers as deputy prime ministers reflects a commitment to reform tempered by the reality of a politically strong opposition.

As we write, for example, debate continues over the question of who will receive ownership of the assets in state enterprises. The government proposes to distribute vouchers to the public for purchase of shares of state-owned enterprises when they are privatized, reserving at least 25 percent of stock for distribution to employees at no cost.[39] The Russian Unity Block, representing the interests of the state-enterprise managers and trade unions, supports instead the leasing and subsequent sale of all assets to labor collectives to prevent the distribution of ownership outside of the existing enterprise arrangements. (Of course, this would result in a common-property arrangement dominated by managers.) Even if the government prevails in the current debate, the opposition will have many opportunities to challenge it in the future before it is irrevocably underway.

Turning from these sketches of the problems of creating private property rights to the problems of maintaining them, we must consider whether the political authority has sufficient resources and commitment to enforce them. Enforcement involves monitoring to detect those who violate rights, as well as punishment to redress actual violations and deter future violations. As enforcement is costly, the political authority faces the problem of establishing credibility that it will continue to enforce rights in the future.

The level of costs that the political authority must bear to enforce a right depends on the informal rules that govern everyday interactions among people — social norms, personal norms, and habits. For example, consider the right to personal property. The size of the criminal justice system required to achieve any desired level of effectiveness of this right depends on the degree to which people view theft as intrinsically morally wrong and outside the range of acceptable personal behavior (a personal norm),

---

[39] Under pressure of threatened strikes by the Federation of Independent Trade Unions, representing sixty million workers, the government agreed to guarantee work collectives access to 51 percent of shares, though at a price to be established by the State Committee on Property. See "Quality Versus Speed in Privatization Discussed," Moscow INTERFAX, May 7, 1992, in *Daily Report, Central Eurasia, Foreign Broadcasting Information Service*, May 12, 1992, pp. 40–43.

as socially improper and deserving of condemnation, including cooperation with authorities or vigilantism to punish violators (a social norm), or simply an option that by experience is so rarely worth considering that it is not routinely considered (a habit). Rights that are consistent with existing norms and habits are more likely to be effectively maintained.

The formerly socialist countries attempting to establish and maintain more effective property rights may be hindered by the existing system of norms and habits that were consistent with state ownership. For example, the managers of state-owned factories may have developed norms that support the trading of state property in violation of official rules to achieve more effective allocations of inputs. These norms may tend to persist and carry over to property that has been allocated to individuals or to firms. More supportive norms may be slow to evolve if people perceive the distribution of rights as unfair.

Indeed, the term "mafia" is used to cover loose associations of people who engage in activity ranging from the unauthorized use of state property to crimes such as extortion. As the creation of market institutions expands opportunities in the private sector, some "mafia" may become legitimate businesses. Others, especially those that now employ force or threats of force, may remain involved in criminal activity, just as bootleggers brought their capacity for violence to the drug and gambling trades after the end of Prohibition in the United States.

The formerly socialist countries face another problem related to enforcement costs if they establish rights to common property as an intermediate step toward private property. The owners of private property have a strong incentive to monitor the use of their property and report violations. Individuals who are members of organizations that own common property have a weaker incentive to monitor, because they bear the full costs of the monitoring but only share in the benefits that are enjoyed by all members of the organization. Organizations usually develop rules and incentives that mitigate, to some extent, such collective-action problems. If such rules do not develop, or develop only slowly, then norms may develop that rationalize use of the common property somewhat, but hinder the enforcement of the private property that follows.

We have already discussed the economic importance of the credibility of property rights and the role that the legal system can play in establishing credibility. One final point is worth raising, namely that the establishment of courts with some independence from the rest of the government offers a way of making a commitment to the future enforcement of rights. The commitment is likely to be more credible, the more independent the courts are from political influence and the more costly to political authorities the courts can make the withdrawal of rights. Indeed, one of the encouraging signs from Russia has been the overturning of several of President Yeltsin's decrees by the Constitutional Court, and Yeltsin's acceptance of these rebuffs. Countries trying to create credible commitments to rights are likely to find that constitutional guarantees by themselves lack credibility. It is the tradition of constitutionalism, as much as the constitution itself, that creates the commitment.

IV. Speculations on Institutional Change from Socialism to Markets

In the preceding sections we have argued that the effectiveness and the credibility of property rights are important determinants of economic performance, that effective and credible property rights generally take shape from the actions of governments, and that the governments of Eastern Europe and the former Soviet Union face great difficulties in achieving effective and credible property rights. These arguments lead us to be somewhat pessimistic about the pace, if not the ultimate degree, of liberalization we should expect to see in the countries of Eastern Europe, and especially the former Soviet Union. The brief comments that follow should be viewed more as speculation than as social science — we have some theory and evidence relevant to understanding the consequences of alternative institutions of property rights, and we have some theory and evidence about incremental changes in institutions, but we have neither theory nor evidence to guide us in predicting the path of so radical a transition as is now being attempted.

We take as our starting point an important insight of Mancur Olson: during the transition from socialism to liberalism, the economy will consist of a mix of the remnants of old institutions and those newly created.[40] Olson emphasizes the role of what he calls "encompassing interests," individuals or coherent organizations that gain when social output increases and lose when social output falls.[41] His argument can be sketched as follows: First, with a strong and relatively powerful leader, socialist institutions can produce economic growth, because the leader identifies his interests with economic performance and has the capability to secure by fear and coercion cooperation that would be achieved in market economies by incentives. Stalin, for instance, seems to have been an effective encompassing interest. Second, over time, coalitions of managers and workers form within the economy to make the central authority relatively less powerful, so that fear and coercion become less effective in achieving cooperation. At some point the coalitions become sufficiently strong so that economic stagnation results. Third, the economic stagnation prompts efforts toward liberalization, but these efforts further weaken the

[40] Mancur Olson, "The Hidden Path to a Successful Economy," in Christopher Clague and Gordon C. Rausser, eds., *The Emergence of Market Economies in Eastern Europe* (Cambridge, MA: Basil Blackwell, 1992), pp. 55–75.

[41] Encompassing interests are to be contrasted with distributional coalitions (special-interest groups) that can gain at the expense of social output. Mancur Olson, *The Rise and Decline of Nations* (New Haven, CT: Yale University Press, 1982), pp. 36–74.

central authority, so that the remaining encompassing interests are weakened even further relative to the coalitions that pursue narrower economic interests. Thus, the initial steps toward liberalization cause further economic decline of the sort we seem to be witnessing now in the former Soviet Union. Fourth, the eventual establishment of individual rights sets the stage for the reemergence of encompassing interests and a resumption of economic growth.

As our earlier discussion might suggest, we think that Olson's scenario can be retold solely in terms of property rights without resort to the notion of encompassing interests. As Olson himself notes, we can think of state ownership under a leader like Stalin as meaning ownership by Stalin himself, so that in effect one person had at least somewhat effective and credible economy-wide property rights! Successive leaders found their ownership rights attenuated as the various coalitions of managers and workers developed to expropriate state property for their own uses. The fluid mix of old and new institutions that make the de facto system of property rights less effective and certainly less credible is, in and of itself and without resort to the notion of the weakening of encompassing interests, an obvious explanation for the economic decline we are now observing. Like Olson, we see the establishment of more effective and credible property rights as the key to the resumption of economic growth.

Thus, though we employ a slightly different model of institutional change, we nevertheless share Olson's prediction (economic performance will get worse before it gets better) and remedy (establishment of individual rights). Yet how will the remedy be achieved if the prediction is correct? As we noted in the introduction, one may fear that the immediate economic decline will shift the political focus to distributional issues, which in turn may slow the creation of a credible economic framework, so that further economic decline will result. How might this vicious circle be broken?

Perhaps a sufficiently productive set of informal relationships will develop within the framework of poorly defined property rights to halt economic decline. People may find creative ways to make the de facto property rights more effective and credible. For example, people may find ways to transfer property like apartments (just as people in New York find ways to pass along rent-controlled apartments illegally), hire thugs to enforce agreements (just as organized crime does in the West), or keep proceeds of joint ventures abroad (as some of the larger Russian state-owned enterprises do now). Countries with market experience in some sectors may find that norms facilitating exchange may spread to other sectors. Similarly, norms promoting efficient exchange may be imported along with goods from foreign trading partners. In any event, if informal rules can evolve to halt economic decline without creating envy directed against those who have been most successful in exploiting them, then it may be possible to move beyond distributional politics to create formal rules that will contribute to long-term economic growth.

Openness to foreign trade and investment may also help stop the vicious cycle. Trade itself imposes price discipline if the economy is kept open. Those wishing to invest in these countries provide a voice for the establishment of sufficiently credible property rights to guarantee their investments. Foreign aid donors and foreign lenders may play a similar role. These external factors may help focus political debate on rules relevant to long-term economic growth.

Perhaps the vicious circle will be broken by the reemergence of authoritarian regimes that repress open political debate about distributional issues in order to advance more effective and credible property rights. Aside from an immediate loss of political freedom, the reemergence of authoritarian regimes risks a slide back to central planning that would hinder future progress toward both political and economic liberalization. A slide toward a myriad of protected cartels is another possibility that might produce results even worse than central planning.

Of course, our fear of a vicious circle may be unfounded. Ideas can be powerful. The idea of liberalism has influenced many people. Perhaps in some of the countries it will help keep liberalization progressing despite short-term setbacks in economic performance. Unfortunately, with a few exceptions (particularly, Czechoslovakia, Latvia, and Estonia), these countries did not have strong traditions of liberal democracy before Communism. In the end, it may be more the firsthand experience of the failure of Communism than faith in liberal economic and political institutions that propels liberalization forward.

V. CONCLUDING REMARKS

Economic theory and experience point to the establishment of effective and secure property rights as critical to the success of economic liberalization. Empirical observation and political theory suggest that political liberalization will not be viable in the long run without successful economic liberalization. Yet we lack a convincing social-science theory of how societies can simultaneously create liberal political and economic institutions. The appropriate question, therefore, seems to be not what social science offers those leading the transitions now underway, but rather what can the transitions offer social science?

The transitions underway in the countries of Eastern Europe and the former Soviet Union provide a rare "natural experiment" for studying the evolution of institutions.[42] These countries share a stated desire to

---

[42] In September 1992, we assembled political scientists with specializations in China, Czechoslovakia, Hungary, Poland, and the former Soviet Union for a nine-month seminar at the University of Rochester devoted to theories of property rights and to the design of a common research protocol for studying the evolution of property rights in these countries. After spending three to five months executing the protocol in their countries of specialization, the seminar participants will contribute to a comparative volume on the evolution of property rights in the transition from socialism to market economies.

move from socialism to market economies with democratic governments. Yet this general force will play itself out in the context of specific local circumstances, including the already existing institutions. Variations in local circumstances allow for the "testing" of existing theories, such as those related to path dependence, as well as providing rich comparisons to support the creation of theory inductively. The system of property rights adopted by each country is a very appropriate dependent variable in the near future. As systems of property rights become more stable and begin to manifest their long-run economic effects, economic performance and political stability can become dependent variables to be explained to some extent by the property rights systems that have emerged. In any event, we believe that it is important for social scientists to at least document the institutional evolution underway, so that the value of this natural experiment will not be lost to future scholars.

Political Science, University of Rochester
Political Science and Public Policy, University of Rochester

DEMOCRACY, MARKETS, AND THE LEGAL ORDER: NOTES ON THE NATURE OF POLITICS IN A RADICALLY LIBERAL SOCIETY*

By Don Lavoie

On the extreme wing of libertarian ideology are the individualist anarchists, who wish to dispense with government altogether. The quasi-legitimate functions now performed by government, such as the administration of justice, can, the anarchists claim, be provided in the marketplace.

George H. Smith[1]

The collapse of socialist regimes constitutes the defeat of the leading form of radicalism in this century. Radical socialist ideology in the West was parasitic on the survival and apparent success, at least in some dimensions, of what was called "really existing socialism," the Soviet-type system. The collapse of the system has exposed the fact that it never really succeeded in serving any but a narrow power elite in those societies. The long-run effect of this exposure, I believe, will be the extinction of the major ideological force of our time.

For many commentators, the end of socialism represents simply a victory for "the West," for a conservatism that declares the existing systems of Western "democratic-capitalist" states, such as the United States, the United Kingdom, Germany, and Japan, to be the best possible political-economic arrangement. For me, on the contrary, the end of socialism is an opportunity to reconsider the nonsocialist form of radicalism that was supplanted by the socialist episode, radical liberalism.

By "radical liberalism" I mean liberalism in its classical European sense, the ideology of the American and other "bourgeois" revolutions that held the oppositional high ground before the rise of socialism. We should recall that the original "left," the radicals of the eighteenth-century Enlightenment, were the French, English, and American liberals. John Locke, David Hume, Adam Smith, Jean-Baptiste Say, Thomas Jefferson, James Madison, et al., were bold critics of "the right," the mercantile state, and its systems of privilege. Their heroes were the likes of Algernon Sidney,

*I would like to thank Ellen Frankel Paul and the other contributors to this volume for helpful comments.

[1] George H. Smith, "Justice Entrepreneurship in a Free Market," in *Atheism, Ayn Rand, and Other Heresies* (Buffalo, NY: Prometheus Books, 1991), p. 295.

© 1993 Social Philosophy and Policy Foundation. Printed in the USA.

an uncompromising radical who, for example, debated the merits of regicide.[2] They aspired to a radicalization of economic and political liberalism, to the principled extension of the ideals of both democracy and markets.

Just as socialism transformed almost everything else in this century, it transformed liberalism, but I want to focus on the ideology in what we might call its pre- and post-socialist forms. The form in which it arose, before the socialist episode, aspired to be a genuine radicalism, and the form it may now be able to take in the aftermath of socialism will, I think, be radical again. Pre-socialist liberalism was, like the ideology if not the practice of socialism, highly distrustful of governments in regard to civil liberties and the conduct of war; but unlike socialist ideology, it was also distrustful of the state in regard to the economy. Many of the intellectual leaders in the emerging societies of Eastern Europe are unmistakably liberal in this classical, pre-socialist sense.[3]

Unfortunately, this classical-liberal radicalism failed. Although the original liberalism of Locke, Sidney, et al. was radical in spirit, it failed to achieve its own ideals. The view among even the most radical liberals was that democracy is a form of government, and that government is a necessary evil whose scope in society needs to be strictly limited, so that democracy has a necessarily constricted role at best. This essay suggests that the cost of this position on democracy was the loss of liberalism's radicalism, and that those who would like to re-radicalize the ideology today should reconsider the role of government and the nature of democracy.

I. DEMOCRACY AND MARKETS

Liberals from the newly liberated countries typically differ from Western liberals on what democracy and markets are, and on whether they ultimately fit with one another. The Eastern European liberals seem to idealize democracy and markets, and to think of them as fully complementary. Western liberals, who have experienced "really existing liberalism" in the democratic-capitalist societies, have certainly enjoyed more democracy and markets than the Eastern European liberals, and seem to be far less enthused about the ideals, and to think of them as in some sort of necessary tension with one another. Liberalism in this view is a pragmatic compromise between its own two ideals, neither of which can be radicalized—that is, taken to its logical extreme—without endangering the other. The ideals that won together in Eastern Europe have been having

---

[2] See Algernon Sidney, *Discourses Concerning Government* (1698; Indianapolis: Liberty Classics, 1990).

[3] Classical liberals are well-represented throughout Eastern Europe; they include Vaclav Havel and many of Boris Yeltsin's economic advisors. But those I have particularly in mind are a number of young radical liberals I met in Warsaw, Moscow, and St. Petersburg.

trouble coexisting in the West, which thinks of itself as their natural home.

Conventional wisdom in the West would have it that it is we who understand the ideals better, and thus who see why in fact they fit only imperfectly with one another. When the Eastern European liberals experience liberal institutions in practice as we have, it is said, they will see that democracy involves empty campaign slogans and irresponsible governance, and that markets are no panacea for the ills of society. We feel a touch of embarrassment when we hear Eastern European liberals wax eloquent about democracy, as we think of the crass sideshows we call presidential elections. We have become jaded about democratic politics, the cynicism of electoral campaign promises, the corruption of popular government, and the manipulation of public opinion. We have doubts as well about a consumerist society that delivers wondrous gadgets but leaves our streets unsafe.

To be sure, nobody today denies that the imperfect liberalism we live in is superior to Communist totalitarianism. We do not begrudge the Eastern European liberals' celebrations for throwing off the system that tried to dispense altogether with bourgeois democracy and markets. But we tend to believe that their joy will come to be tempered by the hard reality that the liberal ideals are flawed.[4]

These notes are an attempt to rethink the liberal notions of democracy and markets from the point of view that it is the liberals in Eastern Europe who sense their true nature, and the true relationship between them.

I admit that residents of Western democratic-capitalist countries typically know more about important details of how a relatively democratic polity works, and of how market institutions work. But if our notions of political and economic liberalism are *informed* by our having lived in a really existing liberalism, they are also to some extent *imprisoned* in preconceptions based on that experience. We "know" from experience that taking democracy too far undermines markets and that taking markets too far undermines democracy. We know, for example, that if income distribution is left entirely to democratic processes, the resulting redistribution would seriously damage the market, and that if we insist on letting it be entirely market-driven then we would have to put significant limits on the scope of democracy. This view of markets and democracy as limiting one another is the source, I think, of liberalism's gradual drift into compromises with conservatism and socialism.[5]

[4] A good example of the disillusion with democracy is expressed in Vaclav Havel's article "Paradise Lost," *New York Review of Books*, April 9, 1992.

[5] The compromises have divided liberalism into two kinds, each of which bears little similarity to the original ideal. Some self-styled liberals favor conservative policies such as aggressive militarism; others favor socialist ones such as intrusive welfare statism. Gone is the principled opposition to government so characteristic of classical-liberal doctrine.

Our Western liberalism is old, tired, worn out, and compromised. Perhaps, then, it is those who have been denied the ideals of liberalism, by being forced to get by in a system that systematically tried to crush democratic and market processes, who know them in their essence, who know them *as ideals*. Maybe out of the newly liberated societies' enthusiasm for liberal values can be forged a more radical sort of liberalism, a liberalism that is more true to its own ideals.

Liberalism needs to reinterpret its notions of markets and democracy in such a way that they fundamentally fit with each other. The principles of political and economic liberalism can be understood in a manner that makes them essentially complementary, but this will require some profound changes in the way we think about both. Seeing democracy and markets as *essentially* complementary suggests the possibility that we do not need to balance them off one another, and that they can each be taken considerably further than we have yet taken them.

Liberalism lost in its confrontation with the ideology of socialism because it never really reconciled its own two ideals with one another, or even came to a very satisfactory understanding of what they are. Socialism arose in the late nineteenth and early twentieth centuries by taking the moral high ground away from liberalism, claiming to go radically beyond mere bourgeois democracy and exploitative capitalism. Marxism saw the conflict between liberalism's two ideals and proposed to radicalize the one by eliminating the other. It challenged liberalism for not going far enough with democracy by limiting it to the election of representatives to run government. Government under capitalism, Marx said, is always in the pocket of the capitalists. And I would have to admit that there is some truth to this charge. Any government, no matter how democratically formed, needs to watch the stock market, and if its policies seem to contradict the "wishes of Capital," so to speak, they will be revised.

Classical liberalism understood the institutional preconditions of markets better, I think, than it understood the nature of democracy. It accepted too narrow a formulation of democracy as merely a useful form of government, the very institution that most of its rhetoric criticized. It aspired not to achieve any high ideals with democratic government but merely to immunize the legal order from democratic government's manipulation. Government, whether democratic or not, needs to have its hands tied to keep it from undermining markets. The result was that liberalism lost to socialism the claim of being democracy's natural ideological home.

Socialism promised to do what liberalism could not: combine and radicalize economics and politics. It would replace a hollow, hypocritical system of voting — in which democracy is at the mercy of Capital — with a genuine, direct participation in the planning of economic activity. The economy would no longer be a separate force limiting democracy, but a direct consequence of conscious, rational, and democratic decision-making processes. Next to this radical economic democracy, the old bourgeois ideals seemed ordinary and partial. What was the big deal about voting for a representative when you could collectively fashion your own history? What was the marvel of the market's invisible hand when visible, deliberately designed policies could engineer economic growth? Socialism succeeded in taking the wind out of liberalism's sails, scoffing at its achievements, confidently predicting its inevitable decline, and derisively trashing its most cherished values.

This whole democratic-socialist vision never bore much resemblance, of course, to really existing socialism, but the democratic vision and the repressive reality supported one another, indeed were absolutely necessary for one another. The vision served the really existing socialists by supplying them with a motivating ideology to convince enough citizens of the ideology's noble aspirations to give its advocates power, and to let them keep it for seventy years. Really existing socialism, in turn, served the visionaries by making it seem that eliminating, or at least suppressing, the market is an effective path to successful economic performance.[6]

Throughout the past century, liberalism in the West has been primarily challenged — and of course, gradually but deeply influenced — by radical ideals of the left. Liberalism compromised with both the right and the left throughout the century, until in some sense it became the establishment.[7] It split off into warring factions of moderate conservatives who were embarrassed about democracy, and moderate social democrats who were embarrassed about markets. In the process it lost its idealism, lost its standpoint of principled opposition.

The unraveling of really existing socialism affords contemporary liberals the opportunity to pose challenges to the status quo of really existing liberalism from a wholly different radical standpoint. The established form of moderate liberalism, no longer threatened from the left, can now be productively challenged from another side, from a standpoint that tries, not to reject its principles, but to take them further than established liberalism ever dared.

It is time to reclaim the old liberal ideals of democracy and markets and give them back the dignity they had before socialism trashed them. But I do not think we should go back to the classical-liberal notions. We have learned a few lessons from the philosophical and economic illusions of

---

[6] Western ideological socialism was also parasitic on really existing socialism in its notion of totality, which presumed that the standpoint of the proletariat was a kind of privileged, totalistic view of history which gave it meaning. The gradual loss of faith in this totality has meant a loss of historical meaning, and thus a collapse of the whole socialist perspective on the world. See Martin Jay, *Marxism and Totality: The Adventures of a Concept from Lukács to Habermas* (Berkeley: University of California Press, 1984).

[7] For a concise critique of the decline of radical liberalism, see Albert Jay Nock, "Liberalism, Properly So Called," in *The State of the Union: Essays in Social Criticism* (1943; Indianapolis: Liberty Press, 1991).

the socialist epoch.[8] What is needed is a fresh attempt to articulate a radical liberal vision that recovers not the details but the original essence of classical liberalism: democracy and markets.

Conventional, moderate liberalism advocates the two ideals of democracy and markets, but it does not truly embrace them. It all too quickly assumes that the existing institutional framework of Western democratic-capitalist societies constitutes a practical realization of liberal ideals. It defines markets and democracy as completely distinct values, articulated in the artificially separated domains of economics and political science. Democracy is a form of government in which citizens can vote for their leaders. Markets are apolitical forces driven by self-interested activities. One is in the private sector, the other is in the public sector. One is epitomized by the (impersonal) act of voting, the other is epitomized by the (impersonal) act of buying and selling. Markets are judged according to the efficiency of their exchange outcomes in giving consumers what they want. Democracy is judged according to the efficiency of its electoral outcomes in giving voters what they want.

This conventional understanding takes for granted a meaning of democracy and markets that does not correspond to the real processes that have made Western democratic capitalism so much more successful than the Soviet experiment.

Francis Fukuyama makes the dramatic claim that the collapse of the anti-democratic and anti-market Communist regimes represents the last gasp of liberalism's opponents.[9] The pattern of history from the turn of the century to the thirties, when classical liberalism was overcome by the ideologies of fascism and Communism, has been reversed. Now that liberalism's right- and left-wing challengers have been utterly defeated, he argues, we have arrived at the End of History, in Hegel's sense. Western liberalism—by which he seems to mean the combination of a relatively democratic form of government with a relatively market-oriented economy—is simply the best possible political-economic system.

Fukuyama is right in seeing the end of Communism as a victory for economic and political "liberalism," but his vague use of the term conceals the fundamental problem. The manner in which democracy and markets are generally understood is such as to set them *necessarily* at odds with one another. The problem with conventional liberalism's combination of democracy and markets is that, the way they are each understood, the more one of them advances, the less room there is for the other. Radicalized democracy would seem to imply that decisions that now are left to the (unconscious) forces of the market, would instead be (consciously) undertaken by a democratic government. Radicalized free markets would seem to imply that decisions that are now taken by (persons on behalf of)

---

[8] The next section will briefly summarize the two main correctives I believe a post-socialist liberalism needs to be built upon, pertaining to the illusions of modernism in philosophy and social engineering in economics.

[9] Francis Fukuyama, "The End of History," *The National Interest*, Summer 1989, pp. 3–18.

democratically legitimated governments, would be left instead to the (impersonal) market. The ideals, as they are understood, cannot be taken too seriously, or they will collide head-on with one another.

It seems to me that the underlying notions of democracy and markets have more in common than the fact that totalitarian ideologies hated them both. The fact that they have been thought to be in fundamental conflict with one another might be a reflection of the incompleteness of our liberalism. Maybe we in the West have not understood either democracy or markets well enough. Perhaps the societies we live in are not really the living embodiments of political and economic liberalism that Fukuyama seems to imply they are.

As someone who considers our established political-economic system far from ideal on both political and economic grounds, I find Fukuyama's complacent attitude about Western systems disturbing. I too consider the collapse of socialism to signal a triumph of political and economic liberalism, but I want to insist that the liberalism that is triumphant is not what we in the West already have, but is an incomplete project. Liberalism has not realized its own political and economic aspirations. There is a great deal of history left to happen in the development of a *genuine* liberalism, that is, one which truly advances both democratic and market processes.

A reinterpretation of liberalism might take its cue from the collapse of the Soviet system, on the hunch that the totalitarians had an insight about the essence of liberalism from which we can learn: the insight that the ideals of democracy and markets are essentially complementary. The defeat of the Soviet system was a victory for *both* political *and* economic liberalism, for both democracy-oriented politics and market-oriented economics.

II. LIBERALISM AS OPENNESS

What, then, should we mean by democracy and markets, if we are to start not from our own jaded view of them but from the recent experience in Eastern Europe? In what direction does liberalism need to move in order to radicalize its views of democracy and markets? I think we need to correct for the Enlightenment prejudices in our economics and politics. In economics we need to purge our thinking of its Cartesian rationalism, which takes as its locus of analysis the isolated, asocial individual.[10] In politics we need to keep that same rationalism from identifying democracy with explicit control over social outcomes by a conscious will.[11] In both cases what is needed is a theory of political culture. Our economics

---

[10] See, for example, Charles Taylor's critique of atomistic liberalism in "Cross-Purposes: The Liberal-Communitarian Debate," in Nancy L. Rosenblum, ed., *Liberalism and the Moral Life* (Cambridge: Harvard University Press, 1989).

[11] See David L. Prychitko, "Socialism as Cartesian Legacy: The Radical Element within Hayek's *The Fatal Conceit*," *Market Process*, vol. 8 (1990).

needs to move beyond the model of the atomistic individual and take into account the cultural underpinnings of markets. Our politics needs to move beyond the model of the exercise of some kind of unified, conscious democratic will and understand democratic processes as distributed throughout the political culture.

The most important lesson to be learned from the experience of socialism is that economic development cannot be engineered but depends on the decentralized knowledge of market participants. The classic challenge the Austrian economists Ludwig von Mises and F. A. Hayek issued to socialism some seventy years ago shows why we need open competitive markets in order to marshal knowledge effectively. The price system involves what one might call a system of *distributed* intelligence. Market prices are our "eyes" on the economy, so that attempting to eliminate them, as traditional Marxism did, or to interfere with them, as all Western democratic-capitalist governments have, blinds or clouds our vision.[12] In principle, then, wherever possible, free-market competition should dictate economic change, and government should get out of the way.[13]

I suspect a similar line of argument can be made in regard to politics and our view of democracy. The force of public opinion, like that of markets, is not best conceived as a concentrated will representing the public, but as the *distributed* influence of political discourses throughout society. These open discourses are our eyes on the polity, and the attempt to resolve their differences into a single political will embodied in a monopoly institution destroys our political vision. We must not reduce our understanding of democracy to a view of the form of government which allows periodic elections. We should recognize, rather, that for a society to be democratic it is neither necessary nor sufficient for it to be ruled by a particular form of government. More important than whether the government permits regular elections is the issue of whether all the other institutions of human interaction are imbued with a democratic spirit, with an open political culture.

[12] On this critique of socialism and the view of markets as knowledge-conveyance and discovery mechanisms, see F. A. Hayek, ed., *Collectivist Economic Planning: Critical Studies on the Possibilities of Socialism* (London: George Routledge & Sons, 1935); Hayek, *The Fatal Conceit: The Errors of Socialism* (London: Routledge, 1988); and Don Lavoie, *Rivalry and Central Planning: The Socialist Calculation Debate Reconsidered* (New York: Cambridge University Press, 1985). For an interesting view along these lines of markets as themselves a kind of language, see Steven Horwitz, *Monetary Evolution, Free Banking, and Economic Order* (Boulder: Westview Press, 1992); and Horwitz, "Monetary Exchange as an Extra-Linguistic Social Communication Process," *Review of Social Economy*, forthcoming.

[13] The chief difficulty with extending this critique of government to a radical position that seeks its elimination altogether is the well-known argument that there are certain "public goods," such as national defense (and, many would argue, courts), which cannot be supplied adequately by the market. See Jeffrey Rogers Hummel and Don Lavoie, "National Defense and the Public Goods Problem," in Robert Higgs, ed., *Arms, Politics, and the Economy: Historical and Contemporary Perspectives* (New York: Holmes & Meier, 1990), for a discussion that suggests that this line of argument may not necessarily establish a case for government provision.

What are the qualities of the political culture which characterize liberalism? What I think we should mean by democracy is the distinctive kind of *openness* in society which the Soviet system crushed, and which began to recover under the banner of *glasnost*.[14] *Glasnost* is the making public of things. The Russian word translates better into "openness" than it does into "democracy." Some Western defenders of democratic governments have complained about the common translation into "democracy" on the grounds that openness is not the same thing as the holding of periodic elections, so that the *glasnost* movement should not be called a democratic movement at all. I suspect, on the contrary, that the movement captures the underlying essence of democracy better than our Western democratic institutions do.

It seems to me that this openness and publicness, not some particular theory of how to elect the personnel of government, is the essence of democracy. Like the market, a democratic polity exhibits a kind of distributed intelligence, not representable by any single organization which may claim to act on society's behalf. Democracy is not a quality of the conscious will of a representative organization that has been legitimated by the public, but a quality of the discursive process of the distributed wills of the public itself. The Soviet system had no democracy in the liberal sense, because it had no public opinion.

Traditional thinking about democracy has presupposed the need to assign to one monopoly institution the role of representing the democratic will, as expressing a boiled-down version of the distributed public opinion. But we can question what happens to democracy in the boiling-down process. We can question whether the nation-state, historically the most significant enemy of democratic values, is well-suited to this role as the primary vehicle for democracy. The force of public opinion is there in a free society whether or not a single representative body is set up to embody it. Is not the essence of democracy rather a matter of the openness of the system to bottom-up influence over social rules by the distributed wills of the public? The state can be undemocratic, in the sense of not open to electoral politics, as in Hong Kong, and yet the power of democratic forces can be great.

Democracy is all too often identified with a particular democratically legitimated institution, with the narrow idea of a government that risks itself to periodic elections. Radicalizing it is too often imagined as moving toward "direct democracy," voting directly for social outcomes. But there

---

[14] For a more extensive argument along these lines, see Don Lavoie, "Glasnost and the Knowledge Problem: Rethinking Economic Democracy," *Cato Journal*, vol. 2, no. 3 (Winter 1992), pp. 435–55. The idea of openness has been elaborated by hermeneutical philosophy in its account of the conditions for mutual understanding in everyday life, in the humanities, and in science. See, for example, Richard J. Bernstein, *Beyond Objectivism and Relativism: Science, Hermeneutics, and Praxis* (Philadelphia: University of Pennsylvania Press, 1983); Hans-Georg Gadamer, *Truth and Method*, revised translation by J. Weinsheimer and D. Marshall (1960; New York: Crossroad, 1989); and Georgia Warnke, *Gadamer: Hermeneutics, Tradition, and Reason* (Cambridge: Polity Press, 1987).

is much more to democratic processes than voting, and much more to politics than government. Wherever human beings engage in direct discourse with one another about their mutual rights and responsibilities, there is a politics. I mean politics in the sense of the public sphere in which discourse over rights and responsibilities is carried on, much in the way Hannah Arendt discusses it.[15] What was crushed by the Soviet system and revived under *glasnost* was not voting, but democratic discourse in all interpersonal relations, and most importantly, in public. Democracy should not be reduced to government institutions, but understood to apply to the whole range of our discourses with one another.

From this point of view, the common law is a good example of a democratic institution. A legal order that is subject to the influence of public opinion, and that evolves according to the application of the liberal principles of openness to human interaction, can be said to be democratic, no matter what its form of government. Democracy should not privilege what people *say* they want in the very imperfect mode of communication we call voting, over what they indicate they want in other ways, by their actions and their other communicative efforts. It should not privilege explicit, conscious action by a single institution that is supposed to "speak for" the public, over the tacit, distributed wisdom that is embedded in our evolved legal rules.[16]

And publicness, I think, is the essence of markets as well. Again we can take our cue about what markets are from the system that attempted to suppress them. The Soviet system had no markets in the liberal sense, because it had no fully public marketplaces. Activities which superficially bore resemblance to democratic politics, such as voting, existed, and activities which looked like market exchange activity, indeed, commodity production on an enormous scale, existed. What made Soviet elections and Soviet official, gray, and black markets only pale imitations of genuine democracy and markets was their utter lack of openness.

Markets are understood, by both individualist liberals and their critics, as apolitical confrontations of atomistic individuals. They are not only taken to be apolitical by definition, in the sense indicated by the language of the public and private sectors. They are thought to be unrelated even to the broader concept of politics as discourse.

Markets are taken to be external mechanisms that are disconnected from political discourse, either because they are understood as impersonalized, or because they are understood as narrowly materialistic. Impersonalized markets put such distance, or as Marx would have said,

---

[15] See Hannah Arendt, *Between Past and Future: Eight Exercises in Political Thought* (1954; New York: Penguin, 1977).

[16] On the common law, see F. A. Hayek, *Law, Legislation, and Liberty: A New Statement of the Liberal Principles of Justice and Political Economy*, vol. 1, *Rules and Order* (London: Routledge & Kegan Paul, 1973); and Arthur R. Hogue, *Origins of the Common Law* (Indianapolis: Indiana University Press, 1966).

alienation, between agents that there is no possibility of democratic discourse. This line of critique remains a crucial element of the contemporary left. The neo-Marxian social theorist Jürgen Habermas, whose approach to democratic politics is very much in the spirit of what I have been saying, retains the traditional Marxist's distrust of markets as inherently undemocratic institutions. His worry that markets threaten to "colonize the life-world" derives from this widespread interpretation of markets, shared by their supporters as well as their critics, as essentially impersonalized mechanisms.[17]

To be sure, not everyone who advocates the spread of markets really sees them this way. As one liberal put it, the pro-market philosophy is frequently attacked with the "tired canard that classically liberal rights deny the essentially social nature of human beings, that they are crafted for self-sufficient 'monads' complete unto themselves."[18] But is this charge really groundless? A significant component of liberal literature — certainly much of its economic analysis — projects exactly this view of individuals as asocial monads, whose preferences confront one another in impersonal markets.[19] Liberalism was born in the Enlightenment, and its writings often show its modernist pedigree. Only recently have a significant number of liberals begun to take seriously the philosophical critique of modernism and the social nature of human beings.[20]

Likewise, seeing markets as driven by narrowly materialistic motivations excludes the realm of democratic politics. Agents in markets are supposed to be motivated by the narrow pursuit of profit instead of noble ideals. Marketplaces are understood to be the locus of antisocial conflicts among bickering traders. People selfishly bickering over price cannot, it seems, by truly engaged in a democratic discourse over their mutual rights and responsibilities as citizens.

[17] See Jürgen Habermas, *The Theory of Communicative Action*, vol. 1, *Reason and the Rationalization of Society* (Boston: Beacon Press, 1984), and vol. 2, *Lifeworld and System: A Critique of Functionalist Reason* (Boston: Beacon Press, 1987). For a particularly stark presentation of this image of markets as impersonal, see Elizabeth Anderson, "The Ethical Limitations of the Market," *Economics and Philosophy*, vol. 6 (1990), pp. 179–205.

[18] See Loren E. Lomasky, "Duty Call," *Reason*, April 1992, p. 51.

[19] For examples of analyses of economic phenomena that take culture seriously, see Mary Douglas and Baron Isherwood, *The World of Goods: Towards an Anthropology of Consumption* (London: Allen Lane, 1979); and Georg Simmel, *Essays on Interpretation in Social Science*, translated, edited, and introduced by G. Oakes (1907; Totowa, NJ: Rowman & Littlefield, 1978). Even writings in the Austrian school, although far less guilty of this modernist vice than neoclassical economics, evidence an acultural view of human agents. See, for example, my critique of Israel Kirzner along these lines in "The Discovery and Interpretation of Profit Opportunities: Culture and the Kirznerian Entrepreneur," in Brigitte Berger, ed., *The Culture of Entrepreneurship* (San Francisco: Institute for Contemporary Studies, 1991).

[20] The postmodern liberalism that is occasionally being presented in the pages of the journal *Critical Review* is beginning to correct for this atomistic element in traditional liberalism. See also G. B. Madison, *The Logic of Liberty* (New York: Greenwood Press, 1986), and Madison, "Getting Beyond Objectivism: The Philosophical Hermeneutics of Gadamer and Ricoeur," in Don Lavoie, ed., *Economics and Hermeneutics* (London: Routledge, 1991), pp. 34–58.

Liberals should not concede so much to the socialist view of the world. Markets are not essentially impersonal confrontations. Of course, modern markets make possible more distanced interactions with people. But Marx's claims that markets made people atomistic is on weak empirical grounds. Inside the firm, in business lunches, at street corners, interpersonal discourses are constantly going on in markets. In all those places there is a politics going on, a politics that can be more or less democratic.

Nor are markets inherently or typically a matter of crass, merely materialistic motivations. Critics often find repulsive the liberals' ideas of leaving such services as education or medicine, much less the provision of legal services, "to the market." The repulsion arises, I think, from the apolitical notion of individuals and markets. The services we buy and sell from one another are not necessarily "mere commodities," and our mutual relations are not necessarily distanced. On the contrary, many of the things we buy and sell are deeply imbued with social meaning. We pay for services to satisfy our desires for health, companionship, musical pleasure, peace of mind; and these goals are not necessarily cheapened just because they can be bought. Leaving a service to "the forces of supply and demand" does not remove it from human decision making, since everything will depend on exactly what it is that the suppliers and demanders are trying to achieve.

If we redefine markets and democracy in terms of the more fundamental value of openness, we may find that the radicalization of these principles poses a challenge to the traditional interpretation of liberalism.

III. POLITICAL CULTURE AND THE LEGAL ORDER

Nowhere is the conflict between traditional notions of democracy and markets more evident than in the political discourse within radical liberalism over the provision of legal services. Although historically most liberals have insisted that the legal system needs to be provided by government, there have been a few radical liberals in recent times who have challenged this view, and who suggest that legal services could be provided in a competitive market. Two particularly interesting examples of the so-called anarchist extreme of liberalism are economists Murray Rothbard[21] and David Friedman,[22] whose controversial and highly polemical works have provoked counterarguments by the philosophers Robert Nozick[23] and John Hospers.[24]

---

[21] Murray N. Rothbard, *For a New Liberty* (New York: Macmillan, 1973).

[22] David Friedman, *The Machinery of Freedom: Guide to a Radical Capitalism* (New York: Harper & Row, 1973).

[23] Robert Nozick, *Anarchy, State, and Utopia* (New York: Basic Books, 1974).

[24] John Hospers, "Will Rothbard's Free-Market Justice Suffice? No," *Reason*, May 1973, pp. 18–23.

These debates may seem a bit arcane and remote from real-world problems, but the free-market anarchist positions represented by Rothbard and Friedman are not as absurd as they appear, and are worthy of serious attention.[25] As Bruce Benson's recent scholarship shows, there are many cases in history of legal systems working quite effectively without government.[26] The articulation of a utopian society that claims to eliminate politics altogether highlights the question this essay is raising about what we ought to mean by politics and by democracy. These debates over ways of establishing a legal order offer an opportunity to rethink the relationship between democratic politics and the market economy.

A radically liberal society might be imaginable in which there is nothing left for government, a monopoly of the use of force, to do. The legal services government now provides could be provided competitively, according to the laws of supply and demand. According to free-market anarchism, all the fundamental institutions necessary for the market to function—money, police protection, and even justice—would themselves be "for sale on the market." Of course, to say justice would be "for sale on the market to the highest bidder" is to invite ridicule. If a court is deciding law according to which party to the dispute can pay better, then the "service" it is supplying does not deserve the name "justice." But as with any good, everything depends on what specifically the suppliers and demanders actually want. It is imaginable that the demand for legal services could be well-defined, so that competitive pressures could force suppliers to offer fair adjudication according to widely understood principles of the rule of law.

Nozick's well-known critique of the free-market anarchists was a normative challenge, arguing that a competitive legal system could evolve step-by-step toward a monopoly government without ever violating in-

[25] I think that this anarchist policy conclusion is more reasonable than it must appear to most readers; however, I find the atomistic individualist perspective in which it is couched by Rothbard and Friedman unacceptable. This notion of free-market anarchism has to be distinguished, of course, from traditional left-wing anarchism, which does not necessarily share its hyper-individualism, but which has other serious problems. On left-wing anarchism, see Michael Bakunin, "Statism and Anarchy," in Sam Dolgoff, ed., *Bakunin on Anarchy* (1873; New York: Vintage, 1971); and Marshall S. Shatz, ed., *The Essential Works of Anarchism* (New York: Bantam, 1971).

[26] The study by Bruce L. Benson, *The Enterprise of Law: Justice without the State* (San Francisco: Pacific Research Institute for Public Policy, 1990), raises the scholarly level of debate considerably above that of the Rothbard and Friedman polemics. It persuades me that a free-market anarchist society would be workable, at least under certain plausible cultural conditions; but I think it will convince very few readers, mainly because the cultural preconditions are not discussed. Free-market anarchism remains unpersuasive to most people not primarily because of any shortcomings of the arguments its proponents make, but because of shortcomings of our background notions of markets and democracy. Behind the objections most people have to the anarchist position is a fear that it would rob us of a deeply cherished value, democracy. In my own view, a radically market-oriented society with a severely limited or perhaps even abolished government could turn out to be a more "democratic" kind of system, properly understood, than the Western-style democracies we are used to.

dividual rights. Of more interest here is a different issue, not so much normative as positive, raised by Hospers's lesser-known critique: Doesn't the anarchists' whole case depend on the matter of ideology?[27] Whether Rothbard or Friedman's imagined schemes for competitive legal institutions — and indeed whether any particular government-supplied legal system — can work depends completely on what Hospers calls "ideology," and what I prefer to call the "political culture." It depends on what the general public in this particular society considers morally acceptable behavior. To this, Rothbard answers: Of course, everything *does* depend on such general beliefs.[28] I agree with this concession by Rothbard, but I think it suggests that radical liberals have been ignoring what is really the most important issue in the question of the state: the political culture.

Economist Tyler Cowen, commenting on this response by Rothbard, argues that it is cheating to invoke ideology in the case for the feasibility of anarchism. It is not surprising, he says, that if nearly everybody believes in liberal values, then a radically liberal society would be workable. In his own discussion of the issue, Cowen insists he will avoid using ideology as a *deus ex machina*.[29] But he then goes on to assume a political culture of self-interested, atomistic individuals who already believe in the legitimacy of the institution of government.

The source of the difficulty with the anarchists' argument, as well as the arguments of their critics, is, in my view, the economistic vice of analyzing individual human beings as autonomous, cultureless "agents." In practice, each of the disputants presupposes a set of beliefs that seem reasonable to him, beliefs which his critics charge beg the question. The solution is not to pretend to avoid discussion of beliefs altogether, but to make the issue of such beliefs the central theme of political discourse.

What makes a legal system, *any* legal system, work is a shared system of belief in the rules of justice — a political culture. The culture is, in turn, an evolving process, a tradition which is continually being reappropriated in creative ways in the interpersonal and public discourses through which social individuals communicate. Anarchism seems workable to its advocates only because they implicitly assume a certain democratic political culture will prevail. Unless anarchists begin to say something about the kind of political culture that would be necessary for a stateless legal order, they will never get very far.

Everything depends here on what is considered acceptable social behavior, that is, on the constraints imposed by a particular political culture. Where slavery is considered offensive, those who attempt to practice it

[27] The term "ideology" is misleading here, since we are not interested in articulated systems of ideas but rather in the sorts of tacit beliefs that inform concrete practices.

[28] Murray Rothbard, "Will Rothbard's Free-Market Justice Suffice? Yes," *Reason*, May 1973, pp. 19–25.

[29] Tyler Cowen, "Law as a Public Good: The Economics of Anarchy," unpublished manuscript, George Mason University, 1991.

are easily overwhelmed by the horror of the public. Where it is thought by the general public to be justifiable, no amount of constitutional design will prevent it. Where taxes are accepted as morally defensible, they will be deployed; where they are equated with slavery, they will be impossible to collect. The feasibility of slavery or taxation does not fundamentally depend on the (concentrated) opinion of the designated representatives of the public, but on the (distributed) opinions of the public itself.

Leaving aside the practicability of the anarchist idea, though, the idea itself is relevant to the thesis of this essay in that it raises in a striking manner the question of democratic politics. The issue of the market supply of legal services is especially interesting, in that law lies at the intersection of the two great ideals of liberalism, democracy and markets. Law is at once the most important precondition of effective market processes and the most important topic of democratic political discourse. How should a liberal legal order be secured? Radical liberals appear caught on the horns of a dilemma. Is the provision of legal services one of the few legitimate functions of government, or is it susceptible to the usual liberal arguments against government and in favor of markets? If the provision of such services is left open to democratic influence, then markets may lose their institutional underpinnings; if it is immunized from democratic influence, then democracy may lose its significance.

Just as socialism resolved the conflict between democracy and markets by rejecting markets, liberalism ends up marginalizing democracy. The limited-government position to which classical liberals have historically adhered boxes in the role of the democratic state in order to ensure that market processes are not obstructed by the minimal government it permits. It thereby seems to put severe restrictions on the realm of democratic decision making. The anarchist position seems even worse. By trying to take a principled approach to free markets, anarchism winds up apparently rejecting politics, and therefore democracy, altogether. After all, as radical liberals say, if everything is decided by market forces, what is there to vote about?

In that question is contained, I suspect, a fundamental misreading of the nature of both market forces and democratic principles. First of all, as I have been saying, democracy is more an issue of open discourse than it is an issue of voting. And secondly, when decisions are "left to the market" there is plenty to talk about.

The provision of legal services for a liberal polity can be thought of nonpolitically, as the private-sector supply of legal services on the market, no different in principle from the supply of electricity. Here it is conceived as the impersonal satisfaction of the preferences of separate individuals, seemingly having nothing to do with culture. Or it can be thought of noneconomically, as belonging to the public sector, to (democratic) government. Here it is a matter of explicit conscious control over social outcomes and thus an issue wholly separated from (and, of course, only apt to interfere with) the decentralized market sphere. In the debates over the supply of justice services, the anarchists have tended to picture the legal order nonpolitically, and the limited governmentalists to picture it non-economically. I think both of these ways of thinking about the legal order need to be challenged. Each is a one-sided way of viewing political economy, which should be seen as an inseparable whole.

Rothbard and Friedman are a case in point. They take the position that politics (and hence any positive notion of democracy) is by definition a matter of government, so that the whole topic is, as it were, summarily dismissed. There is no need for political discourse in the utopias of these authors, since agents simply "buy" justice services on an impersonal competitive market. Friedman's approach leaves the enforcement, interpretation, and definition of rights to be "decided by the market." In Rothbard's case, enforcement and interpretation are left to private police and courts, but the legal rules are supposed to be derived from natural law, established once and for all by a deductive science of ethics.

In either case, there is no room in these utopias for politics. At most, political discourse is only needed in order to drive the process that brings about a radically liberal society, but once the free society exists, all the work of politics is over.[30] The definition of rights is decided without the need for discourse, either by the force of an impersonal market, or by the force of an unquestionable logic.

Liberals cannot resolve the issue of whether a legal system could be supplied by a free market because the issue depends on what is happening in the political culture, in the ongoing discourses about mutual rights and obligations, which individualist liberalism, in both limited-government and anarchist versions, utterly ignores. Radical liberals have been so intent on establishing a universal system of individual rights that they have failed to address the cultural conditions in which socialized individuals would demand this or that kind of legal services.

To say we should leave everything to be "decided by markets" does not, as radical liberals suppose, relieve liberalism of the need to deal with the whole realm of politics. And to severely limit or even abolish government does not necessarily remove the need for democratic processes in nongovernmental institutions.

The reason liberals in general have had trouble convincing others of the desirability of extending markets—and the reason anarchist liberals have had trouble convincing limited governmentalists to extend them to law—

---

[30] Indeed, this may be giving these authors too much credit. Political discourse presupposes an open exploration of issues of mutual concern. It seems that for Rothbard and his followers, genuine political discourse is not even needed in order to *get* to the free society. Instead, it seems there needs to be what is essentially a religious-conversion experience. The definition of rights is not open to exploratory dialogue but presumed to have been accomplished once and for all in Rothbard's *Ethics of Liberty* (Atlantic Highlands, NJ: Humanities Press, 1982).

is that they have all lacked an adequate theory of politics. Since markets are assumed to be essentially apolitical, their radicalization seems to imply the end of politics. Extending the market, according to individualist liberals, seems to mean that we would become the atomistic monads Marx thought we were becoming.

The weakness of both sides in the debates over anarchism is their neglect of what lies behind the legal order. Why does anybody obey the law, whether it is conceived as being supplied in a competitive or monopolistic manner? Limited-government advocates assume that it is the ultimate threat of force by a monopoly state that ensures that individuals will obey the law. Anarchists assume that there is a demand for genuine justice on the part of individual agents, so that competitive courts will profit most from behaving in a properly liberal manner. Both beg the question of the political culture. What gives legitimacy to a legal system is neither the force of threat by the police, nor the force of pure logic, but the force of public opinion, of the distributed political discourse about rights and responsibilities.

IV. Conclusion

What does all this have to do with contemporary realities of post-socialist societies? Neither limited-government nor anarchist forms of radical liberalism are likely to carry the day in the near future in places like Russia or Poland. A people so recently recovering from the excesses of a failed radicalism are apt to resist leaping directly to another utopian-sounding idealism.

Moreover, the special challenges of these societies, their severe economic problems, their rising and sometimes strident expressions of nationalism, make experimentation with any ideal policies difficult in the extreme. The argument could be made that the political culture of these societies has been systematically shaped in nonliberal ways for decades, so that neither markets nor democracy have much prospects for survival.

On the other hand, the case could be made that the political culture in the newly liberated societies is not far from that which would make a radical liberalism an attractive alternative. First of all, the fact that anti-liberal socialist ideology has been the state religion in those societies for many years should not be taken to mean that the bulk of the population has bought into the religion. The severe economic and political problems of these societies are widely understood to be the legacy of socialism. Nowhere can one find less tolerance for Marxian notions than in this part of the world. Nowhere are people as deeply and consistently suspicious of government. Nowhere are the institutions of markets and democracy valued as highly as where their absence is within vivid memory.

The spirit of nationalism that now sees its expression in violent clashes may yet be transformed into peaceful rivalry. Beneath the nationalism is not so much a passionate love of the nation-state as a sincere pride in one's national culture, a pride which had been suppressed but never destroyed under the Soviet empire. Indeed, the reason for nationalistic strife may be related to the fact that we have not radicalized our notion of democracy. If democracy is conceived in terms of control over government, then violent efforts by different cultural groups to gain mastery over the state are to be expected. If democracy is understood, instead, as an element of the whole society, and if the role of government in both the economy and the polity is minimized—or eliminated—then the nationalistic struggles lose their point. If everything is decided by the market and by open political discourse, then what is there to fight about?

The understandable attitude that the newly liberated societies have now, that they cannot afford to experiment with any more radicalisms, is open to challenge. The moderate government-oriented liberalism that they seem to think is safe has been severely contaminated by the very socialism whose dangers these people understand all too well. It is safer to get as far away from socialism as possible than it is to embrace a liberalism that is compromised with socialism.

Thus, even in the face of the very real difficulties these societies are up against, an optimistic view of the future is possible. Radical liberalism may become a reality in Eastern Europe, and is more likely to take hold there than it is in the West. If one of these societies which survives the immediate challenges moves in the direction of radically liberal policies, the economic and political benefits that will reward them will be extremely attractive to the others, and to the rest of the world. And indeed, we in the West, who nowadays presume we know what democracy and markets are, may find ourselves learning from their example.

Economics, Center for the Study of Market Processes,
George Mason University

LIBERALISM:
POLITICAL AND ECONOMIC*

By Russell Hardin

I. Two Liberalisms

Political liberalism began in the eighteenth century with the effort to
establish a secular state in which religious differences would be tolerated.
If religious views include universal principles to apply to all by force if
necessary, diverse religions must conflict, perhaps fatally. In a sense,
then, political liberalism was an invention to resolve a then current, awful
problem. Its proponents were articulate and finally persuasive. There
have been many comparable social inventions, many of which have
failed, as Communism, egalitarianism, and perhaps socialism have all
failed to date. The extraordinary thing about political liberalism is that it
seems to have succeeded in its authors' initial hope for it. It may have
helped end the turmoil occasioned by religious differences. Political liberalism has since expanded in various ways under other influences, and,
if it were not for Islamic fundamentalism with its seemingly coercive the-
ocratic program, we might no longer today associate religious conflict
with the core of liberalism in its actual practice.

In contrast to political liberalism, economic liberalism more or less
grew. It was analyzed and understood retrospectively rather than pro-
spectively. It came into being without a party or an intellectual agenda.
By the time Bernard Mandeville, Adam Smith, and others came to analyze it, they were analyzing characteristics of their own society. Insofar
as they had programs, these were for reforms of political practice to end
elements of state-sponsored monopoly and protection. But perhaps the
large bulk of daily economic activity was already market-driven. Indeed,
part of Mandeville's purpose was to give a moral (welfarist) justification
for the supposedly immoral greed which drives markets to greater production.

Why such a difference in the intellectual bases of the two liberalisms?
The most transparent reason is that the two liberalisms were addressed
to logically different problems. In its early days, political liberalism was
addressed to how we should collectively resolve what was, after all, es-

* I am grateful to Paul Gomberg for extended discussion of this essay, to Roderick T. Long
and Ellen Paul for careful written commentaries, to the other contributors to this volume for
constructive debate, and to the Andrew W. Mellon Foundation for generous general support.

© 1993 Social Philosophy and Policy Foundation. Printed in the USA.

sentially a collective issue. It required a substantial shift in social views. Economic liberalism was addressed to piecemeal, typically small-number interactions that mattered directly only piecemeal to a few in each case, rather than collectively to all or very many at once. Liberal economic practices could arise spontaneously in some contexts and slowly spread to others.

We may eventually choose to have an overarching regime of economic regulation — as in contract law — that is itself a collective resolution. Indeed, as Thomas Hobbes sees the problem, social order is collectively achieved, and therefore we are able to have stable property relations. Although he does not make the argument, we may reasonably suppose he held that either we resolve the problems of property and exchange the same way for all or we do not resolve them. I cannot alone achieve order in the midst of chaos for all others.

But for Hobbes, order was so paramount that he thought we must have absolute authority to keep us in line. Hobbes may have been right in thinking that the problem of weak sovereignty is political activity, which might lead to chaos. But Hobbes went further, concluding that we must even submit to our sovereign's choice of religious practices, because religious differences cause strife that is grossly disorderly. John Locke supposed we might simply set religious political impulses on the side and let our state regulate only such things as property relations. People might disagree as they will on religion, but they could be prohibited from taking action against one another in furtherance of their beliefs.

Liberalism has come to us bifurcated in another way. It has both welfarist and deontological variants. In the welfarist variant, a liberal principle is judged good for what good it does us. In the deontological variant, the principle may be judged good in its own right, perhaps by intuition, perhaps by deduction from some other principle such as autonomy. As may already be evident, I will generally be concerned with the welfarist tradition. It is only in the welfarist tradition that one might hope to see a coherent joining of political and economic liberalisms. The deontological tradition has manifold conflicting visions within it. Many positions turn on bald intuitions that are not universally or even widely accepted. No deontological position has been developed as extensively as the welfarist position and none has benefited from a comparably rich history of criticism and debate.

II. STRATEGIC STRUCTURES

The problems that the two liberalisms address are strategically quite different. Their role, however, is the same: to make social interaction and life better. To do this well, the major methodological task that each must resolve is to generate information that can direct what the economy and society produce. The liberal market works in such a way that it does not even require aggregate accounting of its achievement, although better information may help agents make better decisions and plans. A liberal polity does require aggregate accounting. Trivially, for example, if it is democratic, it requires accounting of votes. But it may typically require even some central economic accounting, as it might in attempting to correct for nonmarketable external effects of various economic activities, such as pollution (much of liberal debate has focused on nuisance law).

For both liberalisms, the role of the state and government seems itself to be collective—in a given polity, we all have the same government. Hence, one might say that government is a collective issue in liberalism, and one might say that one class of relationships in a liberal society is that between the individual and the government. But the issues government addresses need not be collective. For example, for Hobbes the establishment or maintenance of a sovereign is a collective result, but the purpose of this collective resolution is protection of individuals and dyads (pairs of individuals who enter into exchanges). For Locke, government is a device for resolving or managing issues, such as the protection of property. The strategic structures of liberalism that I wish to discuss in the limited space here are those of the issues government is to address, not the structure of creation or maintenance of government itself, or of the relationship of individuals or groups to government.

Hobbes

Let us simplify the problems of political and economic liberalism by characterizing them as merely the maintenance of certain civil and political liberties for political liberalism and the protection of the market for economic liberalism. To see that these need not be logically tied, although they might be causally related, consider the theory of Hobbes, arguably the greatest of all political theorists. Although Hobbes would not count as a major font of liberal thought, he is particularly interesting for understanding liberalism, because he made material, more-or-less economic concerns paramount and he generally deplored political liberty as likely to interfere with the order necessary for economic welfare. Hobbes did not have an articulate economic theory, but only an economic purpose: welfare. Only later, especially in the works of Mandeville and Smith, was there a compelling theory to connect welfare to economic liberty.

Hobbes's solution of the problem of economic liberalism and related material concerns (preeminently survival, but also stable expectations and material accumulation) entailed wholesale violation of political liberalism. He proposed orderly suppression of political activities by an autocratic sovereign. Contrary to the association more commonly assumed today, Hobbes evidently thought that political liberty is causally associated with the violation of economic liberty. At its extreme, political liberty could produce anarchy and chaotic violence that would destroy economic activities. Even modest efforts at political reform can start a society on the slide into chaos.

In brief, Hobbes's solution of the economic problem is as follows.[1] What we all need to enable us to construct good lives for ourselves is police protection for stable expectations and enforceable agreements. With these, we can escape the constant fear that others will take from us, and the associated incentive to harm others preemptively; we can have property; and we can faithfully enter into exchanges,[2] even over time. As a result, we can make our own lives better. This is a very simple set of requirements, which many possible forms of government could meet. Indeed, given how little we know about the workings of different forms of government, we cannot even say with great confidence that one form is better than others. Hobbes thought the balance favors monarchy, unless we already have some other form. It is often assumed that the basis of his theory is consent, because he spoke of a social contract to resolve the problem of anarchy. But he also spoke of conquest and other usurpations of accidental history as means for achieving sovereignty that works. What really matters is only this: that government provide order.

The order we want is an order that allows each of us to enter into exchanges with others as we choose and not to be coerced or harmed by others. We want orderly dyadic relations. Such relations will tend to be very productive in the long run in ways that Mandeville, Hume, and Smith focused on in their own visions of economic liberalism. This is the core of the problem Hobbes's theory was intended to resolve: dyadic Prisoner's Dilemma interactions in which order and general benefit require that only certain moves be allowed. The allowed moves are those in which both parties gain from an exchange, not those in which one party takes and the other loses. We may split this category into two: dyadic exchange and individual property ownership. Some theorists make exchange a part of ownership, but one might read Hobbes as making ownership derivative from protecting against coerced exchange or theft. In any case, the problem Hobbes resolved was the protection of each individual in potential interaction with each other.

Our problem of sovereignty, when we have such a problem, is not itself a Prisoner's Dilemma. The problem is to succeed in achieving coordination on one of the possible forms of government that could give us order in our dyadic relations. In Hobbes's sociology, achieving this order is a pure coordination problem in which we all share the same interest. There is no conflict over ways for achieving order that would be better for me and others that would be better for you. This is a striking vision to

---

[1] For a fuller account, see Russell Hardin, "Hobbesian Political Order," *Political Theory*, vol. 19, no. 2 (May 1991), pp. 156–80.

[2] Hobbes speaks of enforcing promises. The vocabulary of exchange is a later efflorescence.

anyone who thinks of politics as inherently about conflict of interests (or who thinks of Hobbes as the preeminent conflict theorist). Perhaps Hobbes implicitly agreed that that is what politics more broadly is about, but also supposed government should stay out of such politics and concern itself with order. His actual argument, however, is merely the following two steps. First, if we are in a state of anarchy, as during civil war, our ignorance of the likely details of various governments lets each of us treat some set of these as indifferently equally good and as enormously better than continued anarchy. Second, if we are under a working government that some now know to be not as much in their interests as some other might be, still we should all recognize that any effort to improve it a little bit has too great a risk of tipping us into anarchy. Hence, again, we all share an identical interest in maintaining the current regime, so that we face merely a pure coordination with a single universally best outcome, the easiest of all strategic interactions to resolve if all are properly informed.

There have been many apparent Hobbesians in political power. Such military coup leaders as Park in South Korea and Pinochet in Chile, and the current leadership of China, may have cared primarily about economic development and performance and may have been intent on abridging political liberties in order to maintain a firm hand on the order that they believed would bring economic prosperity.

Hobbes has given us an economic justification for having a regime or even for keeping the regime we have. But we cannot use that justification to argue for what a regime ought to do, because once we delve below the level of justifying the grand regime, we cannot suppose many of the important problems are merely pure coordinations. Eventually, economic and political concerns merge in many areas. The finer points of contract or other law may not be matters of mere coordination. Adopting any particular rule may systematically advantage one class of parties over another. Hence, in its detail, law is not a simple matter of coordination even if the choice of what form of general regime to have was, as Hobbes argued, such a simple matter. Having a political system available to resolve the details of law may be a matter of mere coordination. But the issues that system itself faces are typically not merely coordination problems. For example, in an issue on which law is unsettled, settling it one way or another is likely to benefit one class of parties relative to another class or to apportion benefits in one way rather than another. The recommendation of Coasean law and economics in many contexts is to assign an unsettled right in the way that is productively most beneficial overall — for example, by assigning the right in the way that minimizes transaction costs.[3] One might imagine it eminently reasonable *ex ante* to adopt this

---

[3] For a clear statement and argument, see A. Mitchell Polinsky, *An Introduction to Law and Economics*, 2d ed. (Boston: Little, Brown, 1989), p. 13.

principle for settling new problems, and we might all happily coordinate on this rather than any other rule. Yet in an actual application of the principle, there is no longer a matter of pure coordination. I may lose much of what you gain.

Locke

Both liberalisms can be achieved through collective devices — indeed, they may require collective devices. But the *issue* in early political liberalism is itself collective, whereas the issue in economic liberalism is not. Locke shared much of Hobbes's vision of the need for collective protection of property and exchange and was an economic liberal. But he was also greatly exercised by the political problems of religious diversity.[4] Locke supposed, in part for epistemological reasons familiar from later utilitarian social theorists, that the best way to organize society was on weakly democratic principles. If people participate in their own governance, their interests are likely to be better addressed.

This requirement is inherently collective. It is not merely about dyadic relations, but about group relations, as when, for example, religious beliefs create group interests. The problem is how to incorporate groups into the polity. For a Hobbesian, or even a traditional monarchist, this was not a problem: religious groups need not be incorporated, they need only be controlled or suppressed. But for Locke, incorporation was inherently required by democratic commitment. Locke's way of incorporating religious groups was itself, however, almost Hobbesian. He simply required that they leave their religion out of politics. By implication, Catholics could not be incorporated in England. Because their religion gave them an alternative political authority outside England, their religion was inherently political.[5]

Locke's economic liberalism was intellectually messier than his political liberalism. It focused on property, which was a very broad notion for Locke, including one's body and life, as well as external material holdings. It is a loose category that he used very loosely. His readers may fail to read the term as broadly as Locke did, however, because his central discussion, of coming to own something by mixing one's labor with it, is largely about external holdings. Although there are welfarist sentiments laced through his argument, his principle justification of ownership seems to be deontological. Subject to the constraint that I leave enough for others, I own what I work over. In his own time, Locke seems to have

---

[4] John Locke, *A Letter Concerning Toleration* (1689; Indianapolis: Bobbs-Merrill, 1950).

[5] Locke, ever careful, wrote of Mahometans rather than Catholics (*ibid.*, pp. 51–52). Also, atheists could not be trusted because they could not bind themselves with an oath whose violation would bring punishment after death (*ibid.*, p. 52).

thought this theory could apply to America but not to England. In our time, it cannot apply to anything but philosophical history and, until a few decades ago, the South Pole. Locke was the first major philosopher to advocate both economic and political liberalism, but he made no claim for their being logically or empirically related. Such claims reach their fullest development in the work of Ludwig von Mises and Friedrich Hayek after the rise of the Soviet state.

Mill

Hobbes was centrally concerned with dyadic economic relations. Locke added his concern with large group political relations. In his *On Liberty*, John Stuart Mill turned the focus of political liberalism back down to the individual. He argued forcefully for the protection of various civil liberties. Sometimes he defended these on grounds of their general effect on others. For example, one reason for protecting your right of free political speech is that your exercise of this right increases the chance that others will know what they need to know to make their own political choices. Apart from the strategic move to collective resolution on individual and small-number problems, this may be the most remarkable move in the long development of welfarist liberalism. In this Benthamite move, *collective benefits are secured through protection of individual liberties*. I might actively want to have my liberty, but this is not enough. I must also want to have it on the condition that all others also have it. Only then is the systematic protection of the liberty justified.

In addition to this collective-level defense of political liberties, Mill sometimes defended such liberties for reasons of the individual alone. For example, as did Hobbes and Locke, Mill argued from epistemological failings. Mill supposed we should presume each individual has inherent epistemological advantages in knowing what is in her interest. The presumption could be shown false in certain cases (such as the cases of children and the mentally incompetent), but it is very strong in many other cases. But Mill asserted the individual's right to be left without interference even more strongly than this presumption. Perhaps he had a theory of human welfare that gave autonomy central place. Or perhaps he had a deontological vision of individual liberty.

Mill was even more democratic than Locke, and he shared Locke's concern with political liberalism at the level of incorporating, rather than suppressing, various groups, such as fundamentalist religious groups. And he was a master of political economics who shared Hobbes's basic concern to enable exchange and prosperity. However, the changing economic structure of his time, at the height of the Industrial Revolution, made economic liberalism seem to be no longer merely a dyadic matter. He began to analyze it at the group level, as in his discussions of unions and of restrictions on the length of the workday.[6] It would be wrong to say that the problems Mill saw so clearly were entirely new in the factories of his time. For example, there had been sailing vessels with significant numbers of crew members even in Hobbes's time, and Mill's argument could have applied as well to them as to later factories. But there was growth in the pervasiveness and prominence of collective issues in the market in the centuries between Hobbes and Mill.

The complex view

Although the problems addressed by political and economic liberalism are quite different in structure, the form of resolution in many areas is the same for both problems. Political liberalism involves enforced laissez faire with respect to religious views and practices and with respect to opportunities for participation in political decisions. Economic liberalism seems to work best when it too involves enforced laissez faire to a large extent. Libertarian anarchists sometimes have a very optimistic view of the prospects for cooperative exchange without enforcement, while Hobbes seems to have had a very pessimistic view. Hobbes's actual view may have been relatively modest, despite his violent vision of the state of nature. He supposed that, without enforcement, the few who would take adverse advantage of others would finally drive others to be too defensive to enter into beneficial relations that they could readily have sustained without the threat of the few.

Political liberalism therefore has a complex structure. It was collective (Locke's modal concern in his treatment of religious toleration) and individual (the great concern of Mill's *On Liberty*). Before the utilitarians, it was almost entirely addressed to individuals either alone or in aggregate, but Benthamite utilitarians began to focus their greatest concern on the aggregate or total welfare. This was not even a plausible idea for Hobbes and Locke.[7] Economic liberalism is also complex. It has a threefold focus: individual, dyadic, and collective. It is individual as in Hobbes's and virtually all Anglo-Saxon views of the value to the individual of the stability of property. (Indeed, even a Crusoe on a frontier wants no theft, even when he has no expectation of exchange or collective benefit.) It is dyadic as in Hobbes's and the later political economists' concern with exchange, which dominated the nineteenth-century heyday of the rights of contract. And it is group-level as in Mill's concern with the economic liberty of groups of workers acting as groups.

[6] John Stuart Mill, *Principles of Political Economy* (any standard seventh edition), book 5, ch. 11, sect. 12.
[7] See Russell Hardin, "Efficiency," in *Companion to Contemporary Political Philosophy*, ed. Robert E. Goodin and Philip Pettit (Oxford: Basil Blackwell, 1993).

It is interesting that Locke's arguments for religious toleration are primarily welfarist, while his arguments for the ownership of property seem chiefly deontological. In this, his positions were virtually the opposite of much of the later development, with at least the line of economic liberalism that goes through Smith basically welfarist, and the arguments for political liberties, including even many by Mill, increasingly deontological. Locke's strangely irrelevant and even more strangely captivating concern with the morality of appropriating property through mixing one's labor with it gave a very early deontological twist to economic liberalism and provided the moral foundation for one branch of libertarian thought.

III. COLLECTIVE RESOLUTION

Locke and Mill more or less take for granted that the defense of political liberties is a matter for government. That is, the resolution of both the collective and the individual problems is itself collective, as was Hobbes's resolution of his individual-level and dyadic problems. Why should collective resolution be so readily favored for resolving all of these classes of issues? For dyadic problems of economic liberty and individual problems of political liberty, it seems natural strategically to resort to collective devices to correct problems that cannot be corrected dyadically or individually. But it is not merely that it makes strategic sense to resolve dyadic problems by going to the collective level. More important is that the principle of a strong form of collective protection is mutually advantageous. For Locke's collective issue in the incorporation of groups, it is a defining characteristic of a resolution that it be collective. The collective issues in economic liberalism that interest Mill are issues in part because they are governed by contract and other laws that derive from dyadic principles. Those laws are centrally, collectively enforced; to change them by enabling collectives to enter into contracts requires collective devices.

Collective devices might have greater stability than spontaneous devices. But they may also have potential for far greater effective variance, so that a collective regime might be capable of extraordinary harm. One might suppose that the great value of democratic politics lies in its supposed capacity to produce the best leadership when needed through competitive elections, as though Condorcet's jury or truth theorem were applicable to government as it might be to juries. (This theorem says, roughly, that the likelihood that the majority of a jury will find the truth in their deliberations rises with the number of jurors.) But juries seek factual truth with interests ostensibly ruled out of court. Governments seek compromise in the face of conflicting interests, and there is little reason to suppose they find a relevant truth.[8]

---

[8] See Geoffrey Brennan and James M. Buchanan, *The Reason of Rules: Constitutional Political Economy* (Cambridge: Cambridge University Press, 1985), pp. 38–40.

The real magic of liberal democracy often lies in its tendency — sometimes overcome — to decentralize decisions, to make its government less capable of acting, not more capable. That magic is analogous to the magic of the market. Decentralized decision making in the market, however, solves a virtually impossible information problem, as Hayek and the Austrian school argue.[9] Many complain of the inefficacy of contemporary democratic governments in the face of domestic and international problems, especially problems of welfare and distribution. But the benefits of this incapacity may arguably outweigh its costs. The diffusion of power in liberal democratic forms of government often blocks the capacity for decisions that ignore the interests of many. Under an autocratic regime, the issue of abortion, for example, might be relatively quietly and effectively settled even in a society with diverse views. Under liberal democracy, the issue of abortion may not be settled for generations, because views cannot be quietly blocked or overridden. An anarchist might well conclude that democratic liberalism is a reasonably good second best.

A mild form of this difference may even be exhibited by more centralized democratic regimes as compared to the relatively decentralized federal regime of the United States. In the centralized British system, it was relatively easy to require seat belts in autos at the overall national level. In the United States, libertarian objections to such legal requirements on behavior could be focused at the state level to slow down the adoption of seat-belt laws. In the face of a well-organized and well-financed industrial lobby, on the other hand, national governments in both the United States and the United Kingdom have been unable to take very strong action against tobacco and its use. The decentralized American system, however, allows effective action to be taken at lower levels of government.[10]

Economic liberty evidently leads to the growth of powerful commercial organizations, especially firms. Given their power and relative autonomy, these may become the locus of protection of other liberties for some members (even as they may also have become a source of problems for liberalism). Hence, economic liberty may compete with and therefore constrain government in its regulation of liberties. Twentieth-century trends that increasingly bring property under governmental regulation undercut this constraining power of property.[11] Historically, we have tended to assume that liberties — political and economic — must be defended by central government against the particularist values of various local groups and interests. This assumption may usually be correct. But it is an empir-

[9] Friedrich A. Hayek, "The Uses of Knowledge in Society," in Hayek, *Individualism and Economic Order* (Chicago: University of Chicago Press, 1948; reprinted by Gateway, no date; essay first published 1945), pp. 77–91, esp. pp. 86–89.

[10] Howard M. Leichter, *Free to Be Foolish: Politics and Health Promotion in the United States and Great Britain* (Princeton: Princeton University Press, 1991), p. 257.

[11] See Jennifer Nedelsky, *Private Power and the Limits of American Constitutionalism* (Chicago: University of Chicago Press, 1991).

ical, not an a priori, matter. A varied collection of liberties may enjoy decentralized support from business, communities, religious organizations, and other local institutions. Perhaps we gain more liberty in trumping these institutions than we lose. But we may also increase the likelihood of great variance in achieving protection of liberties.

Finally, the achievement of economic and political liberalisms in a common collective government brings the two together even though they need not be conceptually related. Groups may use liberal political devices to intervene in economic relations. If political liberties are sociologically correlated with economic performance, we may expect governments to have strong incentives to promote liberties. This motivation did not trump lesser urges in Ne Win, Papa Doc, Pol Pot, Idi Amin, and many others.

IV. THE NORMATIVE BASES OF THE TWO LIBERALISMS

The historical anthropologist Leslie White argues that "the economic systems of civil society are impersonal, nonhuman, and nonethical, which, in terms of *human* relationships and values, means impersonal, inhumane, and unethical." [12] On Hobbes's view, White is obviously wrong. The values of survival and prosperity are clearly human and worthy. Maintaining, even with the threat of limited coercion, an economic and enforcement system to provide these things is therefore good. White's further lament about pirates and cheats who abuse their fellows for their own benefit is a lament about humanity, unethical humanity perhaps, but humanity to the core. The market may enable us to do more lying and cheating than we could in a woefully primitive state, in which there might be much less to lie or cheat about, but it also enables us to serve our interests through production and thereby to benefit others. [13] The market, and the political regime that focuses entirely on the market, may scant other moral concerns, such as fairness and political liberties, but they can still do one big, good thing very well.

In a related complaint, Daniel Bell says that society rests on a moral justification of authority and that consumption cannot provide such a justification. [14] Again, Hobbes's vision is compellingly contrary. Surely it is commonly good that we be able to satisfy our urges for consumption, including consumption of education, music, culture, and so forth, as well as consumption of material goods. A supremely successful system of production might provide us with opportunity for satisfying many desires for consumption that Bell and others think not in our interests or not for

[12] Leslie A. White, *The Evolution of Culture: The Development of Civilization to the Fall of Rome* (New York: McGraw-Hill, 1959), p. 346.

[13] It would be anachronistic to call their view Benthamite, but Mandeville and Smith clearly valued economic liberty for its general effects on all.

[14] Daniel Bell, *The Cultural Contradictions of Capitalism* (London: Heinemann, 1976), p. 77.

the good of our characters. But such consumption will happen to some
extent even in a more primitive economy. The difference between the
very primitive economy, or anarchy as Hobbes supposed it must be, and
a very productive economy surely is predominantly good, even on Bell's
view. But if it is good, then the justification of authority that makes the
system work is simply that it is good. Hence, consumption can give a
moral grounding for political authority that is used to enhance opportunities for economic exchange and production.

It follows that the early economic and political liberalisms were moral
positions. They addressed problems of welfare. The actual content of
the resolution of the political problem matters, whereas the choice of res-
olutions of the economic problem could vary over many possibilities, all
roughly as good as far as economic liberalism is concerned. Hence, our
choice is merely a matter of coordination on one of the acceptable forms.
This is Hobbes's argument for government. Recall that the central problems he was concerned to resolve were survival and the economic problem. In his simple vision, government is strictly external to the economy.
It facilitates and enables us to engage in economic activities.

The welfarist core

To use modern terminology that was not his, Hobbes's defense of
maintaining order is essentially utilitarian, not deontological. Government has no value in its own right, it is merely a means to the end of
human welfare. It is therefore subordinate to economics. In his welfarism,
Hobbes is consistent with most of the Anglo-Saxon liberal tradition. The
concern of the Levelers with political equality,[15] Locke's theory of property, and some of Mill's justifications of political liberties were not apparently welfarist. But the general tendency to a utilitarian reading of the
law[16] over the nineteenth and twentieth centuries seems to have been
preceded and accompanied by welfarist readings of the purpose of constitutional law. Perhaps merely as a result of the intellectual tastes of the
era, therefore, the welfarist view of liberty is much more richly developed
than any other.[17]

Another part of the Anglo-Saxon tradition is a commitment to pragmatic skepticism, as in Hobbes's supposition that we cannot really know
enough to choose one particular form of government over another as
more in our interest. Pragmatic skepticism also plays a more clearly fun-

[15] The Levelers pushed for egalitarianism and democracy during the seventeenth-century
English Revolution. Not surprisingly, they appealed both to welfarist considerations — society
will be better off — and to deontological considerations that sound like natural rights.

[16] H. L. A. Hart, "Between Utility and Rights," in Hart, *Essays in Jurisprudence and Philosophy* (Oxford: Oxford University Press, 1983; essay first published 1979), p. 198.

[17] See Russell Hardin, "The Morality of Law and Economics," *Law and Philosophy*, vol. 11,
no. 4 (November 1992), pp. 331–84, esp. pp. 380–84.

damental role in welfarist liberalism. We may simply concede many value commitments to other people: if you like chocolate then chocolate is good for you, at least insofar as it contributes to your pleasure. There may be other considerations that trump this one in a particular instance, but your liking of chocolate makes your consumption of it prima facie good.

For some apparent value commitments, however, we cannot so readily concede. Some values, such as religious values, depend on beliefs about what is true. If I believe god's will is that people X should be destroyed, then I may also believe it is good for people X to be destroyed. If you question my prior belief about what god wills, however, you automatically question the inference I have drawn about the goodness of an action or policy. If we note that there are dozens of religions with contrary visions of what is good or right, and if we can find no way to establish the truth of one of these, we have reason, with Locke, simply to be skeptical. This is a central move in Locke's argument on religious toleration.[18] We should not impose religious views on others when we have such strong, in-principle grounds for skepticism about the correlation of religious truth with political leadership. Unfortunately, this argument can plausibly only convince someone who shares Locke's protestant individualist stance with respect to religious beliefs. In application to the Catholic or Muslim who rejects this stance, the argument is question-begging.

Mill's relatively libertarian views have a similar grounding in skepticism. I cannot know that your tastes and preferences are in truth inferior to mine. There may be some objective truths about welfare, such as that smoking or drinking wine laced with lead is dangerous to your health, and that you most likely value your health. But your preference for reading great literary classics and mine for attending the latest junk movie, while potentially subject to revision after debate and a bit of testing, just are our preferences. A welfarist thinks making people better off is good. Since individuals are the subject of welfarist concern, the welfarist must concede that the individual must have substantial say about what is her good. Hence, the welfarist Mill makes a Hobbesian argument for the defense of political liberties. To do so coherently, one need only reject Hobbes's dismal sociology.

Both liberalisms were de facto directed at welfare in large part. Economic liberalism, with its defense in Hobbesian theory and in increasingly utilitarian thinking from Mandeville to Hume and Smith, is conspicuously welfarist. Political liberalism, with its avoidance of especially destructive religious conflicts, enables individuals to seek their own values. But material welfare is not all that matters even to a welfarist. Welfarists may benefit, and may think that others also benefit, from political criticism, cultural developments, and general freedom from being monitored and controlled by someone else. Hobbes was evidently motivated by such

[18] See Locke, *Letter Concerning Toleration*.

values in his own life. Locke came closer to expressing concern for such values.

At some point, these values seem to involve both economic and political liberties. If they do, then an economic liberal must finally also be a political liberal. Why might Hobbes not be? Perhaps only for the sociological reason that he thought political liberties must threaten economic prospects by leading to civil war. But perhaps he also lacked the more extensive value theory that puts economic and civil liberty benefits into a joint account of welfare — this move comes later in the hands of the utilitarian economists of the nineteenth century. Or perhaps both he and Locke looked upon a society much less wealthy than modern industrial capitalism and naturally, therefore, weighed material considerations relatively more heavily than we might. Without the wherewithal to secure life and well-being, few people will be mightily concerned with civil liberties that they have neither the time nor the resources to take up. One may be forgiven for suspecting that, when Milton Friedman thinks the people of developing and poor nations should be "free to choose," he is more concerned that they be free to choose which car to buy than to choose which government to have. And perhaps Friedman, like a modern Hobbes, can reasonably retort that material well-being is the sine qua non of political liberty for the masses.

Deontological additions

Hobbes's theory requires only one general normative notion: some variant of welfarism that we may call Hobbesian efficiency.[19] In his *Second Treatise of Government*, Locke introduced one and plausibly two normative notions that are not welfarist. First, he presented a deontological rights theory of appropriation under certain conditions (conditions that may generally not be relevant for any society that might take interest in Locke's theory), so that his nascent economic liberalism is, unlike Hobbes's, not strictly welfarist. Second, Locke was a nascent democrat, and his commitment to limited democratic principles may well have been an immediate deontological concern. It is plausible, however, to read his theory of government as welfarist. In bringing the focus of political lib-

---

[19] For further discussion of Hobbesian efficiency and its normative limits, see Hardin, "The Morality of Law and Economics." The concept of Hobbesian efficiency is related to Paretian efficiency (it is Pareto efficient to make a change in distribution that makes one or more individuals better off and none worse off). Hobbesian efficiency is an early grasp of the core concern in Paretian efficiency in contexts of choosing between government and anarchy (which, in Hobbes's view, entails chaos and grievous losses to all). It yields a resolution only because Hobbes supposes that we know too little to distinguish between the benefits we would receive from one form of government (e.g., monarchy) and those from another form (e.g., oligarchy). Hence, epistemological constraints play as strong a role for Hobbes as they do for Locke in his arguments for religious toleration.

erty back around to the individual, Mill also often seems to have had a deontological commitment to "this one inviolable principle" of liberty.

In much of current discussion, political liberalism is seen as a matter of neutrality with respect to life values or plans of life. The notion of a plan of life must seem preposterous to many people who wonder how they got where they are, while wondering where they will go from there. Life is what happens while we are making other plans—and it is often much saner than the plans. But if we can escape the florid rhetoric of the life-plans crowd from Mill forward,[20] most of us may grant that we are moderately to strongly committed to various values. Is the point of liberal protection to let us foster or fulfill those values? This might be a reasonable inference even from Hobbes if we have rejected his dismal political sociology. But clearly, liberalism was not driven by neutrality in earlier times. In particular, it was deployed, as by Locke, to support the suppression of some manifestations of religious belief. Standard Anglo-Saxon skepticism about others' minds and their pleasures might lead us for epistemological reasons to plump for letting them decide their own good, as Mill does. Some of the present commitment to neutrality, however, seems deontological rather than merely welfarist. It is morally grounded with Locke's theory of the appropriation of property. I have the value, and by god therefore it's my right to have it or it's right that I have it.

In contemporary writings, political and economic liberalism are often held separate, either explicitly or implicitly. For example, the recent spate of writings on the liberal's supposedly foundational concern with neutrality is almost entirely about political liberalism. Economic liberalism, through most of its variants, is not neutral with respect to values. It tends strongly to favor welfarist values that can be enhanced through production and exchange. Economic liberals may be neutral with respect to who gets welfare, but they are not neutral on what counts as the central value, which is welfare. If other values are to come into consideration, most of the writers in the long Anglo-Saxon tradition of economic liberalism would have to bring these other values in by treating them as components of welfare. They might even have to make Mill's move of treating these other values as he did free speech—that is, of making them valuable as means to greater welfare.

Incidentally, it seems clear that even in what one might argue is his commitment to economic liberalism, Hobbes has little in common with many contemporary libertarians. Libertarian theory is often deontologically grounded in intuitions about specific rights, such as rights of property ownership and rights to voluntary dyadic exchange. For Hobbes, rights have force or interest only if they are positively backed by a coer-

---

[20] For a clear and important discussion, see John Rawls, *A Theory of Justice* (Cambridge: Harvard University Press, 1971), pp. 407–16.

cive government. Moreover, although it is somewhat tendentious to claim Hobbes has a clear position on an issue he did not explicitly recognize, he seems to have been moved to value property and exchange for their welfare effects, not for their prior rightness in some other sense.

Libertarians often argue from dyadic relations exclusively, not allowing any move that trumps these.[21] This is supposed to follow from a deontological commitment to consent or autonomy.[22] We might more readily think we should move, with Hobbes, from the overall achievement of, say, order or welfare to the dyadic-level achievement of exchange. For Hobbes, the social construction of welfare obviously overwhelmingly trumps what individuals can accomplish. If Hobbes is right about his implicit sociological claim here, then libertarian economic liberalism is, at its base, wrong. It, too, must be pragmatically grounded in the larger social achievement. Moreover, we might wonder with Mill why dyadic agreements must trump collective concerns, as in early state interventions in unionized worker relations with business.

One way to characterize the difference between utilitarianism and libertarianism is to say that the utilitarian would consider the value of the overall result of dyadic choosing to be itself a potential matter for collective choice. Some libertarians would commonly rule out such a move. In his paradox of liberalism, Amartya Sen virtually defines liberalism as a matter of what *at most* dyads would do.[23] In this paradox, each of two players has one right only, and the only additional choice rule is a requirement of unanimity that, whenever both agree, their choice will be the social choice. With these radically limited choice rules, we can still produce what Sen takes to be a paradoxical result, as follows.

You have the single right to have pink walls; I have the single right to have next Sunday free from labor. I hate your pink walls so much, however, that I am willing to spend Sunday painting them chartreuse. You hate chartreuse and have a right to keep your walls pink, but you would enjoy seeing me work all day.[24] We agree to my painting your walls. But that violates your right to pink walls and my right to the day off. Or so Sen perversely argues. Most commentators on this result seem to find no paradox. In ordinary life — no theorist's cute contrivance — I have a right to keep my money from you and you have the right to keep your car from me, and yet we may both happily engage in a trade. Hence, the usual liberal economic right to exchange is strategically an instance of Sen's supposed paradox (if there are no other people affected by our exchange). *Any liberalism that would make voluntary exchange paradoxical is of*

---

[21] Robert Nozick, *Anarchy, State, and Utopia* (New York: Basic Books, 1974).

[22] See Russell Hardin, "To Rule in No Matters, To Obey in None," *Contemporary Philosophy*, vol. 13, no. 12 (November–December 1991), pp. 6–12, esp. pp. 7–8.

[23] Amartya Sen, "The Impossibility of a Paretian Liberal," *Journal of Political Economy*, vol. 78 (1970) pp. 152–57.

[24] Political philosophy ranges from the sublime to the ridiculous.

no interest. Sen's earliest examples of his paradox typically blend material and nonmaterial welfare considerations. In later defenses, Sen implicitly argues that it matters what the content of the violated rights is.[25] He then resorts to particular intuitions about rights that presumably are not grounded in welfare and that he thinks should trump individuals' willingness to trade in their violation.[26] This move puts us in the land of whimsy. Heaven help us if I have the trumping intuition that no one should have pink walls. You say my intuition does not trump? You're wrong.

V. CAUSAL AND CONCEPTUAL LINKS

Political and economic liberalism may not be conceptually tied; they make different contributions to welfare, and they might make their contributions independently. But they can be strategically tied together with either one playing a causal role in determining the other. For example, those who want political liberalism may resort to economic moves, such as strikes, to force a regime to liberalize politically. Moreover, a regime that is committed to high levels of economic productivity and growth may find little point in using illiberal political devices to maintain power when political suppression leads to economic disruptions.

One of Hobbes's seemingly most outlandish claims is that any kind of sovereign government—monarchy, oligarchy, democracy—would do for order. Yet this claim seems to be true enough for economic liberalism, which has arisen under quite varied regimes. Or perhaps the claim is only true during early stages of economic development. Marxist regimes which assumed that economic liberalism was the source of problems they wished to resolve have, of course, been openly hostile to economic liberalism. But that is a result of their ideological position on economic liberalism and not of their authoritarian political structure per se. Economic liberalism has come to be associated with liberal political regimes in the views of many theorists other than Marxists. But, to the limited extent that the association holds, that is generally because the liberal political regimes have followed the prior establishment of liberal economic regimes.

---

[25] If elaborated this way, Sen's paradox requires a fourth condition. In addition to having two individual rights and the principle of dyadic agreement (Sen speaks of unanimity), he now adds the random intuition about the wrongness of a particular outcome. That these conditions cannot universally be satisfied is no paradox. For discussion of further problems with Sen's paradox, see Russell Hardin, *Morality within the Limits of Reason* (Chicago: University of Chicago Press, 1988), pp. 108–13. In particular, Sen speaks of unanimity when what he means is agreement of two people in a two-person society. In such a society, rights talk is pointless.

[26] See, e.g., Amartya Sen, "Liberty as Control: An Appraisal," in *Social and Political Philosophy*, vol. 7 of *Midwest Studies in Philosophy*, ed. Peter A. French, Theodore E. Uehling, Jr., and Howard K. Wettstein (Minneapolis: University of Minnesota Press, 1982), pp. 207–21.

Today, we may have opportunity to watch the reverse order, with liberalizing politics in Eastern Europe before liberalizing economics. Many observers evidently think it an open question whether liberal economics must follow liberal politics. Why? Because more-or-less democratic politics may work against long-term collective interests. One who thinks that in the long run free trade will be mutually beneficial may also think that for the nearer term protection is in our interests. Or the producers in a declining industry may be able, through democratic politics, to secure their jobs through protections and subsidies that violate liberal economic principles.

It is a common misunderstanding of the Pareto principle—itself supremely liberal—to conclude that if all exchange is consensual, no one will be made worse off by generally free exchange. Suppose that in one state of affairs no one is worse off and one or more are better off than in a second state of affairs. Vilfredo Pareto supposed that the first state of affairs is unarguably superior to the second. Consensual exchange seemingly should produce only better-off people unless there are external costs of production imposed on others, for example, through pollution. But if I have a modest restaurant and you open another across the street from me, within days your superior cooking may drive me under. All exchanges that take place in this sad story may be fully consensual. My loss is that I participate in too few of them, although I once participated in many. The dismal fate of my restaurant may await most entrepreneurial activities. These lines were written just as American Airlines not so inadvertently drove Braniff under by making its fares extremely competitive for the summer of 1992. American did not need to violate the Pareto principle, narrowly conceived, for Braniff to lose badly.

Some of the most spectacular losses among major corporations are losses of entire industries as the technological capacities and demands of economies change rapidly. Among the most productive enterprises in Eastern Europe and the former Soviet Union are very large firms in industries that a shortsighted Stalin thought important in the more advanced economies of his time, and on which he improved by making his even larger in scale. Those industries have been in decline for decades in the West, and they will plausibly go through even more rapid decline in the East. Declining industries include steel manufacturing, coal mining, and agriculture in Poland, Czechoslovakia, and much of the former Soviet Union (as well as in much of the industrial world). Hence, the Eastern economies must make a twofold transition: from a discarded central organization to a market organization, and from obsolescent industries to dynamic industries. Most discussion of their problem in the American press focuses on the former transition, while the latter may be the greater obstacle if they try to make a gentle, piecemeal conversion.

Economically threatened groups have long pushed through anti-liberal economic policies in democratic societies, yet we would generally think those societies have tended to maintain basically liberal economies. In the Eastern European experiments of our time, the protectionist politics of groups does not merely threaten to reduce the quality of economic liberalism. Rather, group politics over economic issues threatens to block the introduction of economic liberalism. That would be a perverse causal connection between political and economic liberalism.

There may also be a causal connection between domestic and international possibilities that drives all nations toward market devices in order to stay comparatively viable. For example, the educated elite, who might have options elsewhere, may leave if their nation chooses egalitarianism, collective ownership, or other major policies that block entrepreneurial possibilities. Such policies may virtually require anti-liberal policies on freedom of political activity or on migration, in order to block the options of voice and exit in a personally disagreeable context. Hence, anti-liberal economics may lead to anti-liberal politics. In a nation that was isolated and autarkic, this result need not follow. But for a nation with economic and personal ties to a larger competitive world, it might follow with a vengeance. For example, a nation that gives up 1 or 2 percent of its potential annual rate of economic growth in order to achieve egalitarian distributions might find itself reduced to relative poverty in a generation or two.[27]

At its extreme, we may wonder whether Hobbesian political autocracy, by suppressing political liberties, might boost economic performance. It may sound incredible today, but around 1960, when military juntas took power in both nations, Burma and South Korea had similarly impoverished per-capita incomes. (General Ne Win seized control of the government of what was then Burma in 1958, and General Park ended relatively democratic government in 1960 in South Korea.) After three decades of autocracy, South Korea has very nearly entered the ranks of the wealthy industrial world, while destitute Burma (now Myanmar) has plausibly even declined from its earlier position.[28] During that same period, North Korea, with its autocratic Communist regime, may have achieved greater equality than South Korea. But if it did, it may have done so at a very high cost in productivity. Both these comparisons may be poor cases for present purposes, because South Korea's growth may have been stimulated very much by its special relationship with the United States or by some other special feature. Many Korean observers, however, think that the authoritarian imposition of order, plus protection of economic liberties, did the trick. Debate largely turns on whether specific, inegalitarian,

[27] Russell Hardin, "Efficiency vs. Equality and the Demise of Socialism," *Canadian Journal of Philosophy*, vol. 22, no. 2 (June 1992), pp. 149–61; see especially the section on "Egalitarianism in one society," pp. 156–58.

[28] From 1967 to 1989, gross domestic product per capita in Burma rose 31 percent, from 946 kyats to 1239 kyats (in 1985 prices), for a dismal annual rate of growth of slightly over 1 percent (International Monetary Fund, *International Financial Statistics*, 1991).

entrepreneurial policies hastened or slowed economic growth. In any case, autocratic governments that are hostile to political liberties can evidently have dramatically different economic effects: per-capita GNP was $200 in Burma in 1986, $3,450 in South Korea in 1988, and $1,180 in North Korea in 1985.[29]

Against the vision of a resplendent autocracy, note that autocracy is not typically a choice. It is more nearly like life. It is what happens to us when the autocrat comes in from the wings, typically with military force. Hitler and Khomeini were unusual cases of autocrats who were relatively popular choices.

VI. One Unified Liberalism?

Do the long lines of welfarist liberalism in English political and economic thought cohere? In particular, is the complex liberalism of Mill consistent with the earlier political liberalism of Locke and with the economic liberalism that grew from Hobbes to Smith? To answer such questions we must look to the major turns in the development of liberal thought. First, there were the strategic focuses of various liberalisms, from Hobbes's economic individuals and dyads and Locke's political collectives, through to Mill's political individuals and economic collectives. Then there has been the sometimes acute, sometimes mild concern with religious toleration, which often brings in a value that might give welfarists trouble. Finally, there have been historical changes in capacities for addressing many of the economic issues that drove Hobbes and Locke. With rising wealth, political and economic concerns seem to have merged, perhaps inextricably.

Strategic complexity

Recall Sen's paradox of liberalism.[30] Through all of his examples, the move he necessarily makes is to set off the dyadic-level right of exchange against individual-level liberties analogous to those Mill ardently defends. We may need both, and collective-level protections as well. The whole point of dyadic-level or collective-level liberties or rights is to secure results that cannot be secured with individual-level liberties alone.

One could conclude that the welfarist-strategic account of liberalism is at most a part of our concern, that various deontological rights and liberties could trump welfarist conclusions. There would be no paradox in such a position, although its actual working might make severe demands on intuition to resolve the weighing of numerous concerns. Liberalism does not trivially founder by definition on the mere fact that this

---

[29] *The Statesman's Year-Book 1991–92*, ed. Brian Hunter (New York: St. Martin's, 1991), pp. 254, 781, 787.

[30] Discussed above in Section IV under "Deontological additions."

is the range of problems it must address. Welfarist liberalism might face insurmountable obstacles of measurement of welfare effects and might therefore be uncomfortably indeterminate. Welfarist liberals would do well to cultivate a reasonable tolerance for ambiguity. Such tolerance may be the defining psychological difference between modern welfarists and intuitionist deontologists.

Religious toleration again

Hobbes and Locke both confused the issue of the separation of material and nonmaterial welfare when they addressed religion. Hobbes willingly supposed we must suppress, kill, or banish certain fundamentalist believers. The very issue of survival that Hobbes invoked to justify government he oddly ignored for the fundamentalist. Locke similarly rules religious issues off the political agenda, while counting material issues as acceptable subject matter for a political theory. Their moves against certain fundamentalists are not a matter of mere coordination or of mutual advantage — it is not to the advantage of the fundamentalist to be depoliticized, suppressed, or killed. Implicitly, Hobbes and Locke made substantive value claims that the economic well-being of most people outweighs the religious values of some people. This argument would not survive even in implicit form if they were addressing a severely divided society.

There is a conundrum in the liberal guarantee of freedom of religion. For example, the discussion of the establishment of religion and the freedom of religious practice in the First Amendment to the United States Constitution seems to be internally contradictory. Each person may worship as her beliefs dictate — this sounds like neutrality. But the state will not support any religion.[31] If one's beliefs dictate that one have a religious state (some of the original American colonies were religious states with the death penalty for such minor infractions as taking the deity's name in vain), what is one to do?

One might suppose Mill faced a similar problem when he pushed economic liberalism into collective issues of the rights of groups, as opposed merely to the rights of individuals involved in the market. But, insofar as he had a utilitarian value theory for aggregating welfare, he could escape the automatic inconsistency that troubles the arguments of Hobbes and Locke.

Historical changes

The separation of economic and political liberalism makes less sense in very productive modern societies than it once did. Why? Because the sep-

---

[31] Nor can there be any religious test required as a qualification for any office or public trust in the United States (Article 6 of the Constitution).

aration of contributions to welfare into the relevant material and nonmaterial categories makes less sense than it once did and less sense than it
might still make in much less productive societies today. The change derives from a combination of causal and conceptual changes.

Conceptually, my valuations of matters covered by political liberties are
not decoupled from my valuations of material benefits. This is trivially
true for valuations of political liberties to try to affect economic policy in
my own interest. But it is true more generally in any value theory with
roughly the form of the indifference-curve utility theory. At some point
in the increasing consumption of, say, bread, I will finally be willing to
trade off some further bit of bread for some nonmaterial good. Despite
this fact, however, the level of my consumption of such things as bread
may be so low that I never reach the point of willingness to trade off bits
of them for many nonmaterial goods. If I am very well off—I get all the
bread I could want—I would even trade a great lot of it for Beluga cav-
iar or a night at the opera. Suppose my government says that Mikhail
Baryshnikov cannot do modern dance, because such dance is a manifestation of bourgeois decadence. Now I, who have no worry about the
adequacy of my food, housing, and clothing, and who can afford to indulge my cultural tastes, may suffer a direct loss from this lack of political liberty. It affects what I can consume, just as taking money away from
me affects what I can consume. Many of the peasants who made up the
vast bulk of the populations of Europe until this century would have suffered no direct loss from comparable restrictions on political liberty in
their time.

Unfortunately, if we see political and economic liberalism as joined in
our value theory, then we no longer have available an a priori argument
such as Locke and early defenders of religious toleration used. Material and
nonmaterial interests were relatively decoupled in seventeenth-century
England. These finally blend with nonmaterial interests, and an effort to
hold them separate for the citizen of a modern, wealthy state may be
wrongheaded.[32] We cannot hive off religion and let government and social choice focus entirely on material interests. Hence, separate programs
of economic and political liberalism make less sense in very productive
modern societies. Material and nonmaterial interests were always coupled
in principle in our value theory or our value commitments. Their coupling
now intrudes more frequently or urgently into our opportunities. We now
want additional liberty of, say, life-style and other choices, in part because
such choices are now broadly affordable.

Hobbes, writing in a period of grim turmoil, put survival as the individual's first concern in having government. Locke, taking survival for
granted even in a state of nature, put material interests first. It would be

---

[32] As argued by Kent Greenawalt, *Religious Convictions and Political Choice* (New York:
Oxford University Press, 1988), esp. ch. 3.

silly to suppose that survival and material interests would not be major concerns in justifying states, but nonmaterial interests play a stronger role as the other concerns are increasingly well addressed. But that means — if we may generalize from observed phenomena — that conflicts over what governments ought to do and to protect may get worse in many areas, even while the grand economic policy conflict of this century seems to have been almost universally settled in favor of the market.[33] With survival and material interests comfortably secured, we can afford to fight it out over religious and other divisive issues. David Braybrooke argues that welfare policy should be designed to let needs be satisfied in order that wants might flourish.[34] Hobbes presumably would shudder at the thought of what might follow in the train of this flourishing.

VII. Concluding Remarks

In the end, perhaps a unified welfarist liberalism is an incoherent program. The unification of economic liberalism, which is most focused at the dyadic level, and political liberalism, which is focused at the collective and individual levels, may demand too much complexity. But if that is true, the incoherence is more than merely in liberalism. First, it is in the conflict between society and the individual. Our relations are too intertwined for a theorist to cut out a part of our problem and analyze it alone, as Hobbes, Locke, and others have tried to do. And, second, the incoherence is in our plausible value theories, welfarist and nonwelfarist. Unless we can appeal, as Hobbes, Locke, and Mill did at crucial moments,[35] to our fundamental ignorance of parts of our problem, we may not be able to prune the thicket enough to untangle it.

Historically, the two liberalisms were not related ideologically. Hobbes was a nascent liberal in economics but not in politics. Indeed, Hobbes's solution of chaotic anarchy was an all-powerful sovereign, a solution that might well achieve economic order but that violates liberal political values. For Hobbes the point of politics was to secure order that economy might flourish. It is prima facie a contingent matter just how far toward political liberalism or how far away from it a society can go without harming economic relations. In our time, economic relations are commonly attacked in the name of political liberties (and other, nonliberal concerns, such as fundamentalist religious beliefs) or through the institutions of political liberalism, which can offer losing economic groups an alternative

[33] Even India has abandoned much of its socialist economic program. See *New York Times*, March 29, 1992, sect. I, pp. 1, 9.

[34] David Braybrooke, *Meeting Needs: Studies in Moral, Political, and Legal Philosophy* (Princeton: Princeton University Press, 1987). See also Robert E. Goodin, *Protecting the Vulnerable: A Reanalysis of Our Social Responsibilities* (Chicago: University of Chicago Press, 1985).

[35] One could add Mandeville, Hume, Smith, and others in the long lines of economic and political liberalism to this list.

route to welfare. The most striking case of this phenomenon in our time may occur in the Eastern European and former Soviet nations. But, finally, it seems increasingly difficult to hold separate the values that Hobbes, Locke, and other early writers cavalierly separated. If our vision is welfarist and, at the same time, subjectivist, we cannot a priori rule particular values, such as social, communal, or religious commitments, out of someone's welfare.

Political Science and Philosophy, University of Chicago

SOCIALISM AS THE EXTENSION OF DEMOCRACY

By Richard J. Arneson

Introduction

Are socialists best regarded as those who are most truly and consistently committed to democracy, under modern industrial conditions? Is the underlying issue that divides liberals from socialists the degree of their wholeheartedness in affirming the ideal of a democratic society? On the liberal side, Friedrich Hayek has remarked: "It is possible for a dictator to govern in a liberal way. And it is also possible that a democracy governs with a total lack of liberalism. My personal preference is for a liberal dictator and not for a democratic government lacking in liberalism."[1] No doubt many socialists would wish to quibble with Hayek's free-market oriented conception of liberalism. But I am wondering whether the conceptual map implicit in Hayek's remark is apt. Hayek appears to assume that there are two independent lines of division, one marking greater and lesser commitment to liberal values, the other marking greater and lesser commitment to democratic procedures. According to the conception of socialism as democracy that I wish to examine, a better picture of the political landscape would show one line of division with gradations indicating greater and lesser commitment to democracy. On this continuum, socialists are located at the extreme pro-democratic end, those who favor autocracy at the other end, and liberals somewhere in the middle. The analyst who finds this latter conceptual picture the more illuminating of the two will say that Hayek reveals his rejection of socialism by being less than wholehearted in his support of democracy.

My own view is that Hayek's map is better. It is misleading and probably wrongheaded for the socialist to march so enthusiastically under the banner of democracy. Quite the contrary: The socialist should accept Hayek's half-hearted endorsement of democracy, proceeding from a correct sense that other values are more important. Echoing Hayek, the socialist should say that if it came to a choice, she would favor a liberal-socialist dictator and not a democratic government lacking in liberal socialism. The socialist who understands the logic of her position will dispute

---

[1] From a 1981 interview with Friedrich Hayek, cited after Samuel Bowles and Herbert Gintis, *Democracy and Capitalism* (London: Routledge and Kegan Paul, 1986). I owe this reference to Philippe Van Parijs. Hayek makes a similar observation in *The Constitution of Liberty* (Chicago: University of Chicago Press, 1960), pp. 103–4.

© 1993 Social Philosophy and Policy Foundation. Printed in the USA.   145

Hayek's interpretation of liberal values, not his understanding of the relationship of liberal values to democratic procedures.[2]

No doubt the terms in which I have formulated this issue need to be explicated carefully. And isn't it pointless to quibble about word usage and the names that are assigned to the views one favors? In my view, deliberate mislabeling and stretching the accepted usage of ordinary words often do harm in political theory insofar as they foster confusion of thought. That aside, my aim in what follows is to raise the issue of what foundational values underlie the socialist program and to ask what reasons there are for supposing that pressing the socialist program is the best way to make progress toward achieving those values. Broadly conceived, socialism is public ownership of society's major means of production. This is a policy proposal, not a candidate fundamental value. Further specification of context is needed in order to anticipate the consequences of instituting this policy and to identify the values it might serve.

To this end, this essay analyzes the conception of socialism as the extension of democracy. In Eastern Europe and (to some extent) the Soviet Union nowadays, popular revulsion against Communist dictatorship extends to Communist organization of the economy and indeed to virtually any policies that are identified with socialism, social democracy, or any governmental control of the economy directed toward left-wing goals. Eastern Europeans now seek Western-style capitalism and Western-style democracy, and quite understandably view capitalism and democracy as complementary and mutually reinforcing.[3] Are they confused? They must be so in the eyes of those democratic socialists who believe that "a commitment to socialism follows naturally from a commitment to democracy."[4] Of course it is no news that bourgeois democracies, such as the United States, that combine universal suffrage and capitalist economic institutions have existed since the nineteenth century and are numerous today. According to the democratic socialist, however, these are not real democracies, not democratic enough; and in her view, to achieve real democracy one must replace capitalist institutions with a socialist economy. My first task will be to examine the main arguments to this conclusion.

---

[2] Hayek's liberalism is of the classical, nineteenth-century variety that emphasizes individual freedom under a rule of law that offers wide scope for free-market activity. The liberalism that I take to have affinities with socialism is the contemporary philosophical liberalism exemplified in the writings of John Rawls. See John Rawls, *A Theory of Justice* (Cambridge: Harvard University Press, 1971); and Will Kymlicka, *Contemporary Political Philosophy: An Introduction* (Oxford: Oxford University Press, 1990), ch. 3, "Liberal Equality," and ch. 5, "Marxism."

[3] For some skeptical thoughts on this topic, see Adam Przeworski, "The Neoliberal Fallacy," *Journal of Democracy*, vol. 3, no. 3 (July 1992), pp. 45–59.

[4] Joshua Cohen, "The Economic Basis of Deliberative Democracy," *Social Philosophy & Policy*, vol. 6, no. 2 (Spring 1989), pp. 25–50.

My examination is indebted to Joshua Cohen's recent helpful summary of four such arguments.[5]

I. Left-Wing Arguments on Socialism and Democracy

The structural-constraints argument

In a capitalist economy, investment and savings decisions are made primarily by owners of capital. These decisions are influenced by their expectations of profitability. In turn, the short-term health of the economy is a major concern of incumbent politicians who intend to seek reelection. If capitalist investment drops, in many likely circumstances the health of the economy is negatively affected. Democratically elected politicians will then be unwilling to enact legislation that will unsettle business confidence and cause investment to decline. This dependence of elected politicians on the investment decisions of wealthy capitalists significantly constrains the democratic agenda, the set of proposals that citizens and their representatives might wish to entertain and to enact. The power of capitalist wealth limits the power of the people: so claims the structural-constraints argument. The scope of democratic decision making is limited in this way just as if a powerful neighboring nation constrained democratic choice by threatening that if specified policies it dislikes were to be enacted, severe penalties would be imposed. Following Adam Przeworski and Michael Wallerstein, we might say that popular sovereignty is greater, the less it is the case that the range of decisions available to the people as voters is constrained by the will of powerful individuals or groups. As they put it: "People, by whom we mean individuals acting on the bases of their current preferences, are collectively sovereign if the alternatives open to them as a collective are constrained only by conditions independent of anyone's will."[6]

---

[5] *Ibid.* See also Jon Elster, "The Market and the Forum: Three Varieties of Political Theory," in *Foundations of Social Choice Theory*, ed. Jon Elster and Aanund Hylland (Cambridge: Cambridge University Press, 1986), pp. 103–32; Michael Walzer, *Spheres of Justice* (New York: Basic Books, 1983), pp. 291–303; and Brian Barry, "The Continuing Relevance of Socialism," in his collection *Democracy, Power, and Justice* (Oxford: Oxford University Press, 1989), pp. 526–42.

[6] Adam Przeworski and Michael Wallerstein, "Popular Sovereignty, State Autonomy, and Private Property," *Archives Européennes de Sociologie*, vol. 27, no. 2 (1986), pp. 215–59; see p. 215. It should be noted that Hayek explicitly disavows popular sovereignty in this sense. More popular sovereignty rather than less is not always on balance desirable, according to Hayek. He writes: "The crucial conception of the doctrinaire democrat is that of popular sovereignty. This means to him that majority rule is unlimited and unlimitable. The ideal of democracy, originally intended to prevent all arbitrary power, thus becomes the justification for a new arbitrary power." See Hayek, *The Constitution of Liberty*, p. 106. See also Hayek, "Economic Freedom and Representative Government," reprinted in Hayek, *Economic Freedom* (Oxford: Basil Blackwell, 1991), pp. 383–97.

The structural-constraints argument is incomplete as stated. To round out the argument, one would have to specify some institutional alternative to control of investment funds by capitalists in sufficient detail so that we could ascertain whether the suggested alternative does better than capitalist control in terms of maximizing popular sovereignty. For example, the expropriation of capitalist wealth, coupled with the introduction of a centrally planned economy with economic firms controlled by state-appointed managers, might end up limiting the effective scope of democratic decision making by citizens by vesting effective short-term control of economic resources in enterprise managers. In this scenario, rational voters will decline to vote for laws that they would otherwise favor (but for their expectation that the strategic responses of managers to these laws would cause such bad consequences as to render the laws unattractive options). In general, in order to credit the structural-constraints argument, one would have to be assured that it is specifically capitalist control of investment that constrains popular sovereignty, more so than it would be constrained by the control of specific economic resources by some particular agents in any feasible economic system.

The structural-constraints argument also raises a question about why and to what extent popular sovereignty is desirable. Very few of us would consider unlimited popular sovereignty to be an ideal state of affairs. Imagine that there is a minority of Huguenots in a nation with a stable Catholic majority. The Catholic majority would like to pass laws that place virtually the entire tax burden directly on Huguenots, but these would-be persecutors are dissuaded from this policy by the knowledge that the Huguenots are fierce defenders of their religious liberty and would respond to the imposition of discriminatory taxation by unleashing a civil war that would be costly to all, Catholics included. In this situation, the resisting disposition of the Huguenots limits popular sovereignty, but from a moral standpoint this is not to be regretted. I would argue that even if the Catholic majority is tolerant and not at all inclined to persecution, it is not morally a bad thing if the Huguenots are disposed to resist violations of their rights and if, in this way, the popular sovereignty of the nation as a collective is constrained. In the second case, the erosion of the disposition to resist would not produce any bad consequences, since the Catholics are pacific, but I do not see that the expansion of popular sovereignty to add rights violations to the set of options among which voters are free to choose is in any sense desirable.[7]

This point can be brought home swiftly. Whether we should regard the limitation on popular sovereignty constituted by capitalist control of

---

[7] Joseph Raz makes a parallel point regarding the question of whether or not it is valuable from the standpoint of individual freedom that an individual should have greater rather than lesser freedom to do evil. See Joseph Raz, *The Morality of Freedom* (Oxford: Oxford University Press, 1986).

investment as on balance desirable or undesirable depends on whether we think the capitalists are morally entitled to the wealth that gives them sovereignty-constraining power. If the answer is affirmative, I submit that we should not be distressed by the entailed loss of popular sovereignty. If the answer is negative, the reasons that support this answer are the true reasons for expropriating capitalist wealth, and the discussion of popular sovereignty is just a diversion.

Notice that for exactly the same reason that capitalist control of bank-account wealth counts as a constraint on popular sovereignty, ownership by talented individuals of their marketable talents also counts as a constraint on popular sovereignty. To some extent, the health of the economy depends on the work-versus-leisure decisions of the talented, and these will be affected by such legislative acts as raising the income-tax rate for the top brackets, where the talented are clustered. In Sweden, where income-tax rates are high in comparison to U.S. rates, doctors work at their medical practice many fewer hours per year on average than their U.S. counterparts. We could then increase popular sovereignty by finding a feasible way to expropriate the natural talents of specially talented individuals. I do not intend on this occasion to go into the difficult issue of whether personal property in individual skills and talents should ideally be expropriated in the service of an egalitarian program. My own leaning on this issue happens to be egalitarian.[8] The point I wish to make is that the considerations that should weigh heavily in discussion of the morality of self-ownership versus talent pooling would not be concerned with the impact of self-ownership or its abolition on popular sovereignty.

So far I have not denied that a commitment to popular sovereignty does plausibly lead to a commitment to abolition of private ownership of capital, just as full-blown commitment to popular sovereignty entails abolition of any private right (or individual or sectoral power) that in any way constrains popular sovereignty. My question is: Is it really the case that unstinting commitment to popular sovereignty is a premise that a reasonable democrat should endorse? Reflection on this question makes me suspect that the fact that capitalism might be incompatible with "real" maximal popular sovereignty is not, after all, one of its faults.

---

[8] By "egalitarian" here I intend to refer to the position that better-off persons are morally obligated to lend aid to worse-off persons, when they can do so at tolerable cost to themselves and when the cost-to-benefit ratio of this aid would be favorable. These obligations come into play quite independently of whether or not the better off have voluntarily committed themselves to provide such aid; and the obligations are legitimately enforceable, in appropriate circumstances, by third parties. For discussion of egalitarianism in this sense, see Thomas Nagel, *Equality and Partiality* (New York and Oxford: Oxford University Press, 1991), and the references cited by Nagel. See also Richard Arneson, "Liberalism, Distributive Subjectivism, and Equal Opportunity for Welfare," *Philosophy and Public Affairs*, vol. 19, no. 2 (Spring 1990), pp. 158–94; and Arneson, "Property Rights in Persons," *Social Philosophy & Policy*, vol. 9, no. 1 (Winter 1992), pp. 201–30.

The psychological-support argument

Here the argument begins with the observation that the way institutions are organized beyond the formally political realm has a psychological effect, for better or worse, on the dispositions and traits of the members of society who are called on to perform the tasks of democratic citizens. In particular, two types of effects on individual dispositions give cause for concern. First, the character of nonpolitical institutions can affect individuals' capacities to perceive the common good, their interest in having correct awareness of the common good, and their willingness to comply with policies that are directed toward the common good. Second, the character of nonpolitical institutions can influence the extent to which individuals believe that public affairs are subject to control and that they themselves can effectively intervene to make a difference in the outcomes of public controversies. Let us call citizens who rank high on both of these measures *public-spirited*. The claim, then, is that the organization of economic institutions is particularly significant in determining the extent to which people become public-spirited, and that the hierarchical organization of capitalist firms does poorly at fostering widespread and intense public-spiritedness compared to what we might expect on this score from state-mandated workplace democracy. Hence, workplace democracy should be instituted; democracy should be extended to the economy.

The first comment to be made about the psychological-support argument is that its claim that instituting workplace democracy will inculcate democratic personalities in citizens is quite speculative. Large-scale society-wide experimentation with state-mandated workplace democracy of a sort that could confirm or disconfirm these speculations has not occurred. One can cite the (ambiguous) evidence gained from the experience of state-mandated workers' control in Yugoslavia, but the linkage of workers' control to an autocratic state means that the sorts of connections that the psychological-support argument postulates could not be expected to be called into existence by the Yugoslavian experience even if the psychological-support argument were correct.[9] And small-scale experiments are a biased sample from which one would hesitate to extrapolate to predict likely effects of broadening the experiment even if the evidence we have were encouraging, which it is not.

[9] The statement in the text is controversial, because some authors who have drawn negative lessons from the Yugoslavian Communist experience with workers' self-management schemes have offered analyses that would not be affected by the substitution of a democratic government in place of the actual autocratic Yugoslavian state. See, for example, Ellen Comisso, *Workers' Control under Plan and Market* (New Haven: Yale University Press, 1979); E. Furubotn and S. Pejovich, "Property Rights, Economic Decentralization, and the Evolution of the Yugoslav Firm, 1965–1972," *Journal of Law and Economics*, vol. 16, no. 2 (October 1973), pp. 275–302; and the voluminous literature on the "soft budget constraint" in centrally planned public-ownership economies experimenting with decentralization of authority and control.

A few cautionary points should be noted just at the level of a priori speculation.

First, there is no particular reason to think that the experience of participating in the democratic management of one's firm, even if it sharpened one's desire to see the common good of the firm membership advanced, would have any tendency to increase one's desire to see the common good of the entire society advanced. After all, in identifying more strongly with one's firm, one identifies with it against other firms and other industrial sectors with opposed interests.

Second, we should consider the cynical public-choice theorist's conjecture that a rational voter who perceives that his vote is extremely unlikely to make a difference in a city, state, or national election, will rationally invest no resources in informing himself about election issues and will vote irresponsibly. Supposing that this tendency exists to some extent, it would be mitigated at least in a small firm, where one might calculate that one's vote — and more plausibly one's informed contribution to democratic discussion — would have a significant chance to affect the outcome of elections and hence one's interests. So the voter in the firm might be somewhat better informed than the voter in the polity, though one should still expect the dilution of interest, due to the low chances that one's vote will matter, to degrade the quality of decision making in the firm as well as in the democratically organized state. But why suppose that the voter who invests in political participation in his firm will thereby be more likely to invest in political participation in the wider polity? The costs and benefits are very different in the two cases.

Third, if one supposes there are only so many hours in the day and that to some extent more resources of time and personal energy invested in one place leave fewer personal resources to invest elsewhere, then workplace democracy may well compete for scarce personal resources with ordinary political-democracy obligations of citizenship. The good citizen in the firm could then be expected to be a less public-spirited citizen of the nation, just because she has given her all at the workplace. Obviously, the effects of increased political participation at the workplace level on ordinary political participation will be different for different individuals. But it is far from clear that the overall effect of multiplying opportunities for participation will increase participation in regular politics.

Fourth, whether participation in workplace politics has a positive or negative effect on one's public-spiritedness will obviously depend to a great extent on the success of workplace democracy. If firms are on the average badly run, and if corruption and favoritism are rife, the effect would probably be negative. If shining incorruptibility and efficiency prevail at the workplace level, one would expect that workers will generalize from this experience, expect that citizens whom they cannot monitor are probably voting conscientiously and complying faithfully with duly enacted law, and act accordingly. The effects can tilt either way.

Finally, an obvious and relatively uncontroversial point should be noted. There are several steps that societies could take that would be likely to increase the capacities of their members for participation in democratic decision making and reduce their degree of alienation from the political decision making process. I have in mind such steps as raising the minimum level of education that is supplied to all citizens, increasing the opportunities for further educational attainment available to the less-educated citizens, ensuring that all or nearly all citizens have decent employment opportunities and access to a tolerable level of health care, and significantly improving the nurturing quality of parental or substitute parental care afforded to children so as to enable them to develop a sense of justice. Since it is less controversial to hold that these measures (which are desirable on independent grounds) would increase the average level of citizens' public-spiritedness than that mandating workplace democracy would have this effect, the psychological-support argument for workplace democracy is weak.

The parallel-case argument

This argument proceeds by identifying the features of ordinary politics that justify democratic procedures in that realm and urging that these features are present in the economic realm as well, and thus that rights of democratic citizenship should be extended to the workplace. This extension of rights of democratic citizenship to workplaces entails abolishing or curtailing the rights of private owners of firms. Here I quote Joshua Cohen's clear statement of the argument:

> The best justification for the requirement of democratic governance of the state is that a political society is a cooperative activity, governed by public rules, that is expected to operate for the mutual advantage of the members. Anyone who contributes to such an activity, who has the capacity to assess its rules, and who is subject to them has the right to participate in their determination.[10]

But these characterizations hold true of workers in capitalist firms. So the argument that justifies political democracy also justifies economic democracy.

In response, I would deny that the best justification of democracy is what Cohen says it is. Here I will just indicate an alternative point of view and forgo any attempt to argue for it. I think the best justification of democracy is that it is (in many, not all, circumstances) of all political constitutions the one that works best to achieve the fulfillment of significant

---

[10] Cohen, "The Economic Basis of Deliberative Democracy," p. 27.

individual moral rights.[11] It may not do terribly well on this score. But other forms of government such as monarchy, autocracy, and aristocracy have an even worse track record. When different political constitutions might be expected to do equally well at respecting rights, the choice between them should be made by considering which one would do better at furthering the goals of the members over the long run. Cohen postulates, in effect, that individuals have a right to a democratic say in institutions in which they are subject to orders and which are supposed to work for their benefit. I suspect that our willingness to endorse such a right is a function of our confidence that democratic processes will produce morally nice outcomes. Democracy is to be valued as a tool, not as valuable for its own sake or as a right that people are endowed with regardless of the consequences of exercising it. To elicit one's intuitions on this issue, imagine that Cohen's conditions all obtain, so that one undeniably has the right to a democratic say on his view, but that the consequences of instituting democracy in this case are horrible. The democratically assembled associates vote to pollute the North Sea, to give special benefits to white-skinned persons, and so on. This does not look to me to be a genuine instance of rights in conflict. If democracy performs poorly to protect individual rights, and a nondemocratic mechanism does better, there is no right to democracy to be balanced against the bad consequences of democracy. Whether one is plausibly viewed as having a right to democratic procedures is entirely conditional on their outcomes.

On the instrumental view of democracy that I advocate, the case for a democratic political constitution at the level of the nation-state is likely to be very strong, because the nation-state imposes commands backed by force on its members that are normally unavoidable or at least onerous to avoid. Democratic political rights are the only means at the disposal of the citizen, short of emigration, for reducing the chances that she will be subject to intolerable laws that must be obeyed. But this prima facie case for democracy does not apply at the level of voluntary associations within the state. In the case of voluntary associations that unlike the state do not enforce compulsory membership, the individual has the option of exit, which may serve to guard her essential interests in the absence of a voice. In the case of churches, business firms, football associations, political clubs, and so on, the individual can quit the association if the association's policies are not to her liking. But one can hardly quit the state. Hence, there is a strong presumption in favor of democracy at the level of the nation-state, and of free association on mutually agreed-upon terms, democratic or not, for nonstate organizations. This is not to deny that there might be a case to be made for state-mandated workplace de-

---

[11] The formulation in the text leaves it unspecified what individual moral rights are at stake here. I leave this matter unspecified because I believe that on any remotely plausible position on the content of justifiable, important individual moral rights, under modern conditions a democratic mode of government provides the best chance of fulfilling them.

mocracy on other grounds. I merely reject the parallel-case argument for mandatory workplace democracy.

The criticism just made seems to me to go to the heart of the parallel-case argument. Independently of this criticism, which rejects the case for democracy that is supposed to apply both at the level of the state and the workplace, I want to register another objection, which accepts the case for democracy for the sake of the argument but denies that the workplace is a parallel case. According to the parallel-case argument, one of the conditions that must be present if democracy is to be morally required is that the society is expected to operate for the mutual benefit of its members. But since many institutions in civil society are not and should not be expected to operate for the mutual benefit of their members, this argument for mandatory democracy does not apply to these institutions. I am ready to grant that the expectation-of-mutual-benefit condition is met if the society in question is the nation-state. Hence, whatever warrant for democracy this argument provides is provided for democracy at the level of the nation-state. But the condition is not obviously or standardly met at the level of the workplace.

Consider first of all that some employment settings are organized causes. Greenpeace is organized to act for the benefit of endangered animals and threatened natural habitats, and Oxfam is organized to prevent famines worldwide. In a less explicit way, something similar is true of many private businesses as well. The point of running a bar and greasy spoon restaurant in the remote Sierras may well be partly to cater to the welfare of mountain travelers, and not merely to serve the interests of those who manage and operate this establishment. And many business people would say that the purpose of their business is to make profits for the owners and that the interests of workers are catered to only in contractually specified ways. Under some versions of market socialism, enterprise managers might similarly assert that the purpose of the enterprise is to make profits for the benefit of the general community, and not specifically to serve the interests of the workers.[12] I raise this point only to note that tucked away in what purports to be a sweepingly single-minded justification of socialism from the value of democracy alone is an assumption that could be justified only by invoking values quite distinct from democracy and more closely associated with traditional arguments for versions of socialism that do not construe it as democracy extended to the limit.

The resource-constraint argument

This argument appeals to a hitherto unmentioned democratic norm: in a democratic association, each member should have an equal capacity to

---

[12] See John Roemer, "The Morality and Efficiency of Market Socialism," *Ethics*, vol. 102, no. 3 (April 1992), pp. 448–64.

influence the outcomes of democratic deliberation leading to majority-rule voting. The formal equality of one-person-one-vote does not suffice to ensure equal power to affect outcomes. In particular, large inequalities of wealth and income result in greatly unequal access to media of communication, to the deferential consideration of political parties looking for campaign contributions, and to other sources of political influence. A more equal distribution of material resources would go far to satisfy this equal-influence norm, and socialism can do better than capitalism at providing this more nearly equal distribution.

I agree with the idea that formal equality of votes cast is not sufficient for democratic association. If citizens have insufficient resources which they can put at the disposal of political projects, their participation opportunities are revealed as merely formal, not effective.

The goal of rendering the participation opportunities of the poorest citizens more substantially effective may, but need not, require increased equality of material resources. To some extent, one secures more effective opportunities for the poorest simply by enlarging the stock of material resources at their disposal. And the goals of equalizing resources and maximinning resources can obviously conflict.[13] I do not think there is a general answer to the question of whether equalizing or maximinning resources is the better strategy for increasing the effective participation opportunities of the poorest citizens.

Equalizing is important insofar as there is a fixed and limited supply of democratic forums, and access to the forums goes to the highest bidder. For example, if there are one thousand available minutes of political advertising on network commercial-television networks and the broadcast time is auctioned to the highest bidder, then the richest can, if they wish, dominate communication.

But suppose the forum in question is distributing leaflets and flyers door-to-door. Within limits of the attention span of voters who receive leaflets and flyers, the process is not competitive. If you have sufficient funds to purchase flyers to blanket your desired audience, it does not limit your opportunity if others more richly endowed also target this same audience with leaflets. This forum expands to accommodate those who wish to enter it. Insofar as political forums have this character, maximinning is the appropriate means to achieving effective opportunity for the poorest citizens. This point has political relevance if one believes that capitalist institutions, together with redistributive taxation, might do better than any feasible socialism insofar as the aim is to maximin material resources.

In contemporary political culture, financial contributions to campaigns as a means of influence are important determinants of the political pro-

---

[13] With respect to a group of people, to maximin is to make the position of the worst-off person as advantageous as possible (or in other words, to maximize the minimum resource holding of the worst off).

cess and would seem to be amenable to an equalizing, not a maximinning solution. But here one should mention the possibility of insulating political campaigns from the influence of money rather than trying to equalize the money endowments of citizens. For instance, one might at the extreme require that political campaigns be wholly financed by public funds from general tax revenues and strictly limit campaigning between delimited electoral seasons. In the United States, the Federal Election Campaign Act of 1971 took moderate steps in this direction, the most significant of which, perhaps, was prohibiting any individual from spending more than a certain sum of money per year "relative to a clearly identified candidate."[14]

A more difficult issue emerges once one notices that equalizing wealth would not render equal the capacities of citizens to influence political outcomes. Breaking down the dominance of wealth would render the dominance of education, intelligence, political skill, and personal connections more salient. These sources of unequal capacity to influence political outcomes are, if anything, less tractable than the inequality of bank-account wealth. I raise this point in order to ask whether the person who favors reduction of wealth inequality in order to foster equal capacity to influence political outcomes is really committed to the latter. If so, why is this goal not dismissable as utopian, unapproachable by any means? In contrast, if there is a special morally unattractive taint that attaches to the disproportionate control of political outcomes by possession of relatively great wealth, this special opprobrium should be more fully characterized.

No doubt in an ideal democratic deliberation, in which only the force of the better argument sways the assembly, the capacity to identify and formulate these better arguments would surely be unequally distributed across the citizenry. Short of genetic engineering carefully orchestrated (or the provision of schooling inversely to native talent in order to counterbalance native talent), no social policy would eliminate unequal capacity to influence political outcomes. Perhaps the idea is that inequalities in political capacity are only bad insofar as they tend to prevent the realization of the ideal deliberative assembly in which only better arguments have influence. But this move might precipitate a larger slide away from a commitment to political equality. Perhaps John Stuart Mill's conjecture is correct that denying some citizens rights of citizenship or conferring plural votes on more qualified citizens would tend to enhance the responsiveness of the deliberative assembly to the force of the better argument.[15] In this eventuality, some tradeoff between the value of political equality and the value of intelligent responsiveness in deliberation would have to be made.

---

[14] See the Supreme Court opinions on the constitutionality of the provisions of this act in *Buckley v. Valeo*, 424 U.S. 1 (1976).

[15] John Stuart Mill, *Considerations on Representative Government*, in *Collected Works*, vol. 19, ed. J. M. Robson (Toronto and Buffalo: University of Toronto Press, 1977), ch. 7.

In short, the resource-constraint argument introduces an important set of problems for normative democratic theory. But the agenda that is thereby revealed is sufficiently unsettled that we cannot confidently at this time assert that overturning capitalism and introducing socialism is obviously the best way to make progress on this agenda.

II. Hayekian Arguments on Socialism and Democracy

The arguments just canvassed have some force, despite my doubts and reservations. But in order to clarify further the relation between the ideas of democratic association and socialism, these left-wing arguments should be set against some right-wing arguments that also have the ring of a priori plausibility. The two arguments this section discusses are drawn from Friedrich Hayek's critique of socialism and centralized planning. Hayek argues that the introduction of socialism would pose a danger to the continued existence of democratic order at the level of the nation-state. According to Hayek, socialism is in conflict with democracy, and also with the rule of law. (The latter conflict is more significant for Hayek, because he is more committed to the ideal of the rule of law than to democracy.) I argue that the conflict that Hayek describes can be reduced to a tolerable level without abandoning socialism. Section I of this essay denied that a commitment to socialism is usefully viewed as flowing from a commitment to democracy. This section holds that a commitment to democracy is not, under plausible factual assumptions, incompatible—or even seriously in tension—with a commitment to socialism.

Democracy, economic planning, and strife

In the eyes of some political theorists, notably Hayek, the market mechanism has the considerable virtue of settling "automatically" in a relatively uncontroversial fashion many issues that would immediately become highly contentious if they were explicitly placed on the political agenda and made the stuff of democratic politics.[16] Most obviously, market determination of the incomes and wealth holdings of individuals over time comes about impersonally, through the combined effects of many separate economic decisions, none of which are intended to produce the overall results that actually ensue. In this system the economic fate of individuals is not settled by anyone's deliberate choice. A democratic political order is regarded as a fragile mechanism prone to collapse if overburdened with controversy. We can best preserve a functioning democracy by insulating it from intractable controversy that we can foresee will destroy it.

---

[16] See Friedrich Hayek, *The Road to Serfdom* (Chicago and London: University of Chicago Press, 1944), for a simple exposition of this line of thought.

With this aim in view, we might follow the advice of Mill and try, other things equal, to have the boundaries of modern states with free institutions drawn so that each state includes only one nationality group that strongly desires political sovereignty for itself separate from other nationalities.[17] Disparate tribes and ethnic groups should be bound together in a single state only insofar as proto-nationalist consciousness centered on any single tribe or ethnic group is weak and diffuse. The reason to bring it about that each state should be organized as far as possible to correspond to a single nationality grouping is that if hostile tribes and ethnic groups, each clamoring for independent national existence, are fenced together in a single regime, nationalist ethnic and tribal conflict is likely to tear the state apart. In the interest of preserving democratic order, excess strain of controversy on that order should be averted when this is possible.

On the same principle, the Hayekian recommends leaving matters of economic distribution to the vagaries of the market. Market outcomes will be good for some people and unfortunate for others. Those who lose in any given round of fluctuating market outcomes will usually be able to regard themselves as unlucky rather than oppressed. They are the victims of impersonal market forces that operated in such a way as to produce an outcome that was not deliberately sought by any agent and for which no agent can (or must) bear responsibility. Making one's living in a market economy, one is inevitably a gambler, whether one wills it or not, even if one hedges one's bets with insurance. It is as though one has no choice but to ride a giant roulette wheel that stops where it will, distributing payoffs that share one (to Hayek) marvelous quality: they are not the result of the deliberate policy pursued by any government agency or indeed by any human agency. A similar point occurred to Mill back in the mid-nineteenth century when he compared capitalism to a thoroughgoing Communist system intent on equality of distribution. He worried that Communism "has also some disadvantages which seem to be inherent in it, through the necessity under which it lies of deciding in a more or less arbitrary manner questions which, on the present system, decide themselves, often badly enough, but spontaneously." Deciding such questions by deliberate political choice would engender "squabbles and ill-blood" according to Mill.[18]

All of this changes dramatically, according to Hayek, if the society takes on the responsibility for economic planning and entrusts this task to government. If the economy is run according to a plan set by a democratic political process, inevitably the detailed economic fate of individuals and

---

[17] John Stuart Mill, *Considerations on Representative Government*, ch. 16.

[18] John Stuart Mill, *Chapters on Socialism*, in *Collected Works*, vol. 5, ed. J. M. Robson (Buffalo and Toronto: University of Toronto Press, 1967). The first quote is from p. 743; the second is from p. 744.

groups is amenable to political decision. A democratic political assembly assigned the task of setting planning goals will then be buffeted by interest groups lobbying for favored treatment under the plan. The greater the scope and magnitude of planning, the greater the political conflicts: no one wants his ox to be gored, and everybody will fight to protect what he naturally regards as his just and fair entitlement. These lobbying and string-pulling activities are inherently wasteful: resources that could be put to productive use are now deployed in endless redistributive squabbles. Even those who would like to maintain their integrity above the fray will be drawn into the political combat in order to offset the aggressive lobbying of others. In this setting the democratic political order will deteriorate into corruption or collapse entirely. Moreover, an economy run by democratic plan will in practice be sluggish. Under the pressure of swiftly changing circumstances, any modern economy in order to adapt efficiently must cause constant social dislocation as old jobs are ended and new jobs are created. Even if a planned economy could be arranged so that accurate signals and indicators are transmitted to the planners, the democratic planners enmeshed in arm-twisting politics could not respond to these signals with market-like dispatch.

Instead of commenting straightaway on this argument it will be helpful to consider it in conjunction with a tandem argument.[19]

The chimera of social justice

The problems just described could be alleviated to an extent if citizens could agree on planning goals, justified by agreed-upon ethical norms, which would command their allegiance even on occasions when their implications cut against some people's self-interest. And indeed one does

---

[19] For the argument above, see Hayek, *The Road to Serfdom*, ch. 8. See also Hayek, *The Constitution of Liberty*, ch. 6; and Hayek, *Law, Legislation, and Liberty*, vol. 2, *The Mirage of Social Justice* (London: Routledge and Kegan Paul, 1973). In calling attention to Hayek's arguments to the conclusion that refraining from socialist policies and a regime of central-planning preserves political democracy, I do not mean to imply that these arguments from democracy exhaust his case against socialism. Hayek asserts that the attempt to run an economy by state planning must destroy the rule of law, governance by general and abstract rules that are not directed at helping or hurting particular individuals. In turn the rule of law is closely connected to the maintenance of individual freedom, for Hayek holds that an individual is free "if he is not subject to unjustifiable coercion" (Chandran Kukathas, *Hayek and Modern Liberalism* [Oxford: Oxford University Press, 1990], p. 132). The rule of law does not unjustifiably coerce, hence does not limit individual freedom. In Hayek's mind, sustaining a genuine rule of law requires that the state limit itself to legislating rules of procedure that facilitate the working of the extended order constituted by property rules, common-law rules, and traditional moral rules enjoining socially useful virtues, including honesty and forbearance from theft and aggressive violence. Once the state goes beyond rules that facilitate private ordering and legislates social goals, the rule of law is eroded, for with changing circumstances the rules enforced on individuals must change erratically in order to meet these goals. I do not attempt a full survey of Hayek's arguments here, and a fortiori I do not try to assess the full range of his arguments.

find in the public culture of modern democracies an impressive-sounding rhetoric that appeals to the common good, the general welfare, the national interest, the common heritage, moral traditions, principles of fairness and fair play, and common-sense social-justice norms. Upon cursory inspection, however, these lofty ideals will be found to be pitched at such a high level of abstraction as to be capable of doing very little of the necessary work of forging agreement on detailed questions of policy. The problem is not that there is no plausible interpretation of social justice but that there are too many. When there is controversy involving conflict of interest, each of the parties to the controversy can pick out from the spectrum of interpretations of justice one that favors her interest, so conceptions of justice do not bind citizens together in social unity, but become ideologies, weapons for individual, group, and class conflict. Indeed, as Hobbes first intimated, ascending from low-minded conflict of interest to high-minded conflict of principles does not tend to render the adversary parties more tractable and more inclined to compromise when the principles advanced by the parties are proxies for their interests.[20] The situation seems to be that the party most likely to be sincerely persuaded by an argument of principle is that party whose interests are aligned with that principle, but sincere assent to a principle can motivate entrenched commitment beyond what cool, self-interested calculation would have dictated.

In short: The threat to democratic political order introduced by placing economic planning on the political agenda could be averted if stable consensus among citizens on an ideal of social justice that would guide planning could reasonably be expected. But it cannot.

In response: Like many Hayekian arguments in political theory, the arguments just sketched tend to present as extreme, dichotomous choices what are really choices on an array of alternatives. The claim is that either there is society-wide consensus on a detailed plan of justice that dots every "i" and crosses every "t" or there is no practical agreement at all. But it is not utopian to strive for a broad consensus encompassing most major points of view in society at a mid-range level of principle that leaves room for disagreement at lower levels of abstraction but is not the same as no agreement at all. The claim is that either distribution is essentially left to free-market mechanisms or the state must undertake the full task of centralized planning. But, once again, these options do not exhaust the alternatives. The claim is that if society takes on the task of addressing economic-justice issues, then either there is a broad consensus on every last detail of justice goals or the democratic political order is entirely ground down to the point of collapse by the incessant unprincipled lobbying and manipulation of interest groups. But an obvious feature of

---

[20] Thomas Hobbes, *Leviathan* [1651], ed. C. B. Macpherson (Harmondsworth, Middlesex: Penguin Books Ltd., 1981), pp. 109, 111, 120, and 166.

modern democracies, which is disconcerting to the tidy mind, is that they can lumber along quite well despite continuing deep fissures and rifts among citizens. Sometimes conflict and disagreement about fundamental values and the rules of the game threaten the stability of democracies. Often, however, these conflicts are nonthreatening. And so it goes, for virtually every either-or conjured up in the Hayekian line of thought.

Another odd feature of the conservative argument for adherence to something close to laissez-faire economic policy is that once it is recognized that society acting collectively through the agency of governments can exert considerable influence for good or ill on economic outcomes, the choice of laissez faire is from that point on just that: a deliberate policy choice. But then one can no longer continue to expect that if the unregulated market outcome leads to famine, say, and government chooses not to intervene, then informed citizens who are suffering from this famine will regard themselves as the accidental victims of impersonal forces rather than the victims of governmental neglect: after all, the government could have acted but chose not to. Of course, there are constitutional devices and other means available to a government to tie its hands in advance, so at the moment when there is a call for intervention the public officials can say with a straight face that there is nothing they can do. But at any rate they will be held responsible for creating or acquiescing in the state of affairs that was designed to tie the government's hands at the crucial moment. So I am inclined to say that if we accept the conservative analysis, then we are in the soup: we have lost the possibility of naive laissez faire regarded as anything other than one policy choice among alternatives.

I am convinced that additional flaws in these conservative arguments could be found if they were examined further. But instead I wish to take a stab at stating what I take to be the kernel of truth in the conservative analysis.

Economic-justice rights of the sort the socialist wishes to implement are highly vulnerable to the tug and pull of interest-group lobbying that is inseparable from democratic politics. If these rights give special protection to the vulnerable, the nonvulnerable will be negatively affected, and will be tempted to seek to manipulate the political process so that the rights are diluted in the implementation process. Now the Hayekian might be right in his hunch that either there is no such thing as a correct set of principles of social justice, or this possibility is irrelevant to democratic politics because no feasible conception of social justice, correct or not, could secure a stable consensus. Just for the sake of the argument, let us suppose the Hayekian is wrong: there can be objective judgment of social-justice principles, and workable conceptions can gain a working consensus across citizens. Even if this is so, and even if we suppose our society can attain a consensus that is on the right track, the consensus will be fragile in the sense that it will continuously affect for the worse the material interests of groups and individuals who are very capable of acting successfully to protect their interests if they choose to do so. The situation might be akin to the situation that currently prevails in many constitutional democracies with respect to civil liberties like freedom of speech. In the abstract there is considerable popular support for freedom of speech, but in everyday policy settings many who think of themselves as supporters of free speech are strongly inclined to trim it down here and there in many particular cases. When this situation obtains, it may be appropriate to use constitutional means to entrench civil liberties and to displace decision making regarding their application to cases from democratic assemblies to an independent judiciary insulated from control by the electorate. My suggestion is that rights of socialist justice, once we get clear on their proper formulation (which need not be detailed), should perhaps be insulated from majority-rule control in much the same way and for the same reasons that we constitutionalize other fundamental liberties. Here we might say we are taking a leaf from the Hayekian book and protecting the orderly integrity of the democratic process by removing from its purview the direct dispatch of issues likely to be overly contentious.

III. The Distributive Conception of Socialism

To summarize the argument to this point: There is a certain attraction in conceiving of socialism as the extension of democracy, what you get if you follow through rigorously on the logical implications of commitment to the ideal of a democratic association. The trouble is that on any ordinary understanding of what majority rule is and what a democratic decision procedure is, democracy is not even a remotely plausible candidate for the status of ur-value, the foundational norm from which all else flows. Consider that a society is more democratic — popular sovereignty in the society is less constrained — if the members are collectively free to pass laws closely regulating the details of what we would regard as private individual behavior. If the society is collectively free to legislate the sex life of each of its members, the scope of democracy is wider than it would be if constitutionally entrenched rights of individual privacy, or the fighting disposition of individuals jealous of their private freedom, set severe constraints on what the society collectively is free to decide by way of sexual commandments. But I submit that there is no value in collective self-determination on matters that are properly the self-regarding business of each individual. If privacy rights secure decision-making authority to each individual and deny decision-making authority to the set of individuals taken collectively, then if we are for even minimal rights of privacy we are to that extent against unlimited majority rule. I would further submit that even if we could mark out (1) a self-regarding sphere where individuals should be individually sovereign and (2) an other-regarding sphere where the decisions of individuals are the business of the group of those who might be affected by the decisions, democracy is still a procedure to be valued for its results, not for its inherent value or anyone's inherent right to it.

If the value underlying socialism is not democracy, then what is it? Briefly, I suggest that public ownership of the means of production should be regarded as a means of implementing the anti-exploitation norm that is central (along with the ideal of ending alienation) in Karl Marx's critique of capitalism. The anti-exploitation norm holds that it is morally undesirable that some people take advantage of undeserved ownership (or possession) of assets in ways that render them better off than others. This undesirable feature is what is common to the various phenomena that Marx views as exploitive: the exploitation of slaves by masters, peasants by state bureaucrats, serfs by lords, workers by capitalists, and untalented by talented economic agents.[21] The intuitive idea shaping the norm is that if society assigns you ownership rights in a factory, or in other people's labor, or in your own unusually talented labor, and you do not deserve to own these assets, then other things equal it is morally undesirable that you use these assets to gain special benefits for yourself above what other people get. It is morally undesirable that you obtain special benefits in the absence of special desert, but you might not be in any way at fault for this bad state of affairs: in turning these owned assets to your advantage, you might be acting entirely in conformity with the dominant common-sense morality of the time and locale.

The other-things-equal clause in this rationale of the anti-exploitation norm allows deference to these contingencies: (1) Other things are not equal if it is the case that if you do not benefit from ownership of an undeserved asset, no one else will benefit either. If the fruit on a tree I own through no merit of my own is about to turn rotten, it is better that I eat it than that it rots, even if this renders me better off than others. The same point applies, but more weakly, if the owner stands to gain a lot from deployment of her asset whereas no one else could gain more than a little from it. (2) Other things are not equal if it is the case that even though you do not deserve to own the asset, there is some other morally considerable reason to assign ownership to you.

My statement of the anti-exploitation norm tries to register the moral objections implicit in Marxist characterizations of what are viewed as ca-

---

[21] The textual warrant for including conflict of interests between talented and untalented individuals as a source of exploitation is in Karl Marx, "Critique of the Gotha Program," in Karl Marx and Friedrich Engels, *The Marx-Engels Reader*, ed. Robert Tucker (New York: W. W. Norton and Co., 1978), p. 530. The best discussion of the possible underlying moral bases of Marx's views on exploitation is a pair of articles by John E. Roemer: "Property Relations vs. Surplus Value in Marxian Exploitation," *Philosophy and Public Affairs*, vol. 11, no. 4 (Fall 1982), pp. 281–313; and "Should Marxists Be Interested in Exploitation?" *Philosophy and Public Affairs*, vol. 14, no. 1 (Winter 1985), pp. 30–65. See also Richard Arneson, "What's Wrong with Exploitation?" *Ethics*, vol. 91, no. 2 (January 1981), pp. 202–27.

nonical instances of exploitive arrangements, such as capitalist wage-labor relations. This task calls for some interpretation, because the Marxist account of exploitation is a complex, perhaps a tangled, skein of threads. For example, the Marxist conception of exploitation involves an element of force or coercion not reflected in the anti-exploitation norm. But intuitively it would seem that the unfair treatment that troubles the Marxist can occur in the absence of force or coercion. Imagine that an agent has no option except to work for a capitalist on terms the Marxist will regard as exploitive. The worker is forced to submit to exploitation, let us stipulate. Now vary the example by imagining that the worker also has the option of refusing the capitalist offer and surviving by a combination of government dole and self-employment. This latter option is less attractive to the worker than the deal the capitalist offers. As we vary the example further by imagining this outside option to be increasingly attractive, it becomes decreasingly plausible to say the worker is forced to accept the wage-labor bargain. But even if the outside option is made just as attractive to the worker as the capitalist wage-labor offer, it still should remain the case that the worker who takes this wage-labor offer is being exploited, even though the worker is no longer forced to take this offer. The terms of the offer itself make it exploitive, not the alternatives (or lack of alternatives) available to the worker. Being exploited and being forced to submit to exploitation are distinct matters. The anti-exploitation norm should characterize what is wrong with the former, not the latter.

To call this norm an "anti-exploitation" norm deviates from ordinary usage in at least two ways.

First, to exploit someone is to interact with her in a way that is (a) unfair to her and (b) profitable to the exploiter.[22] The anti-exploitation norm formulated here casts a wider net. For example, imagine that there are just two persons in the universe and that each lives alone on an island. One is lucky to be talented and to have access to rich natural resources. The unlucky agent has less talent than the other along all significant dimensions of talent, and the island he lives on is poor in natural resources as well. The lucky person knows of the unlucky person's existence and could assist him by placing aid packages in unmanned boats that would float on the prevailing currents to the shore of his island home. No other causal interaction between the two agents is possible. The lucky person declines to assist the unlucky one. Since the two persons in this example do not interact at all, a fortiori neither interacts with the other in an unfair way that could constitute exploitation. But in this example the anti-exploitation norm is violated, since the lucky person exploits her assets in a way that is unfair by the standards of that norm.

---

[22] For more careful and nuanced discussion of the ordinary-usage concept of exploitation, see Joel Feinberg, *The Moral Limits of the Criminal Law*, vol. 4, *Harmless Wrongdoing* (Oxford: Oxford University Press, 1988), chs. 31 and 32.

Second, in ordinary usage, whether Smith exploits Jones depends on the relations between them, not on how their benefit and burden levels resulting from their interaction compare to those of other people. In contrast, of two otherwise identical interactions between Smith and Jones, it might be the case that one violates the anti-exploitation norm and the other does not, owing to third-party comparisons. The anti-exploitation norm, as I have formulated it, is concerned with the overall distribution of benefits and burdens among persons in society, not just with the quality of interaction among particular persons.

The anti-exploitation norm is a moral hybrid. It melds together a principle regulating the distribution of benefits and burdens and a deontological norm against unfair use of advantages that an individual gains by sheer luck, without special merit. In my formulation of the norm, this deontological element is attenuated.

If one sets aside the deontological element altogether,[23] what remains is an egalitarian distributive norm similar to the general conception of justice that plays a central role in John Rawls's analysis.[24] This egalitarian ethic holds that priority in bringing about benefits or avoiding losses should be given to the worse-off members of society. The principle is more fully elaborated as a two-part requirement: (1) the moral value of gaining a small benefit (or avoiding a small loss) for a person is directly proportional to the size of the benefit and inversely proportional to how well or badly off the person was prior to receipt of this benefit, and (2) social arrangements should be set so as to maximize moral value. Benefits and losses here are to be measured from the standpoint of each individual's scale of values. The idea of bringing about an end to exploitation is not to impose some particular conception of the good life on anyone; rather, we wish to enable every member of society to make intelligent decisions about the sort of life she wishes to lead and then to enable every last member to flourish in living out the life she has (one hopes) intelligently chosen. Perhaps the spirit of this ethic is captured in Friedrich Engels's unwillingness to speculate about the content of sexual morality in a society of equals:

> That will be settled after a new generation has grown up: a genera-
> tion of men who never in all their lives have had occasion to pur-
> chase a woman's surrender either with money or with any other
> means of social power, and of women who have never been obliged
> to surrender to any man out of any consideration other than that of
> real love, or to refrain from giving themselves to their beloved for

[23] Perhaps the deontological element should be retained via the notion of deservingness. Arguably, a liberal-egalitarian theory of justice should include a ground-level notion of deservingness in such a way that one's deservingness status affects the treatment one should receive.

[24] Rawls, *A Theory of Justice*, p. 62.

fear of the economic consequences. Once such people appear, they will not care a rap about what we today think they should do. They will establish their own practice and their own public opinion, conformable therewith, on the practice of each individual — and that's the end of it.[25]

On this view the socialist is not opposed in fundamental ethical beliefs to the contemporary egalitarian liberal.[26] The socialist position is defined by the public-ownership proposal, regarded as a means to egalitarian-liberal ends. Regarded as a means, proposed socialist arrangements should be evaluated in comparison to social-democratic arrangements, welfare-state capitalism, and so on. The egalitarian goal is to enable each individual to acquire resources adequate for living a good life according to her own standards (which would withstand rational scrutiny), with priority accorded to the claims for resources of those individuals whose life prospects are currently substandard.

This essay does not aim to show that the distributive conception of socialism expresses a defensible ethic that is a suitable fundamental norm for the regulation of a modern society. I have indicated a connection between the socialist project and an egalitarian-liberal principle, but this essay does not reach the question of whether this principle is justifiable, all things considered, or whether the socialist proposal for reorganizing society is the best means, all things considered, for satisfying this principle. The issue for this essay is whether the democratic conception or the distributive conception is the better interpretation of the socialist project. There are two aspects to this issue. One aspect is good fit: Does the democratic or the distributive conception better explain the criticisms of capitalism and class-divided societies that Marx and socialists advance? A second aspect is normative appeal: Does the assumption that a distributive, rather than a democratic, constellation of values is implicit in the socialist critique of capitalism and program of social reconstruction, enhance the normative appeal of that critique and program? This essay has tried

---

[25] Friedrich Engels, *The Origin of the Family, Private Property, and the State*, reprinted in *The Marx-Engels Reader*, p. 751. I say only that "perhaps" this quote expresses an egalitarian-liberal perspective. One can also read this passage as merely asserting that it is futile to attempt now to determine what the content of the future socialist ethical culture will be or should be. On this reading Engels is neither asserting nor denying that in a mature socialist society public opinion will be a law to individuals on matters of individual sexual conduct, a law that will exert repressive force on individuals who would wish to deviate from the majority norm.

[26] Egalitarian liberalism encompasses two doctrines: (1) a view about the fair distribution of resources that individuals need in order to lead good lives according to their own values, and (2) a view about fair and worthy processes by which individuals acquire their values. Freedoms of association, thought, and expression fall under (2). My discussion ignores (2) not because it is unimportant but because the socialist tradition has little to say by way of contribution to it.

to make the case for the distributive conception by concentrating on the aspect of normative appeal.

I have already indicated some respects in which the transition from a socialist nonexploitation ethic to a contemporary egalitarian ethic is not smooth. Some concerns that are important to the former ethic do not register in the latter ethic. But I wish to defend myself against the objection that generalizing the nonexploitation ethic along Rawlsian lines entirely misstates the socialist ethic because exploitation is not the sole consideration shaping that ethic.

Marxism, along with the socialist tradition influenced by Marxism, is inspired by two master ideals: the idea of a society free of exploitation, and the goal of eliminating alienated labor. In focusing solely on exploitation, I admit I have ignored half of the ethics of socialism. Hence, the reader might suspect that my interpretation of that tradition bowdlerizes it.

The narrow focus of my discussion in this section reflects my personal judgment of the comparative value of the two master ideals animating the socialist tradition.[27] In my judgment, the alienation ideal is illiberal if construed as a standard that is valid for assessing the worth of any individual's life regardless of her own values and preferences. But insofar as what is at stake in this discussion is the adequacy of the democratic conception of socialism, it makes little difference whether or not the reader agrees with my comparative judgment. Ending alienation, no less than ending exploitation, is a distributive concern.

Roughly, a worker's labor is alienated to the degree that (a) she does not control the disposition of her product, and dislikes the disposition that is imposed; (b) she is unfree with respect to the character of the labor process that she engages in, and she dislikes that process; (c) she does not produce in order to serve the human community; (d) she does not freely develop and exercise her talents at work; and (e) she sustains unfriendly, purely instrumental relations with those persons whom she interacts with in the course of laboring. Evidently, the ideal of unalienated labor bundles together heterogeneous values. The ideal of unalienated labor is a Marxist contribution to the normative theory of the good life. Marx's critique of capitalism reflects the norms that basic institutions should minimize alienated labor, and that insofar as some alienated labor is unavoidable, basic institutions should fairly divide this necessary alienated labor among the members of society. In short, the account of alienated labor is a contribution to the Marxist account of what constitutes benefits and burdens and how their distribution should be regulated.

---

[27] See Richard Arneson, "Meaningful Work and Market Socialism," *Ethics*, vol. 97, no. 3 (April 1987), pp. 517–45; and Arneson, "Is Socialism Dead? A Comment on Market Socialism and Basic Income Capitalism," *Ethics*, vol. 102, no. 3 (April 1992), pp. 485–511; see esp. pp. 486–88.

However, to conceive the socialist ethic as a principle regulating the distribution of benefits and burdens is one-sided. What the distributive conception ignores or downplays is the theme of socialist solidarity versus capitalist acquisitiveness. The socialist traditionally objects to capitalism not merely as a form of society that offers too few opportunities to the downtrodden, but also as a form of society that promotes human selfishness. The socialist aims at a transformation of human nature along with the reconstruction of institutions. Indeed, the institutional changes which the socialist recommends are supposed to be not just a mechanism for distributing social benefits but also a device for altering motivation. This prominent aspect of the socialist critique and vision deserves a comment.

The socialist who raises the problem of acquisitiveness is troubled by the thought that the steps that a society takes in order to harness existing selfish motivations to socially beneficial ends might block the steps that the society should be taking to change socialization practices so that the total quantity of selfish motivation that must be harnessed in the future is less. In other words, the socialist conjectures that there is a tradeoff between minimizing the net loss to society that existing human selfishness will cause and minimizing the net loss to society that will arise from the avoidable production of human selfishness. The socialist further conjectures that the capitalist free-market mechanism for coping with human selfishness, even if successful in its own terms, is a bad long-term choice because this mechanism also produces ever more selfishness to be negotiated.

I have no quarrel with the animus against selfishness that motivates the socialist who seeks to cure what R. H. Tawney once called "the sickness of an acquisitive society."[28] We can distinguish two levels of aspiration here. Overcoming selfishness might be conceived as inculcating in all individuals an effective sense of justice, so that no one is disposed to behave unfairly in order to gain some advantage for herself. Nice as it would be to attain a society all the members of which are perfectly disposed to be just, it would be still nicer to bring about a state of affairs in which selfishness is further dampened. We could imagine a society all the members of which are (a) perfectly disposed to conform to obligations of justice and (b) disposed not to give "too much" extra weight to their own interests and the interests of close kin and friends in competition with the interests of strangers in decision problems that do not involve any obligations of justice. I believe that Tawney's ideal of a nonacquisitive society envisages the overcoming of selfishness in the stronger of the two senses just distinguished.

---

[28] R. H. Tawney, *The Sickness of an Acquisitive Society* (London: Fabian Society, 1920). Compare Hayek's more sympathetic construal of the motivations of agents successfully pursuing their aims within an extended order, in *The Fatal Conceit: The Errors of Socialism* (Chicago: University of Chicago Press, 1988), p. 81.

However, in practice the tradeoff between the goals of coping with self-ishness and reducing it is virtually irrelevant to issues of social reconstruction and constitutional design, because neither socialist theorists nor anyone else has any clear ideas about how to organize institutions so as to alter human motivation for the better.[29] Pending the development of new and compelling social theory that is not yet on the horizon, we must be content to leave the campaign against acquisitiveness at the level of utopian speculation.

IV. DEMOCRACY IDEALIZED: THE IDEAL OF SOCIALISM AS AN IDEAL DELIBERATIVE DEMOCRACY

So far, I have been deliberately unfair to the viewpoint that regards a commitment to socialism as following naturally from a commitment to democracy. The advocates of the extension-of-democracy conception of socialism are perfectly aware that in the ordinary sense of the term "democratic," a society could be as democratic as you like, yet thoroughly unjust — thoroughly exploitive. Packed into the ordinary idea, I intend to include certain counter-majoritarian rights that must be sustained if the outcomes of votes are to count as genuinely democratic votes. For example, a society must respect freedom of expression regarding public affairs and the conduct of politics, or else votes are a plebiscitary mockery. Also, in a democratic society all adult citizens are equally eligible to vote and to stand for office in open elections, controlled by fair election-campaign laws. And so on. Nonetheless, a society might be scrupulously true to what we might call the full sense of democracy and yet the outcome of democratic votes might be, for instance, that a majority of whites passes laws that impose unjust burdens on those with black or brown skin. Democracy is a procedural norm, not a theory of justice.

Hence, the most developed articulations of the democratic-extension idea of socialism tend to downplay the role of majority rule and democratic procedures. Instead, they uphold the ideal of the rational consent of all, following ideally extended democratic debate among competent and conscientious citizens who are striving to achieve the common good.[30] The ideal is recognizably drawn from the thought of Jürgen

---

[29] The absence of any theory of motivation change vitiates much of the interesting discussion in Richard M. Titmuss, *The Gift Relationship: From Human Blood to Social Policy* (New York: Random House, 1971). See also Kenneth Arrow, "Gifts and Exchanges," *Philosophy and Public Affairs*, vol. 1, no. 4 (Summer 1972), pp. 343–62; Peter Singer, "Altruism and Commerce: A Defense of Titmuss against Arrow," *Philosophy and Public Affairs*, vol. 2, no. 3 (Spring 1973), pp. 312–20; and Richard Arneson, "Commerce and Selfishness," *Canadian Journal of Philosophy*, supp. vol. 8 (1982), pp. 211–32.

[30] For good discussion, see Elster, "The Market and the Forum"; and Joshua Cohen, "Deliberation and Democratic Legitimacy," in *The Good Polity*, ed. Alan Hamlin and Philip Pettit (Oxford: Basil Blackwell, 1989). See also Jürgen Habermas, *Communication and the Evolution of Society*, trans. Thomas McCarthy (Boston: Beacon Press, 1979).

Habermas. The ideal of deliberative democracy shades over into the ideal speech situation ethic, the idea that any ethical claim implicitly supposes that it could be redeemed in an ideal deliberative procedure in which no force except the force of the better argument prevails. If sufficient stress is laid on the idea of *rational* consent to rules directed toward the common good, the possibility of conflict between majority-rule procedures and the attainment of substantively just outcomes can be eliminated. But this very idealized democratic conception at this lofty level of abstraction is then left virtually without links to any recognizable notion of socialism in the sense of public ownership. In fact, the ideal of Habermasian deliberative democracy does not clearly support movement in the real world toward democratic rather than authoritarian political institutions. What has happened is that the ideal of deliberative democracy, so idealized, has become a hypothetical-rationality test, roughly a restatement of the Rawlsian ideal of wide reflective equilibrium. But this is a purely formal notion that has in itself no substantive ethical or political content.

To appreciate this point, imagine a king or Communist Party official who accepts the Habermasian deliberative-democracy ideal but denies that it has practical implications regarding the dismantling of autocratic state structures. The king or bureaucrat seeks to justify the policies of the state by showing that these are policies that all citizens qua rational and moral would endorse if they underwent an ideal process of deliberation with full information. To show that this "hypothetical-rationality" test is met, one would need to argue for the rationality and morality of the policies pursued by the autocratic regime. Doing this need not involve actually setting up democratic deliberation procedures with actual members of society. Since citizens do not in fact come remotely close to conforming to the hypothetical-rationality norm, whether they *actually* consent or not to state policies (the autocrat argues) does not bear on the justifiability of those policies. Nor would it necessarily be wise to try to do as much as we can to create circumstances in which the conditions of free, rational dialogue among all citizens are approximated as fully as possible. We could not come close at all, due to the ineliminable limited rationality of the vast majority of citizens. To try to create free, rational dialogue would recreate the unholy chaos of the Tower of Babel. In the real world, given the strikingly different capacities for rational dialogue possessed by individual citizens, something approximating free dialogue is best limited to elite circles, the memberships of which are carefully screened. Or so the autocrat argues. To argue against the autocrat, one cannot simply invoke the ideal-deliberation norm, since the autocrat I am imagining accepts it. The norm identifies moral truth with whatever ideally rational and conscientiously motivated people would agree to in an ideal conversation. Acceptance of this norm in no way commits one to the democratic faith that political decision making should be made to conform to the results of the best real-world deliberation one can achieve among nonideal citizens followed by majority vote.

The Habermasian ideal is that society should be governed by a rational unanimous consensus. I have been interpreting the ideal as a purely formal counterfactual test for correct norms and policies: society should be governed by the rational norms that would emerge from an ideal conversation leading to unanimous consensus among fully rational dialogue participants. One could instead interpret the norm as the claim that society should be governed by the decisions emerging from an actual democratic process that is made to approximate as closely as possible an ideal conversation that would precipitate unanimous rational consensus. This latter construal does support democracy here and now. But on the latter construal, the norm strikes me as an unstable hybrid. Why should we wish to be governed by the decisions reached through democratic deliberation unless we think that these decisions are more likely to be substantively correct than the decisions that would be reached by some other procedure? If the noncounterfactually construed democratic-deliberation norm says we should be for democracy whatever the consequences, the norm deserves to be rejected. In the real world, whether we should take steps to try to alter democratic procedures in order to bring it about that they maximally resemble an ideal conversation depends on the likely consequences of putting these alterations into effect.

In short, the ideal of deliberative democracy is uncontroversial only if formally interpreted as a counterfactual test of moral claims on the lines of the Rawlsian wide reflective equilibrium idea. Interpreted nonformally, the ideal of deliberative democracy is a highly controversial democratic faith—an unlikely substitute for a conception of social justice and surely no substitute for a socialist conception of social justice.

CONCLUSION

I have argued that the democratic conception of socialism, the view that socialism is an extension of the democratic ideal, is flawed. I have examined various facets of the democratic conception. In some cases the democratic claims that form this conception are ethically unappealing regarded by themselves; in some cases these claims have no plausible connection to the socialist program of reconstruction straightforwardly construed; and in some cases both objections hold. On the democratic interpretation, socialism aims to facilitate collective self-determination. On the distributive interpretation that I favor, socialism aims to enhance the quality of the individual lives of all members of society, but particularly the disadvantaged. On neither interpretation is the socialist program reasonably thought to be discredited by the recent welcome collapse of autocratic Communist regimes in Eastern Europe and the Soviet Union.

Philosophy, University of California, San Diego

LIBERALISM, WELFARE ECONOMICS, AND FREEDOM*

By Daniel M. Hausman

With the collapse of the centrally controlled economies and the authoritarian governments of Eastern Europe and the former Soviet republics, political leaders are, with appreciable public support, espousing "liberal" economic and political transformations—the reinstitution of markets, the securing of civil and political rights, and the establishment of representative governments. But those supporting reform have many aims, and the liberalism to which they look for political guidance is not an unambiguous doctrine.

In this essay, I shall be concerned to explore what light, if any, is cast on practical problems facing liberal reformers in Eastern Europe by an examination of some abstract problems concerning the foundations of liberalism and the relations between liberalism and economic theory. I have my doubts about the practical relevance of this philosophical inquiry. Liberal reformers in Eastern Europe and the former Soviet republics have so few humane and nontotalitarian alternatives that the question of which are the most faithful to liberalism may be moot. But I shall nevertheless indulge in the luxury of thinking about the foundations of liberalism and about how a liberal should appraise forms of economic organization. I shall argue that liberalism is not committed to assessing policies by their impact on individual preferences and that despite the many affinities between liberalism and contemporary economic theory, liberals should be wary of welfare economics. There is a good liberal argument for markets, but there are also good reasons for liberals to be concerned to regulate and limit markets.

Unfortunately, this essay is not informed by detailed knowledge of the circumstances in the former Soviet bloc, but then neither is most of the advice provided by Western economists. Although I try to apply my general conclusions about the character of a liberal attitude toward markets to the circumstances of contemporary reformers in Eastern Europe and the former Soviet republics, my focus is on the relations between liberalism and economics and on clarifying what a liberal attitude toward markets should be.

All variants of liberalism highly value "negative" liberties—the absence of coercive interference with the actions of individuals. Why? Although

* I am indebted to Andrew Levine, to Michael McPherson, and to the other contributors to this volume, for helpful criticisms.

© 1993 Social Philosophy and Policy Foundation. Printed in the USA.

liberties might be regarded as themselves intrinsically valuable (as an essential aspect of intrinsically valuable human activities and experiences), I shall suppose that negative liberties are so highly valued mainly because they are means to something else that is highly valued. What might that something else be? I shall examine three related answers:[1] Liberties are valuable because they enable people to get what they want, because they are necessary if people are to live autonomously, and because they are entailed by principles of equal respect. If autonomy is getting what one wants, and equal respect presupposes autonomy and demands its promotion, or if all people want to live autonomously, then these answers may coincide. So we cannot take for granted that these answers are distinct, though later I shall argue that they are.

There is some basis within liberalism for all three answers. Although liberals have been deeply concerned with individual welfare, I do not think that welfare concerns are distinctively liberal, and, as I shall argue below in Section IV, neither is the identification of welfare with the satisfaction of preferences. In my view, the second account of the value of liberty, which stresses autonomy, best explains why liberals think liberty is so important to individuals. Equal respect or impartiality,[2] on the other hand, provides the best account of the political importance of liberties. It matters which answer one offers, for the answers lead to different normative social theories and to different practical advice for contemporary reformers. Interpreting autonomy and equality as the central values of liberalism — with autonomy grounding individual concern with liberties and equal respect providing the foundation for the political case for liberty — gives a better rationale for central theses of contemporary liberalism and a better way of appraising plans for the restoration of markets.

I. Why Are Liberal Reforms Wanted?

At a superficial level, the answer to this question is obvious enough. Most of the Eastern European economies have virtually collapsed. Individuals and groups are angry about restrictions on speech, religion, movement, and life style, and about the violence, suspicion, and fear con-

---

[1] There are some echoes here of C. B. Macpherson's contrast in "Maximizing Democracy" between justifying liberal regimes by claiming that they maximize utility and justifying them by claiming that they maximize individual powers. See Macpherson, "Maximizing Democracy," in his *Democratic Theory: Essays in Retrieval* (Oxford: Clarendon Press, 1973), pp. 2–10.

[2] As authors such as Samuel Scheffler and Thomas Nagel convincingly argue, equal respect does not in general entail impartiality, and it is certainly not the same thing. But in the context of political theory or of the theory of social justice, equal respect is equivalent to a certain interpretation of impartiality. See Scheffler, *The Rejection of Consequentialism* (Oxford: Clarendon Press, 1982), chs. 2 and 3; and Nagel, *The View from Nowhere* (Oxford: Oxford University Press, 1986), ch. 11, and *Equality and Partiality* (Oxford: Oxford University Press, 1991).

sequent on the enforcement of these restrictions. And individuals and interest groups want more of a voice in decision making. The liberal reforms are motivated by desires for economic betterment, for freedom, and for political power.

Even the dissatisfaction with the economies has multiple sources. The collapse of the centrally planned economies was not a matter of their failure to function at all, but of their failure to function "well enough." In particular, (1) they failed to provide the same variety, quality, and abundance of consumer goods that successful market economies have provided; (2) they were plagued by persistent and irritating shortages, by long waits for an arbitrary and ever-changing miscellany of commodities or services;[3] (3) their inefficiencies and environmental catastrophes were blatant, and they failed to encourage innovations in products or production techniques; and (4) their economies, like their political systems, restricted individual liberty. Centrally planned economies did not provide the goods; they were clumsy, wasteful, destructive, and inefficient; and they did not leave individuals free to pursue their own projects. The current stampede toward the reintroduction of markets is thus driven by multiple motives. It is not clear what people want markets for, and it is not clear how they are going to respond to the myriad changes, many of which will be painful, that the introduction of markets will bring. Greater affluence will take time. Markets have their own wastes, inefficiencies, and irrationality, which may take some getting used to. And the freedom markets provide to those who are extremely impoverished takes some philosophical sophistication to appreciate (though the population in Eastern Europe may be in a particularly good position to appreciate it). If those regimes and policies that best satisfy preferences do not coincide with those that best protect liberty and rights, one can expect these theoretical tensions to issue in political conflict.[4]

To varying degrees, citizens of former Soviet-bloc countries also seek liberal political regimes that guarantee civil and political rights and pro-

---

[3] A joke circulating in Leningrad (now St. Petersburg) in 1988: Two men are waiting in a long line to buy something. They wait and they wait. Finally one says, "I've had it. I'm going to shoot Gorbachev." And he runs off. Two hours pass and he returns. His friend, who is still in line, asks, "So what happened? Did you shoot him?" "No, the line was too long."

[4] Market socialism has been almost entirely removed from the agenda because of the association of socialism with authoritarian government and because of the association of capitalism with affluence. Even many of those who have studied market socialism seriously are dismissive. For example, Jànos Kornai comments in *The Road to a Free Economy — Shifting from a Socialist System: The Example of Hungary* (New York: W. W. Norton & Company, 1990), p. 58: "I wish to use strong words here, without any adornment: the basic idea of market socialism simply fizzled out. Yugoslavia, Hungary, China, the Soviet Union, and Poland bear witness to its fiasco." It seems to me that the evidence is inconclusive and that some forms of market socialism might in fact be better able to satisfy the conflicting aims governing the current transformations. See John Roemer, "The Morality and Efficiency of Market Socialism," *Ethics*, vol. 102 (1992), pp. 448–64.

vide some measure of democracy. The sort of democracy that is at issue is "a system in which parties lose elections."[5] The rallying cries are "freedom" and, owing to the Soviet rewriting of twentieth-century history, "truth."[6] Democracy is desirable not only because it interferes with monopolies of political control and makes possible a measure of political power for groups representing more of the population, but also because it helps insure individual liberties. Democratic political reforms are thus also driven by the value of freedom. Although the severe problems in consolidating democratic reforms and liberal regimes constrain the pace and character of economic reform, I shall not be directly concerned with issues concerning democracy or political structure. My focus is instead on markets.

The values that lie behind the reforms are freedom, empowerment, welfare, and efficiency. Since these values are prominent in liberalism and since liberalism has traditionally been aligned with the institutions the Eastern Europeans seek to acquire, it is easy to see the attraction of liberalism to the reformers. But what exactly *is* liberalism?

II. What Is Liberalism?

No doctrine, such as liberalism, which has evolved over centuries and has excited the passions of millions,[7] can be cleanly defined. Although the word "liberalism" can be treated as referring to one or another well-defined philosophical view, the term refers in the first instance to a powerful ideology.

In calling liberalism an ideology, I do not mean to criticize it. The term "ideology" has well-known pejorative uses, and indeed these uses are so well known that it is dangerous to use the term nonpejoratively. For my purposes, the defining feature of ideologies is that they provide a general picture of how human beings and society "in essence" (but for various interferences) are, which is simultaneously a picture of how they ought to be.

---

[5] Adam Przeworski, *Democracy and the Market: Political and Economic Reforms in Eastern Europe and Latin America* (Cambridge: Cambridge University Press, 1991), p. 10. This book is a brilliant recent study of the problems that arise when one attempts to introduce democracy at the same time as attempting economic transformation. Contemporary "democracies" are, of course, not what the Greeks or Rousseau had in mind when they spoke of "democracy," and their undemocratic features are well known.

[6] But one should not exaggerate: "In spite of Vaclav Havel's eloquent eulogies to the subversive power of truth, the spiritual force that provided the lasting source of opposition to communism was not a yearning for liberty (as distinguished from independence from the Soviet Union), but religion and nationalism; indeed, the historically specific amalgam of the two" (Przeworski, *Democracy and the Market*, p. 93).

[7] A friend regarded this phrase as comical, and commented that "liberalism has always been a recourse of those whose passions for more and better have been for one reason or another quashed." It is hard to picture the romantic liberal revolutionary. But I shall stand by this phrase.

Liberalism, like all ideologies, embodies a simplified vision of human nature and of the character of social relations. Nobody believes that this vision is the whole truth, or indeed any truth at all, without qualifications and disclaimers. But this vision provides a caricature in terms of which human and social phenomena can be interpreted. In the liberal sketch, human beings are rational, self-interested individuals who pursue many different ends. They are individuals who are capable of choosing their own course and who are responsible for their choices. Inequalities are mainly the result of social contingencies rather than reflections of fundamental differences among individuals.[8] Social phenomena consist mainly of voluntary interactions among these individuals.

But ideologies are not just simplified visions of human nature and society. They also embody ideals concerning how people and society ought to be, and they identify the way people and society in their simplest outlines are (or would be, but for some interferences) with the way they ought to be. So liberals not only regard individuals as fundamentally equal and rational, they believe that they should be. People deserve equal respect in virtue of their common capacity to form and act on life plans. Diversity is unavoidable and desirable, for individuals are not only capable of choosing their own way, but autonomous self-development is an ideal. Perhaps self-interest is not an ideal, but it is unavoidable. And with the freeing of human beings from the shackles of feudal restraints or the intrusions of socialist experiments, social phenomena can become what they ought to be — the voluntary transactions of rational and autonomous individuals commanding equal respect and pursuing their own separate and diverse ends. Social phenomena ought ideally to consist only of voluntary arrangements, because individuals value freedom itself and because when they are freer, they are better able to achieve their ends. Government is a necessary evil.

The core values implicit in this ideal are, I believe, freedom (in some sense) and equality. By "equality," the liberal means something more like a Kantian notion of equal respect or equal worth than distributive egalitarianism. Equality is, in Ronald Dworkin's view, the central liberal value.[9] In Dworkin's view, individuals and institutions treat people

---

[8] In chapter 13 of part I of Thomas Hobbes's *Leviathan*, equality is reflected in the ability of individuals to kill one another. Adam Smith makes a more radical claim: "The difference of natural talents in different men is, in reality, much less than we are aware of; and the very different genius which appears to distinguish men of different professions, when grown up to maturity, is not upon many occasions so much the cause, as the effect of the division of labour." See Smith, *An Inquiry into the Nature and Causes of the Wealth of Nations* [1776] (New York: Modern Library, 1937), book I, ch. 2. But the relevant sense of equality has less to do with people's abilities than with how they should be treated.

[9] Ronald Dworkin, "Liberalism," in Stuart Hampshire, ed., *Public and Private Morality* (Cambridge: Cambridge University Press, 1978); reprinted in and cited from Dworkin, *A Matter of Principle* (Cambridge: Harvard University Press, 1985), p. 183. See also Charles Larmore, *Patterns of Moral Complexity* (Cambridge: Cambridge University Press, 1987), pp. 59–66.

equally when they show equal concern for everyone's fate, treat the ambitions, talents, and objectives of all as equally worthy of respect, and show no favoritism among different lives.[10] It is in virtue of their capacity for autonomy that individuals deserve equal respect. The freedoms the liberal values include civil, political, and economic liberties as well as *autonomy*. The term "autonomy" can be used to refer to a *capacity* to govern oneself, a *condition* of self-governing, an *ideal*, or a matter of moral *authority*.[11] The liberal values both the capacity for autonomy, which provides the basis for equal respect, and the condition of autonomy, which is what I am referring to when I speak of "autonomy." That condition is itself very complex.[12] Autonomy is not the satisfaction of preferences, even if one's preferences are themselves rationally defensible and result from no coercive manipulation. For autonomy is active. It involves satisfying one's own preferences rather than having them satisfied. And autonomy also involves aspects such as self-possession, individuality, authenticity, integrity, self-control, initiative, and responsibility.[13] So preference satisfaction, autonomy, and equality are indeed distinct values. Although I have not said much about rights, which liberals have traditionally emphasized, my account is fully consistent with this emphasis. For rights are grounded on the fundamental concerns with liberty and equal respect.

The connections between ideology and any sophisticated body of liberal theory are often too obvious to be worth pointing out. One learns relatively little, I think, about Locke's or Mill's views by pointing out that they place flesh on skeletal liberal views of how society is and ought to be. This is unsurprising. Ideologies are typically of more interest to sociologists than to philosophers. But awareness of an underlying ideological commitment may help one to appreciate the motivation behind some bit of theory. It may point to implicit connections between separate views. And it may reveal significant tensions, particularly when ideological commitments are put into action. For ideologies, much more than sophisticated theories, motivate and direct social movements; and ambiguities or tensions within ideologies can consequently have great practical significance.

As this essay will maintain, there is an important ambiguity or conflict within liberalism concerning whether liberties are highly valued as impli-

---

[10] Dworkin, "Liberalism," pp. 192–93.

[11] Joel Feinberg, *Harm to Self* (Oxford: Oxford University Press, 1986), p. 28.

[12] See especially *ibid.*, pp. 31f.; Gerald Dworkin, *The Theory and Practice of Autonomy* (Cambridge: Cambridge University Press, 1988), ch. 1; Arthur Kuflik, "The Inalienability of Autonomy," *Philosophy and Public Affairs*, vol. 13 (1984), esp. pp. 271f.; and John Christman, "Liberalism and Individual Positive Freedom," *Ethics*, vol. 101 (1991), esp. pp. 347f. See also John Christman, ed., *The Inner Citadel: Essays on Individual Autonomy* (New York: Oxford University Press, 1989).

[13] Feinberg, *Harm to Self*, pp. 32, 40–44.

cations of equal respect, as prerequisites of autonomy, or as facilitating the satisfaction of preferences. Recognizing this ambiguity helps one to appreciate the complex relations between standard economic theory and liberal ideology, and it helps one to recognize the hard choices to be made by those who currently seek to reinstitute markets. Again, let me caution that in linking economics to liberal ideology, I intend no criticism of either liberalism or economics. For even if liberal ideology were false and wicked, a particular articulation of it might not be either false or wicked, and the fact that liberalism is an ideology implies nothing about its truth or virtue. In fact, I shall for the most part write as if I were a committed liberal.

III. Liberalism, Economics, and Economic Welfare

Liberalism seems to be closely linked to contemporary "neoclassical" economic theory. In standard "positive" economic theory, as in liberal ideology, individuals are rational and self-interested, though now in very precise senses. They interact voluntarily; and the economy is, as a first approximation, nothing but the consequences of the voluntary interactions of these individuals. Only distantly in the background is there a legal order with an assignment of legal rights. Positive economics provides a partial articulation of the liberal vision of human nature and social life.

On the normative side, the unfettered operation of the market guarantees a certain sort of economic freedom. Indeed, the market accomplishes the seemingly impossible task of providing social organization without any social organizer, of harmonizing individual plans without overt coercion. Although there are inequalities in income and wealth, markets show a sort of equal respect (or equal lack of respect) to individuals. Dollars, commodities, and services count, not individuals. Furthermore, as thinkers such as Milton Friedman have argued, the separation of political and economic power and the diffusion of economic power are the best protection of the whole range of individual and political liberties.[14]

Although economists take individual liberty seriously and are attracted to markets because of the liberty they permit, it is remarkable how few argue for markets on the grounds that they protect individual freedom. On the contrary, the main issue in standard normative economics is to what extent market economies enable individuals to satisfy their preferences. Theorems in theoretical economics establish the existence of perfectly competitive equilibria coordinating the plans of rational individuals. The two central theorems of welfare economics then show that every perfectly competitive equilibrium is Pareto optimal and that every Pareto-optimal allocation is obtainable as a perfectly competitive equilibrium given

---

[14] Milton Friedman, *Capitalism and Freedom* (Chicago: University of Chicago Press, 1962), ch. 1.

the appropriate distribution of initial endowments among the agents. Although a Pareto optimum is typically defined as a state of affairs in which it is impossible to make anyone better off without making someone worse off, this purported definition is misleading. R is a Pareto improvement over S if nobody *prefers* S to R and somebody *prefers* R to S. S is a Pareto optimum if and only if there are no Pareto improvements over S. If one identifies, as economists commonly do, preference and well-being, then this last definition implies the misleading standard definition.

At the foundation of both positive and normative economics lies a thin normative theory of individual rationality.[15] An agent A chooses (acts) rationally if A's preferences are rational, and A never prefers an available option to the option chosen. Preferences are rational only if they are complete and transitive.[16] If an agent's preferences are complete and transitive, one can assign numbers to the objects of preference. These numbers, which are arbitrary apart from their order, merely indicate preference ranking. They are "utilities," and the theory of rationality may be restated this way: Agents are rational if and only if their preferences may be represented by ordinal utility functions, and they act in a way that maximizes utility.[17] I intentionally avoided the more natural phrase that they act "in order to maximize utility." For utility is merely an index or indicator. It is not a substantive aim or an object of preference. Maximizing utility is just doing what one most prefers to do. Rationality is having complete and transitive preferences and choosing what one most prefers.

Other things being equal, it is a good thing to be rational. Indeed, the word "rational" is a synonym for "prudent." But it is not necessarily in one's best interest to do whatever one prefers to do. For one's preferences may be based on ignorance, or one may prefer to sacrifice one's own well-being for something that matters more. Satisfying Gertrude's desire for wine in the last act of *Hamlet* failed to make her better off, probably for one of these reasons.[18] To some extent, economists paper-over these difficulties by appropriating the evaluative term, "rational." In addition, since most economic models assume that agents have full in-

---

[15] The view of economics sketched over the next few pages is developed at length in my recent book, *The Inexact and Separate Science of Economics* (Cambridge: Cambridge University Press, 1992). See particularly chapters 1, 2, 4, and 15.

[16] An agent A's preferences are complete if and only if for all alternatives x and y, A prefers x to y or y to x or is indifferent between x and y. A's preferences are transitive if for all alternatives x, y, and z, whenever A prefers x to y and y to z, then A prefers x to z, and similarly for indifference.

[17] If there is an uncountable infinity of options, then the existence of a continuous utility function also presupposes that an agent's preferences are continuous. See Gerard Debreu, *The Theory of Value* (New York: Wiley, 1959), pp. 54–59.

[18] Apart from these obvious difficulties, there are subtler philosophical objections which I shall not comment on. See James Griffin, *Well-Being: Its Meaning, Measurement, and Moral Importance* (Oxford: Clarendon Press, 1986), part I; and Richard Arneson, "Liberalism, Distributive Subjectivism, and Equal Opportunity for Welfare," *Philosophy and Public Affairs*, vol. 19 (1990), pp. 158–94. My interpretation of *Hamlet* is, no doubt, contestable.

formation and are self-interested, they typically exclude the difficulties mentioned above. Most positive theory also treats preferences for commodities and services as givens. There is little work on preference formation, on "adaptive preferences,"[19] on cognitive dissonance,[20] or on other grounds for the criticism of actual preferences. Markets are not a political forum in which one's *reasons* matter. All of this makes it easier to accept the view that what people prefer is what is good for them. Because of these features of positive economics, into which the model of rationality is incorporated, economists feel little discomfort in identifying rational and prudent action with doing whatever one most prefers to do.

This account of rationality is also an account of individual well-being, which is one crucial component of ethical theory. Economists are implicitly saying that x is better than y for A if and only if A prefers x to y. This theory of rationality is a theory of human well-being. So normative economics and the theory of economic rationality are closely linked.

The theory of rationality is embedded directly into positive economics. If one adds to the theory of rationality the generalization that real people are to some extent rational in the sense defined, then one has the central nomological components of the positive theory of economic choices. More is added, of course, concerning the objects of preference and rates of substitution. But in economics the theory of rational choice is simultaneously the theory of actual choice.

Positive economics can be formulated without using the word, "rational." Rather than first defining "rational" and then stating that individuals are in fact to some extent rational, one can instead assert directly that to a considerable extent the preferences of individuals are in reality complete and transitive and that individuals in fact usually choose whatever they most prefer. But the identification of the actual with the rational is not a trivial feature of a given formulation. As already noted, the identification of rational and actual choice permits peculiarities of positive economic theories to cloak inadequacies in the theory of prudence that is implicit in the theory of economic rationality. Acceptance of the positive theory leads to acceptance of the theory of rationality. Conversely, as I have argued elsewhere, the fact that the economic theory of rational choice is simultaneously a theory of actual choice increases the plausibility of the positive theory and makes it more resistant to disconfirmation.[21] Commitment to the theory of rationality leads to commitment to the positive theory.

[19] Jon Elster, "Sour Grapes—Utilitarianism and the Genesis of Wants," in Amartya Sen and Bernard Williams, eds., *Utilitarianism and Beyond* (Cambridge: Cambridge University Press, 1982), pp. 219–38.

[20] See George Akerlof and William Dickens, "The Economic Consequences of Cognitive Dissonance," *American Economic Review*, vol. 72 (1982), pp. 307–19.

[21] Hausman, *The Inexact and Separate Science of Economics*, ch. 12.

Via the theory of rationality, one thus finds tight connections between positive and normative economics. These are the sorts of links that one would expect to find in an articulation of an ideology. Noticing these links helps resolve an apparent paradox. For, on the one hand, economists do not see themselves as moral philosophers, and they attempt to steer clear of controversial ethical commitments when doing theoretical welfare economics. Indeed, economists have sometimes supposed that theoretical welfare economics was independent of all value judgments whatsoever. Yet, on the other hand, when welfare economists address policy questions, they speak with apparent moral authority. They purport to know how to make life better.

What explains this apparent contradiction is that economists do not regard the identification of well-being with the satisfaction of preferences as a controversial ethical judgment. It is just part of the standard view of rationality. And once one accepts this identification, one need only add an uncontroversial principle of minimal benevolence to get strong policy recommendations via the following argument:[22]

Suppose that one identifies individual well-being with the satisfaction of preferences and that one accepts the moral principle of minimal benevolence: other things being equal, it is a morally good thing if people are better off. Then it is, other things being equal, a morally good thing to satisfy an individual's preferences. So Pareto improvements are (other things being equal) moral improvements, and Pareto optima are (other things being equal) morally desirable. Given the first welfare theorem (that perfectly competitive equilibria are Pareto optimal), one can conclude that, other things being equal, perfectly competitive equilibria are morally desirable and market imperfections that interfere with the achievement of competitive equilibria are morally undesirable. Note that this is a defense of perfect competition, not a defense of actual markets or of a laissez-faire policy.

That it is a good thing to satisfy preferences follows unproblematically from minimal benevolence and the identification of well-being with the satisfaction of preferences. Given the demonstration that perfectly competitive equilibria are Pareto efficient, the conclusion follows that such equilibria are, *ceteris paribus*, morally good and that market failures are, *ceteris paribus*, bad. This moral conclusion is highly theoretical, because real economies are not perfectly competitive and because of the "other things being equal" qualification. The conclusion is sufficiently abstract that both conservative defenders of laissez faire and liberal defenders of activist government economic policy can accept it.

A consideration of the "other things" that are morally relevant leads to ethical controversy, which many economists would like to avoid. Indeed,

---

[22] This argument is presented in more detail in *ibid.*, section 4.6.

I conjecture that economists so rarely make the case for markets on the grounds of individual liberties and rights, because they believe (mistakenly, in my view) that the liberty and rights arguments are more philosophically controversial and ambitious than the benevolence argument.

Among the "other things" that must be equal is justice, and a Pareto improvement that leads to distributional injustice may be morally undesirable. But the argument above may be continued. Given the second welfare theorem, which says that all Pareto-efficient states of affairs can be obtained as competitive general equilibria from the right initial distribution of endowments to individuals, one can conclude plausibly, although not validly, that all other moral concerns, including concerns about justice, can be satisfied merely by adjusting initial holdings. The conclusion does not follow, because there may be no Pareto-efficient state of affairs that satisfies all other moral constraints. But enough has been said to make explicit how economists can speak with moral authority.

Whether defenders of laissez faire or of extensive government intervention to address market failures, most economists share a moral commitment to the *ideal* of perfect competition. It is this commitment that gives point to the analysis of market failures. (For why should they matter if market successes are not a good thing?) The fact that this commitment appears to presuppose nothing more controversial than minimal benevolence explains how economists can feel themselves possessed of moral authority, without the trouble of doing moral philosophy. Standard theoretical commitments permit moral conclusions (*ceteris paribus*) that apparently rely on only an uncontroversial principle of benevolence. With one big step into the theoretical world of economics (which is a refinement of the liberal vision of human nature and society), rationality, morality, and the positive theory of economic choices become tightly interlinked.

IV. Is Welfare Economics Liberal?

The above argument depicts market arrangements as morally desirable because of their consequences for the satisfaction of given individual preferences. Insofar as liberals are beneficent, they are, of course, concerned with the well-being of others, and, other things being equal, they prefer that others be better off. But the same may be said of beneficent non-liberals. There is nothing peculiarly liberal about a concern with people's well-being. The distinctive normative concerns of liberalism are freedoms, rights, and equality. Qua liberal, one should be more concerned about the extent to which markets serve individual freedom and respect human equality, than with the extent to which markets promote well-being. Thus, many Austrian economists, who identify themselves as classical liberals, are more concerned with the character of economic processes than with economic outcomes;[23] and they defend markets in terms of the liberties they promote and protect. And, as liberals of a very different sort (such as Amartya Sen) have argued, the promotion of freedom and of welfare may not always be compatible.[24]

Nevertheless, I think most economists would be surprised at the charge that welfare economics is nonliberal. Most regard their views as distinctively liberal, for they take the identification of well-being with the satisfaction of preferences as itself a crucial *liberal* premise.

Is it? Is it, as many economists feel, paternalistic to assess people's preferences or to claim to know better than others do what is good for them? Can one maintain that standard welfare economics takes freedom seriously, because it accepts each individual's view of his or her own good? Welfare economists might argue that in its concern with satisfying preferences, normative economics necessarily aims to help individuals to pursue their own projects. It does not attempt to carry out some view of the good endorsed by a paternalistic authority. Even if direct arguments for markets on grounds of freedom and rights are seldom made, one might maintain that the accepted theory of well-being itself embodies a liberal commitment to accepting the judgments of individuals and helping them to get what they want.

Although this argument is seldom made explicitly, it is nevertheless, in my view, tremendously influential. I think that it misconstrues liberalism — though, as I suggested at the very beginning, it might be better to say instead that it points to an ambiguity within liberalism. The liberal's basic commitment is to permit people freely to act on their views of what is good, unless the rights of others are at stake; it is *not* to accept these views as correct. Liberalism is not mainly a theory of human well-being, and indeed many contemporary liberals have stressed the *neutrality* of liberalism among various theories of well-being.[25] It appears that the liberal

---

[23] See particularly James Buchanan and Viktor Vanberg, "The Market as a Creative Process," *Economics and Philosophy*, vol. 7 (1991), pp. 167–86. Robert Nozick's influential defense of libertarianism, *Anarchy, State, and Utopia* (New York: Basic Books, 1974), argues that questions of justice are completely independent of welfare appraisals.

[24] See Amartya Sen, "The Impossibility of a Paretian Liberal," *Journal of Political Economy*, vol. 78 (1970), pp. 152–57, and "Liberty and Social Choice," *Journal of Philosophy*, vol. 80 (1983), pp. 5–28.

[25] As Joseph Raz points out in chapter 5 of *The Morality of Freedom* (Oxford: Clarendon Press, 1986), one can interpret neutrality as a constraint on the *effects* of policies or on the kinds of *arguments* one can use in support of policies. Will Kymlicka — in "Liberal Individualism and Liberal Neutrality," *Ethics*, vol. 99 (1989), p. 884 — calls these two notions of neutrality, "consequential" and "justificatory." I follow Kymlicka in regarding justificatory neutrality as the correct interpretation. See also Larmore, *Patterns of Moral Complexity*, p. 44. Although defenders of neutrality are not always clear on the point, neutrality is intended as a constraint on *political* argument. Liberalism itself is not uncommitted or neutral concerning views of the good.

is committed not to helping individuals to get what they want but to enabling them freely to pursue their projects.[26]

But is this appearance correct? What if individuals do not want to struggle with their own projects? What if they prefer comfort to autonomy? What if they read *Brave New World* as a genuine utopia? If the liberal is truly neutral among conceptions of the good life, should not the liberal then be concerned about satisfying these preferences rather than increasing freedom? And if under real circumstances, the liberal is concerned with permitting people freely to pursue their own projects, is this not because people *want* this freedom? Isn't the liberal, after all, committed to identifying well-being with the satisfaction of preferences and to supporting those social policies which best satisfy preferences? If the point of freedom is to enable people to get what they want, then welfare economics encompasses the crucial liberal value of freedom. Or so a defender of the liberal credentials of welfare economics might argue.

The first thing to notice about this argument is that does not support identifying well-being with the satisfaction of *actual* preferences. The concern to permit Gertrude to pursue her own projects, to respect her decisions, or to treat her as of equal worth does not commit one to hand over the poisoned wine without argument. And indeed, the concern to permit people to live their own lives may justify frustrating preferences when they are the result of mistake or coercive manipulation. In response to these obvious objections to identifying well-being with the satisfaction of actual preferences, most economists would probably deny that they are defending any philosophical theory of well-being. The satisfaction of actual preferences is intended only as a good indicator of increasing welfare. Further conditions must be met before it is true that satisfying preferences necessarily increases well-being. Preferences may need to be "laundered" in various ways. But for practical policy purposes, these conditions can be ignored. Liberal neutrality commits policy makers to identifying well-being for practical purposes with the satisfaction of actual preferences. In Richard Arneson's words:

> [T]he primary concern of the liberal state should be the impact of its policies in utility terms on all affected persons. "Utility" here is a measure of the value of each individual's life from that very individual's perspective. The preferences and values of each individual regarding how she wishes her life to go (corrected by hypothetical rational deliberation with full information) supply the proper measure of value for that individual's life. The proper business of the state is to assist the individual in living the life she wants, getting

---

[26] See Loren Lomasky, *Persons, Rights, and the Moral Community* (Oxford: Oxford University Press, 1987), esp. chs. 2 and 3, for a powerful argument that libertarianism derives from an appreciation of the centrality of individual *projects*.

what she most wants from life, and, in addition, to bring it about that the process by which each individual's basic preferences are initially formed, and perhaps altered over the life course, is healthy, fair, and nonmanipulative.[27]

A welfare economist might then go on to argue that, given the purposes of economic policy and the informational constraints on political action, this liberal concern with satisfying and cultivating rational and unmanipulated preferences reduces in practice to the task of satisfying actual preferences. So welfare economics *is* liberal.

This argument fails in two ways. First, even if liberal neutrality supported identifying well-being with the satisfaction of rational, informed, or laundered preferences, it does not follow that satisfying actual preferences is the best practical expedient. It might, for example, be better to address policy to meeting needs. Second, liberal neutrality does not support identifying well-being with the satisfaction of properly spruced-up preferences. For to say that well-being is the satisfaction of rational preferences is to espouse one theory of well-being, not to be neutral among theories of well-being.

The state must not espouse a single theory of the good because, in John Rawls's view, doing so would undercut the nonsectarian justification of principles of justice as fair terms of cooperation for individuals, regardless of their conception of the good.[28] Liberal political institutions are a *modus vivendi* which individuals and groups with widely different views of the good can accept.[29] In Ronald Dworkin's view, the state fails to treat citizens with equal respect if it favors the conception of the good held by some individuals over that held by others.[30] Provided that their actions do not violate principles of justice or the rights of others, those who deny that the good is the satisfaction of rational preferences must be treated equally, and liberal principles of justice should be justifiable to them. These must be principles "which no one could reasonably reject as a basis for informed, unforced general agreement."[31] Liberal neutrality is not itself a "comprehensive moral doctrine" with its own theory of the good. It is instead a political implementation of impartiality or equal respect.

One might complain that the above objection is just philosophical pedantry. The requirement that the state not espouse a view of the good ap-

---

[27] Richard Arneson, "Liberalism, Freedom, and Community," *Ethics*, vol. 100 (1990), p. 377.

[28] John Rawls, "Justice as Fairness: Political not Metaphysical," *Philosophy and Public Affairs*, vol. 14 (1985), pp. 245–46.

[29] Larmore, *Patterns of Moral Complexity*, pp. 70–77.

[30] Dworkin, "Liberalism," p. 191.

[31] Thomas Scanlon, "Contractualism and Utilitarianism," in Amartya Sen and Bernard Williams, eds., *Utilitarianism and Beyond* (Cambridge: Cambridge University Press, 1982), p. 110.

plies only to *substantive* theories, not to the formal view that the good is the satisfaction of rational preference. For in accepting that theory, one is committed to neutrality among all the particular things that people rationally value. Regardless of what theory of well-being individuals accept, they still prefer what they believe to be good. Insofar as the state aims to satisfy rational preferences and weights everyone's preferences equally, it gives their views of well-being equal weight. The only exceptions are views of well-being that demand that the state act in a non-neutral and paternalistic way or that would have the state do less than it can to help individuals achieve their goods.

There are three responses to this argument. First, one might object that basing "neutrality" on a theory of the good as the satisfaction of preferences does precisely what Rawls and Dworkin seek to avoid: it makes political neutrality the doctrine of a particular ethical sect. Indeed, one might go on to maintain that although political neutrality can have many justifications, some of these must themselves be neutral.[32] Rather than expressing fair terms to coordinate behavior and to adjudicate conflicts of interest among individuals with different views of well-being, the "neutrality" that results from taking well-being to be the satisfaction of preferences would be a means for pursuing collectively a particular view of well-being.[33]

I am reluctant to place too much weight on this response, because I question whether political neutrality has a neutral justification.[34] I am inclined to think that it is a liberal view that follows from liberal values. Political neutrality can appeal to nonliberals who to some extent share liberal values, and it offers many the opportunity to pursue their own conception of the good (within the constraints of justice). It even holds open the possibility that nonliberal ways of life may flourish, while liberal ideals wither. But I am skeptical that political neutrality can be justified neutrally.

Second, the anti-paternalism that follows from identifying well-being with the satisfaction of preferences may fail in subtle ways to show equal respect. Those who deny that well-being is the satisfaction of preferences — who include among their number many good liberals — are, so it seems, not impeded in their activities, but the justification for their liberty is that they are mistaken about well-being. Does the state treat a per-

---

[32] Larmore, *Patterns of Moral Complexity*, p. 53.

[33] In *The Morality of Freedom*, pp. 138–39, Raz distinguishes "political welfarism," the doctrine that the state should not attend to individual ideals and should focus instead on satisfying desires, from "moral welfarism," the doctrine that what is good for individuals is whatever satisfies their actual or rational desires. Moral welfarism, unlike political welfarism, does not need any principle excluding valid ideals from influencing political decisions, because it denies that there are any. The moral welfarist is not a defender of liberal neutrality.

[34] I am here indebted to Guy Perez.

son P with equal respect, when its reason for not interfering with P's pursuits is its assumption that they are misconceived?

Third, one can question whether taking the good to be the satisfaction of rational preferences really does justify political neutrality. If the state aims to increase well-being, and well-being is the satisfaction of preferences, ought not the state to do what it can (noncoercively and non-manipulatively) to insure that individuals form preferences that can be readily satisfied?[35] Even though the state places no greater weight on satisfying the preferences of a Protestant than on satisfying the preferences of a Catholic, the state might tax Catholic churches more heavily or limit their access to the media on the grounds that the preferences of Catholics are harder to satisfy. A liberal concern that processes of preference formation be free of coercion and manipulation places loose constraints on how far the state can go in such activities, but it does not rule them out. The only grounds for rejecting such policies as not merely impractical in particular circumstances, but as illiberal, lie in the values of autonomy and equal respect.

There is no reason to link political neutrality to a theory of well-being as the satisfaction of preferences. Nor is this theory of well-being central to liberalism (though it is not an anti-liberal view of well-being either). Central to liberalism is a different view of well-being: One lives well only if one lives autonomously.[36] Although there are a wide variety of good lives, they are all autonomous lives. They are all lives of self-determination, in which individuals possess the material and cultural means and the intellectual and emotional capacities to reflect upon their characters and activities and to affirm them or, to some extent, to alter them. Autonomous individuals are capable of "thinking for themselves," and as they mature they refine their intellects and emotions. The good life need not be highly intellectual or devoted to reflection, but it must be a life in which human capacities are cultivated rather than stunted and in which people are capable of choosing for themselves how to live. Liberals value their own freedom from coercion not mainly because it enables them to get what they want, but because it helps them to live autonomously. Liberals support political neutrality not because it enables people to get whatever they prefer, nor because it helps people to live autonomously, but mainly because it is required by their view of equal respect.

Joseph Raz takes an opposing view. In linking nonpaternalistic liberal policies to the value of autonomy, he repudiates neutrality altogether:

> Moral pluralism asserts the existence of a multitude of incompatible but morally valuable forms of life. It is coupled with an advocacy

---

[35] See Nagel, *Equality and Partiality*, pp. 165–66.
[36] See Raz, *The Morality of Freedom*, chapters 12, 14, and 15.

of autonomy. It naturally combines with the view that individuals should develop freely to find for themselves the form of the good which they wish to pursue in their life. Both combined lead to political conclusions which are in some ways akin to those of Rawls: political action should be concerned with providing individuals with the means by which they can develop, which enable them to choose and attempt to realize their own conception of the good. But there is nothing here which speaks for neutrality.[37]

Raz takes his views to be a development of liberalism, but I think he overemphasizes autonomy and underemphasizes equality. Although an advocacy of autonomy and a recognition of diversity support extensive liberties, these liberties do not serve only one particular ideal. They do not specifically promote living autonomously. Liberals are not attempting to impose autonomy. On the contrary, like nonliberals, they can only hope that ways of life they value will thrive under a neutral political framework. Liberals favor political neutrality over state policies to promote autonomy, because of their commitment to equality. Respecting the *capacity* for autonomy constrains state policy to promote the *condition* of autonomy. Although the liberal hopes that ideals of individual autonomy will spread, they must not be imposed by the coercive power of the state. To enforce or promote one kind of life is to fail to respect other ways of living and conflicts with a liberal view of equality.

The liberal recognition that there are many kinds of good lives and that individuals should be responsible for choosing their own way does not support identifying well-being with the satisfaction of preferences. Although liberals are as benevolent as anybody else, what is of peculiarly liberal importance is not whether people get what they want, but that they are treated with equal respect and are consequently free to choose for themselves.

Could this liberal commitment to negative freedom be sustained if individuals were not generally good judges of their interests, and if extensive freedoms made them greatly worse off? Do equality and autonomy have so much importance? If one believes, as liberals have, that freedom, equality, and welfare are not antithetical, that in the long run the surest way to benefit people is to protect their rights and enlarge their freedom, then this question need not be faced.[38] But none of these remarks establishes the liberal credentials of welfare economics. Mistakenly optimistic about the possibility of doing welfare economics free of any appreciable taint of moral philosophy, and enchanted with their model of rationality

[37] *Ibid.*, p. 133.

[38] Unfortunately, it is not clear that such optimism is justified. Consider, for example, the alarming contrast between the slow pace of economic development in India, in which individual rights have been protected, and the much more rapid pace of development in China, in which rights have generally not been respected.

and with the positive economics in which it has been embedded, welfare economists have sold their liberal birthright for a mess of welfarism. And those liberals who have misinterpreted the liberal insistence on neutrality as an endorsement of a preference-satisfaction view of well-being have abetted them in their betrayal of the liberal ideals.

So what? Does this ideological backsliding on the part of welfare economists matter? I think it does. What satisfies preferences best does not coincide with what equal respect requires or with what best protects freedom. But this is not an easy case to make, since it is unclear what policies best satisfy people's preferences, what policies are required by equal respect, or what policies best protect freedom.

V. The Liberal Case for Reintroducing Markets

Liberalism is primarily a political doctrine, not an economic theory. Contemporary economic theory develops liberalism's fundamental sketch of individuals and of society, but what matters normatively to liberals are freedom and equality. Economic arrangements should show equal respect by securing individual rights and should promote rather than hinder freedom. But this formula provides little guidance. For though liberals are deeply concerned with individual freedom, they may disagree on what freedom is and whether its value is intrinsic as well as instrumental. Liberals are deeply concerned that individual rights be respected, but they differ in regard to their lists of rights, their reasons for valuing rights so highly, and their views of the obligations that rights ground. Liberals share a commitment to equality, but they differ on its nature, importance, and extent. So it is hard to be precise about what the liberal view of markets should be.

Without insisting on some precisely formulated moral theory, it is nevertheless still possible to make a genuinely liberal case for replacement of central planning with markets. Despite their detailed philosophical disagreements, different liberals can, I think, all endorse three different arguments in defense of markets. Notice that these are only arguments for markets. They are not necessarily arguments against government involvement in economic life, since government action may be needed to cultivate markets. Furthermore, these arguments do not support one particular set of institutions and property rights among the many that are compatible with the existence of extensive markets.

The first argument is not a narrowly liberal argument at all, though it is one liberals should endorse. Questions of affluence are morally important, and would remain so even if they were irrelevant to the core liberal values of freedom and equality. For freedom and equality are not the only important values, and the liberal, like almost everyone else, would like people to be better off. Since markets make people better off, they are (*ceteris paribus*) morally desirable.

This argument depends crucially on the factual premise that markets do make people better off. It might be thought that theoretical welfare economics shows its importance here through the demonstrations that perfect competition satisfies people's preferences optimally and that all optimal allocations can be brought about by competitive markets. But these demonstrations are of little direct significance. What matters is how well actual markets perform in providing what liberals take to be good things. Given the limits of economic knowledge, the best evidence is the historical record: actual market economies have on most criteria outperformed actual centrally controlled economies.[39] This evidence is far from conclusive, for there are many ways to interpret the historical data. Since there are many different ways to plan and manage an economy and many different economic circumstances, it remains possible that some form of centrally managed economy would perform better in, for instance, Bulgaria than would any feasible market arrangement. But, given the limits of our knowledge, it might be hard to make such a possibility credible.

So the liberal would want to reintroduce markets to provide people with many of the good things in life. Furthermore, a high general level of well-being is not only something that all benevolent people value, but it is important in providing the material prerequisites for political stability and individual autonomy. Thus, even though liberalism is, as I have argued, not welfarist at its core, liberals will have a deep concern with getting people much of what they want, and liberals will favor the reintroduction of markets for this reason.

Second, and more closely tied to the core of liberalism, market life is in important ways itself *freer* than is economic life within a planned economy. There is more scope for individual choice, for individual innovation, for diversity of individual experimentation. As Adam Smith stressed, there is less direct dependence of one individual on another.[40] There is also much less overt personal coercion than there is in a planned economy.[41] Furthermore, markets encourage impartial (if not impersonal) treatment of individuals, and, as Ronald Dworkin has stressed, they preserve certain sorts of equalities.[42] Capitalism scores better on some of

---

[39] But see the last paragraph in this section. The record is hardly unambiguous. Consider, for example, the poor performance of the economies of most of the less-developed nations. Of course, their markets are imperfect, but so are markets in developed nations. Since there are many possible ways in which to implement market socialism, and very few of these have been tried, there is little evidence concerning how well market-socialist economies perform.

[40] Adam Smith, *Wealth of Nations*, book III, ch. 4 (see note 8 above).

[41] But it is questionable whether the range of economic choices available to most people increases. The prospects of unemployment and poverty are so chilling that many of the choices people make are much less than free. But I shall not review these venerable questions here. Even if freedom is in this way restricted for most people, it is also greatly enhanced in other ways.

[42] Dworkin, "Liberalism," pp. 193–94, and "What Is Equality? Part 2: Equality of Resources," *Philosophy and Public Affairs*, vol. 10 (1981), pp. 284f.

these criteria, while market socialism is superior on others. Liberals can argue for the reintroduction of markets because of the freedom, impartiality, and equality that are intrinsic to market relations.

Third, markets help insure political liberties. By separating political and economic power, they limit political power. Authoritarian control of political life is rendered more difficult, although, as examples such as Singapore vividly prove, thriving markets do not guarantee political liberties. Not only is the state weaker, since it does not directly control economic resources, but groups in opposition to the state may be stronger. The means of political resistance are dispersed throughout society, and control over economic resources brings at least the potential of political power. No conscientious liberal should, however, exaggerate the force of this argument. One the contrary, liberals should emphasize, for example, the ways in which the state can dominate privately owned communications media.[43] One must also be concerned about nonstate concentrations of power in economic monopolies. Individual liberties are fragile. But liberties are, other things being equal, easier to protect when the state is weaker, and the state is weaker when it does not control economic activities. So liberals should favor markets.

The liberal case for markets is overwhelming. But it is not so obvious how large a role markets should play in economic life or to what extent they should be regulated. Indeed, the empirical case for markets is more ambiguous than I have acknowledged, for "market" economies are such a miscellaneous lot. The degree of government involvement in economic successes has varied widely. Sweden provides high levels of social services with a small public sector, while in Austria the public sector accounts for more than half of economic output.[44] The United States has one of the freest markets among the developed nations, and the burden of regulation has over the past decade been lightened further, but its recent economic performance has been mediocre. The long and continuing controversies over economic policy show the scope of the disagreements about the extent to which markets should be limited and regulated. It is unclear what makes for economic success, and it is unclear what degree of government interference with economic life best protects markets and best serves equality and freedom in all the germane senses. Markets are desirable only insofar as they implement liberal ideals and increase individual welfare. Liberals must be concerned not only with the rein-

[43] See, for example, Edward Herman and Noam Chomsky, *Manufacturing Consent: The Political Economy of the Mass Media* (New York: Pantheon Books, 1988).

[44] Przeworski, *Democracy and the Market*, p. 125. Furthermore, the combination of extensive markets with private ownership of the means of production does not uniquely determine an economic system. Alan Blinder argues—in "More Like Them?" *The American Prospect*, Winter 1992, p. 53—that Japan does not have a capitalist economic system, despite the small role of government regulation and private ownership of the means of production. For, in his view, the core employees, rather than the shareholders, are sovereign in Japanese corporations.

troduction of market relations where market relations are appropriate, but with controlling markets when they do not promote freedom and equal respect.

VI. Liberal Limits on Markets

Markets can have bad consequences both from a general welfarist perspective and from the distinctive perspective of liberalism. Welfare economists, who have, I think, contributed more to understanding the limits of markets than to defending their virtues, have discussed many of these under the general heading of "market failures." Monopolies can limit efficiency, exaggerate inequalities in wealth and power, and threaten freedom and equality. In recent years, defenders of markets have made an empirical case that monopolies are less of a problem than they may have appeared to be, because of increased international competition and because of less-visible competition from producers of imperfect substitutes. For example, even though only one carrier provides rail service, there may be competition from trucks or barges. Moreover, economists have pointed out that government regulation of monopolies is costly and sometimes perpetuates and strengthens rather than mitigates monopoly power. Such may indeed have been true of regulation of the transportation industry in the United States. Given the weakness of the new regimes in the former Soviet empire, it may be wisest to hope that these critics of efforts to regulate monopolies are right. But the problems are grave, because the power of monopolies in the formerly state-controlled economies is vast, and liberals cannot ignore the threat monopolies may pose to equality and freedom.[45]

Externalities form the second main class of market failures. Negative externalities, such as the dispersion of toxic chemicals into waterways or the greenhouse effect, can cause grave problems. Some markets, such as markets in human beings or their organs, violate human dignity, and these violations may, with a bit of stretching, be regarded as negative externalities. Limiting such markets should be of particular concern to liberals.[46] Welfare economists have shown that it is sometimes possible to address market failures through adjustments in rights, thus extending

---

[45] Michael Burawoy and Pavel Krotov argue that the collapse of central planning in Russia is leading not to capitalism, but to something more like a sort of commercial feudalism in which the distribution of goods is regulated within conglomerates of huge enterprises. See their essay "The Soviet Transition from Socialism to Capitalism: Worker Control and Economic Bargaining in the Wood Industry," *American Sociological Review*, vol. 57 (1992), pp. 16–38.

[46] Even John Stuart Mill's uncompromising anti-paternalism gave way in the case of slavery. See chapter 5 of *On Liberty* [1859], ed. Currin V. Shields (New York: Macmillan, 1985). For a general discussion of goods that should not be exchanged on markets, see Elizabeth Anderson, "The Ethical Limitations of the Market," *Economics and Philosophy*, vol. 6 (1990), pp. 179–206.

rather than limiting markets. Apart from transactions that undercut human dignity, this kind of solution may be particularly attractive from a liberal perspective, since it has much the same virtues in increasing and protecting freedoms that markets in general do.

But not all negative externalities can be dealt with in this way. Economists are divided about the seriousness of problems that are not thus remediable, and about the efficacy of government regulation as a solution. Whatever general view is most defensible, it seems to me that the prospects are dim in Eastern Europe for dealing effectively with externalities without direct state regulation. Given the weakness of markets and the inevitable unclarities in background rights assignments during a revolutionary period, externalities are likely to be especially serious problems, and addressing them without direct government regulation may not be feasible in the short and medium run. Furthermore, the former Soviet-bloc nations also have a sad legacy of environmental damage with which they will have to cope. The social costs and the destabilizing consequences of not intervening are likely to be too large.

Positive externalities can also be of great importance. Particularly in the process of establishing a market economy, there is a crucial role for government in providing collective goods. Effective markets require a legal and financial infrastructure, which the state may need to provide. State incentives or action may also be needed to provide a good transportation and communications network, utilities, education, and protection services. The historical record suggests that markets need lots of help from the state in clarifying and facilitating exchange.[47] State action may be needed to promote markets as well as to ameliorate their unfortunate consequences.

In addition to problems of market failure, there are also troublesome consequences of markets concerning the distribution of wealth and power. Most people in our society, and an even larger majority in Eastern Europe and the Commonwealth of Independent States, see great inequalities in wealth and income as unjust.[48] The inequalities can, moreover, undermine the sense of worth and the capacity for autonomy of those who are worst off. Furthermore, these inequalities give rise to disparities in political power that can threaten liberal political values. These difficulties must be faced immediately, because programs of economic conversion will be

[47] Singapore is a particularly striking example in this regard. Although Jànos Kornai argues passionately in *The Road to a Free Economy* for minimal state interference in markets (see esp. pp. 38–39), he sees the state as developing and enforcing contract law (p. 45), as promoting investment through the provision of credit (p. 47), and even as promoting "social respect" toward the private sector (p. 49).

[48] "Right now, in the beginning of the new era, many people in various political groups, even within strongly anticommunist movements, are still under the spell of their former indoctrination in extreme egalitarian values. They regard profit or high income as the result of unethical practices, and speculation and profiteering as sure signs of unacceptable greed." Kornai, *The Road to a Free Economy*, p. 21.

imperiled if the population regards the reforms as unjust. People will accept hardship much more readily if they regard it as fair and for their own long-term benefit, rather than as an unjust imposition for the benefit of others. The prominence of criminals among the new urban trading classes, and the sudden riches of former Party commissars turned "capitalists," are very destructive, though hardly surprising, developments. To function efficiently, markets depend not only on laws defining property rights and permissible conduct, but also on less-formal norms concerning honesty, fair play, promise keeping, and so forth, which themselves change in character and stringency with the character of the markets. One should not forget that the traditional bazaars of Java and Morocco are markets, too, but they do not lead to economic development, largely because of the norms governing the behavior of their participants.[49] The societies of Eastern Europe need to create a commercial and an entrepreneurial ethos without destroying moral norms that are needed for both prosperity and democracy.[50] To refuse to temper the distributive injustices of a chaotic fledgling market would be political suicide, if it were a political option at all. There is no practical way of sharply separating the political and the economic and of leaving the market to its own devices.

Finally, and of growing contemporary importance, are questions concerning preference formation.[51] If, as I have argued, individual autonomy is a central liberal value, then liberals must be concerned about the processes by which preferences are formed. Traditionally, these processes

---

[49] See Clifford Geertz, *Peddlers and Princes: Social Development and Economic Change in Two Indonesian Towns* (Chicago: University of Chicago Press, 1963), ch. 3.

[50] It is unfortunate that market socialism is so tarnished by the negative associations of the word "socialism," for it might be able to respond to these difficulties better than even a carefully regulated capitalist economic system can. See Roemer, "The Morality and Efficiency of Market Socialism."

[51] There are also important difficulties with markets to which liberals have traditionally been blind. For in instituting markets one removes certain *social choices* from the agenda. Questions about the character of our communities and cultures are not open for rational discussion. The citizens of Southern California never deliberated about whether cities there should sprawl or whether the automobile should be the predominant means of daily transportation. If markets work as they theoretically ought to, such questions are answered through the consumption choices of individuals, which need not coincide with what would be the outcome of rational deliberation. Since liberals reject the notion of collective decision making about such issues, these problems about markets are not problems for liberals. But if the citizens of Eastern Europe learned anything about Marx at all, one can expect them to ask questions about the rational justification of market outcomes. Albert Hirschman — in *Exit, Voice, and Loyalty: Responses to Decline in Firms, Organizations, and States* (Cambridge: Harvard University Press, 1970) — makes the related but more modest point that "while exit requires nothing but a clearcut either-or decision, voice is essentially an *art* constantly evolving in new directions. This situation makes for an important bias in favor of exit when both options are present. . . . The presence of the exit alternative can therefore tend to *atrophy the development of the art of voice*" (p. 43; emphasis in original). Hirschman's point should heighten liberal qualms about markets.

have been extremely diverse, and apart form early industrial phenomena such as child labor and oppressive working hours and working conditions, which were inconsistent with the development and exercise of reflective capacities, there was little in the functioning of markets to raise liberal concerns about the possibility of individuals acquiring the capacities for living autonomously. But technological developments in mass communication should be alarming to liberals. Left to the marketplace, the miracles of contemporary electronics, especially television, can eat away at the intellectual, emotional, and reflective capacities of individuals, and destroy the contexts in which individuals employ and develop these capacities. If controlled by government rather than by market forces, the totalitarian potential of our electronic toys is no less frightening.

Children in the United States spend far more time watching television than talking with their parents. Parents have, of course, always left much of the socializing of their children to others — relatives, peers, parents of peers, servants, teachers, and neighbors. But these other socializers were more diverse than television is, and most of these had some concern for the interests of the child.[52] Commercial television programming has to satisfy sponsors, and consequently children's programs have to catch and hold the attention of children. Thus, especially in the age of the remote controller, these programs cannot demand long attention spans. They can do little to stretch children's minds or emotional capacities. They cannot discourage or disparage exciting fantasies of glamour, power, or violence. And the scenes flash by with an almost stroboscopic rapidity, ruling out those few reflections the one-dimensional and infantile material might possibly provoke.[53]

Even if these problems with the content of television could be solved by state control, which would of course create dangers of its own, all television, whether commercial or not, teaches passivity to children and to adults alike. One cannot argue with it. One cannot do anything but watch or kibitz with other watchers, and the kibitzing interferes with the next event. It is for voyeurs rather than actors.

Since the bad consequences are delayed, cumulative, and collective, while the enjoyment is immediate and private, this is not a problem that individual viewers can easily address — particularly when the viewers are children with limited cognitive abilities and limited capacity to defer enjoyment. Furthermore, among the bad consequences are a growing inability to understand what has been lost, a growing incapacity to enjoy

[52] See James Coleman, *Foundations of Social Theory* (Cambridge: Harvard University Press, 1990), p. 599.

[53] Notice that these problems, unlike some of the other objectionable features of television, are not due to monopoly power and would not be alleviated by greater competitiveness.

or to participate in the activities television replaces, and a growing political incompetence. So television not only poses problems of individual myopia and collective action, but it systematically undermines the capacities to perceive and remedy them.

These problems of preference formation are, however, more pressing for us than for liberals in Eastern Europe and in the former Soviet republics, who have few options with respect to mass media. One complaint against the former regimes was that they censored all mass media and banned Western television, radio, and newspapers. New censorship and control is unwelcome. Western television and radio can have a positive influence, too. They can, for example, provide language skills and familiarity with the products and customs of market societies. Moreover, cosmopolitan media might help counteract the illiberal and divisive nationalism sweeping through the former Soviet empire. On the other hand, the painful contrasts between televised affluence and the hard reality of economic rebuilding can undermine popular patience. Liberals may have no choice except to embrace a free market in mass communications, but the dangers remain. The values of liberalism are the values of a society of literate, reflective, deliberating, and conversing individuals. Can they be the values of an electronic culture? Instead of the necessary implements of liberalism, might not these markets be its ultimate undoing?

Liberals admire markets because they can help create the conditions for individual autonomy. They treat individuals impartially and leave them relatively uncoerced. By limiting political power and by creating the material prerequisites for effective political participation, they contribute to a democratic regime in which civil and political liberties are protected.

Yet because of the importance of externalities and of distributive justice, both in the long run and during the critical period of transition, and because of the long-run danger of surrendering the control of mass communications to market forces, I suggest that liberals regard markets cautiously. They are dangerous institutions, which can serve the cause of liberty and equality if they are properly restricted and regulated, but which can destroy everything liberals value if they get out of control. In my view, the main liberal battle, which is yet to be fought, is not *for* markets but *against* them. In any event, if liberals want to fight for their ideals, they need to see where they demand restricting rather than enlarging and deregulating markets. There are choices to be made between satisfying preferences on the one hand, and promoting autonomy and showing equal respect on the other. Furthermore, I think there is a practical case to be made that an explicit commitment to equality and autonomy will better gird people to withstand the costs of economic transformation and to play a positive part as agents of that transformation. Knowledge of theoretical welfare economics can be of some use in understanding why markets need to be regulated and in appreciating the difficulties involved in different schemes of regulation. But liberals should keep their distance from welfare economics, for its main concerns are not theirs, and economists have provided comparatively little useful knowledge concerning how best to organize economic life to promote freedom and respect equality.

Philosophy, University of Wisconsin–Madison

SOME RULES OF CONSTITUTIONAL DESIGN*

By Peter C. Ordeshook

Introduction

Events in both Eastern Europe and the former USSR illustrate the intimate connection between economic and political processes. Those events also remind us that political and economic institutions are human creations, and that when those institutions are poorly designed, political-economic failure is a direct consequence. It is axiomatic, then, that the transition to stable and prosperous societies in those former Communist states requires careful attention to the design and implementation of democratic institutions.

Unfortunately, research grounded in a well-developed framework of scientific discourse that serves as a practical guide to the construction of stable democratic institutions is virtually nonexistent. There are exceptions, the most important being *The Federalist Papers* and some other parts of the debate surrounding the ratification of the United States Constitution. With respect to the contemporary literature, perhaps the two most evident exceptions are Robert Dahl's *Preface to Democratic Theory* and William H. Riker's *Liberalism against Populism.*[1] However, although there are areas of agreement, Dahl and Riker posit diametrically opposite conditions for a stable political system and reach different conclusions about a constitution's role in facilitating stability. Riker argues that "the fundamental method to preserve liberty is to preserve ardently our traditional constitutional restraints."[2] Dahl, in contrast, asserts that "constitutional rules are not crucial, independent factors in maintaining democracy. . . . Constitutional rules are mainly significant because they help to determine what particular groups are to be given advantages or handicaps in the political struggle [and] . . . to assume that [the United States] remained democratic because of its Constitution seems to me an obvious reversal of the relation; it is much more plausible to suppose that the Constitution has remained because our society is essentially democratic."[3]

* The author would like to acknowledge grants from the United States Institute of Peace and *IRIS* of the University of Maryland that allowed for revision and refinement of this essay.

[1] William H. Riker, *Liberalism against Populism* (San Francisco: W. H. Freeman, 1982); Robert Dahl, *A Preface to Democratic Theory* (New Haven: Yale University Press, 1956). For another exception, see Donald Horowitz, *Democratic South Africa?: Constitutional Engineering in a Divided Society* (Berkeley: University of California Press, 1991).

[2] Riker, *Liberalism against Populism*, p. 252.

[3] Dahl, *Preface to Democratic Theory*, pp. 134 and 143.

198   © 1993 Social Philosophy and Policy Foundation. Printed in the USA.

This essay reconsiders this dispute in light of two ideas. The first is that if we conceive of constitutions as coordinating devices rather than as social contracts, then we can develop a more satisfying view of the way they become self-enforcing.[4] The second idea, from social-choice theory, is that although procedures such as direct presidential elections are subject to the usual instabilities that concern social-choice theorists, those instabilities do not imply that anything can happen—instead, final outcomes can be constrained, where the severity of those constraints depends on institutional details and the content of issues. These ideas strengthen Riker's argument about the importance of a separation of powers, the executive veto, and scheduled elections, and the view that federalism is an essential component of the institutions that stabilize the American political system.

However, this essay seeks also to provide a guide to the construction of a constitutional democracy. Countries in Eastern Europe and the republics of the former USSR do not require theory but practical advice on how to proceed. Thus, this essay attempts to justify a menu (by no means exhaustive) of some "rules of constitutional construction" implied by this essay's theoretical perspective. Some of these rules are well understood and commonly accepted; but others are more controversial, and they are highlighted here not because they are unassailable but because they warrant focused debate.

I. THE SELF-ENFORCING CONSTITUTION

Any attempt at providing a practical guide to the design of a democratic constitution, as well as any attempt at sorting out the influences of political institutions, culture, and social cleavage, must answer at least this question: What is a constitution's fundamental purpose, and how does it achieve that purpose? If Dahl is correct, our task is simply that of deciding who should win and who should lose and how to effect those losses and gains. But if Riker is correct, we must also learn the role of constitutional provisions with respect to aiding or hindering political stability.

We begin by noting that constitutions are commonly viewed as contracts whereby people try to resolve those market failures occasioned by public goods and externalities—by the necessity for finding relatively efficient mechanisms for providing such services as national defense, ensuring the viability of market contracts, and establishing Pareto-efficient redistribution—redistribution that cannot be altered to make some people better off without making others worse off. But this view cannot solve

---

[4] See especially Russell Hardin, "Why a Constitution?" in *The Federalist Papers and the New Institutionalism*, ed. Bernard Grofman and Donald Wittman (New York: Agathon Press, 1989), as well as Peter C. Ordeshook, "Constitutional Stability," *Constitutional Political Economy*, vol. 4, no. 3 (1992).

a critical puzzle, namely how a constitution's provisions are enforced. The particular problem is that if sovereignty resides in the people, then constitutions must be *self-enforcing* and this fact vitiates the contractarian view.

To see the basis of this assertion, consider the two-person Prisoner's Dilemma.[5] This dilemma offers the simplest illustration of market failure and models the problems foremost on the minds not only of the framers of the United States Constitution but of those who seek to establish democratic governments elsewhere — national defense, commerce, and currency reform. Played once, the inefficient equilibrium that characterizes this dilemma is avoided and an efficient outcome is substituted for it only if both persons are coerced by some exogenous force. If the players contract to a third "player" (the state) who administers fines for noncooperation, then both players cooperate and no fines are collected. But notice that what "solves" this dilemma is an abrogation of sovereignty by the contracting players. Unless sovereignty passes to the state, one or both persons can defect and leave the dilemma unresolved.

What is missing from our application of the Prisoner's Dilemma is recognition of the fact that the framers of America's Constitution did not envision solving defense or interstate commerce dilemmas that would exist only for a few years. They saw these as problems of indefinite duration that, unresolved, would lead to the eventual disintegration of the Union. Put simply, constitutions are intended to solve long-term problems and, regardless of the facts surrounding their durability, they ought to have long half-lives.

Suppose then that the Prisoner's Dilemma is played an indefinite number of times instead of once. In this instance, the game that confronts the two players is changed in a fundamental way. The single-play Prisoner's Dilemma offers each participant only two strategies; but if it is played an indefinite number of times, then each player is confronted with

---

[5] Briefly, the Prisoner's Dilemma corresponds to a situation in which each of two persons must choose between two alternatives — to cooperate or not to cooperate. The payoffs (in terms of money, satisfaction, or any such measure) from their joint choices are as follows (where the first number in each cell corresponds to the payoff to the row chooser and the second number corresponds to the payoff to the column chooser):

	Cooperate	Don't Cooperate
Cooperate	10, 10	0, 20
Don't Cooperate	20, 0	1, 1

Notice now that failing to cooperate is the dominant choice for both persons — a person prefers not to cooperate, regardless of what the other person chooses. But these actions yield the (1, 1) outcome even though both persons would prefer to cooperate in order to achieve the outcome (10, 10).

an infinity of alternative strategies (plans of action), such as "cooperate as long as the other person cooperates, but refuse to cooperate in the event that the other person chooses not to cooperate." More importantly, this change expands the set of outcomes that can be enforced without exogenous enforcement from the one in which only the inefficient outcome prevails to an infinity of outcomes, including the one in which the "fair" and efficient outcome prevails every time.[6]

Thus, mere recognition of the fact that all social processes are ongoing would appear to resolve the issue of self-enforcement. However, although there are strategies that yield cooperation at every stage and that give no advantage to one player or the other, there are others that give asymmetric rewards or that are simply inefficient. And another fact with which we must contend is that it is now possible for one player to choose a strategy involved in one equilibrium and the other to choose a strategy involved in some other equilibrium without the conjunction of their two strategies being in equilibrium.[7] Thus, rather than being concerned merely with enforcing some agreement, the players in our example must now be concerned also with coordinating their actions so as to achieve an equilibrium that is acceptable to both of them.

The necessity for some mechanism of coordination in politics and the point that coordination need not require complex mechanisms is revealed by the fact that if the two players in a simple repeated Prisoner's Dilemma simply discuss the matter beforehand and agree to a particular pattern of play in which each agrees to punish the other (by failing to cooperate in subsequent plays of the game), then nearly any agreement can be sustained. If each person believes that the other will abide by the agreement, then both persons have an incentive to act accordingly and nearly any agreement becomes self-enforcing.[8] Moreover, this reasoning does not require that society be concerned only with resolving Prisoner's Dilemmas. This discussion applies to nearly any repeated game, and thereby illustrates the following general facts: (1) any ongoing social process is characterized by countless alternative equilibria that require only coordination to achieve; (2) nearly any pattern of outcomes can prevail regardless

[6] Michael Taylor, *Anarchy and Cooperation* (New York: Wiley, 1976), and Robert Axelrod, *The Evolution of Cooperation* (New York: Basic Books, 1984). Briefly, a sequence of outcomes corresponds to a self-enforcing "agreement" if the pair of strategies that yield that sequence are in equilibrium — if neither player has an incentive to deviate unilaterally from his or her equilibrium strategy.

[7] For example, although the strategy pairs (cooperate always, cooperate always) and (never cooperate, never cooperate) are in equilibrium — neither player has an incentive to shift to a different strategy if the other person does not shift — the pairs (cooperate always, never cooperate) and (never cooperate, cooperate always) are not equilibria.

[8] Notice, moreover, that the precommitment strategies that Sunstein, for instance, sees as the essential character of constitutional agreements are equilibria and self-enforcing. See Cass M. Sunstein, "Constitutionalism, Prosperity, Democracy," *Constitutional Political Economy*, vol. 2, no. 3 (1990), pp. 371–94.

of the efficiency or fairness of this pattern; and (3) without coordination, there is no guarantee that any equilibrium will in fact be achieved.[9]

Hence, theory compels us to Russell Hardin's conclusion that "a constitution does not depend for its enforcement on external sanctions. . . . Establishing a constitution is a massive act of coordination that creates a convention that depends for its maintenance on its self-generating incentives and expectations." It also compels us to Vincent Ostrom's view that if people "have basic confidence that the conditions of life are organized to facilitate the working out of mutually agreeable relationships, they can approach one another in quite different ways than if they have to assume that they are always exposed to threats and exploitation by others," and to Cass M. Sunstein's argument that constitutional "provisions set out rules by which political discussion will occur, and in that sense free up the participants to conduct their discussion more easily."[10] Indeed, we can make an even stronger assertion: Since all political processes are ongoing, since the realization of efficient, coherent, and even "fair" outcomes in politics is achieved only through coordination, and since the agency of the state is an essential part of any society's coordinative mechanisms, a well-drafted constitution, which coordinates society to a definition of the state and a specification of its domain, is (in contrast to Dahl's view but in support of Riker's) essential for democratic stability.

II. Stable Expectations and Stable Constitutions

My interpretation of a constitution as a coordination mechanism has several advantages. Combined with some contemporary game theory, it reveals how unwritten constitutions can function and how written ones can allow for continued ambiguity.[11] Put simply, coordination can be achieved not only with explicitly written documents, but also with tacit agreements. In addition, we know that a great many other factors facilitate coordination in society. Thus, stable constitutions are merely one element of society's fabric, and if we are to begin effectively weaving them into that fabric, they must satisfy at least these three rules:

Rule 1: If a written constitution is to serve as a coordination mechanism for all of society, it ought to be a simple and concise document.

---

[9] See, for example, Drew Fudenberg and Eric Maskin, "Folk Theorems in Repeated Games with Discounting and Incomplete Information," *Econometrica*, vol. 54 (1986), pp. 533–54.

[10] Russell Hardin, "Why a Constitution?" p. 119 and *passim*; Vincent Ostrom, *The Political Theory of the Compound Republic*, 2d ed. (Lincoln: University of Nebraska Press, 1987), p. 51; Cass M. Sunstein, "Constitutionalism and Secession," *University of Chicago Law Review*, vol. 58, no. 2 (1991), pp. 633–70.

[11] See, for example, Michael Foley, *The Silence of Constitutions* (New York: Routledge, Chapman, and Hall, 1990).

Rule 2: A constitution's adoption ought to be accompanied by a public debate that conveys its fundamental character to as wide an audience as possible, where that debate is intended to commit the citizenry to act in accordance with the constitution's rules by establishing the common expectation that all persons will so act.

Rule 3: If a society already possesses a democratic tradition, then any constitutional revision ought to make as few changes in constitutional structure as possible — constitutions ought to accommodate a society's political traditions and those amorphous things we place under the rubric of political culture.

To this list we should add a rule that pertains to a constitution's internal structure. In seeking to avoid the ambiguity of enforcement, crafting a constitution from the perspective that it is a contract leads to the error of trying to "nail down" every detail, to defend against every tyranny, and to plan for every contingency.[12] But this approach merely pushes the problem back a step, so that the only "solution" seems to be to add further prohibitions, and administrative and legislative directives.

The danger into which one can fall in taking this approach is illustrated by the draft Russian Federation (RF) constitution proposed by its Constitutional Reform Commission in October 1991.[13] For example, Article 25 of this draft states that "[e]veryone is entitled to freedom of movement and choice of place of sojourn and residence within the RF. A citizen of the RF is entitled to freely leave it and return without let or hindrance." To this point, the article addresses forthrightly a "right" that cannot be taken for granted in a country that has experienced seventy years of Communist Party domination. However, anticipating the necessity for legislative refinement and fearing that a simple statement of rights is too imprecise in any contractual constitutional design, Article 25 goes on to state that "[a] qualification of these rights is permitted only on the basis

---

[12] One way to attempt to resurrect the contractarian view is with the argument that contracts are self-enforcing owing to the desire on the part of the contracting parties to establish and maintain certain types of reputations. But this argument founders on the fact that constitutions, at least in their ideal conceptualization, are not documents written between specific individuals. Rather, they facilitate collective action within a society regardless of the identities of the members of that society. For additional discussion of the role of reputation building and maintenance in the enforcement of contracts, see David M. Kreps, "Corporate Culture and Economic Theory," in *Perspectives on Positive Political Theory*, ed. James Alt and Kenneth Shepsle (New York: Cambridge University Press, 1990). For a discussion of constitutions from this perspective, see Adam Gifford, Jr., "A Constitutional Interpretation of the Firm," *Public Choice*, vol. 68 (1991), pp. 91–106.

[13] *Rossiyskaya Gazeta*, October 11, 1991. All subsequent references to the draft prepared by this commission pertain to this version, which, although subsequently revised, has not changed greatly.

of federal law," thereby negating entirely the constitutional character of this "right."[14]

Any additional elaboration of this right would, of course, merely compound further the problem of enforcement and interpretation, since it would necessarily add yet additional layers to the document that require enforcement. The result can only be a document that can confuse but cannot coordinate. Indeed, because contracts can only be enforced by a higher authority, this view tempts us to begin a futile search for the philosopher-king, to undertake the dangerous creation of the dictator, or to construct a governmental structure so mired in confusion and countervailing forces that stalemate prevails.[15] Thus:

> *Rule 4:* Constitutions ought to focus on institutional design and the statement of general principles, with the presumption that the need for greater specificity and administrative detail, as well as the resolution of potential ambiguity, will be attended to by the legislative and judicial institutions the constitution establishes.

Of course, wholesale ambiguity in the design of institutions must be avoided. Thus, declaratory statements such as "the system of state power is based on the principles of the separation of legislative, executive, and judicial authority"[16] are at worst too ambiguous to identify institutional structure, and are at best redundant and unnecessary if the constitution defines institutions and jurisdictions that otherwise establish a separation of powers.

More generally, the advantage of my interpretation of a constitution is that it helps identify an *effective constitution.* Briefly, a constitution must establish a set of stable and self-generating expectations about people's actions. The strategy of tit-for-tat solves the repeated Prisoner's Dilemma not only if both players intend initially to choose it, but also only if each expects the other to do the same. Indeed, this expectation must be common knowledge — each person must expect the other to choose that particular strategy; each must believe that the other holds a similar expectation; each must believe that the other believes that this is so; and so on. Without such expectations, one person or the other may think that the interaction is headed toward some other equilibrium, in which case there is

---

[14] Of course, this article could be interpreted as a jurisdictional assignment that precludes autonomous republics and the like from passing laws that restrict mobility. Such an assignment would be wholly reasonable, but if that were the goal, then there are far more direct ways to make such assignments.

[15] Contrast the American Constitution's 23-word prohibition that "Congress shall make no law . . . abridging the freedom of speech, or of the press; or the right of the people peaceably to assemble . . ." with the draft Russian Federation constitution's 191-word (English translation, Articles 26, 31, and 74) treatment of these prohibitions.

[16] Article 8, draft Russian Federation constitution.

no guarantee that a mutually agreeable resolution of the dilemma will prevail.

To the extent that it is in everyone's interest to be certain about process and outcomes, a constitution that cannot provide a self-fulfilling set of expectations cannot survive. This fact yields some additional rules of constitutional design. First, although a constitution ought to be flexible so as to allow for evolutionary change, it cannot be too flexible if it is to be stable and effective.[17] That is:

> *Rule 5:* Constitutions should allow for their own modification, but they should be restrictive enough to allow people to anticipate and adjust to those changes.

Second, in drafting a constitution, people cannot anticipate every possibility. Consider those instances in which a constitution's emergency provisions are used by a despot as an excuse for suspending democratic processes and protections of individual rights (e.g., the Philippines under Marcos, nearly any constitutional government in South America). This is not to say that we can wholly preclude the possibility of tyrants, but allowing for any suspension of provisions is dangerous territory indeed. Other than rules of succession, attempting to plan for even cataclysmic events such as war falls into the trap of supposing that the rules of democratic process ought to be suspended at those times and that a constitution is a contract to ensure against excessive expropriation of powers by the state. Thus:

> *Rule 6:* Rather than plan for every contingency, constitutions define the structure of the "normally" functioning state, with the presumption that the state can function even in times of emergency.

Equivalently:

> *Rule 7:* If, owing to some emergency such as war (or, as in the case of Eastern Europe and the former Soviet Union, economic transformation), there is a near-consensus that a chief executive requires special authority to effectively facilitate social coordination, then it should be assumed that the institutions that a constitution establishes, if designed well, will respond appropriately by granting that authority on a provisional basis and only through statutory provision.

Attempting to define emergency circumstances with vague references to "periods of transformation" and the like, and allowing for executive decrees during those periods, merely opens the door not only to ambiguity,

---

[17] William A. Niskanen, "Conditions Affecting the Survival of Constitutional Rules," *Constitutional Political Economy*, vol. 1, no. 2 (1990), pp. 53–62.

but to a continuing conflict between the various branches of government that destroys the constitution's coordinative role.

Third, if a constitution is effective, it must correspond to an equilibrium in the sense that no member of society has an incentive and the ability to defect to some other mechanism. And since we cannot avoid the possibility that people can collude to act in accordance with some new agreement precluded by the constitution, a stable constitution must be impervious to coordinated defections. That is, a constitution must produce outcomes that are efficient or that cannot be significantly improved upon by different arrangements that can be realized at acceptable costs. A minimal requirement to that end is:

> *Rule 8:* The rules and procedures that a constitution establishes must be sufficiently clear to allow for subsidiary planning.

The failure to satisfy this requirement eliminates the possibility of stable expectations, the effective coordination of political activity, and the generation of efficient policy.

Fourth, because constitutions must be capable of generating fulfilled expectations, their content should not be obscured with unrealizable utopian provisions. This is a problem for the authors of new constitutions for Eastern Europe and the republics of the former USSR, who seem determined to extend the Communist tradition of overloading constitutions with statements of aspirations that no state can meet. Consider, for example, the following provisions of the draft constitution of the Russian Federation:

> *Article 36:* "Each employee is entitled to recreation. Wage workers are guaranteed the working hours, weekly days off, holidays, paid annual leave, and a shorter working day for a number of occupations and industries established by law."

> *Article 37:* "Everyone is entitled to qualified medical assistance in state or local systems of health care from the resources of social insurance."

> *Article 39:* "Everyone is entitled to a dwelling place. No one may be arbitrarily deprived of a dwelling place. The state encourages housing construction and creates the conditions for the realization of the right to a dwelling place. Housing is made available to needy citizens free of charge or on preferential terms from the housing of the RF, the republics, the lands, and local housing."

> *Article 73:* "Children who have come of age and who are fit for work are required to take care of their parents."

The source of such articles is, of course, the attempt by Communist ideology to expand the list of individual rights guaranteed by a constitution to include not only those rights we normally associate with the "Western" democratic tradition (e.g., freedom of speech and of religion), but also more explicitly material things such as housing, medical care, and the like. However, even if we ignore the ambiguity inherent in such provisions and the open invitation they provide for state incursions into nearly every aspect of social endeavor, the inevitable policy failures can only undermine the state's legitimacy and, thereby, the constitution's coordinative function. Hence:

> *Rule 9:* Constitutions ought to avoid vague lists of utopian policy goals that are beyond the capacity of the state to realize, and they ought to focus instead on the minimal institutions and rights that are sufficient to ensure society's ability to coordinate for the realization of policy goals as expressed through such agencies as democratic elections.

In fact, if a constitution otherwise performs its coordinative function, then even if unusual and "unconstitutional" actions are required in times of emergency, a society can informally accede to such actions and treat them as legitimate (e.g., Lincoln's suspension of *habeas corpus*, or restrictions on freedom of the press during war to bar the publication of troop movements).

Finally, "if a constitution is to be essentially a legal document, it must primarily include provisions that courts can enforce without upsetting the proper balance of power among the branches of government . . . without taking on the role of a super legislature."[18] And to be enforceable by the court a constitution's provisions must be implementable by the legislature. Thus:

> *Rule 10:* Constitutional provisions, especially those pertaining to rights and guarantees, must be translatable into policy that can be feasibly implemented by the legislature.

III. Social-Choice Theory

To have any practical value, the preceding ten rules of constitutional design must be transformed, in accordance with Rules 4, 7, and 9, into specific institutional mechanisms. But our design must also contend with some theoretical facts provided by the contemporary theory of social de-

---

[18] Andrzej Rapaczynski, "Constitutional Politics in Poland," *University of Chicago Law Review*, vol. 58, no. 2 (1991), pp. 595–631.

cision making.[19] I begin with Kenneth Arrow's General Possibility Theorem which tells us that there is no guarantee that a "best" social policy can be said to exist.[20]

> *Result 1:* For any nondictatorial rule for aggregating individual preferences, there exist individual preferences such that the social preference as revealed by that rule is intransitive.

That is, barring dictatorship, we cannot preclude the possibility that individual actions, operating through the institutions of the state, will imply a social preference in which policy A is preferred or regarded indifferently with respect to policy B, policy B is preferred or regarded indifferently with respect to policy C, but C is preferred to A.

Although the relevance of Arrow's Theorem is not limited to majority rule, because majority rule plays such an important role in constitutional theory, my remaining results focus on it. First:

> *Result 2:* If we require two or more issues to characterize public policies, then the set of preference configurations that occasion an outcome that cannot be defeated by some other outcome in a majority vote is generically empty.[21]

Another result shows the full consequences of Result 2:

> *Result 3:* If social decisions are made by majority rule and if we require two or more issues to characterize public policies, then in general the social preference order is wholly intransitive over the entire set of possible policy outcomes.[22]

Results 2 and 3 have occasioned considerable research into elections, committees, legislatures, voting procedures, and so on. I cannot review

---

[19] I should emphasize at this point that I eschew the social-choice theorist's definition of instability in favor of the pluralist's concern for governmental stability. That is, I am not equating the instability of individual outcomes with that of the state itself. For further discussion of this distinction, see Nicholas Miller, "Pluralism and Social Choice," *American Political Science Review*, vol. 77 (1983), pp. 734–47.

[20] Kenneth Arrow, *Social Choice and Individual Values* (New Haven: Yale University Press, 1963). I note, however, that Arrow's theorem does not formally establish the possibility of *cycles* (e.g., situations in which society prefers, say, outcome A to B, B to C, and C to A), and, thus, it does not formally preclude "best" outcomes. A slight alteration in Arrow's original axioms, however, secures the requisite result. See Thomas Schwartz, "On the Possibility of Rational Policy Evaluation," *Theory and Decision*, vol. 1 (1970), pp. 1–33.

[21] Otto A. Davis and Melvin Hinich, "A Mathematical Model of Policy Formation in a Democratic Society," in *Mathematical Applications in Political Science II*, ed. J. L. Bernd (Dallas: SMU Press, 1966); and Charles R. Plott, "A Notion of Equilibrium and Its Possibility Under Majority Rule," *American Economic Review*, vol. 57, no. 2 (1967), pp. 787–806.

[22] Richard D. McKelvey, "Intransitivities in Multidimensional Voting Models and Some Implications for Agenda Control," *Journal of Economic Theory*, vol. 12 (1976), pp. 472–82.

that literature here, but one result—Duncan Black's Median Voter Theorem—warrants special attention:[23]

> *Result 4:* If all preferences can be represented by a single issue dimension such that each relevant voter can be characterized by an ideal preference on that issue, and where that voter's preferences decline as we move away from that ideal in either direction, then the median ideal cannot be defeated by any other alternative in a majority vote.

Thus, if two candidates compete under the circumstances described by this result, if all citizens vote for their most preferred candidate, and if each candidate seeks to win the election, both candidates should identify with the median ideal preference.

Three additional results elaborate on the properties of majority rule when the preconditions of Result 4 are not met—when policy alternatives are multidimensional. First, for two-candidate elections:

> *Result 5:* If an election concerns two or more issues, then, in general, there is no policy toward which the candidates must eventually converge; but if there are few "extremist" voters, the candidates will not choose policies far from the electorate's median preference on each issue.[24]

The part of this result that warrants emphasis is that although any incumbent can be defeated by a sufficiently astute challenger, policies themselves—the candidates' campaign platforms—need not be subject to any great change. That is, although the Median Voter Theorem does not apply in multi-issue contests, the centralizing tendency it uncovers is a general property of two-candidate majority-rule elections.

Turning from two-candidate elections to legislatures, considerable research has been directed at uncovering the impact of specific voting rules. This research reveals not only that rules can have a profound effect on outcomes, but also that *the extent to which a particular procedure mitigates against disequilibrium depends not only on the character of that procedure but also on the character of individual preferences.*[25] Although a procedure such as

---

[23] Duncan Black, *Theory of Committees and Elections* (Cambridge: Cambridge University Press, 1958).

[24] Richard D. McKelvey and Peter C. Ordeshook, "Symmetric Spatial Games without Majority Rule Equilibria," *American Political Science Review*, vol. 70 (1976), pp. 1172–84; and Richard D. McKelvey, "Covering, Dominance, and Institution-Free Properties of Social Choice," *American Journal of Political Science*, vol. 30 (1986), pp. 283–314.

[25] See, for example, Kenneth Shepsle and Barry Weingast, "Structure-Induced Equilibrium and Legislative Choice," *Public Choice*, vol. 37 (1981), pp. 503–19; Thomas Hammond and Gary Miller, "The Core of the Constitution," *American Political Science Review*, vol. 81 (1987), pp. 1155–74; and Arthur Denzau and Robert Mackay, "Structure-Induced Equilib-

voting on each issue in sequence can induce a stable outcome when a person's most preferred policy on each issue is independent of what prevails on other issues, such a procedure need not induce stability. Indeed:

> *Result 6:* If a majority-rule committee uses "typical" procedures, then in general, the final outcome will depend on the specifics of those procedures; moreover, a greater variety of outcomes can prevail typically under them than would prevail under a two-candidate election format.[26]

Two final results concern the fact that many constitutional arrangements raise the vote quota necessary to upset the status quo to something greater than a simple majority. The effect of such rules, however, depends on the type of issues under consideration. Briefly, we can distinguish between two broad types—"public-good" and "redistributive" issues. A public-good issue is illustrated by policies that concern the determination of government involvement in such matters as education and defense, and their most important characteristic is that one person does not gain only if someone else loses. Redistributive issues, in contrast, concern tax policy and the allocation of tax revenues across a population, so that if one person's tax or subsidy is increased, someone else's must be decreased. Our two final results now are:

> *Result 7:* If preferences concern several public-goods issues and if the preference distribution is "sufficiently tight," then the status quo cannot be defeated by any other alternative in a majority vote if a vote quota greater than 64 percent is employed.[27]

> *Result 8:* If the allocation of some resource (e.g., money) is to be determined by majority rule, then there is no stable outcome. And short of unanimity, the size of the majority that defines winning merely affects the number of people from whom we can expropriate but not the nonexistence of a stable policy.

IV. DESIGNING STABLE AND EFFECTIVE CONSTITUTIONS

If an effective constitution is a set of rules that facilitates the coordination of political action so as to induce stable expectations about political

---

rium and Perfect Foresight Expectations," *American Journal of Political Science,* vol. 25 (1981), pp. 762–79.

[26] Nicholas R. Miller, "A New Solution Set for Tournaments and Majority Voting," *American Journal of Political Science,* vol. 24 (1980), pp. 68–96; Shepsle and Weingast, "Structure-Induced Equilibrium and Legislative Choice"; and Peter C. Ordeshook and Thomas Schwartz, "Agendas and the Control of Political Outcomes," *American Political Science Review,* vol. 81, no. 1 (1987), pp. 179–99.

[27] "Sufficiently tight" refers to a technical condition on the form of the distribution of preferences. For details, see Andrew Caplan and Barry Nalebuff, "On 64%-Majority Rule," *Econometrica,* vol. 56, no. 4 (1988), pp. 787–814.

process, then such a constitution (1) coordinates social action to an equilibrium and (2) ensures that out of the universe of possibilities, the equilibrium that is in fact achieved is deemed "reasonable" by a sufficiently large portion of society. To see how the results from the previous section flesh out the substantive meaning of these requirements, let us consider an especially simple possibility—a society that confronts annually only a single salient issue. Suppose this issue is of the sort that arises when people divide a government's budget between two alternative services—how much to spend, for instance, on national defense versus social welfare. People will differ in their preferred patterns of spending, but to make a final decision, suppose society, informed of the virtues of majority rule, meets once a year to choose a person at random to campaign against an incumbent. Suppose both challenger and incumbent compete by proposing alternative policies, and suppose society uses a majority vote to determine a new incumbent, implements the policy advocated by that new incumbent, and compensates the winner sufficiently so that winners gain more by implementing their promises than by implementing their ideal policy. The Median Voter Theorem (Result 4) tells us that a stable outcome prevails—society's median preference.

Of course, our society could just as easily implement the median directly with a public opinion poll, but now let matters become more complicated and suppose society confronts an additional issue that requires resolution. Again, people could be polled on each issue and the two medians implemented as policy. But now social-choice theory alerts us to two new problems. First, what a person prefers on one issue may depend on what prevails on the other, in which case a simple poll of society will not suffice and the outcome of any poll will depend on the way questions are posed. Second, even if the issues are wholly disjointed, other policies will be preferred by a majority to the one that corresponds to the median preference on each issue (Results 2 and 3).

A third fact complicates matters further. Even though society may adhere to majoritarian principles, outcomes are influenced by the way those principles are implemented (Result 6), and this fact reveals another problem—*procedures inherit the instability of final outcomes, procedures for choosing procedures inherit this instability, and so on.*[28] If society confronts a single issue so that one outcome dominates the rest, people are indifferent as to how majority rule is implemented. But if every outcome can be upset and if procedures can be designed to lead to any outcome, people will hold different preferences over procedures and any instability over outcomes will transfer to these procedures. So, just as preferences over

---

[28] See William H. Riker, "Implications from the Disequilibrium of Majority Rule for the Study of Institutions," *American Political Science Review*, vol. 74, no. 2 (1980); Peter C. Ordeshook, "Political Disequilibrium and Scientific Inquiry: A Comment on William Riker's 'Implications from the Disequilibrium of Majority Rule for the Study of Institutions'," *American Political Science Review*, vol. 74, no. 2 (1980); and Jules Coleman and John Ferejohn, "Democracy and Social Choice," *Ethics*, vol. 97, no. 1 (1986), pp. 6–25.

procedures will be intransitive (Result 1), preferences over procedures for choosing procedures will also be intransitive, and so on.

Clearly, this infinite regress must terminate, for otherwise society cannot establish stable expectations. Fortunately, although people may have preferences over which procedure to use in resolving current issues, they are less likely to hold such preferences for decisions made in the future, especially if a veil of ignorance characterizes the situation. For example, suppose some card players must choose the game they will play before the cards are dealt. Different players may hold different preferences, depending on which game best matches their beliefs about their comparative advantages in skill. But if they must choose after the cards are dealt, then preferences are unlikely to yield any agreement and the most likely outcome is a decision to choose a game and redeal the cards. Thus:

> *Rule 11:* Constitutions should not focus on the resolution of immediate conflicts over which there is intense disagreement; rather, they should provide for the institutional framework whereby those conflicts and any others can be resolved.

Stating the matter even more strongly, "any attempt to stabilize a country's governmental pattern by means of a formal Constitution while a given revolutionary cycle is in progress and before it has run its course, is doomed to failure."[29] During such periods (which match the circumstances in, say, Yugoslavia and possibly Romania with its "incomplete revolution"), there are, by definition, significant numbers of people who believe they can benefit from the inability to wholly coordinate actions or who believe that the "game" being played is strictly zero-sum and that only subparts of society can coordinate against other subparts. Thus:

> *Rule 12:* If a constitution is drafted in a period of revolutionary change in which political-economic conflict is severe and threatens stability, it is unlikely to ameliorate the causes of that conflict.

In one sense, of course, all the countries of Eastern Europe and the new states that previously formed the USSR confront a period of revolutionary change: "The main difficulty of the constitution makers . . . [there] is that they are operating in a complete vacuum. There are no ground rules; everything is up for arguing and bargaining. The framers have too much freedom, too many possibilities to choose from, and too many decisions to make simultaneously."[30] Hence, at least for these states, the

---

[29] Benjamin Akzin, "On the Stability and Reality of Constitutions," in *Scripta Hierosolymitana III*, ed. Roberto Bachi (Jerusalem: Magnes Press, Hebrew University, 1956).

[30] Jon Elster, "Constitutionalism in Eastern Europe," *University of Chicago Law Review*, vol. 58, no. 2 (1991), p. 480–81.

design of a constitution should not be approached as an exercise in solving immediate problems (especially redistributive conflicts), but rather it should be approached as the design of a device for ensuring the viability of long-term solutions, including problems of the type they confront today.

Returning to "normal" circumstances, consider whether the society in our example can ensure policy stability. If we implement a two-candidate election format, we will observe two things. First, a challenger can find another policy that is preferred by a majority regardless of the incumbent's strategy (Result 3). Thus, no candidate remains in office long, and policies change from election to election. However, policies will not change greatly unless preferences over policy are widely dispersed (Result 5) — indeed, they may not change in a way that is deemed significant. We may observe instability in the winning and losing candidates' identities, but this instability need not translate into any great instability in policy. That is:

> *Rule 13:* Designers of constitutions ought not confuse instability in the identities of elected officials with instability in policy.

V. Redistributive Politics

This last rule appears to undermine Riker's conclusion that liberal institutions ought to be preferred over populist ones, since Riker constructs his case largely on the policy instability inherent in majority rule. However, thus far I have assumed that governments regulate only public goods, whereas there is no actual circumstance in which the state is restricted only to this role. Providing for national defense, highways, or education, for example, confers private benefits and costs, because goods that are public in consumption have private consequences in production.[31] In addition to the consequences of taxation, *someone* must secure the contract to build a weapons system, to lay concrete, and to print textbooks. Put simply, it is impossible for the state to avoid redistribution. Redistribution, moreover, need not take a purely economic form. States with ethnic, linguistic, or religious conflicts must constantly contend with redistributive issues to the extent that the government's actions are perceived as necessarily conferring recognition or power on one group at the expense of another.

Social-choice theory tells us that this change in focus yields a radically different situation. Rule 13 no longer applies, since not only does instability traverse the entire domain of feasible policies with redistributive is-

---

[31] See, for example, Peter H. Aranson and Peter C. Ordeshook, "Public Interest, Private Interest, and the Democratic Polity," in *The Democratic State*, ed. Roger Benjamin and Stephen Elkin (Lawrence: University Press of Kansas, 1985).

sues, but even with a two-candidate election format, final outcomes can include those that reduce some maximal minority to poverty (Result 8). If issues take the form "the government ought to spend 'X' on education, national defense, and so on," and if the methods whereby governments raise the revenues for these services are not salient, then a winner-take-all election format produces outcomes about the center of gravity of preferences. But if issues concern "who pays," or if these services confer differential benefits across society, then there is no stable outcome and candidates can jockey for electoral advantage by advocating extreme policies that pit different categories of voters against each other, thereby threatening the rights and even the existence of minorities.

There are, then, two types of instabilities. One type, derived from different tastes over public goods, can be regulated with simple (populist) constitutional forms such as winner-take-all election procedures, where by "regulated" I mean the establishment of stable expectations about policy outcomes. The second type, which arises if wealth or political power is redistributed, cannot be regulated effectively in the same way. That is:

> *Rule 14:* Simple constitutional procedures such as referenda and direct elections can regulate the provision of public goods, but different mechanisms are required to ensure stable expectations over redistributive issues.

Nevertheless, the instabilities occasioned by redistribution must be regulated, since, in words that are especially relevant to societies emerging from the economic devastation wrought by central planning, "one of the best ways to destroy a democratic system is to ensure that the distribution of wealth and resources is unstable and constantly up for new evaluation. . . . A high degree of stability is necessary in order to allow people to plan their affairs, to reduce the effects of factional or interest-group power in government, to promote investment, and to prevent the political process from breaking down." [32] The question, then, is: What constitutional mechanisms can keep redistributive issues from threatening the stability of the state?

Madison's solution in *The Federalist Papers* is the expansive republic, but because of the dilution in the value of any individual vote that it implies, Madison's prescription, without countervailing institutional devices, increases the problems associated with rational ignorance and the transfer of power to an informed elite.[33] But there is one justification for Madison's argument, summarized by the reasoning: "If I know that any redis-

[32] Cass M. Sunstein, "Constitutionalism, Prosperity, Democracy," *Constitutional Political Economy*, vol. 2, no. 3 (1991), p. 380.

[33] By "rational ignorance" I mean those situations in which a voter rationally chooses not to gather information about the candidates or their parties because the cost of doing so exceeds the incremental benefits associated with making more informed decisions.

tributive coalition is unstable and likely to be replaced with another coalition, and if I am as likely to be included in a losing coalition as a winning one at any point in time, then if I am risk averse, I should prefer that redistributive issues never arise or that some equitable resolution be imposed for all time. And if everyone else feels the same as I do, then surely we can coordinate to such an outcome."

This argument encapsulates Dahl's pluralist theory, and it may be correct if society is divided into innumerable crosscutting cleavages *and if there is nothing that can be used as the basis for forming a permanent winning faction.* This theory is wrong and dangerous, though, if there are ways for factions to coordinate. A society divided into two racial or ethnic groups, for example, will find it easy to coordinate so that one group expropriates from the other. Russians in the USSR and Serbs in Yugoslavia can discriminate knowing that only some minimal socialization will allow ethnicity or language to be a permanent mechanism of coordination. And although it appears that the pluralist argument suggests a way for certain types of societies—those with no minority or a plurality of them—to avert the instabilities occasioned by redistribution, we should not discount the ability of people to *invent* ethnic categories as a mechanism for coordinating redistributive coalitions (e.g., the *Pamyat*-types in Russia and their creation of a "Jewish conspiracy," or similar types in Eastern European states who ignore the fact that there are few Jews in their countries who can conspire to anything). Thus:

> *Rule 15:* Constitutions ought to be designed under the assumption that political decision makers will attempt to raise the salience of (or even create) ethnic, linguistic, religious, or racial categories.

Indeed, the instability of redistributive politics and the ability of ethnicity to coordinate action poses a serious challenge to stable democracy. For example, the conflicts that have emerged or that threaten to emerge in the now dissolved Soviet Union (e.g., between Russians and Ukrainians in Ukraine, between Russians and Tatars, between Georgians and Ossetians, between Russians, Ukrainians, and "Romanians" in Moldova, as well as those that may soon arise in the Moslem republics that entail religious and linguistic cleavages) derive largely from the fact that these cleavages fill a political vacuum—without alternative institutional devices, they are the only available means for coordinating political action. Without any meaningful constitutional tradition and with the destruction of central and authoritarian controls, there is virtually nothing else to coordinate people to political action except ethnic appeals that begin with the believable argument that others are doing the same. Thus:

> *Rule 16:* Constitutions should be viewed as devices that must compete with ethnic, linguistic, religious, or racial cleavages as coordinating mechanisms.

Put differently, constitutions are not devices whereby ethnic cleavages are resolved or are somehow submerged in society's consciousness. Rather, their institutional structure must try to channel the individual and group interests that arise "naturally" from such cleavages in such a way that the state continues to function; and in doing this, the constitution must attempt to provide coordinating mechanisms that will compete with the coordinative function of ethnicity.

Subsequent sections of this essay will examine how constitutional structures can accomplish this redirection. Presently, though, I note that part of the mechanism required is the rights that constitutions prescribe, which accomplish their coordinating task "by reducing the power of highly controversial questions to create factionalism, instability, impulsiveness, chaos, stalemate, collective action problems, myopia, strategic behavior, or hostilities so serious and fundamental as to endanger the governmental process itself."[34] That is, in accordance with Result 8:[35]

Rule 17: Constitutional specifications of rights should be viewed as an attempt to remove issues from the domain of politics so as to reduce the opportunities to create unstable social outcomes.

Finally, insofar as the attitude that the framers of a constitution ought to take toward the state's role relative to that of the private sector, Richard Epstein's argument that "the greater the internal disparity, the more critical it is to have a small list of core government functions on whose discharge all can agree"[36] warrants inclusion as a rule of constitutional design and can be reformulated thus:

Rule 18: The greater the salience of ethnic cleavages, the greater the attention that must be paid to the principle of limited government.

VI. Presidential Systems and the Separation of Powers

One solution to redistributive instability is to require the rule of unanimity, but the danger is that people can hold the state hostage, in which case contemporary bargaining theory shows the impossibility of making precise predictions about final outcomes, thereby undermining a constitution's ability to generate stable expectations. Alternatively, if we raise

[34] Sunstein, "Constitutionalism and Secession" (see n. 10 above), p. 642 and passim.

[35] An important caveat to Rule 17 is that framers of constitutions ought to avoid attempting to specify rights that merely invite the state to expand its domain too easily and too greatly. Consider, for example, the following provisions of the draft Russian Federation constitution: Article 59: "The state protects the rights of the consumer and supports the activity of societies in defense of these rights and other forms of their protection"; and Article 60: "The state guarantees freedom of enterprise."

[36] Richard A. Epstein, "All Quiet on the Eastern Front," University of Chicago Law Review, vol. 58, no. 2 (1991), p. 568.

the vote quota from majority rule to something less than unanimity, then although the threat of expropriation and tyranny is not wholly eliminated (Result 8), expropriation is less profitable. If the "losers" are sufficiently few in number and if the "winners" are sufficiently numerous, then the individual incentives for expropriation diminish. Of course, even near-unanimity rule threatens governmental paralysis, but suppose that we can determine the precise rule that bars "tyrannical redistribution" and that also leaves the government capable of dealing effectively with the traditional matters of policy. The question is: How do we implement this rule?

To see the role of bicameralism here, suppose the modern state requires representative government and that legislation can be authorized only by the requisite extraordinary majority in a unicameral legislature. There are now two difficulties. First, a simple rule of near unanimity may be too tempting a target for constitutional or nonconstitutional revision. Second, such a rule need not translate into a rule of popular vote near-unanimity.[37] However, the first problem is resolved if we impose an institutional structure that is difficult to change. Substituting a bicameral for a unicameral legislature satisfies this objective. A bicameral legislature also addresses the second problem.[38] But bicameralism must be designed with care. Specifically, bicameralism raises a vote quota only to the extent that it provides for different bases of representation in the two houses of the legislature. If the two houses have identical electoral bases, they merely reproduce each other.[39] That is:

> *Rule 19:* Bicameralism raises the vote quota necessary to pass legislation, but only if the houses of the legislature have different bases of representation.

Representative government, though, offers another way to raise vote quotas — a separation of powers. In fact, by multiplying the hurdles that challenges to the status quo must pass, a separation of powers does more. To this point, we have been concerned with subsets of citizens using the state to tyrannize some other subset. But to the list of interests who might

---

[37] For example, if each of n legislators is elected in a single-member district and if $n - x > (n + 1)/2$ votes are required to upset the status quo, then as few as $(50 + \varepsilon)(n - x) < 50\%$ of the voters can control the outcome. That is, if a simple majority in each of $n - x$ constituencies prefers to change the status quo, then the status quo is defeated.

[38] Thomas Hammond and Gary Miller, "The Core of the Constitution," *American Political Science Review*, vol. 81 (1987), pp. 1155–74.

[39] We can speculate, then, that the Seventeenth Amendment (providing that senators should be elected by the people, rather than appointed by state governments) circumvents an important provision designed to raise the vote quota. Although some of the original intent of bicameralism remains owing to the staggered election terms of senators, senatorial and congressional election districts coincide too closely to lead us to believe that bicameralism today imposes a significant constraint on legislative action.

tyrannize we must add the state itself (those who occupy its formal positions, elective or appointive). A separation of powers addresses this problem. Following Madison's admonition that the "great security against a gradual concentration of the several powers in the same department consists of giving to those who administer each department the necessary means *and personal motives* to resist the encroachments of others":[40]

> *Rule 20:* A separation of powers should seek to initiate competition among the state's branches so that a balance of power protects citizens from the state.

With respect to implementing this balance, it is generally assumed that there should be three branches. International relations theory tells us that this number is not accidental. If nations maximize wealth and power, a majoritarian-like system arises in which coalitions with more power can block the ambitions of those with less. This fact and the fact that measuring power is problematical, gives the number three special meaning. A balance among three is assured for wide variations in relative power — as long as one state does not become wholly predominant, the remaining two can always block the ambitions of the third. In contrast, with two states the danger is that one of them will become predominant; and with four or more states, one or more can be inessential.[41] Thus, a three-state system requires a less precise evaluation of each state's power than do other systems.

Matters are even more difficult to quantify in intrastate balances. Part of the "power" of a branch of the state includes not only its constitutionally mandated jurisdictions and vetoes, but also its ability to mobilize public opinion and its susceptibility to that opinion. So in this instance, three is an even more essential component of balance in a separation-of-powers system.

> *Rule 21:* Because power is difficult (impossible?) to measure, a separation of powers should be based on at least three essential branches.

Balance in international affairs also requires each state to possess some measure of power over other states and conflicting objectives among the individual states. The same is true in intrastate balances. We have already indicated that the "power" of the different branches is imprecise, but the most common mechanism of ensuring that branches of the state have power over each other is through the assignment of overlapping jurisdic-

---

[40] *The Federalist Papers*, ed. Garry Wills (Toronto: Bantam, 1982), number 51, p. 262.
[41] Emerson M. S. Niou and Peter C. Ordeshook, "Stability in Anarchic International Systems," *American Political Science Review*, vol. 84, no. 4 (1990), pp. 1207–34.

tions and the assignment of a limited veto to each branch within its jurisdiction. The second component of a balance of power—conflicting objectives—can derive from only one legitimate source:

> Rule 22: In a separation-of-powers system, the branches must be designed so that they do not have identical goals, which is accomplished by assuring that each branch has a different relation to the ultimate sovereign, the people.

To see how this rule is satisfied in a presidential system, notice that legislative districts can become captive of an extended form of the Prisoner's Dilemma in which representatives from each district provide, at national expense, particularized benefits for their constituencies that are largely unrelated to economic efficiency.[42] Suppose constituencies are given a choice between voting for an incumbent legislator who promises to deliver specific benefits to his constituency and voting for a challenger who promises greater efficiency in government even if that entails cutbacks in constituency service and benefits. Although all voters might prefer such cutbacks, a constituency has little incentive to elect the challenger, since a unilateral move merely diminishes its standing relative to all others in the race for governmental resources.[43]

Legislators, then, focus their attention on constituency interests, regardless of whether meeting those interests is economically efficient. And they have little incentive to block other legislators from securing similar benefits for their own constituents, since they are not rewarded for doing so and since acting thus merely opens the door to the possibility that they will fail to secure the benefits their constituents demand. Indeed, it is rational for legislators to respond by focusing even greater energy on constituency services and particularized benefits, since the corresponding deepening of the dilemma increases their reelection chances.

What works against this dilemma in a presidential system is that, when voting for president, citizens can register their dissatisfaction with governmental inefficiency and legislative performance. This does not mean that the ensuing policy conflict between president and legislature is resolved in favor of greater efficiency. But we see here how electoral imperatives can create different political incentives.

---

[42] Aranson and Ordeshook, "Public Interest, Private Interest, and the Democratic Polity" (see n. 31 above).

[43] The term-limitation movement in the United States provides a useful example. Although voters appear to favor such limits in the abstract, they fail to implement them for their national representatives knowing that doing so would put their representation at a disadvantage with respect to all other states. For additional discussion of this dilemma in more general contexts, see Morris P. Fiorina and Roger G. Noll, "Voters, Bureaucrats, and Legislators: A Rational Choice Perspective on the Growth of Bureaucracy," *Journal of Public Economics*, vol. 9 (1978), pp. 239–54; and Emerson M. S. Niou and Peter C. Ordeshook, "Universalism In Congress," *American Journal of Political Science*, vol. 29, no. 2 (1985), pp. 246–58.

With respect to this arrangement's efficiency, because a separation of powers increases the vote quota, the danger is stalemate. Legislation cannot pass unless a significant part of both major political parties ratifies the change. To win control only of the legislature or the presidency is not sufficient — control of both branches must be secured. So, barring joint control, a third branch must break the impasse. Thus, the courts in America have been called on to resolve disputes on nearly every major social issue, including civil rights, presidential prerogatives, social welfare, criminal penalties, election laws, and environmental protection, as well as issues on which the constitution is wholly silent, such as abortion. Thus, as a corollary to Rule 22:

> *Rule 23:* An independent judiciary is an essential component of a presidential system, since it is a primary guarantee against governmental stalemate.

The possibility of stalemate raises other problems. If the president is elected by a popular vote (directly or indirectly), we should be concerned if the victorious candidate receives either "too large" or "too small" a proportion of support. In the first instance, winners may believe that they have a mandate, and the danger, realized all too frequently in countries with only weak or nonexistent democratic traditions, is a presumption of extraordinary executive power. Indeed, in such circumstances, "both the temptation and the ability to weaken the electoral sanction are especially strong . . . [and] it is easy for rulers to believe their programs are the 'true' will of the people and hence more precious than the constitution and free elections." [44] It is impossible, of course, to mandate maximum election pluralities. Instead, the solution is to ensure that electoral institutions allow for competitive elections and to rely on the forces of competition for insurance against mandates. Hence:

> *Rule 24:* Constitutions should make adequate safeguards to ensure an unbiased electoral system, where by "unbiased" I mean an electoral system that is not designed to favor one preexisting party over another.

The second danger is occasioned by a president who is elected with something far less than a majority and in which executive activism in opposition to entrenched interests brings the threat of *coup d'état*. However, this problem is minimized if electoral institutions employ a winner-take-all format that encourages the development of a two-party system. Of course, we can only imperfectly guarantee the existence of two parties and thereby ensure against a scenario in which no presidential candidate

---

[44] Riker, *Liberalism against Populism*, p. 249 and *passim*.

receives a majority. Nevertheless, a president must possess some minimal mandate to successfully "battle" against a legislature, and the route to this end is to allow runoff elections or to employ an electoral college that magnifies pluralities. That is:

> *Rule 25:* Election procedures in presidential systems should be defined so that a victorious presidential candidate receives majority approval at some point in the election process.

The threat of stalemate, though, is not wholly undesirable. Result 1 asserts that the existence of a "best policy" cannot be guaranteed, but it does not preclude the existence of such a policy. Indeed, if there is a sufficient consensus on how citizens conceptualize a policy dispute, then a Condorcet winner exists (Result 4) — that is, an outcome exists which cannot be defeated in a majority vote by any other feasible outcome. Thus, we should not discount the possibility that debate and deliberation can develop such a consensus. Preferences that are initially contradictory can be transformed into something else, as when short-run redistributions promise long-run improvements that benefit everyone in society. This argument leads to the inference that constitutional provisions such as those that allow for presidential dissolution of a legislature are inherently destabilizing. Such provisions disallow conversion, or they allow chief executives to take advantage of coalitions that are themselves temporary and unstable. That is:

> *Rule 26:* Elections should be regularly scheduled, where the president does not have the authority to dissolve the legislature and the legislature does not have the authority to call for the reelection of the president.

VII. FEDERALISM

In presidential systems at least, legislators are more interested in their own reelection than in defeating incumbents from other parties. Indeed, because incumbents have an incentive to collude on such matters, we should not assume that competition is necessarily between parties rather than between incumbents and challengers.[45] The point I want to make

---

[45] For an example of collusion, consider this letter (November 16, 1989) addressed to the Speaker and Republican Party leader of the United States House of Representatives, signed by the leaders of both parties following passage of a legislative pay raise (*Congressional Quarterly*, December 2, 1989, p. 3326).

Dear Mr. Speaker and Mr. Republican Leader:
The ethics reform package that was adopted in the U.S. House of Representatives today provides an opportunity for all federal elected officials to move away from a growing dependence on special interests.

now, though, is that bicameralism makes this collusion more likely, because it makes any individual vote for a representative even more remote from policy than does a simple unicameral system. Bicameralism's unintended consequence is that it exacerbates the problem of rational ignorance among voters.

What is less obvious is whether this consequence is wholly undesirable. On the one hand, a political system in which legislators, once elected, are nearly impossible to displace seems far removed from the idea of a representative government in which citizens are sovereign. Trapped in a Prisoner's Dilemma—the dilemma of seniority—in which each constituency has little incentive to remove unilaterally an incumbent legislator, a political elite evolves in which only death and scandal are grounds for retirement. To anticipate rational public policy from such a state of affairs seems to require an excessive faith in the virtues of democratic practice. On the other hand, there are compensations. Rational ignorance and the dilemma of seniority can not only yield collusion in which "good" issues are suppressed, it can also yield the suppression of "bad" issues—those redistributive matters that can threaten stability. If such issues make challengers more viable (and once again we can appeal to Result 8 to validate this presumption), and if legislators can suppress those issues or otherwise act to reduce their salience, then collusion is stabilizing.

Before we can reach any definitive evaluation of collusion, though, we must consider one additional matter—federalism—because it can be a key determinant of a state's stability and the ways in which collusion affects policy. I begin by differentiating between the two forms of federalism, *constitutional decentralization* and *contingent decentralization*. Contingent decentralization "locates all sovereignty in the central government. That government then decides . . . how much authority to devolve to the constituent units," whereas in constitutional decentralization "the authority of the states . . . is guaranteed as a matter of organic, constitutional law." [46]

As the leaders of our political committees we are well aware of the political dangers that Members of Congress might face if this issue were to be misused in the campaigns of 1990.

The four of us have agreed to issue instructions to our staffs that the vote on HR 3660 is not an appropriate point of criticism in the coming campaigns. Further we will publicly oppose the use of this issue in any campaign in the 1990 cycle.

This agreement demonstrates our commitment to helping provide a positive political and ethical environment in which qualified people can serve in government.

We applaud the House leadership for the work they have done in this difficult and important area and pledge our continuing support for their efforts.

    Sincerely,

        Ron Brown (Chair, Democratic National Committee)
        Guy Vander Jagt (Chair, Nat. Republican Cong. Comm.)
        Lee Atwater (Chair, Republican National Committee)
        Beryl Anthony (Chair, Democratic Cong. Campaign Comm.)

[46] Peter H. Aranson, "Federalism," *Cato Journal*, vol. 10, no. 1 (1990), p. 20.

The argument for contingent decentralization is that it provides a flexible state form. However, we do not know how to construct a constitution that guarantees even an approximate optimal allocation of governmental responsibility—we do not even know how to identify that optimum, since to assume that we can do so is to assume that we can direct the centrally planned state. Moreover, since contingent federalism precludes constitutionally defined barriers between levels of government, we should suppose that the most naturally powerful level—the national—will soon usurp all authority. That is, without strict constitutional prohibitions to the contrary, the size and influence of the national government in a federal system will grow relative to other governmental units, thereby increasing the redistributive matters that require national resolution. Thus:

> *Rule 27:* The only viable federalism, if we are to have a federal structure at all, is a constitutional one.

Of course, some form of constitutional decentralization seems essential if a society consists of hostile ethnic or religious groups that live in distinct, geographically defined regions, as in the former countries of Yugoslavia and the Soviet Union. Without meaningful economies of scale and with military threats coming wholly from within, coordination is at best difficult and federalism can be little more than a treaty in which hostile groups agree to cooperate only on a limited set of issues if they can cooperate at all. Indeed, *it is difficult to reject the hypothesis that decentralized federalism verging on mere treaties of cooperation is the only feasible form in any society with territorial ethnic, linguistic, religious, or racial divisions.* It is arguably this feature that renders the Swiss confederation stable. There it is almost certainly true that a unitary state would not long survive in light of that society's linguistic and cultural differences.[47] But decentralization allows that country to act as a unitary state on those matters for which there are significant economies of scale, while allowing local governments to operate over relatively homogeneous populations. When a population is subdivided, each subgroup has a more compact preference distribution than the whole, thereby expanding the opportunities for stability at the local level (Result 7).

However, there is the temptation, in constitutional design, to create subunits that match as closely as possible a society's ethnic divisions. The Czechoslovak approach offers an example that should not be followed.[48] Dividing a state solely in accordance with ethnic boundaries sets those di-

---

[47] Alvin Rabushka and Kenneth A. Shepsle, *Politics in Plural Societies: A Theory of Democratic Instability* (Columbus, Ohio: Merrill Pub., 1972).

[48] That approach involves a parliament apportioned equally between Czechs and Slovaks, in which most legislative measures require majority approval in each half. For additional details, see Lloyd Cutler and Herman Schwartz, "Constitutional Reform in Czechoslovakia: E Duobus Unum?" *University of Chicago Law Review*, vol. 58, no. 2 (1991), pp. 511–53.

visions in stone, and when there are only two such groups, places the smaller or the less industrialized and prosperous group at a permanent disadvantage—a disadvantage that it will try to correct either through wholly artificial constitutional means or through secession. Instead:

> *Rule 28:* The federal structure of states with territorial ethnic groups should be partitioned into as many districts as is feasible, where this division partitions even ethnically homogeneous regions.

This rule proceeds on the assumption that even ethnically hostile groups can find issues on which to cooperate (e.g., highway construction, development of irrigation systems, bank reform) that will frequently result in coalitions that we might deem examples of "strange bedfellows" when viewed from a purely ethnic perspective.[49] And, taking a page from the pluralist's book, to the extent that such issues proliferate as a political economy develops, the fragility of coalitions will contribute to the diminution of the salience of ethnic matters.

Taken together, Rules 27 and 28 call for a decentralized federalism in which political parties are forced to compete for votes across ethnic categories within political subunits. Such decentralization seeks to facilitate stability by forcing political parties to resolve ethnic disputes at the regional or local level before they "bubble up" to disrupt national politics. It is at this point, however, that we must confront a seemingly inconsistent empirical fact. Specifically (and noting such exceptions as Switzerland), stable federalisms in general are centralized states—states that make provision, in one way or another, for the theoretical supremacy of the national government over local units. Indeed, the two most notable contemporary examples of federal self-destruction—Yugoslavia and the Soviet Union—occurred when central authority evaporated along with the Communist Party, so that all that remained of a national government was a military establishment and the only political choice was between peaceful disintegration and war.[50]

Fortunately, there are at least two reconciliations of this seeming inconsistency that go a long way toward showing how to design a federalism that does not collapse upon itself into a wholly centralized (unitary) state.

First, we know that outcomes afforded by any issue-specific decentralization will be unstable, because in general a majority of the population will prefer different outcomes, especially if the assignment concerns redistributive issues (Results 2, 3, and 8). There are always those who are advantaged by nationalizing issues and undermining constitutional fed-

---

[49] For a discussion of this case and how it fits our discussion, see Donald L. Horowitz, *Ethnic Groups in Conflict* (Berkeley: University of California Press, 1985).

[50] William H. Riker and Jonathan Lemco, "The Relation Between Structure and Stability in Federal Governments," in *The Development of American Federalism*, ed. W. H. Riker (Boston: Kluwer Academic Publishers, 1986).

eralism. However, one protection against nationalization is provided by the collusion of parties and incumbents discussed earlier in the context of bicameralism. Here the argument is that to the extent that an issue threatens incumbents generally, they will try to use federalism as a means of de-nationalizing that issue. To illustrate, consider reapportionment and notice that in the United States, the Supreme Court sets guidelines but the national government does not intervene otherwise in such matters. In accordance with the initial prescription of the constitution, congressional districts are determined by state legislatures and the competition between parties there. That this allocation of responsibilities is stabilizing derives from the fact that reapportionment, which redistributes political power, is inherently destabilizing in the social-choice theorist's definition. But federalism gives incumbent politicians a device with which to protect themselves, and thus indirectly, the state, from instability.[51]

This device, however, seems a weak reed upon which to base a stable federal government, especially if ethnic conflicts render divisive issues especially salient. Fortunately, Riker, in his seminal analysis of the subject, offers a second solution that rests on the convincing argument that the essential property of a stable federal state is that its institutions ensure that *national* parties are themselves federal.[52] The particular purpose that a federal national party system serves is that it acts as a counterweight to the national government's ability to exert its supremacy over its constituent units. That is, much like the Democratic and Republican parties in the United States,

> *Rule 29:* The political institutions of a federal state ought to be designed so that national political parties are themselves federal in the sense that national legislators retain a strong connection to their local constituencies.

The institutions to which Rule 29 refers include, for example, the requirement that legislators reside in the districts they represent, and the requirement that we eschew proportional representation systems such as those employed by Holland and Israel, in which national legislators are elected without any hint of regional representation. However, Rule 29 is not by itself sufficient for stability, because in combination with Rules 27 and 28, it can yield a fragmented national party system in which parties represent each significant (and even insignificant) cleavage within society. In addition, then:

---

[51] Federalism is not the only device that politicians have at their disposal. Issues can also be "depoliticized" by directing them to specific bureaucratic jurisdictions (e.g., allowing a quasi-independent Federal Reserve to set the discount rate and the money supply) or by allowing the courts to adjudicate them. But federalism has the specific advantage that if parties collude to avoid an issue, then it is difficult for challengers to increase this issue's salience in each constituency taken one at a time.

[52] William H. Riker, *Federalism* (Boston: Little Brown, 1964).

Rule 30: The application of Rules 27–29 in the establishment of a stable federalism requires an electoral incentive that induces local party elites to coalesce at the national level and to negotiate divisive issues within party organizations.

The application of Rule 30 is intended, of course, to facilitate such negotiations, because they will be simpler to conduct if local party elites have already been forced to negotiate at the local level. But something else is required, and that something else in a separation-of-powers system is a plurality-rule presidential election (and its electoral imperatives).

VIII. PARLIAMENTARY GOVERNMENT

Any mention of a presidential system as an essential component of a stable federal government requires, of course, that we also consider its chief rival, parliamentary government. This is especially important since the states of Eastern Europe appear well on their way to establishing governments of this type (or, as in the case of Hungary and Bulgaria, electoral systems that mix plurality and proportional schemes).[53]

Briefly, parliamentary systems, which are distinguished from presidential systems by their abandonment of the idea of a separation of powers, are commonly assumed to have at least three advantages: (1) they allow for greater vitality in government; (2) they allow for the proportional representation (PR) of parties; and (3) by linking the selection of chief executive directly to the legislature, they give voters a more direct policy-oriented stake in the election of representatives.

Each of these "advantages," though, becomes a disadvantage if we keep in mind the intent of a separation of powers—to avoid the instabilities associated with populist democracy and to place a check on demagogues (or states in general) who scheme to represent a nonexistent popular will. First, if we grant that combining executive and legislative branches promotes vitality, we must also conclude that this vitality comes at a cost. Since no governmental activity is devoid of redistributive consequences, greater vitality necessarily increases the salience of redistributive issues and the problems of political instability associated with those issues.

Admittedly, this cost will vary across polities. It will be low in small homogeneous societies that lack ethnic, linguistic, religious, or racial divisions (e.g., the Icelands of the world, or for a more relevant example, Hungary). Here there is little to be gained from a separation of powers and much to be gained from a government whose primary responsibil-

---

[53] See, for example, John R. Hibbing and Samuel C. Patterson, "A Democratic Legislature in the Making: The Historic Hungarian Elections of 1990," *Comparative Political Studies*, vol. 24, no. 4 (1992), pp. 430–54.

ity is to act as society's agent as it tries to coordinate its activities in the maze of a complex world economy. Thus:

> *Rule 31:* Parliamentary government is an appropriate governmental form in small homogeneous states with no well-defined majority or minority.

However, before we can evaluate the displacement of a separation of powers by parliamentary government in "larger" heterogeneous societies, we must consider the role of PR. I will not review the evidence documenting PR's propensity to yield a greater number of parties than evolve as serious competitors in winner-take-all systems.[54] Nor do I want to place undue emphasis on F. A. Hermens's view that arguments for PR fail to specify what it is that ought to be represented.[55] Nevertheless, it is one thing to assert that PR allows for the proportional representation of parties; it is another to assert that it allows for the proportional representation of interests.

The assumption that PR allows parliament to be a microcosm of society rests on the assumption that voters vote for the party that is "closest" to them in some policy space. But this assumption presupposes that voters ignore the ultimate consequences of their vote. In fact, people should vote for the party whose platform most closely matches their interests only if doing so moves governmental policies closer to those interests, and there is nothing in the structure of PR or parliamentary procedure that guarantees this result. Although increasing one's vote share may increase one's share of seats, I know of no proposition that argues that increased seat share increases a party's probability of participating in a government or increases its weight in policy deliberations.[56] And barring this connection, if voters are strategic—if they look ahead to final consequences—then PR need not yield a parliament that "faithfully reflects" the character of interests in an electorate. That is, *proportional representation can be assured of guaranteeing a parliament that approximates being a microcosm of the electorate's underlying policy preferences only if voters do not vote strategically.*

The incentives of voters depend critically on the role of parties. In presidential systems, parties are primarily devices to capture the presidency.

---

[54] See especially Douglas Rae, *The Political Consequences of Electoral Laws* (New Haven, Yale University Press, 1967 and 1971); Rein Taagepera and Matthew Soberg, *Seats and Votes* (New Haven, Yale University Press, 1989); Arendt Lijphart, "The Political Consequences of Electoral Laws, 1945–85," *American Political Science Review*, vol. 84, no. 2 (1990); and Peter C. Ordeshook and Olga Shvetsova, "Electoral Laws, Social Cleavage, and Political Party Formation," working paper, California Institute of Technology, 1992.

[55] F. A. Hermens, *Democracy or Anarchy* (Notre Dame, Indiana: The Review of Politics, 1941).

[56] Indeed, for examples of situations in which increasing one's vote share actually decreases one's utility, see Thomas Schwartz, "The Paradox of Representation," working paper, Department of Political Science, UCLA, 1992.

In PR systems, parties evolve to maximize the chance of participating in a government, to maintain a discernable opposition, or to give specific interests a discernable representation. Winning isn't everything, at least if it is defined in terms of capturing a majority of parliamentary seats. This variation in a party's role in different systems occasions quite different behavior on the part of party leaders. Party leaders in winner-take-all presidential systems must continually seek policy compromises in order to expand their coalitions. Correspondingly, much of the negotiation among potentially hostile interests occurs within parties and is negotiated by party leaders. In contrast, party leaders in PR systems must first be concerned about maintaining their primary base of electoral support, since otherwise new competitors can emerge to claim a share of their seats. Compromise must be negotiated elsewhere, ostensibly in parliament when governments are formed. Hence:

> *Rule 32:* The choice between a presidential and a PR parliamentary system should be viewed as a choice between having minorities attempt to reach compromises within party structures or within parliaments.

Of course, the locus of compromise is itself unimportant. What is relevant is whether compromise reached at one point is more stable than that reached elsewhere. To see then why compromises reached in presidential systems are likely to be more stable, we note that "unless there is an incentive to compromise . . . the mere need to form a coalition will not produce compromise. The incentive to compromise, and not merely the incentive to coalesce, is the key to accommodation." [57] What, then, provides the requisite incentive? The answer is that parties must prefer to vote pool — to exchange electoral support — or to attract voters from other parties directly.

The problems associated with a system such as party-list PR, then, are evident. First, it "contains no incentives to vote pooling or compromise and will produce only coalitions of convenience. . . . To promote intergroup accommodation, the need to form a coalition is . . . a necessary but not a sufficient condition." [58] Second, because party leaders have an incentive to ensure that their supporters vote sincerely in order to maintain their base of support, they have a corresponding incentive to raise the salience of those redistributive issues that justify their existence.

This argument applies with special force to ethnic, religious, linguistic, and racial matters, since it is these "permanent" divisions that are most likely to provide a party with its original reason for being. Thus, PR establishes a conflict between the constitution and ethnicity as the two

---

[57] Donald L. Horowitz, *Democratic South Africa?* (see n. 1 above), p. 171.
[58] *Ibid.*, pp. 175–77.

compete for the role of society's chief coordinating mechanism in political-economic affairs. That is, *PR systems legitimize the conflict between a constitution and ethnic cleavages as mechanisms of political-economic coordination.*

One other feature of PR warrants emphasis in terms of how it deals with ethnic conflicts. In two-party presidential systems, nearly any significant interest can be pivotal in determining a winner. Indeed, we are impressed by the multitude of interests in American elections that claim to be pivotal. Moreover, all such claims have a degree of legitimacy to the extent that the strategic imperatives of Result 4 work to produce a nearly evenly balanced two-party system. Those interests, then, can expect some protection and some reward from any administration. In multi-party PR systems, on the other hand, a party and its corresponding interest either is or is not part of the governing coalition, in which case its protection is more of an "all or nothing" proposition. That is, *although PR may give a particular special interest clear representation, presidential systems provide a near-guarantee that that interest can claim to have provided the critical margin for victory.*

Turning finally to the third ostensible advantage of parliamentary government — that it gives voters a more direct policy-oriented stake in elections — I want to suggest that these incentives render the compromises reached in presidential systems more stable than those achieved under PR. First, party leaders with an incentive to maintain the salience of redistributive issues based on ethnic divisions provide fertile ground for the instabilities identified by Result 8. And if parties have well-defined and differentiated positions, then changing a government coalition's composition can produce wide swings in policy — swings that will not be modified by compromise, since coalitions in such a process are more likely to be associated with policy allocation than with concession.[59] The incentives of parties and voters merely exacerbate this problem. If the parties advocate centrist positions in a two-party presidential system (Result 4), then voters will rationally fail to seek information about policy positions (since the outcome will not greatly affect their welfare) and the parties will fail to generate such information. These consequences, in turn, allow political leaders to collude and to submerge divisive issues. In contrast, parliamentary systems, to the extent that they give voters a more direct stake in the election of representatives and give parties greater incentives to differentiate themselves by their policies, may succeed in creating a more informed electorate that votes with great frequency. But they also create an electorate that is less tolerant of collusion and, thereby, more susceptible to the allure of politicians who take up the cause of redistributive issues.

---

[59] Michael Laver and Kenneth Shepsle, "Subgame Perfect Portfolio Allocations in Parliamentary Government Formation," working paper, Harvard University, 1991. Briefly, "allocation" refers to the practice of giving parties in the governing coalition control of specific issues; "concession," in contrast, requires negotiation on each issue. Allocation, then, can yield outcomes that are not Pareto efficient; concession cannot.

In summary, then, although I have no great objection to the use of parliamentary forms of government and proportional representation in ethnically homogeneous states, a presidential system seems more appropriate in societies that are heterogeneous. Of course, if there are well-defined minority and majority ethnic groups, as in Czechoslovakia and Ukraine, then the minority will oppose a presidential system for fear that that office will be controlled by the majority. However, rather than reject the presidential form, minorities ought to consider other adjustments, such as a more extensive devolution of jurisdictional authority to federal subunits and a president with weaker powers than is found in, say, the American example.

CONCLUSION

A democratic constitution not only defines the state but also is designed to preserve and protect individual liberties and rights. The great puzzle of constitutional democracy, however, is determining how a piece of paper can preserve and protect anything and how societies such as those in Eastern Europe and the republics of the former USSR, ravaged by decades of deception, can have faith that words on paper offer any resolution of their problems.

The answer to this query requires that we consider two alternative philosophical views of constitutional design. The first sees a constitution as a social relationship, a contract, between citizen and state, similar to a contract that sets the terms of market exchange. The second view sees a constitution merely as a mechanism of political coordination that augments those social norms that informally regulate social activity.

Crafting a constitution from the first perspective leads to at least two errors, which come from the way we must try to ensure that a contractual constitution's provisions are enforced and that governments remain subservient to the ultimate sovereign, the people. First, seeking to avoid the ambiguity of enforcement, such constitutions seek to do too much, and readily become documents that justify governmental incursions into all aspects of people's lives. In attempting to avoid this undemocratic outcome, and to defend against every potential tyranny, the unavoidable temptation is to add further prohibitions, administrative and legislative directives, and vague admonitions of rights. But this approach merely compounds the problem, because it succeeds only in adding another layer to our document that requires enforcement. A second and related error is the excessive use of words. The details of a contractual constitution can be specified only with words; unfortunately, this merely opens the door to further ambiguity. For each word used, we may need ten to define it, each of which in turn requires ten additional words, and so on. Formulating a constitution as a contract leads inevitably to these problems because of a simple logical fact—a contract cannot enforce itself.

The alternative view is that constitutions are coordination devices that merely define the general character of the state and, with brevity, specify the mechanisms whereby citizens direct the state to act as their agent. On this view, constitutions are like the social norms that evolve and are accepted by society in general and unconscious ways.

Briefly, a social norm is an implicit or explicit prescription of acceptable or unacceptable social behavior, such that if everyone (alone and together) acts in accordance with it, everyone is better off than if no norm whatsoever existed. Without its norms, a society exists in a state of anarchy and all patterns of social interaction must inefficiently be reinvented at every occasion. Thus, norms arise and are sustained, because they occasion stable expectations about the behavior of others and thereby efficiently coordinate social activity. Their enforcement, in turn, is endogenous to society and is an expression of a popular, consensual will.

A constitution is like a social norm in that it seeks to coordinate action in politics. It establishes a consensus on rights, on the legitimate processes of the state, and on the relation of the state to society. Correspondingly, a stable constitution becomes part of society's social fabric and is enforced not by edicts, threats of force, or the comprehensiveness of its written promises, but by the people's consensual determination to abide by and to protect it.

This second view of constitutions is not mere utopian philosophy—it in fact provides a practical guide to the construction of a stable democracy. First, and with special relevance to the constitutions being crafted today in Eastern Europe and the former USSR, just as social norms are rarely complicated so as not to make it difficult to transmit their meaning across generations, a constitution that can coordinate the political actions of a complex and multicultural society must be simple and capable of being understood by nearly everyone. Second, such constitutions do not provide menus of promises of a better life that the state may not be able to meet. Housing, pensions, security, or children who respect and care for parents obviously are desirable ends. But even reasonable failures to meet such constitutionally mandated goals can undermine the legitimacy of the entire document and the state. The state must be directed to secure the rights of life and liberty, but such words take on meaning only after they are codified by the legislation enacted by elected representatives, who themselves act in accordance with the electoral imperatives that the people establish. Thus, the coordinating constitution may assert general goals to remind us of our values, but it does so briefly and focuses its attention instead on governmental structure—because it is this structure that provides the only guarantee that those goals can be realized.

A third and related feature of such constitutions is that they do not attempt to legislate details. A constitution is not merely the "supreme law of the land"; rather, it is the supreme mechanism that coordinates society in the varied processes of creating and administering laws. A constitution is not a piece of legislation; it is the mechanism people use to guide the formulation of legislation and law. It completes this task in two ways. First, it creates institutions and thereby establishes stable expectations about legitimate process. Indeed, the primary characteristic of this view of constitutions, in contrast to the pluralist view, is that not only do institutions matter, institutions are of primary importance. Second, through bills of rights and other such provisions, a constitution limits the state's "legitimate" functions and removes specific issues from the domain of renegotiable agreements. However, both mechanisms—institutional and jurisdictional—are sustainable only to the extent that they in fact successfully coordinate people's actions to intended equilibria.

I should, however, end this essay with a final rule that would occur to any engineer operating in the physical world. Briefly, the ethnic, religious, racial, or linguistic conflicts that characterize many of the emerging democracies of Eastern Europe and the former USSR may be sufficiently severe that no amount of constitutional engineering can create a stable democratic order. Thus, the only "solution" may be to subdivide such states into independent entities. Put differently:

Rule 33: To the extent that constitutional design is an exercise in political engineering, the drafters of constitutions ought to recognize that there are engineering problems without a solution.

Political Science, California Institute of Technology

THE MORALITY OF INCLUSION

By ALLEN BUCHANAN

I. NEW STATES, NEW ECONOMIES, AND THE PURSUIT OF SELF-INTEREST

Today we are witnessing two dramatic processes: the fragmentation of old states and empires, followed by the emergence of new states and new forms of political association; and the construction of new economies out of the ruins of state socialism. These two processes—the redrawing of political boundaries and the creation of economies—are not independent of one another. In some cases, the desire for a new, more productive economy supplements other motives for state-breaking and state-making. In others, even if the fragmentation of political union results from other factors, such as ethnic divisions or the resurgence of nationalism against a weakened imperial center, the fragments may sort themselves out into new states, federations, or commonwealths, according to what they believe to be maximally productive economic units.

These momentous, largely unanticipated developments make it difficult to evade certain fundamental and perplexing questions about what may be called *the morality of inclusion* — questions upon which political philosophy has generally remained unhelpfully silent. The chief question is this: What general obligations, if any, do we have, either as individuals or collectively, to endeavor to include others in our states or our economies (when they would find it beneficial to be included)? (By "general" obligations I mean to exclude special obligations arising from past joint activity as well as those arising from promises, contracts, or agreements.)

A few examples will suffice to illustrate both that the scope of issues involving the morality of inclusion is quite broad and that the issues themselves are urgent and practical, not just abstract possibilities of moral theory.

(1) If Quebec secedes from Canada, some predict the demise of the Canadian Federation. Once the federal structure is shattered by the departure of Quebec, the richer Western Provinces may band together in closer connection with the United States, leaving the poorer Maritime Provinces to fend for themselves or to remain in what is left of Canada after the Western Provinces go their own way. The hypothesis is that once the status quo is irretrievably destroyed, new political associations may arise according to the perceived self-interest of the members.

© 1993 Social Philosophy and Policy Foundation. Printed in the USA.

(2) The decision of Slovenians to secede from Yugoslavia appears to have been motivated in significant part, if not exclusively, by their realization that their more developed region would fare better alone.

(3) In 1960, just as the Congo was gaining its independence from Belgium, Katanga Province, by far the richest in resources, seceded. (The secession was bloodily suppressed, with the help of United Nations forces.)

(4) In 1970, Biafra, the most economically developed region of Nigeria, seceded. (This secession, too, was unsuccessful.)

(5) The Lombardy Party includes in its platform a resolution calling for the secession of Northern Italy, the richest region of the country.

The last three cases are instances in which the "haves" secede (or, in the case of Northern Italy, threaten to secede) from the "have nots" in an *existing* state, in order to further improve their economic situation. The first, second, and possibly the third, are cases in which the previous state is *already broken* and some of the fragments either take the path of independence or unite with others to form new political units based strictly on self-interest.[1]

All five cases raise the question: Are there any general moral obligations to include others, obligations that place limits on the justified pursuit of self-interest in redrawing political boundaries and in reconstructing economies? And if so, what are the scope and limits of such obligations, and what is their source? More specifically: Do individuals have rights to be included in states, or rights to have access to participation in economic systems, or both, and if so what is the basis of these rights?[2] In this essay I will concentrate chiefly on the morality of political, rather than eco-

---

[1] In some cases in which the "haves" secede from the "have nots" or the "haves" simply refuse to include the "have nots" in new arrangements once the state is shattered, the "haves" may view themselves as morally justified in taking either of these courses because they believe that the preexisting state engaged in regional exploitation or discriminatory redistribution (also called "internal colonialism") toward them. (For a discussion of this grievance and its role in secessionist movements, see Allen Buchanan, *Secession: The Morality of Political Divorce from Fort Sumter to Lithuania and Quebec* [Boulder: Westview Press, 1991], esp. ch. 1.) In what follows I will leave this moral complication aside and focus on whether self-interest alone, rather than the endeavor to escape exploitation, can justify excluding some from the state in these circumstances.

[2] Again, I wish to emphasize that the question that concerns us here is whether there are general obligations of inclusion. Even in the absence of any general obligations, longstanding patterns of cooperation may generate legitimate expectations of continuance, which in turn may ground what may be called "transitional" special obligations. These are obligations on each party not to cease cooperation unilaterally, precipitously, and without compensation or special transitional arrangements designed to minimize the adverse impact of a cessation of cooperation on the other party.

nomic inclusion. However, it will turn out that the two issues are intimately connected.

II. POLITICAL PHILOSOPHY'S SILENCE ON THE MORALITY OF INCLUSION

It is both surprising and disturbing that political philosophy has had so little to say about the morality of secession in particular and the morality of inclusion in general.[3] Past and contemporary political philosophers have concerned themselves with the justification for the state, the conditions under which political authority may be resisted or overthrown, and the proper functions of the state in protecting the rights of its citizens. However, nothing approaching a moral theory specifying the rights of persons to be included in states or the duties of some to include others in states has been proposed. Similarly, political philosophers who have directed their attention to the theory of justice have generally taken membership in an economy or "cooperative scheme" as given, and then asked: What are the appropriate principles to regulate the distribution of burdens and benefits among those who are participants in an economy or "cooperative scheme"?[4] Questions concerning the morality of inclusion in states and economies have, with a few exceptions, been sadly neglected.[5] Pursuing answers to questions about the morality of inclusion, I shall argue, forces us to confront, in a fresh and illuminating way, two central questions of political philosophy, as well as their connection with one another: *What is the state for?* and *To whom is justice owed?*

III. CONFLICTING VISIONS OF THE FUNCTION OF THE STATE AND OF THE SCOPE OF JUSTICE

Even though questions of the morality of inclusion have rarely been explicitly addressed (and never in a systematic way), there are two major traditions in political philosophy which have diametrically opposed implications for the morality of inclusion. The first tradition, which I shall call *justice as self-interested reciprocity*,[6] views justice as applying only to relations among participants in mutually beneficial cooperation and conceives of the state as a mechanism for enforcing principles of justice so

[3] I attempt to begin the task of remedying the lack of a moral theory of secession in *Secession: The Morality of Political Divorce*.

[4] See, for example, John Rawls, *A Theory of Justice* (Cambridge. Harvard University Press, 1971), pp. 11–17; and Brian Barry, *A Treatise on Social Justice*, vol. 1, *Theories of Justice* (Berkeley, California: University of California Press, 1989), pp. 9–11.

[5] Among the exceptions are some rather unsystematic works on the morality of immigration and emigration and on the decision not to grant full citizenship to "guest workers." See, for example, Michael Walzer, *Spheres of Justice* (New York: Basic Books, 1983), pp. 31–94.

[6] Allen Buchanan, "Justice as Reciprocity Versus Subject-Centered Justice," *Philosophy & Public Affairs*, vol. 19, no. 3 (1990), pp. 227–52.

understood. According to justice as self-interested reciprocity: (1) Only those who are one's co-participants in a mutually beneficial cooperative scheme have rights, and it is only toward fellow participants that one owes duties. (2) Furthermore, it is permissible for one to decide with whom one will cooperate solely out of considerations of self-interest. If Jones and Smith can each do better for themselves by cooperating with Brown than with Davis, then they have no obligation to include Davis in their cooperative scheme. In other words, there are no obligations of inclusion that place any restrictions on the pursuit of self-interest in choosing optimally beneficial cooperative schemes and excluding less than optimal participants from them. The implication of the conjunction of theses (1) and (2) is as harsh as it is clear: (3) The scope of justice—the membership of the class of those to whom justice is owed—is determined solely by the requirements of self-interest. Even though duties to respect others' rights impose restrictions on the pursuit of self-interest in interactions with others *within* a given cooperative scheme, no one is obligated to include anyone in such a scheme who is not an optimal partner, and no one is obligated to choose a cooperative scheme which will include more rather than fewer participants.

A fourth defining thesis of justice as self-interested reciprocity is this: (4) The function of the state is to articulate, institutionalize, and enforce principles of justice (understood as applying only to co-participants in the cooperative scheme). According to justice as self-interested reciprocity, then, individuals are free to associate with like-minded others to form cooperative schemes according to what will maximize their self-interest; justice applies only to relations among co-participants in a mutually beneficial cooperative scheme; and the boundaries of the cooperative scheme determine the boundaries of the state.

In sum, on this view the *function* of the state is to make possible optimal mutually beneficial cooperation; and individuals, being free to pursue their self-interest in choosing optimal partners in cooperation, are therefore free to determine who shall be within the state and who shall be outside of it. Since there are no obligations of inclusion in cooperative schemes, and since states exist to support cooperative schemes by enforcing rights and duties among participants in them, there are no obligations to include individuals in states.[7]

---

[7] It might be thought that some representatives of the tradition I have labeled "justice as self-interested reciprocity," such as Hobbes, hold that one is obligated to form cooperative schemes with enforced rules of peaceful cooperation and that this amounts to an obligation to include others in such arrangements. In support of this claim, one might cite Hobbes's Second Law of Nature: "That a man be willing, when others are so too, as farre-forth, as for Peace, and defense of himselfe he shall think it necessary, to lay down his right to all things; and be contented with so much liberty against other men, as he would allow men against himselfe" (Thomas Hobbes, *Leviathan* [New York: Penguin Books, 1968], p. 190). However, all the Second Law requires is that one include whoever is necessary in order to achieve security from one's physical destruction (and to achieve commodious living). The

Justice as self-interested reciprocity is a venerable view in political phi-losophy. Its proponents include Epicurus, Glaucon in Plato's *Republic*, Thomas Hobbes, perhaps David Hume, and, most recently, and rigor-ously, David Gauthier.[8] Gauthier's work is especially instructive, since he most explicitly embraces justice as self-interested reciprocity and does not shrink from its implications concerning the scope of justice. According to Gauthier, principles of justice (and indeed moral principles generally) are the outcome of a bargain among rationally self-interested individuals. Those who are not desirable as co-participants in a mutually beneficial

---

Second Law does *not* imply that there are any obligations of inclusion that represent restric-tions on the pursuit of self-interest.

A proponent of justice as self-interested reciprocity might more plausibly argue that this view does allow the possibility of different levels of strengths of obligations and can encom-pass some obligations, though of an inferior nature, to individuals who are not within the boundaries of the state. For example, purely rationally self-interested citizens of one state (who have toward one another what we might call "primary obligations," due to their di-rect and actual cooperative relationships with one another) might have "secondary obliga-tions" toward citizens of other states, to whom they are perhaps only indirectly related in more limited schemes of cooperation, or with whom they may become co-participants in a cooperative scheme in the future. Thus, justice as self-interested reciprocity might be thought to be capable of explaining the existence of some limited obligations to those who lie beyond the boundaries of one's state. The central point, however, is that justice as self-interested reciprocity, so far as it includes a view about the state, maintains that the function of the state is to enforce obligations among those who are co-participants in a cooperative scheme, and that whatever obligations exist to include individuals within the state are owed only to those who are co-participants in the cooperative scheme.

[8] In *The Republic*, Glaucon offers a version of justice as self-interested reciprocity:

> People say that injustice is by nature good to inflict but evil to suffer. Men taste both of its sides and learn that the evil of suffering it exceeds the good of inflicting it. Those unable to flee the one and take the other therefore decide it pays to make a pact nei-ther to commit nor to suffer injustice. It was here that men began to make laws and covenants, and to call whatever the laws decreed "legal" and "just."

Plato, *The Republic*, trans. and ed. Raymond Larson (Arlington Heights, IL: AHM, 1979), bk. 2, section 359, p. 32.

Epicurus suggests a similar view in his *Kuriai Doxai* ("Key Doctrines"). See, for example, Key Doctrine 32: "Nothing is just or unjust in relation to those creatures which were un-able to make contract over not harming one another and not being harmed"; and Key Doc-trine 33: "Justice was never anything *per se*, but a contract regularly arising at some place or other in people's dealings with one another, over not harming or being harmed." See *The Hellenistic Philosopher*, trans. A. A. Long and D. N. Sedley (Cambridge: Cambridge Univer-sity Press, 1987), p. 127.

In *Enquiries concerning Human Understanding and concerning the Principles of Morals*, Hume at least hints at justice as self-interested reciprocity when he speculates that creatures oth-erwise like us, but powerless to harm us, would at most hope to be treated mercifully, but could not expect to be treated justly. See Hume, *Enquiries*, ed. L. A. Selby-Bigge and P. H. Nidditch, 3d ed. (Oxford: Clarendon Press, 1975), pp. 190–91.

Epicurus, Glaucon, and (perhaps) Hume present what might be called the "negative" ver-sion of justice as self-interested reciprocity—emphasizing that it is the ability of others to *harm* us (and our self-interest in avoiding that harm) that is the basis of their rights and our obligations. David Gauthier, the most explicit, rigorous, and systematic proponent of jus-tice as self-interested reciprocity, expounds the "positive" version of the view, emphasiz-ing the idea that justice (and morality generally) applies only to those who are or can be co-participants in a mutually beneficial cooperative scheme. See Gauthier, *Morals by Agree-ment* (Oxford: Oxford University Press, 1986), pp. 113–56.

cooperative scheme have nothing to bargain with and therefore fall outside the scope of justice.[9] From the standpoint of justice as self-interested
reciprocity, what qualifies one as a being to whom justice is owed is a
strategic capacity — one's ability to be a net contributor in the cooperative
scheme.[10]

A second major tradition in political philosophy is *subject-centered justice*. According to this view, what determines an individual's inclusion
within the domain of justice is not her capacity for contribution to a maximally beneficial cooperative scheme. Instead, inclusion in the domain
of justice is determined by what may be called subject-centered or nonstrategic characteristics. Different versions of the subject-centered view
propose different characteristics of the subject as those which qualify an
individual for possessing rights. According to utilitarianism, it is the
capacity for happiness; according to Kantianism, the capacity for rational
agency. From a Lockean perspective (at least according to some interpretations) what qualifies one as a possessor of rights and the object of others' duties is the rational nature bestowed by the Creator. Whether other
persons have duties of justice toward one depends upon whether one has
these characteristics, not upon whether one has the strategic capacity of
being a participant (or having the potential for being a participant), in a
cooperative scheme which is optimally beneficial for them.

Unlike justice as self-interested reciprocity, subject-centered justice, at
least on some of its versions, is capable of grounding *universal* rights and
duties. For example, if, as on Kantian versions of the view, the characteristic which determines inclusion in the domain of justice is the capacity for rational agency, then all beings who have this capacity are subjects
of justice — all have whatever rights justice confers. Similarly, for Locke,
it is a characteristic shared by all persons, the ability to understand and
follow the laws of their God-given reason, that confers rights.

Utilitarianism, in contrast, is a subject-centered theory which does not
ensure that rights, even the most basic rights, are universal. Whether a

[9] Gauthier does allow the possibility of one pre-cooperative right — the right not to have
one's condition worsened by the action of others (the Proviso). (See Gauthier, *Morals by
Agreement*, pp. 205, 214–23). However, in my view this one exception to the general thesis
that rights are derived from an agreement among rational bargainers and that rights and
obligations exist only among those who are net contributors to a cooperative scheme, is an
ad hoc and thoroughly unmotivated addition to the basic conception of justice as self-interested reciprocity with which Gauthier operates. The function of the Proviso is to soften the
harshness of the theory — by importing some considered moral judgments which reflect limitations on what we may do to others in the pursuit of our own interests. However, the
appeal of justice as self-interested reciprocity is supposed to be that it does not rely on considered moral judgments, but instead accepts only those moral principles and judgments
which can be shown to be grounded in self-interested rationality.

[10] As noted earlier, according to some versions of justice as self-interested reciprocity,
including that of Epicurus, the ability to harm is said to be what qualifies one for membership in the community of beings to whom justice is owed. The notion that what makes one
a being who falls within the scope of justice is one's strategic capacities (either to benefit or
to harm) is broad enough to encompass these views.

particular individual or class of individuals has rights will depend upon whether the general recognition that they have rights will maximize utility. It is not inconceivable that in certain circumstances greater utility might be gained by not ascribing rights to certain classes of individuals — for example, those who are seriously retarded from birth.[11] So although at least one subject-centered theory, utilitarianism, does not provide a firm grounding for universal rights, other subject-centered theories do, including two of the most prominent ones, Kantian and Lockean theories.[12]

In contrast, according to justice as self-interested reciprocity, rights obtain only within a cooperative scheme. Those outside the scheme have no rights, and none has a right to be included within a cooperative scheme, nor, hence, within the domain of justice. In sum, while some of the more prominent subject-centered theories do ground universal rights, theories of justice as self-interested reciprocity are incapable of doing so.

It was noted earlier that justice as self-interested reciprocity includes a thesis about the function of the state: the state is a mechanism for articulating, institutionalizing, and enforcing principles of justice, the latter being understood as specifications of the general duties co-participants in the cooperative scheme owe one another. The state exists only to support mutually beneficial cooperation among those who, on the basis of their own self-interest, choose to cooperate together. Subject-centered theories also hold that the function of the state is to enforce duties of justice. For example, according to Locke, the function of the state is to uphold the natural rights to life, liberty, and property.

For justice as self-interested reciprocity, there can be no question of *obligations* to enforce rights beyond the limits of the cooperative scheme, since rights (and duties) apply only within the cooperative scheme. However, since on at least some subject-centered views all persons have these rights, the question arises as to what the proper *scope* of the state's enforcement function is. And if the boundaries of the state are the limits of its domain of enforcement, that is, the jurisdiction within which it performs the function of enforcing rights, then the question is whether there are general obligations to include individuals within the state if their being included is necessary in order to protect the rights which they, like all persons, have. In other words, because subject-centered theories, un-

---

[11] Allen Buchanan, "The Right to a 'Decent Minimum' of Health Care," *Philosophy & Public Affairs*, vol. 13, no. 1 (1983), pp. 55–78.

[12] Utilitarianism is a subject-centered theory, but it can be argued that it does not provide a secure grounding for universal rights. According to rule utilitarianism, attributions of rights are appropriate when and only when the recognition of these rights for those to whom they are attributed maximizes overall utility. A utilitarian case can be made for *not* attributing rights to some persons who are so disabled that they are unable to make net contributions to overall utility, even if they are capable of rational agency. Thus, utilitarianism may lead to the exclusion of some persons from the domain of justice when Kantianism, for example, would not, even though both are subject-centered theories.

like justice as self-interested reciprocity, allow for the ascription of rights to all persons, not just to members of one's cooperative scheme, they at least leave open the possibility that there are general obligations of inclusion in states.

Surprisingly enough, the major subject-centered theories are silent or at least far from clear on the question of what the scope of the state's enforcement of rights is supposed to be. For example, Locke argues that individuals have a right to enforce rights (their own and others') in the state of nature, and that this individual right is the foundation of the right of the state to perform the enforcement function.[13] He does not, to my knowledge, state explicitly that individuals have any *obligation* to enforce their own rights, nor does he so much as suggest that individuals have any obligation to establish an enforcement mechanism that will protect the rights of individuals generally. Instead, Locke seems to concentrate only on showing that individuals who *choose* to do so *may* create a mechanism to enforce *their* rights. There is no suggestion that a group constituting a political association is obligated to include others in that association or to aid in any other way the enforcement of their rights. One plausible interpretation of Locke, then, is that he believes that individuals who interact with one another may set up a mechanism for the impartial enforcement of their rights vis-à-vis one another (if private enforcement is "inconvenient"),[14] but that no one is under any obligation to help facilitate the protection of the rights of persons generally, or of any persons with whom one is not now or not likely to be in contact if one chooses not to be. On this reading of Locke, there are no general obligations of inclusion in a regime for the enforcement of rights, not even weak and defeasible ones.

In contrast, Kant does explicitly state that there is an *obligation* to create a state, understood as a mechanism for articulating, institutionalizing, and enforcing rights. In the *Rechtslehre*, he enunciates "the postulate of Public Right [or Justice]," namely, that "[w]hen you cannot avoid living side by side with all others, you ought to leave the state of nature and proceed with them into a rightful [*Rechtlich*] condition. . . ."[15]

This passage actually says only that one is obligated to help create a state to govern relations with those one cannot avoid interacting with. It does *not* say that one has any sort of obligation, even a very limited or defeasible one, to help ensure that all persons' rights are enforced.

However, in an explanatory note to the paragraph that follows the passage just cited, Kant seems to say that persons as such—all persons— have a right to be included in a state. By failing to contribute to the

[13] John Locke, *Second Treatise of Civil Government*, ed. C. B. Macpherson (Indianapolis: Hackett Publishing Co., 1980), p. 11.

[14] *Ibid.*, pp. 11–16.

[15] Immanuel Kant, *The Metaphysics of Morals*, trans. Mary Gregor (Cambridge: Cambridge University Press, 1991), p. 122.

establishment of a regime (or regimes) which enforces all persons' rights, we "do wrong in the highest degree" and "subvert the Right of men as such." [16] This passage suggests that every person has a right to inclusion in some state and that every person has a duty to help ensure that each person enjoys such inclusion so that her rights may be protected.

My point in making this brief excursion into Kant and Locke is only to make clear that the major figures of the subject-centered justice tradition speak equivocally, when they speak at all, on the issue of whether the enforcement of persons' basic rights is obligatory, rather than merely permissible. Yet on the face of it, it seems a thoroughly odd view to hold that all persons have certain basic rights and that individuals may make collective provision for their own rights, while at the same time denying that we have any obligations at all to help ensure that persons' rights are protected, unless those persons are already included in (or we choose to include them in) the regime which protects our own rights. To put the matter bluntly, it is an odd view because whatever considerations point to the conclusion that all individuals *have* these basic rights (which we are obligated to respect) seem to point beyond it to the conclusion that we are obligated to contribute to the establishment of reliable institutional mechanisms for ensuring that those rights are respected. (This is not to say, of course, that we are obligated to so contribute no matter what the cost.)

Now if our duties not to kill or enslave or steal from others were *not* correlatives of their rights — if we only had duties *regarding* others rather than duties *toward* them and did not *owe it to them*, in virtue of the sorts of beings they are, to refrain from treating them thus — then it might be more plausible to say that we have no obligations to contribute toward the enforcement of their rights. For example, if the sole basis of our duties regarding other persons were the command of God that we not kill, not steal, etc., then we might have no reason to view ourselves as being obligated to help ensure that others do not violate their duties (unless God had also commanded us to do this).

However, according to subject-centered theories of justice, as I understand them, our duties of justice are *owed to* others in virtue of *their* (nonstrategic) characteristics. Moreover, a proper appreciation of these characteristics entails the conviction *that the beings who have them are not to be treated in certain ways*, not simply that *I* am not to treat them in those ways. But if this is so, then, barring any countervailing moral considerations, it would appear that I am obligated not only to refrain from violating persons' rights, but also to contribute to institutional arrangements for ensuring that their rights are not violated.

What I am suggesting is that given a subject-centered view of justice, as opposed to justice as self-interested reciprocity, or a divine-command view, there is at least a strong presumption that we have obligations to

[16] *Ibid*.

help foster arrangements for the enforcement of persons' rights. The burden of argument should be on those who would deny such an obligation.

A theory of justice which recognized that all persons have certain basic rights because of certain characteristics that all persons have, but which recognized no obligations to help facilitate arrangements for protecting those rights, might not be logically inconsistent, but it would surely manifest a deep incoherence. In the absence of any sound argument to rebut the presumption that there are obligations of inclusion, the denial of obligations of inclusion would, for such a view, seem arbitrary and unmotivated.

What sorts of countervailing moral considerations might defeat the presumption that we have obligations to help ensure that everyone is included in a rights-protecting regime? As far as I can ascertain, there is only one prospect for blocking the inference from the obligation to respect rights to the obligation to help ensure that rights are respected, and hence to the obligation to include others in one's state if that is the only feasible way for ensuring that their rights are respected (assuming the costs are not excessive). This would be to argue that any such obligation would be an unwarranted restriction on individual autonomy or a burden that would detract in unacceptable ways from one's pursuit of one's own projects.

However, this is not really an argument for denying that obligations of inclusion exist. It is only a reason for understanding them as being limited obligations which do not entail the impositions of excessive costs or risks.

It is tempting to think that the obligation of political inclusion necessarily would be unduly burdensome, if one makes the mistake of assuming that the obligation is to include any person who presently does not enjoy protection of his rights in *one's own* political unit. But this is an excessively onerous interpretation of what the obligation is. If, instead, the obligation is merely to do one's fair share in helping to create a situation in which everyone has access to *some rights-protecting regime or other*, then it is hard to see why the obligation's existence can be denied on the grounds that it necessarily intrudes too deeply into personal autonomy and well-being.

Furthermore, what our obligations require will vary, depending upon the circumstances. In some cases, all that will be required will be allowing those whose rights are being violated to emigrate to our state or to some other state that will protect their rights. Moreover, a fair sharing of the burdens of accepting such emigrants might be achieved by multilateral agreements among the better-off states, to avoid excessive burdens on any particular state. Notice also that nothing said so far requires that those whom we allow to enter our borders in order that their rights may be protected are to be granted all the privileges of full citizenship. All that is required is that their basic rights be protected, and the rights of full citizens may exceed these. For example, full citizens may run for office, while resident aliens may not.

The most extreme case in which the obligation of political inclusion might apply would be one in which a group that hitherto had been included in a state would lose its basic rights if another group in the state seceded and left the first group in a condition of anarchy, or in a position in which it would be invaded by a third, rights-violating state. In such a case, the only way to protect the rights of the first group might be to continue to include it within the state. If this were the case, then the obligation of political inclusion would speak in favor of the second group not seceding and leaving the first group in a condition in which its members' rights would be violated. Whether this obligation would be morally decisive would depend upon a number of factors—for example, upon the moral cogency of the second group's reasons for seceding, and upon the costs to them of continuing to include the first group within their political boundaries in order to protect them. But to say that the obligation of political inclusion will require different policies in different situations—from allowing emigration to refraining from fragmenting the state—and to recognize that this obligation is not absolute, is not to deny that it exists. As we have already seen, any subject-centered theory which ascribes certain basic rights to all persons would have great difficulty with such a denial.

There is, of course, no presumption of obligations of inclusion for the proponent of justice as self-interested reciprocity, because that view does not, and indeed cannot, support the thesis that all persons have rights. So, in that sense, the proponent of justice as self-interested reciprocity, unlike the advocate of subject-centered justice, does not owe us either an account of such obligations or an argument to rebut the presumption that they exist.

However, if we take it to be a criterion of adequacy for a theory of justice that it include the tenet that there are some basic rights which all persons have, simply because they are persons, then justice as self-interested reciprocity fails to measure up. So justice as self-interested reciprocity avoids the task of providing a theory of obligations of inclusion, but only at what many will regard as a prohibitive price—the inability to recognize rights that are in any sense universal.

Subject-centered justice views, such as those of Kant and Locke, do satisfy this criterion of adequacy—they make sense of the notion of universal rights. But, precisely because they do, they cannot evade the question of whether there are obligations of inclusion, and they run the risk of a deep incoherence if they stop short of the conclusion that there are obligations to help include persons in rights-enforcing arrangements.

The same point can be made from a different angle. Unlike justice as self-interested reciprocity, subject-centered justice does not determine the domain of justice by following the dictates of self-interest. Persons have rights because of the kinds of beings they are, not because they happen to have what it takes to be optimal partners in mutually beneficial schemes of cooperation. But if, as the subject-centered theorist asserts, the domain of justice is not determined solely by considerations of self-interest, then why should we assume that we ought to include others in our arrangements for protecting our rights only if it is in our interest to do so? For a theorist of subject-centered justice to maintain that there are universal rights but no obligations of inclusion in rights-protecting regimes, he would have to hold that we have obligations to help enforce rights only to those with whom we choose to unite in a cooperative scheme for the enforcement of rights. But this latter view appears to be much more consonant with justice as self-interested reciprocity than with a subject-centered view.

IV. Obligations of Justice or of Charity?

To say that there are obligations to facilitate the inclusion of persons generally in rights-protecting regimes is not by itself to say that persons generally have a *right* to such inclusion. Not all obligations are correlatives of rights. Thus, it might be argued that the considerations that support the position that all persons have certain basic rights imply, at most, that we have obligations of charity, but not of justice, to ensure that everyone's rights are protected.

There is some dispute about exactly how the distinction between obligations of justice and obligations of charity is to be construed, what its basis is, and how we are to draw it in particular cases.[17] Usually it is said that what distinguishes obligations of charity is that they are "imperfect," in that the individual has discretion both with respect to the choice of a recipient of his benevolence and with respect to the amount and nature of his assistance. Moreover, it is often said that although an individual's failure to act charitably may be wrong, it is not a wronging of the one whom he failed to act charitably toward, because obligations of charity have no correlative rights. In other words, if I fail to act charitably, I wrong no one, since no one has a right corresponding to my obligation. It is otherwise with obligations of justice, which are correlative with and grounded in individuals' rights. To fail to fulfill an obligation of justice is to wrong someone, to violate her right.

Unfortunately, there is a good deal of disagreement as to which of our obligations are obligations of charity and which are obligations of justice. It might be thought that we can distinguish the two by a simple phenomenological test: For any given obligation, one can ask whether, in recognizing a failure to discharge it, one has the conviction that someone was

---

[17] Allen Buchanan, "Justice and Charity," *Ethics*, vol. 97, no. 3 (April 1987).

thereby wronged, that there is an aggrieved party, with a valid claim to redress. If so, then it is an obligation of justice; if not, then it is merely an obligation of charity.

The difficulty with the phenomenological test—with this appeal to intuitions about the nature of the failure when the obligation is not discharged—is that persons with different theories of justice will have different intuitions on just this point. For example, an extreme libertarian may believe that failure to help the starving children in one's own neighborhood shows a lack of charity, but does not constitute an injustice. Believing as he does that persons have no rights to welfare, he will not feel that the children, in being allowed to starve, are being wronged. Especially for those who have thought explicitly about the principles to which they subscribe, intuitions may be too closely congruent with principles to provide a neutral, independent standard for adjudicating between rival theories.

Given the difficulty of distinguishing convincingly between obligations of justice and those of charity, especially in just the interesting and controversial cases which concern us, it is well to ask precisely what is at stake in the distinction. The usual answer is that obligations of justice may be rightly enforced, while obligations of charity may not.

If this latter claim is to be understood as an analytic truth, then I have little quarrel with it—though I also find little interest in it. If one simply *means* by an obligation of justice any obligation that may rightly be enforced, and if one reserves the term "obligation of charity" for those obligations that may not be rightly enforced, then there may be no harm in such a stipulation. However, such linguistic fiat will not itself tell us *which* obligations may rightly be enforced. My own view, which I have argued for at some length previously, is that any genuine obligation carries with it a very weak presumption that enforcement may be employed, if necessary, but that this presumption may be overridden either on grounds of impracticality or because there are weightier moral considerations against enforcement.[18] The most obvious candidate for a countervailing moral consideration, of course, would be that enforcement would violate someone's rights. What I am suggesting, then, is that, given that persons have rights, we have an obligation to help ensure that those rights are respected, an obligation that may be enforced if necessary, *unless* the enforcement of this obligation violates rights (or unless some other weighty moral reason speaks against enforcement).

A libertarian such as Robert Nozick might well accept this last statement, but then argue that enforcing the obligation to ensure that all persons have access to a rights-protecting regime *does* violate individual rights and that, therefore, this obligation of inclusion is not an obligation which could ever be rightly enforced. The libertarian would then have to

[18] *Ibid.*, pp. 556–57.

show that *every* instance of enforcing an obligation to facilitate inclusion would involve a violation of some individual right or other (or run contrary to some other weighty moral consideration).

Presumably, the right in question would be the individual right to private property. For example, when the United States allows some persons whose rights had been violated in their own country to come to this country, costs are thereby imposed on U.S. taxpayers. "Processing" emigrants as they enter the country costs money, as does providing them with various social services, whether or not they are granted full citizenship rights. The libertarian would say that using citizens' resources (gained by taxing them) to cover these costs violates their rights to private property, even if the emigration policy in question was the result of sound democratic processes.

It is not my intention here to rehearse various familiar arguments against libertarianism.[19] Instead, I only wish to point out that in order to show that obligations of political inclusion may never rightly be enforced, the libertarian must not only show that there is a basic moral right to private property, but also that this right is so broad in scope and so absolute that any effort to exact contributions from individuals for the sake of discharging obligations of inclusion must violate this right.

There are, it seems, two main strategies available for making good the claim that there is such a right to private property. On the one hand, the libertarian might attempt to provide a positive argument for such a right. On the other hand, one might provide a negative or indirect argument for a broad and virtually absolute right to private property by showing that recognizing anything less than such a robust property right would result in unacceptable intrusions into individuals' lives and would undermine the stability of expectations associated with the rule of law. Nozick's famous Wilt Chamberlain example can be interpreted as an argument of this second, indirect or negative sort. The idea is that (a) any principle of justice that sanctions forced redistribution will require unacceptable intrusions and will disrupt expectations, and (b) to prevent such intrusions and disruptions it is necessary to recognize (and institutionalize) a very broad and virtually absolute individual right to private property which will rule out forced redistribution. This interpretation is consonant with a long tradition of libertarian thinking which argues for a strong individual right to private property, not as a basic moral right, but as an institutional bulwark against those infringements of liberty and economic inefficiencies which are thought to follow inevitably from attempts to implement redistributive policies or to establish positive rights.

---

[19] See, for example, G. A. Cohen, "Wilt Chamberlain and Robert Nozick: How Patterns Preserve Liberty," in *Justice and Economic Distribution*, ed. J. Arthur and W. H. Shaw (Englewood Cliffs, NJ: Prentice Hall, 1978), pp. 246–62; and Allen Buchanan, *Ethics, Efficiency, and the Market* (Totowa, NJ: Rowman and Littlefield, 1982), pp. 64–70.

The first libertarian strategy, that of providing a positive grounding for a very broad and virtually unlimited right to private property, has not (so far) been successful. In particular, neither Nozick, nor his predecessor Locke, provides such an argument.[20]

The second libertarian strategy does seem capable of showing that *very ambitious* (or very clumsy) redistributive programs—for example, those that aim at equality rather than at providing a "decent minimum" or "safety net"—are incompatible with any significant right to private property and will intrude unacceptably on individual liberty, preventing the individual from being able to lead his own life and pursue his own projects. Yet none of these arguments seems capable of showing that less ambitious, more carefully crafted redistributive programs, such as those that actually exist in the less extreme welfare states, are incompatible either with the stability of expectations we associate with the rule of law, or with an acceptably broad sphere of individual freedom.[21] For example, redistributive programs designed to ensure that all citizens have some insurance for unemployment and major disabilities need not require frequent, unpredictable, and disruptive takings, if they are funded through longstanding, publicized tax laws. Virtually all developed countries, including those that approximate the liberal ideal of the rule of law, make use of such provisions.

It seems, then, that neither the positive nor the negative libertarian strategy makes a convincing case for an individual moral right to private property so broad and absolute as to rule out any enforced redistributive policy whatsoever. If this is the case, then it is hard to see why *all* enforced redistribution for fulfilling obligations of political inclusion is necessarily prohibited. For this reason, I think it would be unwarranted to assume that whatever obligations of political inclusion we have are obviously not enforceable obligations under any circumstances. My main purpose here, however, is to argue that, at least on subject-centered theories of the universalist sort, there are such obligations. Whether, or under what circumstances, it is permissible to enforce them is of secondary importance for present purposes. My brief critical comments on the libertarian objection to the permissibility of enforcing obligations of political inclusion are merely meant to show that it would be a mistake to assume that such rights may *not* be enforced.

---

[20] In *Anarchy, State, and Utopia*, pp. 26–35, Nozick does suggest some reasons in favor of the libertarian rights he largely assumes. The leading idea is that only these rights meet the fundamental moral imperative of not treating persons as mere means but as ends in themselves. However, although this line of argument may be able to support the claim that there is a right to liberty and a right to private property, it seems incapable—at least without further premises which Nozick nowhere supplies—of showing that only the very strong libertarian versions of these rights capture this basic requirement of morality. See Robert Nozick, *Anarchy, State, and Utopia* (New York: Basic Books, 1974).

[21] Buchanan, *Ethics, Efficiency, and the Market*, pp. 64–70.

V. Subject-Centered Justice Versus Justice as Self-Interested Reciprocity: How Are We to Adjudicate the Theoretical Dispute?

We have seen that how one answers the question "Are there obligations of inclusion?" depends, ultimately, upon which type of theory of justice one subscribes to. If the theory is some version of justice as self-interested reciprocity, then the scope of justice is restricted to the class of those who are co-participants in a mutually beneficial cooperative scheme, and individuals transgress no moral duties if they seek to cooperate only with those who will be optimal partners. Since the state is merely a mechanism for enforcing the terms of cooperation among those who choose to cooperate together, there can be no obligations to help ensure that all individuals have access to inclusion in states.

Subject-centered justice, in contrast, allows for the possibility that there are universal rights. For those subject-centered theories which ascribe basic rights to all persons, all persons have obligations, not only to respect all others' rights, but also to help ensure that all others' rights are respected. And if ensuring that a person's rights are respected requires that he be included in some state or other, then universalist subject-centered theories of justice include an obligation to help ensure that everyone is included in some state or other.

Whether there are obligations of political inclusion depends, then, upon whether the correct theory of justice is justice as self-interested reciprocity or some universalist version of subject-centered justice. But how are we to adjudicate this dispute among rival types of theories of justice? Although I cannot hope to provide a decisive answer to this fundamental question here, I will attempt to set out the main factors that should be considered in arriving at an answer, and I will venture a tentative judgment in favor of subject-centered justice.

I wish to suggest three salient candidates for criteria on the basis of which to evaluate the two types of theories — at least if the evaluation is to be made from within what might be very broadly called the liberal tradition. (By the "liberal tradition" here I mean something very broad indeed. Any view which holds that there are some human rights, which recognizes that persons have even very limited obligations to prevent violations of human rights, and which acknowledges the moral priority of individual liberty, would fall within the compass of the liberal tradition in this broad sense.) First, we may ask, which type of theory provides the best match with and grounding for our most confident and widely held moral judgments about obligations of inclusion? Second, which type of theory can support the ascription of at least some basic moral rights to all persons? Third, which type of theory provides the strongest justifications for the principles of justice it advances?

Subject-centered justice, at least in its Lockean and Kantian forms (which ascribe basic rights to all persons) fares better on the first criterion. These types of theories are not only consistent with, but also explain, our reasons for taking the question of whether to intervene in the current genocidal ethnic conflict in Yugoslavia to be a moral issue, not just a question of choosing the most prudent policy. On the one hand, we feel that it is wrong to sit idly by while thousands of persons' most fundamental rights are being violated. On the other hand, we feel a reluctance to intervene, for a number of reasons, some moral, some purely prudential. Not only is intervention in such a situation likely to be risky and costly, but there are also sound moral reasons for a strong presumption against military intervention in other countries, the most compelling being that what is touted as disinterested intervention to protect individuals' rights is very frequently a cover for hegemonic designs.

Subject-centered theories, at least those of the universalist variety, can explain why we are morally uncomfortable with a policy of nonintervention in such circumstances, and why we feel it incumbent on ourselves to provide sound moral or prudential reasons for not intervening. Justice as self-interested reciprocity, in contrast, cannot account for any sense of obligation to help protect the rights of persons as such, as opposed to those persons who are co-participants in optimally beneficial mutual cooperation.

On the second criterion, subject-centered justice, at least in its nonutilitarian variants, is a hands-down winner. Justice as self-interested reciprocity cannot support the thesis that all persons have some rights. Of course, it is open to the theorist of justice as self-interested reciprocity to bite the bullet here and embrace the position that there are no universal (that is, human) rights. For those of us who believe that all persons do have some basic rights, this is not an option.

It is important to note that justice as self-interested reciprocity is incompatible even with what might be called the "conditional universality" of basic rights. This is the view, espoused by Rawls (in *A Theory of Justice*, not just in later papers) that the priority of basic individual rights obtains only when the society in question has reached the level of material well-being and political culture that makes these rights preeminently valuable.[22] The point is that even such a historically conditioned ascription of basic rights to persons is incompatible with justice as self-interested reciprocity, which makes the ascription of rights depend solely upon whether the individual possesses the strategic capacity of being able to be a partner in optimal cooperation.

Some advocates of justice as self-interested reciprocity are willing to concede that their view fails to satisfy the first two criteria, *because* they

---

[22] Rawls, *A Theory of Justice*, pp. 243–48.

maintain that it is the clear winner on the third. Once again, Gauthier is instructive, because he is the most explicit and unblinking advocate of justice as self-interested reciprocity. Gauthier admits that the principles of justice that would be agreed upon by rational, self-interested bargainers cannot support some of our considered moral judgments, but maintains that it is only those principles that would be so agreed upon that are justified. The conclusion he draws is that any considered judgments that cannot be derived from justified principles ought to be disregarded or recognized as mere preferences, not dictates of morality, so far as morality is rational.

Essential to this line of argument is a thesis about what counts as *justification* for moral principles and, hence, for the particular moral judgments to be derived from them. The thesis is that justified principles are those which rationally self-interested individuals — those who maximize their expected utility — would choose. However, to move from this thesis to the conclusion that justified principles of morality are those which would be agreed upon in a rational bargain among self-interested individuals, something further is needed. The nature of the bargaining situation, including the *options* the rational bargainers face, must be specified. According to Gauthier, and to his predecessors, such as Hobbes, the bargaining situation is one in which the only alternatives open to individual utility maximizers are (a) a state of pure noncooperation (the state of nature, in which none can be counted on to restrain the pursuit of his self-interest), and (b) unanimous agreement on some set of principles of morality (or, in Hobbes's case, some mechanism for enforcing principles of morality). It is all-important to recognize that the view in question (the Hobbesian-contractarian version of justice as self-interested reciprocity) includes not only the first element, the thesis that justified principles are those that a rationally self-interested individual would choose, but also the second, a specification of the choice situation, including the options, in which rational self-interest is to operate.

It is only when these two elements are combined that it is even possible to arrive at the conclusion which Gauthier and other proponents of justice as self-interested reciprocity seek: namely, that a principle is justified only if all rational, self-interested individuals who are in a state of nature — a state in which there are no mutually beneficial cooperative arrangements — and who are faced with the problem of creating such arrangements, would choose and comply with it. It is not enough to defend the identification of justification with the choice of a rationally self-interested individual (understood as an individual utility maximizer). Proponents of this view must also show why theirs is the correct specification of the choice situation in which rational self-interest is to operate. This means that it is necessary to show that the only options for choice are a pure state of noncooperation or cooperation through restraints on rational self-interest. (As we shall see presently, this last assumption is indefensible: rationally self-interested individuals are not typically, much less always, faced with these stark alternatives.)

Since he believes that only those principles which govern the relations of co-participants in a mutually beneficial cooperative scheme are justified in the sense of being those which rationally self-interested individuals would choose, Gauthier is willing to concede that his view of justice cannot accommodate either our considered judgments about obligations of inclusion in particular circumstances (such as the case of Yugoslavia) or the conviction that all persons have some basic rights.[23] In other words, because he thinks that justice as self-interested reciprocity—and only that theory—meets the standard for justification he believes to be correct, he is willing to acknowledge that his view cannot accommodate some of our strongly held judgments and convictions. After all, the quest is for morality so far as it is rationally justifiable. And morality so far as it is rationally justifiable may turn out to be more austere than we assumed.

There are two ways in which one might attack this attempt to show that justice as self-interested reciprocity is superior to subject-centered justice even if it fails to measure up on two of the three criteria for evaluating theories. The first is to challenge the conception of justification that the justice as self-interested reciprocity theorist assumes. A Kantian, for example, might deny that rationality is reducible to self-interest, proposing instead an alternative conception of rationality which includes a requirement of universality capable of grounding both our considered judgments that we have obligations of inclusion and our conviction that there are some universal rights. A second, less ambitious strategy would be to argue that justice as reciprocity fails to meet *its own* criterion for justification, and hence that its failure to satisfy the first two criteria for a sound theory of justice cannot be compensated for by its superiority on the third. It is the second strategy which I endorse and will now sketch.[24]

There are two complementary objections to the thesis that principles of justice (or of morality generally) are the outcome of a rational bargain among self-interested individuals. The first is that even if it is true that such an individual would agree on certain principles (to regulate his interactions with co-participants and to distribute the burdens and benefits of cooperation), his self-interested rationality would lead him to defect

---

[23] Gauthier, *Morals by Agreement*, p. 18 n. 30.

[24] I am indebted to Tom Christiano for clarifying this strategy. In an excellent and original unpublished paper entitled "The Incoherence of Hobbesian Justifications of the State," Christiano makes the important point that this claim about justification is essential to contractarian views such as those of Hobbes and Gauthier. He then argues that such views necessarily fail to satisfy their own standard for adequate justification. His argument can be seen as one interpretation of what Rawls views as a "natural" objection to contractarian views and which I consider presently.

from the agreement, whenever acting contrary to the agreed-upon principles would maximize his own utility. This is the free-rider problem. In other words, one can agree that certain principles for constraining self-interest would be chosen and agreed upon from a self-interested point of view, yet deny that the rationally self-interested individual would in fact comply with them.

Gauthier attempts to avoid the free-rider problem by arguing that rationally self-interested bargainers would undertake to cultivate in themselves an effective disposition to comply with the agreed-upon principles (so long as they have good reason to predict that enough others will do the same), even in particular instances in which self-interest would favor noncompliance. However, as a number of his critics have pointed out, there are two problems with this scenario.[25] The rationality of cultivating the disposition depends upon the "translucency" of others—one must be able to predict reliably whether they are compliers. The assumption that the required degree of translucency will be distributed widely enough among those who are potential cooperators appears to be entirely ad hoc and lacking any adequate empirical support. In addition, and more importantly, even if the translucency assumption can be adequately supported, Gauthier fails to show why it would not be rational for the individual to cultivate a more selective disposition to cooperate—a disposition to cooperate only when one will not be able to refrain from cooperating without being detected, but merely to feign cooperation when it is more advantageous not to comply. If either of these objections is sound, then justice as reciprocity fails to satisfy its own standard of justification because it does not rule out free-riding.

The second major objection is in a sense more subtle, but also more profound. Rawls seems to have voiced it over two decades ago in *A Theory of Justice*, in an effort to fend off an interpretation of his theory that would have construed it as a version of justice as self-interested reciprocity. There Rawls noted that a certain "natural" objection arises concerning the attempt to derive principles of justice as the outcome of an agreement or contract. Why, one might ask, should you or I take any interest at all in the fact (if it is a fact) that certain principles would be chosen by ideal contractors who are deciding on what principles will govern the most fundamental institutions of society, given that we are not those ideal contractors and given that we actually live in a society whose institutions are governed by quite different principles?[26] Suppose that you or

---

[25] See Buchanan, "Justice as Reciprocity Versus Subject-Centered Justice," pp. 239–41 (see note 6 above).

[26] John Rawls, *A Theory of Justice*, p. 21:

We shall want to say that certain principles of justice are justified because they would be agreed to in an initial situation of equality. I have emphasized that this original position is purely hypothetical. It is natural to ask why, if this agreement is never actu-

I are among those who are unjustly advantaged by our fortuitous places in the actual social structure of the society in which we live. Why should the fact that a being who *did not* know he was the beneficiary of unjust social arrangements would agree upon certain principles of justice, convince a being who *does* know he is unfairly advantaged to agree upon those principles?

It is worth pointing out that Rawls's formulation of the natural objection is broad enough to cover both the free-rider problem discussed above and what I shall call the "agreement problem." Given that you and I are not those hypothetical parties in that idealized choice situation, we may well ask not only why we should comply with whatever principles would be agreed upon, but also why we should agree upon principles that would work to our disadvantage. Since I have already considered the free-rider problem, I will now concentrate on the agreement problem.

In contractarian versions of justice as self-interested reciprocity, such as Gauthier's, principles of justice are said to be those which rationally self-interested individuals would agree upon to govern their interactions in a cooperative scheme. The claim is that all rationally self-interested individuals, when confronted with a choice between remaining in a state of noncooperation (a state of nature) and agreeing to certain principles that constrain the individual's pursuit of self-interest, would choose the latter. However, these same theorists also hold the view that only a rational choice is justified and that a rational choice is a purely self-interested choice, one in which the individual maximizes his or her expected utility. The difficulty is that the choice which maximizes one's expected utility is that option *among the alternatives one actually has* which promises the greatest utility for oneself. But the alternatives facing actual individuals will almost never be a state of pure lack of cooperation (a state of nature), on the one hand, and a set of principles of justice that confer no arbitrary advantage on anyone, on the other.[27] A rich and powerful person who is now benefiting and can expect to continue to benefit from an unjust social arrangement will not typically be limited to those options. He will instead rank proposed principles of justice according to how well they serve his actual interests, given the actual situation he is in and the actual options it presents.

Rawls himself does offer an answer to the natural objection. But his purpose in answering is to make it clear that he is not a contractarian, if by a contractarian is meant one who holds the view about *justification*

---

ally entered into, we should take any interest in these principles, moral or otherwise. The answer is that the conditions embodied in the description of the original position are ones that we do in fact accept. Or if we do not, then perhaps we can be persuaded to do so by philosophical reflection.

[27] This point is made by Tom Christiano in "The Incoherence of Hobbesian Justifications of the State."

that theorists such as Gauthier advance—namely that principles of justice are justified only if they would be agreed to by rationally self-interested individuals. On the contrary, Rawls's answer to the natural objection, interpreted here as referring to what I have called the agreement problem, is *not* that we ought to agree on the principles that would be chosen by ideally rational beings in a hypothetical choice situation because it is in our rational self-interest to do so. Instead, he says that we ought to agree upon (and regard ourselves as bound by) such principles because the perspective from which they would be chosen—what he calls the "original position"—fits our considered judgments about the nature of the appropriate conditions for choosing principles of justice, and, more specifically, captures an ideal of moral objectivity or fairness to which we already subscribe, or to which perhaps we will come to subscribe "upon philosophical reflection."[28]

There is no indication, either in *A Theory of Justice* or in his subsequent writings, that Rawls believes that any amount of philosophical reflection will induce all purely self-interested individuals to converge upon the same principles of justice. (Some readers of Rawls have failed to understand this fundamental point, because they have taken him to be saying that the parties in the original position are rationally self-interested individuals, and have then gone on to assume, quite wrongly, that if he holds that the parties would choose his principles then he also holds that actual individuals motivated solely by self-interest would do so as well.) In fact, Rawls *never* suggests that it is in the rational self-interest of every actual individual—regardless of his place in the distribution of wealth and power in the actual society in which he lives—to agree on, much less to comply with, those principles that would be chosen in the original position.[29] Whether it is in the rational self-interest of a rich and powerful in-

---

[28] Rawls, *A Theory of Justice*, p. 21.

[29] Rawls contends that the correct principles of justice for the most fundamental social institutions are those which would be agreed upon from a choice situation (the "original position") which exemplifies our deeply held conceptions of fairness and the normative conception of persons as being free and equal. An important feature of the original position which is designed to ensure fairness or impartiality in the choice of principles of justice is the "veil of ignorance." We are to imagine the parties in the original position as choosing under severe informational constraints: no one knows his or her place in the distribution of wealth, nor even the content of his or her particular conception of the good. Rawls argues that one of the principles that would be agreed upon under such conditions is the difference principle, which requires that social and economic inequalities are to work to the greatest advantage of the worst off. In criticizing Rawls ("Rawls and Marxism," *Philosophy & Public Affairs*, vol. 3, no. 2 [1974], pp. 167–91), Richard Miller argues that parties in the original position would not agree on the difference principle because conflicts of interests among classes would undermine the possibility of agreement in the original position. For example, if one considers the possibility that one will be a capitalist in an unjust capitalist society, then one would not agree to the difference principle, though one might be willing to agree to it if one only considered the possibility of being a poor worker. Since one is supposed to evaluate proposed principles of justice from the perspective of each representative

dividual in an unjust society to agree upon any set of principles of justice, will depend upon whether his agreeing serves a strategic purpose in preserving or enhancing his unfairly advantaged position, not upon whether rationally self-interested individuals who are in a state of noncooperation, and wish to achieve cooperation, would agree upon them. His problem is not their problem. *He* exists in a cooperative scheme—one from which he is deriving special advantages. *They* must achieve agreement on principles of cooperation in order to move from a state of noncooperation to cooperation. What they would agree upon is utterly irrelevant to what he would, as a matter of rational self-interest, agree to. As I have noted, Rawls refrains from replying to the natural objection by saying that it is in one's rational self-interest to agree upon those principles that would be agreed upon in a hypothetical state of nature. I suggest that he does so because he, unlike proponents of justice as self-interested reciprocity such as Gauthier, is acutely aware that it is a gross mistake to think that there is any single set of principles of justice which it is in the rational self-interest of all individuals to agree upon, regardless of their position in the actual distribution of wealth and power in society. Once the magnitude of this error is appreciated, it is hard to see how anyone could make it. After all, is it really plausible to contend that it is always in the rational self-interest of those who are the beneficiaries of an unjust social order to subscribe to principles of justice that would be chosen by rationally self-interested beings who were bargaining on principles of justice for a new

position in society, no agreement on a principle such as the difference principle is possible in the original position, according to Miller.

What has gone wrong here is that Miller has raised against Rawls the natural objection, without realizing that Rawls himself raised this objection precisely in order to dissociate his own view from the sort of view against which that objection is telling! Rawls's point is not that principles of justice must be acceptable from the point of view of the actual self-interest of every individual, even the most arbitrarily advantaged individual in a radically unjust society. (That would be an excessive criterion, after all.) For Rawls, the parties in the original position are not to rank principles of justice from the perspective of the actual interests of real-world individuals (including those of the recipients of unjust benefits). They are to rank principles from the standpoint of the interests which Rawls ascribes to *them* as idealized parties in the original position. Those interests, according to Rawls, are the two "highest-order" interests (a) in critically formulating, revising, and effectively pursuing a conception of the good, and (b) in expressing their sense of justice. To my knowledge Rawls never makes the mistake Miller attributes to him. He never mistakenly contends that even the greatest beneficiaries of injustice will, strictly from the standpoint of their self-interest, agree to principles of justice that would deprive them of their ill-gotten gains. Nor does he embrace the extremely implausible assumption that an adequate justification for a set of principles of justice requires that they be acceptable to the greatest beneficiaries of injustice. Rawls would be committed to both of these views if he subscribed to the view of justification held by Gauthier and other proponents of justice as self-interested reciprocity, but a charitable reading of both Rawls's response to the natural objection and his description of the parties in the original position clearly shows that he does not. For a more detailed analysis of Miller's objection, and for my reply to it in defense of Rawls, see Allen Buchanan, *Marx and Justice: The Radical Critique of Liberalism* (Totowa, NJ: Rowman and Littlefield, 1982), pp. 145–47.

society? It should be clear now that even if the theorist of justice as self-interested reciprocity can avoid the free-rider problem and show that rationally self-interested individuals would actually comply with whatever principles of distributive justice they would *agree upon*, this will be of no avail in answering the natural objection, since the point of the natural objection is that what *they* would agree upon is irrelevant to the question of justifying principles to *actual* rationally self-interested individuals.

For the rationally self-interested hypothetical beings Gauthier describes, the only alternatives are striking a rational bargain among all potential participants in mutually beneficial cooperation or remaining in a state of nature in which there are no constraints on the pursuit of self-interest. But which principles would be agreed upon in *this* choice situation is entirely irrelevant to the question of whether it is rational for a rich person in an unjust society to agree to such principles. It is irrelevant for the simple reason that the alternatives faced by the rational bargainers are not those open to the rich person. His options are not agreement upon principles that would be chosen by rational bargainers in a state of nature or remaining in a state of nature. Instead, his choice is between continuing to support an unjust regime which benefits him more than a regime regulated by those principles of justice, or agreeing to a set of principles of justice which will make him worse off than he is. Thus, what rational bargainers faced with that different choice would agree upon is quite irrelevant to what he, as the rationally self-interested individual he is, ought to agree upon.

Of course, *if* one assumed that among every individual's most important interests is a desire to cooperate on fair terms, then it might be possible to argue that it is in the rational self-interest of all individuals to agree to (and actually comply with) principles that would be chosen in a bargain among rationally self-interested individuals. But the attractiveness of justice as self-interested reciprocity, at least to its proponents, has been that it refrains from making any such substantive assumptions about the content and nature of individuals' interests. To answer the natural objection by attributing moral preferences or a sense of justice to all rational individuals would be to abandon justice as self-interested reciprocity, not to amend it.

If either the free-rider objection or the natural objection is cogent, then justice as self-interested reciprocity fails to satisfy its own criterion for justification. If this is so and if, in addition, justice as self-interested reciprocity fares worse than at least some versions of subject-centered justice on the criteria of fit with considered judgments about obligations of inclusion and the conviction that there are some human rights — some rights that all persons have regardless of their strategic capacities — then, at least on these three criteria of theoretical adequacy, justice as self-interested reciprocity ought to be rejected. And if this is so, then the way is clear for taking the morality of inclusion seriously — for attempting to work out the implications of the more plausible subject-centered theories for the nature, scope, and limits of our obligations to ensure that all persons have access to inclusion in states that will protect their fundamental rights. Only a systematic understanding of the morality of inclusion will enable us to answer some of the most urgent and difficult questions concerning the dramatic political and economic developments in the world today. A theory of the morality of inclusion would provide substantive guidance on a wide range of moral issues of national and international policy, from immigration to secession.

In this essay I have not attempted to provide such a theory. Instead, I have endeavored to clarify the concept of a morality of inclusion, to show that two opposing traditions in theorizing about justice yield radically different conclusions about such a morality, and to clear the way for taking the morality of inclusion seriously by making a tentative case against the tradition which would dismiss the entire enterprise of theorizing about it.

Philosophy, University of Arizona

A NEW CONTRACTARIAN VIEW OF TAX AND REGULATORY POLICY IN THE EMERGING MARKET ECONOMIES*

By Robert H. Frank

Introduction

Recent decades have seen a resurgence of contractarian thinking about the nature and origins of the state. Scholars in this tradition ask what constraints rational, self-interested actors might deliberately impose upon themselves. In response, Hobbes, Rousseau, Locke, and other early contractarians answered that laws of property were an attractive alternative to "the war of all against all." More recently, James Buchanan, Russell Hardin, Mancur Olson, Gordon Tullock, and others have used contractarian principles to justify laws that solve a variety of Prisoner's Dilemmas and other collective-action problems.[1] And in the distributional realm, John Rawls and others have applied contractarian analysis to investigate how material wealth ought to be allocated among people.[2]

Contractarianism is of special interest now as the countries of Eastern Europe and the former Soviet Union face the task of forging new political and economic institutions. With contractarian thinking already evident in the discussion surrounding the current transition, it is an opportune moment to reexamine the foundational assumptions of contractarian analysis.

At the heart of contractarian analysis lies the assumption that people are rational, self-interested actors. In this essay, I will argue that contractarianism's reliance on the self-interest model has obscured the true rationale behind many of the West's most important laws and institutions. I will argue for a more general version of contractarianism, one based on a characterization of preferences that is more easily defensible, on both theoretical and empirical grounds, than that of the self-interest model. Without abandoning the essence of the contractarian mode of analysis,

---

* Much of this essay is developed from material in my *Choosing the Right Pond: Human Behavior and the Quest for Status* (New York: Oxford University Press, 1985), and *Passions within Reason: The Strategic Role of the Emotions* (New York: W. W. Norton, 1988).

[1] James Buchanan, *The Limits of Liberty* (Chicago: University of Chicago Press, 1975); James Buchanan and Gordon Tullock, *The Calculus of Consent* (Ann Arbor: University of Michigan Press, 1962); Russell Hardin, *Collective Action* (Baltimore: Johns Hopkins University Press, 1982); Mancur Olson, *The Logic of Collective Action* (Cambridge: Harvard University Press, 1965).

[2] John Rawls, *A Theory of Justice* (Cambridge: Harvard University Press, 1971).

 © 1993 Social Philosophy and Policy Foundation. Printed in the USA.

this alternative approach promises a more complete and coherent account of the activities of the state. It also recommends tax and regulatory policies that are substantially different from the ones most commonly employed in the Western market economies.

The essay is organized into five parts. Section I explains why economists, contractarians, and others rely for the most part on a standard of rationality that assumes egoistic preferences. Section II then argues that people with such preferences often perform poorly when confronted with important problems of social and economic interaction, and goes on to outline a theory of how specific, nonegoistic preferences often help solve these problems. Section III examines how concerns about relative position affect the laws and tax policies we adopt. Section IV employs nonegoistic preferences in the construction of a contractarian alternative to the Rawlsian account of distributive justice. Finally, Section V examines how the principles developed in the preceding sections might translate into practical policy advice for the emerging market economies.

I. Rationality and the Self-Interest Motive

Two important definitions of rationality are the "present-aim" and "self-interest" standards.[3] Under the present-aim standard, a person is rational if she is efficient in the pursuit of whatever aims she happens to hold at the moment of action. No attempt is made, under this standard, to restrict preferences in any way, or, indeed, even to assess whether the preferences themselves are coherent. The self-interest standard, by contrast, commits itself to a very specific assumption about preferences: people are taken to be narrowly self-interested. Motives like altruism, fidelity to principle, a desire for justice, concern about relative position, and the like are simply not considered under the self-interest standard.

In textbook accounts of rational choice, economists generally embrace the present-aim standard.[4] Tastes are given exogenously, we say, and there is no logical basis for questioning them. A taste for Rachmaninoff is no more valid than a taste for the Rolling Stones.

The difficulty with the present-aim standard is what the late George Stigler might have called the "crankcase oil" problem. If we see a person drink the used crankcase oil from his car, and he then writhes in agony and dies, we can assert that he must have *really* liked crankcase oil. And given a sufficiently strong preference for crankcase oil, the present-aim standard would hold that it was *rational* for him to drink it. Now, this leads to obvious difficulties for the present-aim standard as a theory of human behavior. For under this standard, virtually any behavior, law, or

---

[3] Derek Parfit, *Reasons and Persons* (Oxford: Clarendon Press, 1984).
[4] See, for example, Edgar K. Browning and Jacqueline M. Browning, *Microeconomic Theory and Applications*, 3rd ed. (Glenview: Scott Foresman, 1989), p. 51.

institution, no matter how bizarre, can be "explained" after the fact by simply assuming a taste for it. Thus, the chief attraction of the present-aim model turns out also to be its biggest liability. Because it allows us to explain everything, we end up explaining nothing.

With this difficulty in mind, most economists, and virtually all contractarians, assume some version of the self-interest standard of rationality when they construct formal models of human behavior. This approach has generated many powerful insights into human behavior. It explains, for example, why divorce rates are higher in states with liberal welfare benefits; why car pools form in the wake of increases in gasoline prices; why the members of "service" organizations are more likely to be real-estate salespersons, dentists, chiropractors, insurance agents, and others with something to sell than to be postal employees or airline pilots; why we instruct the state to force us to install catalytic converters on our cars; and so on.

Yet apparent contradictions abound. Travelers on interstate highways leave tips for waitresses they will never see again. Participants in bloody family feuds seek revenge even at ruinous cost to themselves. People walk away from profitable transactions whose terms they believe to be "unfair." The British spend vast sums to defend the desolate Falklands, even though they have little empire left against which to deter future aggression. People approve of redistributive measures that are almost certain to reduce their incomes. And they do not disconnect their catalytic converters, even though they could do so with virtually no chance of being penalized. In these and countless other ways, people do not seem to be maximizing utility functions of the egoistic sort.

II. THE FUNCTIONAL ROLE OF PREFERENCES

Elsewhere I have argued that nonegoistic motives can be accounted for if we view tastes not as ends but as means for attaining other material objectives.[5] The role of nonegoistic motives derives from the fact that we face important problems that simply cannot be solved by self-interestedly rational action. The common feature of these problems is that they require us to make commitments to behave in ways that may later prove contrary to our interests.

The functional role of nonegoistic motives can be seen clearly with the help of an example of a simple ecology in which egoists are pitted against nonegoists in a struggle to survive. The commitment problem they face is the classic Prisoner's Dilemma. The specific version of it is a joint venture, the monetary payoffs from which are given by the entries in Table

[5] Robert H. Frank, "If *Homo Economicus* Could Choose His Own Utility Function, Would He Want One With a Conscience?" *American Economic Review*, vol. 77 (September 1987), pp. 593–604; and Frank, *Passions within Reason*.

TABLE 1. *Monetary Payoffs in a Joint Venture*

		X	
		Cooperate	Defect
Y	Cooperate	4 for each	0 for Y 6 for X
	Defect	6 for Y 0 for X	2 for each

1. These payoffs depend on the particular combination of strategies chosen by the participants. Note that X gets a higher payoff by defecting, no matter what Y does, and the same is true for Y. If X believes Y will behave in a self-interested way, he will predict that Y will defect. And if only to protect himself, he will likely feel compelled to defect as well. When both defect, each gets only a 2-unit payoff. The frustration, as in all dilemmas of this sort, is that both could have easily done much better. Had they cooperated, each would have gotten a 4-unit payoff.

Now suppose we have not just Y and X but a large population. Pairs of people again form joint ventures and the relationship between behavior and payoffs for the members of each pair is again as given in Table 1. Suppose further that everyone in the population is of one of two types — cooperator or defector. A cooperator is someone who, possibly through intensive cultural conditioning, has developed a genetically endowed capacity to experience a moral sentiment that predisposes him to cooperate. A defector is someone who either lacks this capacity or has failed to develop it.

In this scheme, cooperators are hard-core altruists in the sense that they refrain from cheating even when there is no possibility of being detected. Viewed in the narrow context of the choice at hand, this behavior is clearly contrary to their material interests. Defectors, by contrast, are pure opportunists. They always make whatever choice will maximize their personal payoff. The task here is to determine what will happen when people from these two groups are thrown into a survival struggle against one another.

For concreteness, suppose that sympathy is the emotion that motivates cooperation, and that there is an observable symptom present in people who experience this emotion (perhaps a "sympathetic manner"). Defectors lack this observable symptom; or, more generally, they may try to mimic it, but fail to get it exactly right.

If the two types could be distinguished with certainty at a glance, defectors would be doomed. Cooperators would simply interact with one another, thus earning a higher payoff than the defectors. But suppose it requires effort to inspect the symptom of cooperation. For concreteness, suppose inspection costs 1 unit. For people who pay this cost, the veil is lifted: cooperators and defectors can be distinguished with 100 percent accuracy. For those who do not pay the 1-unit cost of scrutiny, the two types are perfectly indistinguishable.

Now consider the problem confronting a cooperator who faces the payoffs given in Table 1 and is trying to decide whether to pay the cost of scrutiny. If he pays it, he can be assured of interacting with another cooperator, and will thus get a payoff of $4 - 1 = 3$ units. If he does not, his payoff is uncertain. Cooperators and defectors will look exactly alike to him and he must take his chances. If he happens to interact with another cooperator, he will get 4 units. But if he interacts with a defector, he will get zero. Whether it makes sense to pay the 1-unit cost of scrutiny thus depends on the likelihood of these two outcomes.

If r_c denotes the share of the population composed of cooperators, the expected payoff to a cooperator when cooperators do not pay the cost of scrutiny is given by

$$E_c = 4r_c + 0(1 - r_c) = 4r_c.$$

Against this payoff, the cooperator weighs the certain payoff of 3 units he would get if he paid the cost of scrutiny. The resultant decision rule is to pay the cost of scrutiny whenever $3 > 4r_c$, or whenever $r_c < 3/4$.

With this rule in mind, we can now say something about how the population will evolve over time. When the population share of cooperators is below 75 percent, cooperators will all pay the cost of scrutiny and get a payoff of 3 units by cooperating with one another. It will not be in the interests of defectors to bear this cost, because the keen-eyed cooperators would not interact with them anyway. The defectors are left to interact with one another, and get a payoff of only 2 units. The population growth rule is that higher relative payoffs result in a growing population share. Thus, if we start with a population share of cooperators less than 75 percent, the cooperators will get a higher average payoff, which means that their share of the population will grow.

In populations that consist of more than 75 percent cooperators, the tables are turned. Now it no longer makes sense to pay the cost of scrutiny. Cooperators and defectors will thus interact at random, which means that defectors will have a higher average payoff. This difference in payoffs, in turn, will cause the population share of cooperators to shrink.

For the values assumed in this example, the average payoff schedules for the two groups are plotted in Figure 1. As noted, the cooperators' schedule lies above the defectors' for population shares smaller than 75 percent, but below it for larger shares. The sharp discontinuity in the defectors' schedule reflects the fact that, to the left of 75 percent, all co-

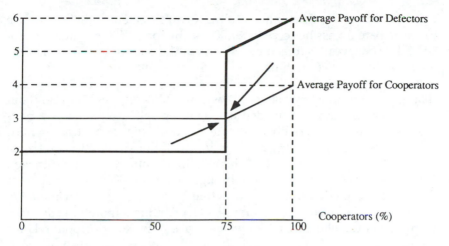

FIGURE 1. Average payoffs with costs of scrutiny.

operators pay to scrutinize while, to the right of 75 percent, none of them does. Once the population share of cooperators passes 75 percent, defectors suddenly gain access to their victims. The population growth rule makes it clear that the population in this example will stabilize at 75 percent cooperators.

Now, there is obviously nothing magic about this 75 percent figure. Had the cost of scrutiny been higher than 1 unit, for example, the population share of cooperators would have been smaller. A reduction in the payoff when cooperators pair with one another would have a similar effect on the equilibrium population shares. The point of the example is that when there are costs of scrutiny, there will be pressures that pull the population toward some stable mix of cooperators and defectors. Once the population settles at this mix, members of both groups have the same average payoff and are therefore equally likely to survive. There is an ecological niche, in other words, for both groups. This result stands in stark contrast to the traditional sociobiological result that only opportunists can survive.

A taste for favorable relative position is another preference that may have utility for a rational egoist because, as the following discussion will suggest, it can help solve time-inconsistency problems that arise in the course of interpersonal bargaining. An established tenet of bargaining theory is that the party who needs the fruits of exchange least has the strongest bargaining position. Suppose X and Y can perform some task that they alone can carry out, and that the reward for this task is $10,000. The task is neither pleasant nor onerous, which means that each party would be better off by performing his share of it as long as the payment he receives is greater than zero. Now suppose that X is wealthy and Y is poor. And that, because of his wealth, X can threaten credibly to refuse to participate unless he receives $9,000 of the total. If Y is a rational egoist and he believes X's threat, he will accept the offer of $1,000, which, after all, is better than nothing.

But now suppose that Y is not a rational egoist in the Rawlsian sense; that instead of caring only about his own wealth level, he cares also about how economic gains are divided between himself and his trading partners. When the terms of trade are one-sided in favor of his trading partner, Y experiences disutility independently of the effect of the exchange on his absolute wealth level. If this sentiment operates with sufficient force, Y will refuse X's offer, even though doing so will leave him poorer than if he accepted it. But if X knows that Y feels this way, X will not demand one-sided terms in the first place. Y is thus a more effective bargainer by virtue of caring not only about absolute but also about relative income.

As with the earlier model of the payoff to sympathy, here too we see a reason for at least some rational egoists behind a veil of ignorance to include concern about relative position among their preferences. The model does not claim that envy is a beneficial motive from the collective vantage point, only that individuals can profit by holding this motive in an environment in which their bargaining counterparts are aware of its presence.

To recapitulate briefly, the result of allowing rational egoists to choose their preferences from behind a veil of ignorance is that at least a certain proportion of them will choose not to be rational egoists. Rather, it will be attractive for at least some of them to choose sympathy, concern about relative position, and various nonegoistic preferences before attempting to make their way in the material world.[6]

A constraint on the present-aim standard

The view of tastes as means rather than ends helps constrain the openended nature of the present-aim standard of rationality. The difficulty, recall, is that the current description of that standard allows it to explain too much. The functional view of preferences suggests that the repertoire of tastes be expanded beyond the simple egoistic tastes assumed in the selfinterest model, but only upon showing that the holding of a specific taste is advantageous (or at least not fatally disadvantageous) in a material sense.

What we assume about the nature of the utility function can make a great deal of difference in the kinds of conclusions that follow from for-

---

[6] Pursuing a similar line of thinking, David Gauthier argues that rational persons might want to predispose themselves to behave in a variety of seemingly irrational ways. See Gauthier, *Morals by Agreement* (Oxford: Oxford University Press, 1985).

mal analysis.[7] In the sections that follow, for example, I will argue that the inclusion of nonegoistic tastes substantially alters the contractarian interpretation of many Western tax and regulatory policies.

III. POSITIONAL CONCERNS AND COLLECTIVE ACTION

Our model of the instrumental role of tastes makes clear that people who care only about absolute wealth will be less effective bargainers than those who care also about how gains are divided. Concern about relative position acts as a commitment device that prevents people from accepting profitable, but one-sided, transactions. People with such concerns often behave irrationally according to the self-interest standard, but there is genuine material advantage in being an effective bargainer.

Irrespective of whatever functional role concerns about relative position may play, there is evidence that such concerns are widely held.[8] For example, surveys conducted over time in a variety of countries, which ask people to report whether they are "very happy," "fairly happy," or "not happy," find that happiness levels within a country at a given moment are strongly positively correlated with position in the country's income distribution. These surveys find no long-term trends in average reported happiness levels, even for countries whose incomes have been growing steadily over time. Looking at different countries at a given point of time, the happiness surveys also find little relationship between the average income level in a country and the average happiness level reported by its citizens.

While surveys call for purely subjective responses about happiness levels, there is evidence that they measure a real phenomenon. For example, numerous other studies have found strong positive relationships between reported happiness levels and observable physiological and behavioral measures of well-being.[9]

Positional concerns focus on many outcomes, one of which is the distribution of monetary income. Our concerns about where we stand in this distribution lead us to impose a variety of restrictions on how we spend our incomes.

Workplace safety

Consider, for example, the worker's implicit decision about how much of his total compensation to spend on workplace safety. Economists fre-

---

[7] For a discussion, see Frank, *Choosing the Right Pond*, ch. 12.

[8] For an extensive summary of this evidence, see *ibid.*, ch. 2.

[9] People who report that they are not happy, for example, are more likely to experience headaches, rapid heartbeat, digestive disorders, and related ailments. Those who rate themselves as very happy are more likely than others to initiate social contacts with friends. For a more detailed survey of this evidence, see *ibid.*

quently argue that government makes us worse off when it requires us to spend more on job safety than we would choose to spend as individuals.[10] By this argument, the competitive labor market offers the worker a choice between relatively safe jobs at one wage and riskier jobs at higher wages. Workers who are most concerned about safety will choose the safer jobs; and the higher wages of riskier jobs will supposedly fully compensate the others for the extra risks they take.

But if people care about relative position, the incentives for choosing between such pairs of jobs are distorted. From each individual's perspective, the riskier jobs promise an upward movement along the economic totem pole. Yet the laws of simple arithmetic stand in the way of *everyone* moving upward in relative terms. For when everyone gets higher pay for performing riskier tasks, relative position remains unchanged. As in the familiar stadium metaphor, everyone leaps to his feet to get a better view, only to find the view no better than when all were seated. Here, an emotion (envy) helps solve one commitment problem (the bargaining problem), only to create another. The quest for relative advancement is a Prisoner's Dilemma, one that leads individual workers to purchase too little safety even when labor markets are perfectly competitive. By regulating safety, we attempt to solve this Prisoner's Dilemma.[11]

Savings

Concerns about relative position also affect the decision of how much to save.[12] A family can save some of its income for retirement, or spend more now on a house in a better school district. For most parents, the lure of providing relative educational advantages for their children is powerful. Yet no matter how much each family spends on housing, only 10 percent of the children can occupy seats in the top decile of the educational quality distribution. Saving less and bidding for a house in a better school district serves only to bid up the prices of such houses. Positional concerns thus cause the individual payoff from spending to appear spuriously large, the payoff to saving spuriously small. There is, in fact, clear evidence that most families would have grossly inadequate savings for retirement were it not for the Social Security system and other forced-savings programs. As in the case of workplace safety, concerns about relative position create a Prisoner's Dilemma with respect to savings. Forced-savings programs may be viewed as an attempt to solve it.

[10] Milton and Rose Friedman, *Free to Choose* (New York: Harcourt, Brace, Jovanovich, 1979).

[11] Frank, *Choosing the Right Pond*, ch. 7.

[12] James Duesenberry, *Income, Saving, and the Theory of Consumer Behavior* (Cambridge: Harvard University Press, 1949).

Hours regulations

Positional concerns also suggest why we might regulate the length of the workweek. The Fair Labor Standards Act currently requires employers to pay premium wages to hourly employees who work more than forty hours per week. The effect of this requirement has been to cause most firms to adopt a standard forty-hour workweek. Without it, workers would confront yet another Prisoner's Dilemma in their decisions about how many hours to work. By working an extra hour, a worker could increase his pay and provide additional material advantages for his family. But if some people work longer hours, others will feel compelled to do likewise, lest their families fall behind in relative terms. Yet when all work longer hours, relative position is left unchanged. By regulating the length of the workweek, we curtail yet another "positional arms race."

Legislating employee control over working conditions

Adam Smith was the first to formally recognize the enormous gains in productivity that arise from the division and specialization of labor. Smith illustrated the basic idea with the following description of work in a small Scottish pin factory:

> One man draws out the wire, another straightens it, a third cuts it, a fourth points it, a fifth grinds it at the top for receiving the head; to make the head requires two or three distinct operations. . . . I have seen a small manufactory of this kind where only ten men were employed . . . [who] could, when they exerted themselves, make among them about twelve pounds of pins in a day. There are in a pound upwards of four thousand pins of a middling size. Those ten persons, therefore, could make among them upwards of forty-eight thousand pins in a day. Each person, therefore, making a tenth part of forty-eight thousand pins, might be considered as making four thousand eight hundred pins in a day. But if they had all wrought separately and independently, and without any of them having been educated to this peculiar business, they certainly could not each of them have made twenty, perhaps not one pin in a day. . . .[13]

As even Smith recognized, however, such fragmentation of workplace tasks can exact a heavy psychological toll on workers. That this toll was yet another manifestation of economic exploitation became one of Karl

---

[13] Adam Smith, *An Inquiry into the Nature and Causes of the Wealth of Nations* [1776] (Indianapolis: Liberty Classics, 1981), vol. 1, bk. 1, p. 15.

Marx's central themes, captured in the following passage written nearly a century after the publication of Smith's *Wealth of Nations*:

> [A]ll means for the development of production transform themselves into means of domination over, and exploitation of the [workers]; they mutilate the laborer into a fragment of a man, degrade him to the level of an appendage of a machine, destroy every remnant of charm in his work and turn it into hated toil. . . .[14]

To the extent that such criticisms of industrial life ring true, they pose a sharp challenge to the Western economist's traditional arguments about welfare and competition. The division and specialization of labor increases productivity, just as Smith claimed, and this, in turn, enables firms to pay higher wages. At the same time, fragmentation makes life less pleasant. The best attainable outcome thus involves a compromise. We should continue dividing tasks until the wage gain from the last division is just sufficient to compensate for the added psychological discomfort it brings. As in the case of safety devices, traditional economic models suggest that competition should bring about this optimal degree of specialization.

When critics then observe that the degree of specialization seems unreasonably high, they conclude that labor markets must not have been competitive after all—that workers are here too the victims of exploitation by powerful economic elites. But this conclusion simply does not follow. If workers care not only about absolute income but also about relative income, then economic theory simply does not predict an optimal level of specialization in the first place. As do choices about safety levels, choices about specialization confront individuals with an opportunity to increase their relative income by accepting less desirable working conditions. Yet if all workers make this trade, each worker's relative income remains the same as before.

It is thus easy to see why people might favor laws, like the ones passed in several Western European countries,[15] that mandate higher levels of employee control over working conditions within the firm. In Germany, for example, a 1976 codetermination law called for employees to constitute half of the membership of corporate boards of directors, and outlined detailed procedures regarding worker grievances. But here again, the attraction of such laws is much more plausibly attributed to positional arms races among individuals than to exploitation by powerful economic elites.[16]

---

[14] Karl Marx, *Das Kapital* [1856] (New York: Modern Library, 1936), pp. 708–9.

[15] For a discussion of these laws, see James S. Coleman, *Foundations of Social Theory* (Cambridge: Harvard University Press, 1990), ch. 16.

[16] Conflicts arise, naturally, when not all workers share the concerns that give rise to positional arms races. For an extensive discussion of how rights might best be allocated in such conflicts, see Frank, *Choosing the Right Pond*, ch. 11.

The labor regulations discussed above have been vigorously opposed on the grounds that they abrogate constitutional protections of the freedom to contract. But once we introduce positional concerns into the analysis, it becomes clear why we might want a constitution to restrict our freedom in just these ways.

IV. Moral Sentiments and Rawlsian Justice

In his celebrated book, *A Theory of Justice*, John Rawls constructs a contractarian theory of distributive justice. The essence of the Rawlsian exercise is that it asks people to choose distribution rules without any knowledge of their own talents and abilities. When people are behind a veil of ignorance, Rawls argues, their natural impulse is to be cautious. Indeed, if there were N contractors faced with the task of dividing a fixed economic pie, the consensus formula would almost surely be for each person to receive one-Nth of the pie.

The practical difficulty, of course, is that the economic pie is not fixed. Its size depends on the risks people take and the effort they expend to produce it. With these links in mind, Rawlsian contractors anticipate the incentive problems inherent in a completely egalitarian sharing scheme. The difficulty is that when N is large, no single person's effort and risk have an appreciable effect on her own reward. And if effort and risk-taking are unappealing, each person's incentive will be to free-ride on the efforts and risk-taking of others. The aggregate result is an inefficiently small economic pie.

Rawlsian contractors are thus willing to tolerate some inequality to preserve incentives:

> If there are inequalities in the basic structure that work to make everyone better off in comparison with the benchmark of initial equality, why not permit them? The immediate gain which a greater equality might allow can be regarded as intelligently invested in view of its future return. If, for example, these inequalities set up various incentives which succeed in eliciting more productive efforts, a person in the original position may look upon them as necessary to cover the costs of training and to encourage effective performance.[17]

But Rawls is quick to argue that there are sharp limits in the extent to which his contractors would be willing to permit greater inequality in the name of higher output. Specifically, he suggests that they will choose distributional rules to maximize the income of the poorest member of society; that is, they will choose according to the celebrated maximin criterion.

---

[17] Rawls, *A Theory of Justice* (see n. 2 above), p. 151.

TABLE 2. *Incomes Under Three Rules of Distribution*

		Incomes of Persons		
		I_1	I_2	I_3
	R_1	5	5	5
Distribution Rule	R_2	20	8	6
	R_3	4	15	30

Suppose, for example, that each of three Rawlsian contractors is faced with a choice between three distribution rules, R_1, R_2, and R_3, that yield the incomes shown in Table 2. These three rules have the property that greater inequality in the distribution of income goes hand in hand with larger total income. Thus R_1, which is completely egalitarian, generates the smallest total income, while R_3, which is the least egalitarian of the three, generates the largest total. Rule R_2 dominates rule R_1 because the income of each person is higher under R_2. R_3, despite yielding the highest total income, is the least desirable of the three rules under the maximin criterion because the poorest person receives the smallest possible income under R_3.

The choice of R_2 illustrates another assumed property of the Rawlsian contractors, namely that they are not envious of the incomes earned by others.[18] While someone with strictly egalitarian preferences would choose the distribution under R_1, the inequalities that exist under R_2 are assumed to be of no concern to the Rawlsian contractors.

The Rawlsian exercise is a thought experiment that invokes the theory of choice under uncertainty. Some of Rawls's most forceful critics have focused on his use of the maximin criterion as a mechanism for making such choices.[19] This criterion, after all, is a bold departure from the most widely accepted normative rule for choice under uncertainty, the von Neumann–Morgenstern model of expected-utility maximization. Under von Neumann–Morgenstern, the decision maker chooses not the option that maximizes the worst possible outcome, but the one that maximizes his expected utility.

If the incremental satisfaction afforded by additional wealth tends to diminish as wealth increases, as is conventionally assumed, the von

[18] *Ibid.*, p. 143.
[19] See Brian Barry, "Reflections on 'Justice as Fairness,'" in *Justice and Inequality*, ed. Hugo Bedau (Englewood Cliffs: Prentice Hall, 1971).

Neumann–Morgenstern rule is qualitatively like the maximin rule in that both favor more-certain outcomes over riskier ones. But although the two rules are alike in this qualitative respect, in actual application they often exhibit dramatically different quantitative responses to risk. Notice, for example, that in Table 2 the two largest entries in the distribution under R_3 are much higher than the two largest entries under R_2, while the worst entry under R_3 is only slightly worse than the worst entry under R_2. With these comparisons in mind, many people find it easy to imagine themselves strongly attracted to R_3 from behind the veil of ignorance, and this choice is completely plausible under the expected-utility model. Suppose, for example, that the contractors have utility functions given by $U_i = \sqrt{I_i}$, $i = 1, 2, 3$. If each of the three outcomes under each rule in Table 2 is considered equally likely, the expected utilities under the three rules will be $EU_1 = 2.24$, $EU_2 = 3.25$, and $EU_3 = 3.78$, respectively, making R_3 the most attractive alternative.

Rawls himself is well aware of the appeal of the expected-utility model. He offers several reasons for his choice of the maximin alternative. He stresses, for example, that his contractors lack any knowledge of the probabilities necessary for computing expected utilities. This fact, he argues, should make them much more sensitive to the possibility of adverse outcomes. Rawls goes on to argue that the once-and-for-all nature of the choice posed by his thought experiment will also tend to make contractors more risk-averse. A mistaken decision, after all, cannot be rectified in some future period.

If these arguments are correct, they have testable implications for the behavior of ordinary consumers with respect to a variety of major risks that arise in the course of everyday life. In many ways, for example, a person's being society's poorest member is not materially different from his having a multimillion-dollar lawsuit awarded against him, or from his falling victim to an illness that destroys his earning power. The same reasons that motivate Rawls's contractors to adopt the maximin criterion should also motivate ordinary consumers to insure against major losses like these. And yet is common for people to leave many such losses uncovered. For example, most people who live on flood plains do not purchase flood insurance, even when it is offered by the government at heavily subsidized rates. Many people do not buy comprehensive personal-liability insurance, disability insurance, or even major-medical insurance, even though the relevant probabilities are no smaller than that of a Rawlsian contractor ending up as society's poorest member. At the very least, these behaviors seem to rule out any confident claim that people would employ a maximin criterion when choosing distributional rules from behind a veil of ignorance.

A second difficulty with the Rawlsian exercise is that while it helps develop intuitions about fairness, it does little to explain why societies actually limit the dispersion of income.[20] After all, people decide distribution rules not behind a veil of ignorance, but with reasonably full knowledge of their individual talents and abilities. Neither the Rawlsian exercise, nor traditional contractarian extensions of it, can explain why abstract standards of fairness would motivate talented, self-interested contractors to share their wealth with others.

Both problems can be addressed by the following simple modification of Rawls's thought experiment. Let the exercise begin as before, with rational, self-interested contractors behind a veil of ignorance. This time, however, let their first task be to choose their preferences with an eye toward solving the kinds of problems they will encounter once the veil is lifted. Having emerged from behind the veil with these preferences, let them then decide the distribution rules for society.

Anticipating the commitment problems they will encounter in economic and social life, rational agents behind the veil would choose not the egoistic preferences of contractarian models, but the richer complex of motives we actually observe: sympathy for the disadvantaged, concern about relative position, concern about living up to agreements, and so on. Self-interest would still be an important concern, but it would now be tempered by other important motives.[21]

What sort of rules would contractors with such motives adopt? If the probability of being the poorest member seems small behind the veil of ignorance, it quickly shrinks to zero for most people once the veil is lifted. The people who actually enact our laws and constitutions are nonetheless likely to call for income transfers to society's poorest members. But they are far more likely to share their wealth out of sympathy for the disadvantaged than out of fear of being disadvantaged themselves. The outcome may be much the same as in the Rawlsian account, but the motivation behind the choice is much more descriptive.

Concerns about relative position provide still another reason for the rich to share their income. I have argued elsewhere that, at the micro level, such concerns motivate precisely such behavior within competitive firms.[22] On first examination, the wage structure within many private firms seems much more egalitarian than would be warranted under the conventional marginal-productivity theory of wages. Many firms, for example, follow strict salary formulas based on experience, education, and length of tenure within the firm, even when there are large visible differences in the productivity of workers paid the same under these formulas. Indeed, pay patterns of the sort predicted by the marginal-productivity theory are virtually never observed in practice.

---

[20] Of course, it was not Rawls's intent to explain the actual practices that societies adopt.

[21] As noted above (n. 6), Gauthier pursues a similar line of thinking; see his *Morals by Agreement*.

[22] See Frank, *Choosing the Right Pond*.

A simple amendment to our theory helps to square it with the wage distributions we observe in practice.[23] The amendment rests on two simple assumptions: (1) most people prefer high-ranked to low-ranked positions among their co-workers (a consequence of the envy motive); and (2) no one can be forced to remain in a firm against his wishes.

By the laws of simple arithmetic, not everyone's preference for high rank in the wage distribution of his firm can be satisfied. After all, only 50 percent of the members of any group can be in the top half. But if people are free to associate with whomever they please, why are the lesser-ranked members of groups content to remain? Why don't they all leave to form new groups of their own in which they would no longer be near the bottom? Many workers undoubtedly do precisely that. And yet we also observe many stable, heterogeneous groups. Not all accountants at General Motors are equally talented; and in every law firm, some partners attract much more new business than others. If everyone prefers to be near the top of his or her group of co-workers, what holds these heterogeneous groups together?

The apparent answer is that their low-ranked members receive extra compensation over what they could earn elsewhere. If they were to leave, they would gain by no longer having to endure low status. By the same token, however, the top-ranked members would lose. They would no longer enjoy high status. If their gains from having high rank are larger than the costs borne by members with low rank, it does not make sense for the group to disband. Everyone can do better if the top-ranked workers induce their lesser-ranked colleagues to remain by sharing some of their pay with them.

Of course, not everyone assigns the same value to having high rank. Those who care relatively less about it will do best to join firms in which most workers are more productive than themselves. As lesser-ranked members in these firms, they will receive extra compensation. People who care most strongly about rank, by contrast, will want to join firms in which most other workers are less productive than themselves. For the privilege of occupying top-ranked positions in those firms, they will have to work for less than the value of what they produce.

Workers can thus sort themselves among a hierarchy of firms in accordance with their demands for within-firm status. Figure 2 depicts the menu of choices confronting workers whose productivity takes a given value, M_0. The heavy lines represent the wage schedules offered by three different firms. They tell how much a worker with a given productivity would be paid in each firm. The average productivity level is highest in Firm 3, next highest in Firm 2, and lowest in Firm 1. The problem facing persons with productivity level M_0 is to choose which of these three firms to work for.

---

[23] For a more complete development of the argument to follow, see *ibid.*, chs. 3–6.

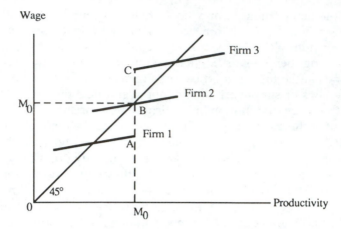

FIGURE 2. The wage structure when local status matters.

Workers who care most about status will want to "purchase" high-ranked positions such as the one labeled "A" in Firm 1. In such positions, they work for less than the value of what they produce. By contrast, those who care least about status will elect to receive wage premiums by working in low-ranked positions such as the one labeled "C" in Firm 3. Workers with moderate concerns about local rank will be attracted to intermediate positions such as the one labeled "B" in Firm 2, for which they neither pay nor receive any compensation for local rank.

Note also that in Figure 2, even though not every worker in each firm is paid the value of what he or she produces, workers taken as a group nonetheless do receive the value of what they produce. The extra compensation received by each firm's low-ranked workers is exactly offset by the shortfall in pay of its high-ranked workers.

High-ranked positions within firms are seen as valuable by those who hold them, but such positions can exist only if others hold low-ranked positions. If workers are free to choose the firms they work for, no one will accept a low-ranked position within a firm unless he receives extra compensation for doing so. By the same token, no worker will be able to occupy a high-ranked position unless he is willing to compensate the lesser-ranked workers without whose presence his own position would be unsustainable.

At the macro level, there is likewise considerable advantage in occupying a high-ranked position in society's income distribution. But, here too, such positions are possible for some only if others agree to occupy low-ranked positions. If people are free to choose their own associates, it follows that the low-ranked members of society must be compensated to remain.[24]

We may thus interpret Rawlsian redistributive tax systems as compensation payments whereby high-ranked members of society "purchase" their privileged positions from their lesser-ranked countrymen.[25] Virtually every civilized country has such a tax system. Far from being a burden on the rich, as the rich so often say, these systems are the glue without which societies would fragment into countless homogeneous groups.[26]

High-ranked positions in society's income distribution are of great value to the people who occupy them; this value exists only because others bear the costs of occupying low-ranked positions in the same distribution. In the absence of redistributive taxation, high-ranked members of the income distribution would be getting a valuable privilege for free.

To recapitulate, in this section I have tried to extend the contractarian discussion of distribution to include choices made by contractors who experience sympathy, envy, and various other common emotions. I have argued that the egalitarian measures described by Rawls are much more likely to be chosen by such contractors than by the purely self-interested contractors described by Rawls. Another dividend of the expanded framework is that the theory now has a positive dimension in addition to the traditional normative one. Thus, the expanded theory helps shed light on why egalitarian measures might look attractive not only behind a veil of ignorance, but also under the conditions confronting actual decision makers in the emerging market economies.

V. Practical Implementation Problems

Alternatives to direct regulation

Critics of the free-market system have interpreted unsafe jobs and alienating working conditions as the inevitable result of exploitation by powerful economic elites. This view motivated different responses in different economic systems: Communist countries assumed direct owner-

---

[24] This is not to say that the rich derive satisfaction from comparing themselves to the poor. But among the rich, as among other groups, it is better to have high rank than low rank. Group A, which is rich, benefits from its comparison with Group B, which is also rich, but slightly less so. B, in turn, benefits from its comparison with C, and so on down to the poorest group. The poorest group thus benefits the richest group indirectly. It constitutes the first link in a chain of comparisons that would unravel if the poorest group were to withdraw.

[25] Frank, *Choosing the Right Pond*, ch. 6.

[26] Pressures toward such fragmentation were indeed very much in evidence during the period preceding passage of the Sixteenth Amendment to the Constitution. See Sidney Ratner, *American Taxation* (New York: W. W. Norton, 1942).

ship of the means of production, while their capitalist counterparts enacted a variety of regulations of the labor contract.

Experience has shown that economic survival is more likely under the regulatory approach than under state ownership. But if the problems at issue are the result of positional arms races, as I have argued, it would be a great coincidence indeed if the regulations motivated by the spurious exploitation model turned out to be optimal.

The regulatory experience in the West has shown that it is, in fact, often difficult to achieve goals like enhanced workplace safety by having bureaucrats draft detailed prescriptive regulations governing the activities of private firms. Consider the following passage on safety requirements for ladders, taken verbatim from the U.S. Occupational Safety and Health Administration's 1976 manual of workplace safety standards:

> The general slope of grain in flat steps of minimum dimension shall not be steeper than 1 in 12, except that for ladders under 10 feet in length the slope shall not be steeper than 1 in 10. The slope of grain in areas of local deviation shall not be steeper than 1 in 12 or 1 in 10 as specified above. For all ladders, cross grain not steeper than 1 in 10 are permitted in lieu of 1 in 12, provided the size is increased to afford at least 15 percent greater strength than for ladders built to minimum dimensions. Local deviations of grain associated with otherwise permissible irregularities are permitted.[27]

This befogged passage appears in a section of the OSHA manual devoted to ladders that is thirty pages long, two columns to the page. It is easy to imagine the managers of a firm deciding that their best bet is to eschew any attempt to master these regulations and instead simply abandon any of their current activities that require ladders.

The problem with regulation in general is that conditions within firms are so idiosyncratic that no set of regulations, no matter how intricately detailed, could possibly track the costs and benefits of alternative production methods. Regulations are clearly not as disastrous as direct state ownership, but there is also no assurance that they are an improvement over the government simply doing nothing.

If the problems to be solved are the result not of exploitation but of positional arms races between individuals, then there is a much more direct and less cumbersome solution readily at hand. Under the positional-arms-race interpretation, recall, the problem is that positional consumption goods are misleadingly attractive. People accept greater safety risks, for example, hoping to advance their relative positions in the consumption distribution, only to discover that, when all take this step, everyone's

---

[27] Quoted by Robert S. Smith, "Compensating Differentials and Public Policy: A Review," *Industrial and Labor Relations Review*, vol. 32 (1977), pp. 11, 12.

relative position remains the same. There is a general principle in economics that when the problem is that an activity is too attractive, the most efficient solution is to tax that activity, thereby lowering the incentive to engage in it.

Taxation is more efficient than direct regulation for two reasons. First, unlike regulation, taxation does not require that bureaucrats have detailed knowledge of people's production and consumption alternatives. And second, whereas regulation imposes the cost of curtailing harmful activities on all parties indiscriminately, taxation concentrates this cost in the hands of those parties who can curtail the activities in the least costly way. Taxing positional consumption alters overall incentives in the desired direction, while preserving for individuals the latitude to take their own circumstances into account.

The significance of these advantages is clearly illustrated by the following example comparing taxation and regulation as a means of curtailing pollution. (Activities that generate pollution are like positional-consumption activities in that each imposes harmful effects—"negative externalities," in the economist's parlance—on others.) Suppose two firms, X and Y, have access to five different production processes, each of which has a different cost and gives off a different amount of pollution. The daily costs of the processes and the corresponding number of tons of smoke are listed in Table 3.

If pollution is neither regulated nor taxed, each firm will use A, the least costly of the five processes, and each will emit 4 tons of pollution per day, for a total pollution of 8 tons/day. Suppose the city council wants to cut smoke emissions by half. To accomplish this, they are considering two options. The first is direct regulation—to require each firm to curtail its emissions by half. The alternative is to set a tax of T on each ton of smoke emitted each day. How large would T have to be in order to curtail emissions by half? And how would the total costs to society compare under the two alternatives?

If each firm is required to cut pollution by half, each must switch from process A to process C. The result will be 2 tons/day of pollution for each firm. The cost of the switch for Firm X will be 600/day − 100/day = 500/day. The cost to Y will be 140/day − 50/day = 90/day, which means a total cost for the two firms of 590/day.

TABLE 3. *Costs and Emissions for Five Production Processes*

Process (smoke)	A (4t/day)	B (3t/day)	C (2t/day)	D (1t/day)	E (0t/day)
Cost to Firm X	100	190	600	1200	2000
Cost to Firm Y	50	80	140	230	325

How will each firm respond to a tax of T per ton of pollution? First, it will ask itself whether switching from process A to B will increase its costs by more or less than T per day. If by less, it will pay to switch, because process B, which yields 1 ton less smoke, will save the firm T per day in taxes. If process B's costs exceed A's by more than T, however, the firm will not switch. It will be cheaper to stick with A and pay the extra T in taxes. If the switch from A to B pays, the firm will then ask the same question about the switch from B to C. It will keep switching until the extra costs of the next process are no longer smaller than T.

To illustrate, suppose a tax of 50/ton were levied. Firm X would stick with process A because it costs 90/day less than process B and produces only 1 ton/day of extra smoke, and thus only 50/day in extra taxes. Firm Y, by contrast, will switch to process B because it costs only 30/day more and will save 50/day in taxes. But Firm Y will not continue on to C because it costs 60/day more than B and will save only an additional 50/day in taxes. With Firm X staying with A and Firm Y switching to B, we get a total pollution reduction of only 1 ton/day. A tax of 50/ton thus does not produce the desired 50-percent reduction in pollution.

The solution is to keep increasing the tax until we get the desired result. Consider what happens with a tax of 91/ton. This tax will lead Firm X to adopt process B, and Firm Y to adopt process D. Total emissions will be the desired 4 tons/day. The cost to Firm X will be 190/day − 100/day = 90/day, and the cost to Firm Y will be 230/day − 50/day = 180/day. The total cost for both firms is thus only 270/day, or 320/day less than the cost of having each firm cut pollution by half.[28] Indeed, the taxation approach achieves the desired result at the lowest possible total cost because it concentrates pollution reduction in the hands of Firm Y, which can accomplish the task more cheaply than Firm X can.

Taxing positional consumption would produce an analogous advantage over the alternative of direct regulations on safety, hours, and other detailed features of the labor contract. If relative consumption is important, it follows that each person's consumption imposes negative externalities on others—externalities that are the logical equivalent of pollution. When any one person increases his consumption, he raises, perhaps imperceptibly, the consumption standard for others. As the British economist Richard Layard once put it: "In a poor society a man proves to his wife that he loves her by giving her a rose, but in a rich society he must give a dozen roses."

Consider, for example, a young man's decision about how big a diamond to give his fiancée. Because the function of this gift is to serve as

---

[28] Note that the taxes paid by the firm are not included in our reckoning of the social costs of the tax alternative, because this money is not lost to society. It can be used to reduce whatever taxes would otherwise have to be levied on citizens. A more complete account of the effects of such taxes would have to account for monitoring and enforcement costs, and the possible waste associated with efforts at tax avoidance.

a token of commitment, the one he buys must necessarily cost enough to hurt. If he is an American, his jeweler will tell him that the custom is to pay two months' salary for a stone and setting. If he makes $36,000 per year, he will have to come up with $6,000 or else be considered a cheapskate.

From the perspective of the economy as a whole, the outcome would be better if there were a 500-percent tax on jewelry. The after-tax price of what is now only a $1,000 diamond would then rise to $6,000. In buying this smaller diamond, the young man would incur the same economic hardship as before. And since this is the essence of the gift's function, his goal would not really be compromised by the tax. Nor would the young man's fiancée suffer any real loss. Because *everyone* would now be buying smaller diamonds, the smaller stone would provide much the same satisfaction as the larger one would have. On the plus side, the government gets an additional $5,000 to finance its expenditures. The only loser is the deBeers diamond cartel of South Africa, which would earn $5,000 less than before the tax.

Diamonds are, of course, a special case in the sense that their relative size and clarity accounts almost exclusively for the satisfaction that people derive from them. Yet positional considerations also figure prominently in the satisfaction derived from many goods that also deliver utility in absolute terms. Indeed, the standards that define acceptable schools, houses, wardrobes, cars, vacations, and a host of other important budget items are inextricably linked to the amounts other people spend on them. Because individual consumers do not take positional externalities into account in their choices, the result is that such commodities appear much more attractive to individuals than to society as a whole. For the same reasons it is often efficient to tax pollution, it will be efficient to tax many of these forms of consumption. On efficiency grounds, such taxes would be an attractive substitute for existing regulations and taxes that interfere with efficient resource allocation (for example, our current income tax, which taxes income saved as well as income consumed, leads to suboptimal rates of capital accumulation).

The mechanics of positional-consumption taxation

Proposals to tax positional consumption raise the specter of forbidding complexity — of citizens having to save receipts for each purchase, of politicians and producers bickering over which products are to be classified as positional-consumption items, and so on. Yet a system of positional-consumption taxation would entail no greater complexity than do the usual systems of income taxation. The need to keep expenditure receipts can be easily avoided by calculating overall consumption as the difference between current income and current savings. There is simply no need to sum the value of each item purchased. The need to debate which items are positional can be avoided by having a standard deduction—by making the first, say, $20,000 of annual consumption expenditures exempt from taxation. This feature would serve two purposes: (1) it would shield nonpositional-consumption items—including necessities like food, basic clothing, shelter, and transportation—from taxation; and (2) it would make the tax system progressive. The positional-consumption tax, like any other tax, invites debate in the political arena about special exemptions. But this tax is no more complex than the existing taxes employed in the United States and Western Europe.

CONCLUDING REMARKS

The contractarian framework has greatly increased our understanding of laws and social institutions. The self-interest assumption on which it has traditionally been based is appropriate for many purposes, but for many others it is not. I have argued that certain laws and institutions can be understood only by reference to nonegoistic motives. The instrumental view of preferences provides a theoretical framework within which such motives can be introduced into contractarian analysis in a disciplined way.

Both the capitalist and Communist countries of the twentieth century saw their primary economic role as that of protecting citizens from exploitation by powerful economic elites. I have argued that the problems that led to this view are the result not of exploitation at all, but of economic competition between individuals. This interpretation suggests that the emerging market economies of Eastern Europe would be much better advised to eschew the regulatory approach adopted by most Western countries in favor of the alternative of taxing positional consumption.

To forestall possible misunderstanding, I should state clearly that my arguments in this essay are not meant to imply that positional-consumption taxation will by itself pave the way for rapid and orderly economic development in the emerging market economies. Such a claim would hardly be plausible for countries like Albania, which can barely feed themselves.

Nor is it my claim that positional-consumption taxation can, or should, completely supplant all existing forms of economic regulation even when a more advanced stage of economic development is achieved. My claim is only that such taxes will often be an attractive substitute for those particular economic regulations that are intended to protect workers from exploitation. Exploitation is, of course, by no means the only rationale offered for economic regulation. Some forms of safety regulation, for example, have been defended as means for reducing informational complexity; other forms, especially those that apply to younger or less well-educated workers, aim to protect workers from the consequences of their own decisions. Positional-consumption taxation clearly would not be an optimal policy response to either of these problems.

Yet for the set of economic problems attributed to exploitation, both in the West and in the former Communist countries, positional-consumption taxation deserves serious consideration. By directly attacking the incentive problem that led to the conditions erroneously attributed to exploitation, it promises to achieve the desired results at the lowest possible cost.

Economics, Cornell University

ASSOCIATIONS AND DEMOCRACY*

By Joshua Cohen and Joel Rogers

Introduction

Since the publication of John Rawls's *A Theory of Justice*, normative democratic theory has focused principally on three tasks: refining principles of justice, clarifying the nature of political justification, and exploring the public policies required to ensure a just distribution of education, health care, and other basic resources. Much less attention has been devoted to examining the political institutions and social arrangements that might plausibly implement reasonable political principles.[1] Moreover, the amount of attention paid to issues of organizational and institutional implementation has varied sharply across the different species of normative theory. Neoliberal theorists, concerned chiefly with protecting liberty by taming power, and essentially hostile to the affirmative state,[2] have been far more sensitive to such issues than egalitarian-democratic theorists, who simultaneously embrace classically liberal concerns with choice, egalitarian concerns with the distribution of resources, and a republican emphasis on the values of citizen participation and public debate (we sketch such a conception below in Section I). Neglect of how such val-

* This essay is drawn from a book-in-progress called *Associative Democracy: Democratic Renewal Beyond the Mischiefs of Faction*. Drafts of the book manuscript have been presented at meetings of the American Political Science Association, Princeton University Political Theory Colloquium, Social Organization Colloquium at the University of Wisconsin–Madison, Society for Ethical and Legal Philosophy, UCLA Center for History and Social Theory, University of Chicago Colloquium on Constitutionalism, University of Maryland Seminar on Political Theory, PEGS (Political Economy of the Good Society), and CREA (École Polytechnique); drafts have also been presented at the conference on "Post-Liberal Democratic Theory" held at the University of Texas at Austin, and at the "Associations and Democracy" conference held at the University of Wisconsin–Madison. We are grateful to participants in those discussions for many useful comments and suggestions, and especially to Bruce Ackerman, Suzanne Berger, Owen Fiss, Charles Sabel, Wolfgang Streeck, and Erik Olin Wright for the same. We also thank the editors of *Social Philosophy & Policy* for comments on an earlier draft of this essay. A shorter version of this essay will appear in *Market Socialism*, ed. Pranab Bardhan and John Roemer (New York: Oxford University Press, 1993).

[1] See John Rawls, *A Theory of Justice* (Cambridge: Harvard University Press, 1971), whose own work is an exception to the generalization made in the text. Another prominent exception is Roberto Unger's *False Necessity*, vol. 2 of *Politics* (Cambridge: Cambridge University Press, 1987).

[2] For examples of the institutional program of "neoliberal constitutionalists" hostile to the affirmative state, see Friedrich A. Hayek, *The Constitution of Liberty* (Chicago: University of Chicago Press, 1960); *idem, The Mirage of Social Justice*, vol. 2 of *Law, Legislation, and Liberty* (Chicago: University of Chicago Press, 1976); and James M. Buchanan, *The Limits of Liberty: Between Anarchy and Leviathan* (Chicago: University of Chicago Press, 1975).

© 1993 Social Philosophy and Policy Foundation. Printed in the USA.

ues might be implemented has deepened the vulnerability of egalitarian-democratic views to the charge of being unrealistic: "good in theory but not so good in practice."

In this essay we address this vulnerability by examining the constructive role that "secondary"[3] associations—labor unions, employer associations, citizen lobbies and advocacy groups, private service organizations, other private groups—can play in a democracy. Our central contention is that, as a practical matter, implementing democratic norms requires a high level of secondary group organization of a certain kind. Roughly speaking, the "level" required is one in which all citizens, irrespective of their initial endowment, enjoy the political benefits of organization; the "kind" required is one which delivers those benefits in ways consistent not only with political equality but with other democratic norms. The problem is that the required level and kind of group activity do not arise naturally, and those groups that do arise often frustrate, rather than advance, democratic aspirations. Our proposed solution to this problem is to supplement nature with artifice: through politics, to alter the environment, incidence, activity, and governing status of associations in ways that strengthen democratic order. We call this deliberate politics of associations "associative democracy."[4]

We would recommend the pursuit of "associative democracy" for a wide range of administrative and property regimes. Here, however, we assume the context of modern capitalism, where markets are the primary mechanism of resource allocation and private, individual decisions are the central determinant of investment. Admitting the limits this context places on the satisfaction of egalitarian-democratic norms, our argument is that associative democracy can improve the practical approximation to those norms.

What motivates our argument are concerns about the likely future of even such approximation. Due principally to changes in the organization of capitalism, many of the most important institutional sources of egalitarian achievement under modern capitalism—from strong unions and employer organizations, to a variety of popular political organizations—have recently fallen into disarray. The egalitarian project is weakened by a widening organizational deficit at its base. Recognizing that most social clocks cannot be turned backward, that new as well as revived institutional structures are needed, we offer associative democracy as a strategy to rebuild that base—to provide egalitarian democracy with necessary associative supports.

[3] So-called because they are, by convention, the large residual of the "primary" organizations of the family, firm, and state.

[4] We share the term "associative democracy" with John Mathews, *Age of Democracy: The Political Economy of Post-Fordism* (New York: Oxford University Press, 1989). But we arrived at the term independently.

We sketch the associative conception in four steps. First, to identify the need for an associative strategy of democratic reform, we note three barriers to egalitarianism and indicate how each implicates questions of associative order. Second, to underscore the potential contribution of groups to democratic governance, we distinguish four general types of contribution and then draw from comparative experience to illustrate how the potential has been realized in different areas of public policy. Third, we defend the associative strategy for netting this contribution against two objections: that it is impossible, because groups are intractable to reform; and that it is undesirable, because the increase in group power needed to secure contributions poses unacceptably high risks of group abuse of power. Fourth and finally, we illustrate the associative strategy by discussing how it might be used to guide reforms of industrial relations and vocational training in the United States.

I. Why Associative Reform?

Associative democracy aims to further an egalitarian-democratic view of politics defined by simultaneous respect for norms of political equality, popular sovereignty, distributive equity, deliberative politics, and the operation of society for the general welfare. We interpret these norms in the following ways. *Political equality* requires a rough equality across citizens in their chances to hold office and to influence political choices. *Popular sovereignty* requires that the authorization of state action be determined (within the limits set by fundamental civil and political liberties) by procedures in which citizens are represented as equals.[5] *Distributive equity* obtains when inequalities of advantage, if they exist, are not determined by differences of inherited resources, of natural endowments, or simple good luck. Collective choice is *deliberative* when it is framed by different conceptions of the common good, and public initiatives are defended ultimately by reference to a conception of the public interest. Society operates for the *general welfare* when there is both economic and governmental efficiency.

These norms are routinely frustrated in the everyday politics of contemporary mass democracies. While there are many sources of frustration, here we note three that are of special relevance to our discussion of associations.[6]

---

[5] This procedural formulation of the idea of popular sovereignty does not assume a people with a single will, and thus is immune to the criticisms directed against that assumption by, for example, William Riker, *Liberalism against Populism: A Confrontation Between the Theory of Democracy and the Theory of Social Choice* (San Francisco: W. H. Freeman, 1982).

[6] Among the fundamental issues we will put to the side here are intense national and religious divisions and the destructive conflicts associated with them.

Three problems of egalitarian governance

The first problem is that government programs directed to achieving a more equitable distribution of advantage (e.g., welfare services, active labor-market policies, much economic and social regulation) are widely perceived as unacceptably costly and inefficient. Whatever their theoretical attractions, critics assert, in practice such programs generate economic rigidities and a wasteful expansion of government aims beyond government capacities. During a period of slowed productivity growth and intensified economic competition, this makes egalitarianism at best an unaffordable indulgence, at worst a betrayal of government obligations to "promote the general welfare."

While claims of government inefficiency are often grossly exaggerated, they have sufficient basis in fact to give popular resonance to their constant amplification.[7] And especially in more liberal societies — where choices about social governance are seen largely as choices between states and markets, and no associative alternative is perceived — popular acceptance of those claims is devastating to the practical pursuit of egalitarian ends. Most publics are unwilling to forgo economic growth in the interest of equality. None enjoys literally wasting its tax dollars. So if state programs are successfully defined as inimical to growth and wasteful, and if market governance is the only alternative, egalitarianism is politically doomed.

The second problem is that egalitarian efforts are deeply compromised by representational inequalities. Capitalist property relations are, of course, defined by inequalities in economic power, and political power is materially conditioned. So economic inequalities characteristically translate into political inequalities in violation of the norm of political equality. Until recently, however, at least in most rich, Western, liberal societies, it was possible to speak of a relatively steady advance in the social democratization of capitalist societies. Gains in political equality accrued from gains in the political representation of economically disadvantaged interests.[8]

Today, any such optimistic assessment needs to be revised. Unions and virtually all other mass popular organizations representing working people are in palpable decline, while success in the organized representation

---

[7] For discussion of some prominent exaggerations, see George W. Downs and Patrick D. Larkey, *The Search for Government Efficiency: From Hubris to Helplessness* (New York: Random House, 1986). In the United States, increased public doubt about government capacity to achieve egalitarian ends is coincident with increased support for those ends. The "politics of happiness" that some saw in the reformist projects of the 1960s has been succeeded by a "politics of sadness" in which the public knows that it is not getting what it wants, but has no confidence that government can provide it.

[8] Many saw this as irreversible. See, for example, Jürgen Habermas, *The Legitimation Crisis of Late Capitalism* (Boston: Beacon Press, 1973).

of the interests reflected in the "new social movements" of feminism, environmentalism, and racial justice is distinctly limited.[9] With a widening range of interests lacking an effective voice, the defining idiom of much politics is not equality, but exclusion.

The third problem is that those whose voice is organized often speak with a strident particularism. On both sides of the many lines of privilege, the narrow assertion of group interest is very nearly a norm. Whether motivated by simple selfishness or by the fear of cooperation that comes from weakness, the result is a politics of group bargaining that, undisciplined by respect for the common good, inevitably conflicts with norms of popular sovereignty and deliberative politics.[10] Group particularism makes democratic governance more difficult, and it lessens the appeal of inclusive politics by inspiring doubt that inclusion in fact enhances democracy.

The problems of government incompetence, political inequality, and particularism feed one another. Inequalities in representation diminish support for any egalitarian effort. The particularism of existing groups prompts substantial reliance on statist means in those efforts. The adoption of such means, even where ends could in theory be better accomplished by or with the aid of associations, compromises government efficiency. And the fact and perception of government inefficiency, working directly or through the consequent erosion of political support, weakens those efforts and thus underscores inequality.

An associative strategy of reform

The idea of associative democracy is to break this cycle by curing the associative disorders that help to fuel it. Using conventional tools of public policy (taxes, subsidies, legal sanctions), as applied through the familiar decision-making procedures of formal government (legislatures and administrative bodies, as overseen by the courts), it would promote associative reform in each of the three problem areas.[11] Where manifest inequalities in political representation exist, it recommends promoting the organized representation of presently excluded interests. Where group particularism undermines democratic deliberation or popular sovereignty, it recommends encouraging the organized to be more other-regarding in their actions. And where associations have greater competence than pub-

---

[9] On unions, see Jelle Visser, "Trends in Trade Union Membership," *OECD Employment Outlook*, July 1991, pp. 97–134.

[10] For the American case, see the classic characterization of the resulting "interest group liberalism" offered by Theodore J. Lowi, *The End of Liberalism: The Second Republic of the United States*, 2d ed. (New York: W. W. Norton, 1979).

[11] Throughout, respect for the associational liberties of group members, recognition of the resistance of many groups to change, and rejection of concessionist views of associations mean that the strategy stops well short of legislating associative practice or its relation to the state. Associative democracy is not a distinct form of order, but a strategy to reform aspects of current practice.

lic authorities for achieving democratic ends, or where their participation could improve the effectiveness of government programs, it recommends encouraging a more direct and formal governance role for groups.

This last point may be the most immediate. In many areas of economic and social concern — from the environment and occupational safety and health, to vocational training and consumer protection — egalitarian aims are badly served by the state-market dichotomy that still dominates mainstream debate about how those aims should be pursued. Often, the right answer to the question "should the state take care of the problem, or should it be left to the market?" is a double negative.

This seems to be so in three ideal-typical classes of regulatory problems. In the first, nonmarket public standards on behavior are needed, and government has the competence to set them, but the objects of regulation are so diverse or unstable that it is not possible for the government to specify just how those standards should be met at particular regulated sites. Much environmental regulation presents problems of this sort. In the second, public standard-setting is needed, and government has the competence to do it, but the objects of regulation are sufficiently numerous or dispersed to preclude serious government monitoring of compliance. Consider the problems of occupational safety and health enforcement. In the third, uniform public standards are needed, but it lies beyond the competence of either markets or governments to specify and secure them, as doing either requires the simultaneous coordination of private actors and their enlistment in specifying the behavior sought. Here, consider the difficulties of getting private firms to agree on standards for vocational training, and to increase their own training efforts.

Where these sorts of problems are encountered, associative governance can provide a welcome alternative or complement to public regulatory efforts because of the distinctive capacity of associations to gather local information, monitor behavior, and promote cooperation among private actors. In such cases, the associative strategy recommends attending to the possibility of enlisting them explicitly in the performance of public tasks.

In sum, the idea of the associative strategy is to encourage the use of associations to address concerns about unequal representation, particularism, and the excessive cost and inefficiency of egalitarian programs, and through that address to satisfy more fully egalitarian-democratic norms. In the next two sections, we will explore in more detail the features of associations that provide foundations for the strategy and underlie our assessment of its promise.

II. The Potential Contribution of Groups

The cornerstone of the argument for associative democracy is that groups have a significant contribution to make to democratic governance. In the ordinary operation of mass democracies, groups are generally acknowledged to be capable of performing at least four useful, democracy-enhancing functions: providing information, equalizing representation, promoting citizen education, and implementing alternative governance.

Information. Associations can provide information to policy makers on member preferences, the impact of proposed legislation, or the implementation of existing law. As the state has become more involved in regulating society, and extended the reach of its regulation to more diverse sites, technically complex areas, and processes subject to rapid change, this information function has arguably become more important. Good information is needed to assess the effectiveness of a myriad of state policies, commonly operating at some distance from the monitoring of state inspectorates, and to adjust policies to changed circumstances or behaviors. This is especially so given social and policy interdependence — the interaction of social welfare policy and economic growth, for example, or environmental regulation and technical change — which underscore the value of accurate, timely intelligence on policy effects. Because of their proximity to those effects, groups are often well positioned to provide such information. When they do, they contribute to satisfying the norm of popular sovereignty, since good information improves citizen deliberation, facilitates the enforcement of decisions, and clarifies the appropriate objects of state policy.

Equalizing representation. Politics is materially conditioned, and inequalities in material advantage, of the sort definitive of capitalism, translate directly to inequalities in political power. Groups can help remedy these inequalities by permitting individuals with low per-capita resources to pool those resources through organization. In making the benefits of organization available to those whose influence on policy is negligible without it, groups help satisfy the norm of political equality. Similarly, groups can promote a more equitable distribution of advantage by correcting for imbalances in bargaining power that follow from the unequal control of wealth. Groups can also represent interests not best organized through territorial politics based on majority rule. These include functional interests, associated with a person's position or activity within a society; "categoric" interests of the sort pursued by the new social movements, interests whose intensity is not registered in voting procedures; and, at least in systems without proportional representation, the interests of political minorities. Here, groups improve an imperfect system of interest representation by making it more fine-grained, attentive to preference intensities, and representative of diverse views. This, too, furthers political equality.

Citizen education. Associations can function as "schools of democracy." Participation in them can help citizens to develop competence, self-confidence, and a broader set of interests than they would acquire in a more fragmented political society. Alexis de Tocqueville provides the classic statement of this educative power of associations: "Feelings are recruited, the heart is enlarged, and the human mind is developed only by the reciprocal influence of men on one another," and under democratic conditions this influence can "only be accomplished by associations." [12] In performing this educative function, associations help foster the "civic consciousness" on which any egalitarian order, and its deliberative politics, depend. That is, they promote a recognition of the norms of democratic process and equity, and a willingness to uphold them and to accept them as fixing the basic framework of political argument and social cooperation, at least on condition that others do so as well.

Alternative governance. Associations can provide a distinctive form of social governance, alternative to markets or public hierarchies, that permits society to realize the important benefits of cooperation among member citizens. In providing a form of governance, associations figure more as problem solvers than simply as representatives of their members to authoritative political decision makers, pressuring those decision makers on behalf of member interests. They help to formulate and execute public policies, and take on quasi-public functions that supplement or supplant the state's more directly regulatory actions.

Such associations facilitate cooperative dealings in two ways. First, their sheer existence reduces the transaction costs of securing agreement among potentially competing interests. The background of established forms of communication and collaboration they provide enables parties to settle more rapidly and reliably on jointly beneficial actions. Second, groups help to establish the trust that facilitates cooperation. They effectively provide assurances to members that their own willingness to cooperate will not be exploited by others. Often directly beneficial to society, associative governance can also support public efforts to achieve egalitarian aims.

Lessons from comparative experience. While examples of all these sorts of group contributions can be found in the United States, in recent years it is students of comparative politics, in particular the politics of Western Europe, who have been especially attentive to these positive features of associations. They have argued more particularly that certain sorts of group organization play a central role in resolving, in egalitarian fashion, problems of successful governance in mass democracies.

The rediscovery in the 1970s of liberal "corporatist" systems of interest representation in Northern European democracies was the key to one such argument. [13] Students of liberal corporatism suggested that the in-

---

[12] Alexis de Tocqueville, *Democracy in America* (New York: Vintage, 1945), vol. 2, p. 117.

[13] See Philippe C. Schmitter, "Still the Century of Corporatism?" *Review of Politics*, vol. 36 (1974), pp. 85–131; Suzanne Berger, ed., *Organizing Interests in Western Europe: Pluralism, Corporatism, and the Transformation of Politics* (Cambridge: Cambridge University Press, 1981);

corporation of organized interests into the formation of economic policy helped produce, simultaneously, better satisfaction of distributive concerns, improved economic performance, and gains in government efficiency. Of particular note was the negotiation and compromise between organized business and organized labor within such systems, which appeared to permit their joint realization of many gains from cooperation.

The Scandinavian social democracies of Norway and Sweden provided a particularly advanced example of such labor-business cooperation. There, encompassing union and employer federations, both speaking for virtually all of their respective populations of interest, would meet regularly to negotiate the terms of their essentially peaceful coexistence, with the state serving to ratify and support those terms. Unions exchanged wage restraint for guarantees of low unemployment and a high social wage. Employers traded employment security and industrial upgrading for union moderation. The state, backed by both "social partners," calibrated fiscal policy to stabilize employment, social policy to provide insurance against market misfortune, and industrial policy to maintain competitiveness on foreign markets.[14]

More recent discussions, even as they have dissented from claims made about corporatism, or paused to note its devolution or collapse, have also stressed the importance of associative activity to economic performance. Students of the successful alternatives to mass production that are marked, simultaneously, by high wages, skills, productivity, and competitiveness have argued that this success requires a dense social infrastructure of secondary association and coordination. This organizational infrastructure provides the basis for cooperation between management and labor, among firms, and between firms and the government on issues of work organization, training, technology diffusion, research and development, and new product ventures. And that cooperation, it is argued, is essential to ensuring economic adjustment that is both rapid and fair.[15]

---

and John H. Goldthorpe, ed., *Order and Conflict in Contemporary Capitalism* (Oxford: Clarendon Press, 1984).

[14] For useful description and analysis of such coordination in Scandinavia, see Walter Korpi, *The Democratic Class Struggle* (London: Routledge and Kegan Paul, 1983); Gøsta Esping-Andersen, *Politics against Markets* (Princeton: Princeton University Press, 1985); for a good comparative treatment of the Swedish and German cases, and the role played by corporatist institutions in facilitating wage stability and industrial upgrading, see Peter Swenson, *Fair Shares: Unions, Pay, and Politics in Sweden and West Germany* (Ithaca: Cornell University Press, 1989); and Lowell Turner, *Democracy at Work: Changing World Markets and the Future of Labor Unions* (Ithaca: Cornell University Press, 1991). For a general review of problems that have beset social democracies since the mid-1970s, see Fritz W. Scharpf, *Crisis and Choice in European Social Democracy* (Ithaca: Cornell University Press, 1991).

[15] See Charles F. Sabel, "Flexible Specialization and the Re-emergence of Regional Economies," in *Reversing Industrial Decline: Industrial Structure and Policy in Britain and Her Competitors*, ed. Paul Q. Hirst and Jonathan Zeitlin (Oxford: Berg, 1989), pp. 17–70; and Wolfgang Streeck, "On the Institutional Conditions of Diversified Quality Production," in *Beyond*

The reemerging (or more newly visible) regional economies of Western Europe—Italy's Emilia-Romagna, Sweden's Smaland, Germany's Baden-Württemburg, Denmark's Jutland peninsula—provide particularly striking examples of such associative economic governance. They feature complex public-private partnerships on training and technology diffusion, flexible manufacturing networks that facilitate inter-firm cooperation in performing discrete and varied production tasks, more formalized consortia and industry associations to realize economies of scale in some functions (e.g., marketing or research and development) among otherwise competing firms, joint training activities among firms, occupational credentialling of labor through industry-wide or regional labor and management associations, and close linkages between regional development and welfare policies. Indeed, the object of state economic development policy in most of these regions prominently includes efforts to build the private associative framework upon which such efforts rely.[16]

For an example of the sorts of associations being fostered, consider CITER, an association of small knitwear firms in the town of Carpi, in Emilia-Romagna. Its six hundred dues-paying member firms are generally tiny, averaging fewer than eight workers each. But by pooling resources in the association itself, as well as countless joint-production schemes facilitated by the association, they are able to flourish in the fiercely competitive and unstable business of international fashion. Through CITER, they share information on trends in technology, production processes, and emerging markets, underwrite a sophisticated forecasting service on fashion trends, gain access to and training in the use of sophisticated business software, and enjoy other services no one firm could afford on its own. CITER is not a cartel. Its member firms still compete with one another. They simply do not forsake the obvious gains to all that can come from associative cooperation.[17]

The virtues of associative forms of governance are, however, not confined to economic cooperation. Associative governance has also been credited with achieving more effective social regulation and welfare delivery. Within the heavily procedural and litigious "command and control" regulation favored in more liberal systems and particularly dominant in the United States, groups commonly appear to frustrate regulatory efficiency. Evidence from systems in which associations are assigned a

---

Keynesianism: The Socio-Economics of Production and Employment, ed. Egon Matzner and Wolfgang Streeck (London: Edward Elgar, 1991), pp. 21–61.

[16] For examples of state policy, see Stuart A. Rosenfeld, *Technology Innovation and Rural Development: Lessons from Italy and Denmark* (Washington: Aspen Institute, 1990). We emphasize that state policy is in fact needed in all these cases: the appropriate infrastructure does not emerge naturally from the interactions of economic actors or from favorable cultural tradition. For further discussion, see Section III below.

[17] For this and other examples of "flexible manufacturing networks," see C. Richard Hatch, *Flexible Manufacturing Networks: Cooperation for Competitiveness in a Global Economy* (Washington: Corporation for Enterprise Development, 1988).

more central and open governance function, however, suggests that they can powerfully contribute to the success of regulatory programs. Instead of acting only or chiefly as "special interests" intent either on capturing public powers or limiting their efficacy, groups supplement traditional public authority by helping to define policy, to monitor its implementation, and to enforce it. Rather than acting as obstructions, they serve as private multipliers on public capacities.

Associations have been shown to play this role for a wide range of regulatory purposes, extending from the enforcement of occupational safety and health, wage and hour, and environmental regulation, to the promotion of curricular reform and better learning opportunities in education and training systems. Admitting variations in national success, the general result appears to be a style of regulation, and the affirmative promotion of egalitarian ends, at once more effective, flexible, and efficient than command and control, or simple state administration of programs.

Consider occupational safety and health. Instead of relying exclusively on a centralized state inspectorate to enforce occupational safety and health laws, virtually all European systems supplement their inspectorates with mandated workplace health and safety committees. These committees operate with delegated public powers: they monitor, and in some measure are empowered to enforce, compliance with the regulatory regime. While bringing new costs in its train (e.g., the costs of training worker deputies), the general result of this strategy is a health and safety policy more effective and efficient than an inspectorate-alone approach. It is more effective because it supplements public capacities for monitoring compliance with the capacities of workers themselves. It is more efficient because it permits public efforts to be left largely to standard setting, and enlists the local knowledge of regulated actors in devising the least costly means, in particular settings, of satisfying such standards.[18]

Or consider the use of associations in education. A striking example is provided by the German system of youth apprenticeship. Employer associations and unions determine training standards and requirements, monitor the provision of training at both school and work, and provide much of the workplace-based instruction. The role of the state is essentially to inform the social partners about emerging labor-market trends, ratify the results of their deliberations, help enforce the occupational standards that result, and encourage widespread participation in the associa-

---

[18] For a review of worker participation in safety regulation focusing on Europe, see the contributions to Sabastiano Bagnara, Raffaello Misiti, and Helmut Wintersberger, eds., *Work and Health in the 1980s: Experiences of Direct Workers' Participation in Occupational Health* (Berlin: Edition Sigma, 1985); for a particularly useful country study, see Bjørn Gustavsen and Gerry Hunnius, *New Patterns of Work Reform: The Case of Norway* (Oslo: Universitetsforlaget, 1981); for the contrast with the United States, see Charles Noble, *Liberalism at Work: The Rise and Fall of OSHA* (Philadelphia: Temple University Press, 1986), and Eugene Bardach and Robert Kagan, *Going by the Book* (Philadelphia: Temple University Press, 1982).

tive effort. From top to bottom, the system is driven off the associations, albeit acting in concert with public authority. The result is generally recognized as the most successful and inclusive vocational training program in the developed Western world.[19]

Taken together, these different investigations and examples underscore the range of important contributions associations can make to a functioning democratic order. What assures that contribution, moreover, is not the sheer "quantity of associability" found in such systems, but the care of public authorities within them in matching the qualitative characteristics of different groups to public functions, and in working with groups to encourage the appropriate qualitative characteristics.[20] The deliberate conditioning of state fiscal and welfare assistance on the outcomes of wage bargaining under corporatism; the explicit state efforts to build the associative infrastructure of regional economies; the laws mandating the workplace safety committees; the support provided by the German state to the social partners in education: here we have examples of the sort of public encouragement of appropriate group forms recommended by the associative strategy.

III. Impossibility and Undesirability: A Response to Objections

Thus far we have discussed problems of government incompetence, political inequality, and particularism that now thwart egalitarian-democratic politics; we have proposed that a partial remedy for those problems lies in an improved organization of secondary associations pursued through a politics of associations; and we have presented some analytical considerations and comparative experience to support and illustrate our proposal. We want now to consider a pair of related objections to it. Both objections accept (at least for the sake of argument) the attractiveness of egalitarian-democratic norms and both agree that associations can contribute to the satisfaction of those norms. But they reject the use of an associative strategy to engender the "right" sort of associative environment. According to the first objection, it is not possible to create a favorable associative environment through politics; according to the second, efforts to create such an environment are more dangerous than the disease they aim to cure.

---

[19] For a close examination of the different public powers enjoyed by the "social partners" in the German case, see Wolfgang Streeck, Joseph Hilbert, Karl-Heinz van Kevelaer, Frederike Maier, and Hajo Weber, *The Role of the Social Partners in Vocational Training and Further Training in the Federal Republic of Germany* (Berlin: European Center for the Development of Vocational Training, 1987).

[20] The phrase and the point come from Philippe C. Schmitter, "Interest Intermediation and Regime Governability in Contemporary Western Europe and North America," in Berger, ed., *Organizing Interests*, pp. 285–327.

Impossibility

The argument for impossibility begins with the assumption that groups are a product of nature, or culture, or some other unalterable substrate of a country's political life. Just as some countries are blessed with good top soil or a temperate climate, others are blessed with the "right" kinds of groups, at the right level of organization. In countries that are so blessed, group contributions of the sort we note are observed. But since patterns of group organization and behavior lie beyond politics, the observation provides no support at all for an associative strategy for addressing the problems of egalitarianism. Indeed, precisely by highlighting the importance of a favorable social basis for egalitarian democracy, they explain why equality does not travel well.

We think that this objection exaggerates the fixity of the associative environment. Groups are, after all, in important ways political artifacts. Their incidence, character, and patterns of interaction are not merely the result of natural tendencies to association among citizens with like preferences. They reflect structural features of the political economy in which they form—from the distribution of wealth and income, to the locus of policy making in different areas. And they reflect variations across the members of that society along such dimensions as income, information, and density of interaction. Existing political institutions and "culture" may crystallize around certain structural features and patterns of variation along these dimensions. But those features and variations are in no sense natural. They can be changed through public policy.

Public policy can, for example, make the background distribution of wealth and income more or less uneven. It can shift the locus of public decision making from regional to national levels, or concentrate it in a single department, in ways that encourage different sorts of group formation and discourage others. The availability of information can be widened or constricted. The density of interaction among similarly situated citizens can be increased or decreased. The cost of administering joint efforts, or navigating the negotiation antecedent to them, can be subsidized or not. Those subsidies can simply be provided to the most powerful, or tied to antecedent satisfaction of certain requirements of behavior. Consistent with the continued supremacy of formal political institutions, groups can also be assigned public functions, including the power to issue complaints for violations of administrative regulation, to take emergency action in correcting violations, to establish standards for licensing and training in different occupations and industry standards on production, to establish eligibility criteria for receipt of other sorts of benefits (including welfare benefits), and to apply such licensing procedures, standards, and eligibility criteria as part of a general regulatory regime.

All such changes in the environment of group formation, the incentives available to individual groups, and the governing status of groups can manifestly change the group system.

The experience of countries that are now recognized as having the "right" kinds of groups, moreover, bears out the importance of such deliberate efforts to shape the group environment. While corporatist systems of wage bargaining and peak negotiation may have benefited from preexisting religious solidarities, they were commonly built, deliberately, on the wreckage of much more contentious industrial relations. While regional economies may be furthered by the social linkages of independent agrarian communities, today those linkages are fabricated by efforts to seed joint projects and lower information costs. While apprenticeship vocational training may draw on longstanding traditions of craft production and employer obligation, the organizational base of such training, and the base of craft production itself, are secured through legally required memberships in organizations and protection of small producers. There is nothing "natural" about such efforts to secure appropriate associative ends, and nothing in "nature" that has precluded their success.

Undesirability

Still, efforts to enlist associations in democratic governance may be undesirable. While groups can contribute to democratic order, and while their contribution can be secured through public policy, they can also work to undermine democratic order. This threat of "faction" was evident in our own inventory, offered earlier, of the practical problems now faced by democratic egalitarianism. Each problem suggested an impairment of democracy produced by the existing system of secondary association. If our associative strategy entails the further cultivation of groups, and the ceding to them of further public powers, does it not risk making faction truly ruinous?

Before addressing this question, we need to enter some background remarks aimed at clarifying the issues it raises.

The problem of faction has been a particular preoccupation of American politics and democratic theory ever since James Madison announced it as the key issue of American constitutional design.[21] But it must be faced by any liberal order, by reason of one of the defining features of such order: the protection of associative liberties. Once associative liberties are protected, associations inevitably follow. And, inevitably, legitimately, and without malfeasance, some of those associations will use their powers in pursuit of their aims in ways that frustrate the satisfaction of basic democratic norms. They will represent members in ways that undermine political equality; they will capture areas of policy in ways that undermine popular sovereignty and the promotion of the general welfare; in "doing their job" of advancing member interests, they will

---

[21] See James Madison, Federalist 10, in *The Federalist* (New York: G. P. Putnam's Sons, 1907), pp. 51–60. We are concerned here only with what Madison called "minority" faction.

inevitably promote particularism in place of deliberative politics. The threat of faction is, then, inescapable in any regime with associative liberties. Moreover, since those liberties are fundamental, the issue is how to mitigate that threat, not how to remove it.

The characteristic forms of faction were suggested earlier. There is, first, a pathology of inequality. Given inequalities in organization arising naturally from the background of market capitalism, group efforts to represent the interests of their members may simply compound political inequality rather than relieve it. Political inequality may then compound material inequality, as groups use their political powers to improve their material position, in a vicious cycle of privilege. Second, there is a pathology of particularism. Groups are, by their very nature, to some degree particularistic. Only some citizens are represented in them, group leaders are (at best) accountable to their members and not others, and the interests and ideals of groups are not shared by all citizens. Representing their members faithfully, particular groups thus often seek policies that impose costs to the society at large even as they provide gains for their own members, and promote a politics of narrow advantage and bargaining that corrupts the ideal of public deliberation about the common good. Commonly, inequality and particularism both thrive, as overrepresented interests bargain with one another, divide the political spoils, and so preserve their privileges until the next round of bargaining begins.

The problem of faction is serious, then; it is also inevitable, so long as associative liberties are preserved. Since threats of faction are inevitable, it would be a mistake to attribute them to the associative strategy or to expect that strategy to eliminate faction. But since those problems are serious, it would be objectionable if the associative strategy increased the threat of faction. The question raised by the second objection, then, is whether pursuit of associative strategy would make the problem of faction worse.

To address this question fully, we would need to consider the likely effects of the associative strategy on each of the defining norms of egalitarian democracy: popular sovereignty, political equality, distributive equity, deliberative politics, and the operation of society for the general welfare. In the interests of space, we propose to focus here solely on the norm of popular sovereignty, though our treatment of it will suggest the shape of our more general response. Recall that that norm requires that the authorization of state action be determined (within the limits set by fundamental civil and political liberties) by procedures in which citizens are represented as equals. Our question then becomes: Would the pursuit of our associative strategy undermine the ultimate authority of the people in the formation of policy?

In answering this question, we assume that all associations, including those vested with quasi-public powers, will operate within a political system with encompassing formal institutions organizing representation along traditional territorial lines. We assume, then, a possibility of "exit" from the group-based system of interest representation to the more traditionally organized system. Moreover, we assume that the group system is itself regulated by the traditional system. Final formal authority resides with traditional institutions. Associations will depend on them for authorizations of certain of their powers, and for material support in carrying such authorizations out.

With these background assumptions in mind, we want first to indicate four sorts of positive-sum relationship between associations and the democratic state—four ways, that is, that the fuller and more explicit incorporation of groups into governance roles might actually enhance the exercise of popular sovereignty through the traditional institutions and practices of territorial representation.

First, groups provide the state with information, thus permitting better definition of problems, and greater precision in the selection of means for addressing them. By thus sharpening policy instruments, and enabling them to be applied with greater precision, groups promote the capacity of the people to achieve its aims. Second, groups provide additional enforcement power, thus increasing the likelihood that decisions made by the people will be implemented.[22] Third, in mitigating enforcement problems, groups remove one important constraint on political debate. Instead of proposals being short-circuited with the claim that they are unenforceable, a wider range of proposals can be seriously discussed. Fourth, a more open politics of associations makes explicit a condition which is already a standing feature of even the most liberal of societies, namely that secondary associations do in fact perform a variety of functions that affect the conditions of political order. The associative strategy "exposes and brings out into the open, it institutionalizes a factor in lawmaking that we have, eagerly in fact, attempted to obscure."[23] By bringing the role of associations "into the open," it would make the exercise of power by associations more accountable. In combination, better and more flexible means, better enforcement, less-constrained debate about ends and their achievement, and more openness and accountability in the exercise of power all count as important gains for popular sovereignty.

These four contributions are, however, accompanied by three sources of serious concern—of negative-sum relations between the powers of associations and egalitarian-democratic order.

First, there are problems of disjunction of interest between the leaderships of groups and their members—the problem of the "iron law of

---

[22] See, for example, the discussion of "fire-alarm" enforcement in Mathew D. McCubbins and Thomas Schwartz, "Congressional Oversight Overlooked: Police Patrols vs. Fire Alarms," *American Journal of Political Science*, vol. 28 (1984), pp. 165–79.

[23] Louis Jaffe, "Law-Making by Private Groups," *Harvard Law Review*, vol. 51 (1937), pp. 220–21.

oligarchy." A dense world of association may make the government more informed about, and more responsive to, the interests of group "oligarchs" but not members. Second, there is the problem of independent powers — what might be called the "Frankenstein" issue. Endowed with quasi-public status, and commonly subsidized by the state, groups that at one point in time contribute to decent policy may continue to exercise power after outgrowing their usefulness, use that power to freeze their position, and so work to distort future debate and choice. Third, increasing the extent of policy making outside of formal legislative arenas increases threats of improper delegation. In particular, powers delegated to associations are bound to be vague. As in the context of legislative delegations to administrative agencies, then, there are problems about the abuse of the discretion permitted by such vagueness.

What are we to make of these problems? To make the case for associative democracy, it should be clear, we do not need to show that the strategy will solve these problems. They already exist, and will remain in place so long as freedom of association is guaranteed. It is enough to show that associative democracy will not plausibly make the problems worse. Moreover, if the same deliberate politics of association that harnesses group contributions can mitigate the threat of faction, that should count as an added support for the argument. In considering the three problems just noted, it appears to us that this burden can be carried, and that the promise of actual advance on curbing faction can be redeemed.

Beginning with internal democracy, the chief threat of the associative strategy appears to be its potential encouragement of large, encompassing, bureaucratic associations of the sort capable of taking broad responsibility for the coordination of social interests. These, it might be thought, are likely to suffer from even greater problems of internal responsiveness than the existing population of organizations. A recurrent example used in critical discussions is the distant, professionalized leadership of centralized trade-union federations, whose "social responsibility" in dealings with employers and the state is seen to come at the expense of the concerns of actual members.

Given the decline of centralized union bargaining, the example may be of diminished empirical relevance. But it suffices to carry the concern. And it remains an instructive test of the intuitive assumption that responsiveness of leadership to group membership must decline as group encompassingness, size, and social responsibility increase. For in fact it suggests that the intuitive assumption is without foundations. There is no correlation between the opportunities for voice and exit that encourage responsiveness and the conditions necessary for peak bargaining. On a variety of measures of internal union democracy, for example, the Norwegian union movement, among the most centralized and encompassing in the world, is more internally democratic than unions in the United Kingdom, comprising one of the least centralized union movements, which are in turn more democratic than the unions of West Germany, which are intermediate in their level of centralization.[24]

If the union case is credited, internal responsiveness need not come at the expense of external capacity. Moreover, internal responsiveness can be designed into large organizations through their internal procedures. In combination, these points suggest that oligarchy is more plastic than the "iron law" suggests. More immediately, they suggest a natural response to the problem of disjunction: require greater use of internal democratic procedures among groups that are granted quasi-public status. Operationally, the requirement should be that groups accorded this status provide evidence that they in fact represent their members by showing that they actually use some mechanism of responsiveness. Infinite gradations in degree and differences in judgment are certainly imaginable here, just as they are in ongoing disputes over the representativeness of electoral systems. But as the case of electoral systems also suggests, it is possible to articulate a general principle of legitimacy, in this case internal responsiveness, and to use that general principle to guide debate about specific proposals.

Our second problem, the "Frankenstein" problem of independent powers, also carries a natural response, namely some variant of "sunset legislation." The quasi-public status of groups (and subsidies to them) should be reviewed on a regular basis, with a rebuttable presumption that the status (or subsidies) will be withdrawn or amended as group behavior, or perceived social needs, warrant. The general requirements are reasonably clear, though their precise elaboration is not. On the one hand, the threat of withdrawal must be sufficiently credible, and the gains associated with public status sufficiently great, to induce groups to meet accountability requirements and other conditions on their conduct. On the other hand, since continuity in bargaining relations is an important prerequisite of gains, the requirements must not be so exacting as to make them impossible to satisfy.

Of course, the ultimate guard against independent powers is the vitality of the system dispensing the powers in the first place. This fact is precisely what gives normative force to our assumption, above, that systems relying heavily on group-based representation still rest final authority in encompassing territorial organizations. For evaluating associative democracy, the narrow issue here is whether, *ceteris paribus*, that system is made more or less vital by the increase in its democratic capacity that would follow on its enlistment of the energies of representative groups. And to ask that question is to answer it.

---

[24] See Peter Lange, *Union Democracy and Liberal Corporatism: Exit, Voice, and Wage Regulation in Postwar Europe*, Cornell Studies in International Affairs, Occasional Paper No. 16. The measures include rules governing election to union councils, intermediate organizations, and national office; the incidence and support of informal caucuses; and procedures for debate and vote on strikes, contracts, and other sorts of concerted action.

Finally, we offer two thoughts on the third problem noted above: the problem of vague delegations of power and the attendant risks of abused discretion. The first of these is simply a plea for realism and fairness in evaluation. The threat of vague delegations of powers in our associative scheme should not be contrasted with some ideal world, but the one that exists, and alternative reform proposals for that world. When it is, the contrast does not seem particularly damning. In the existing world, there is already much vague delegation to and exercise of discretion by administrative agencies. If we consider a scheme of more limited government as a means to cabin discretion, then we need to keep in mind that such a scheme is unlikely to serve the egalitarian democratic aims at issue here. If we consider a scheme with stronger legislative controls—less vagueness in delegation and more sharply formulated legislative standards—then we should consider familiar cautions that it may lead to an unwelcome politicization of legislative instruction, reflected in unreasonable goals, improbable deadlines on their achievement, or simple legislative deadlock.[25] Nor is there any reason to think that such reasonable requirements as clarity in the statement of statutory goals would be inconsistent with the associative scheme.

Moving now to a more positive engagement with the issue, we propose to address the problem of delegation through performance criteria. Where associations are involved in the enforcement and administration of policy, public institutions should formulate clear performance standards for groups to enforce and administer, while avoiding detailed specification of the means to be used in meeting those standards. For example, in the area of workplace health, there might be performance standards in the form of permissible exposure limits for hazardous chemicals, while decisions about the means for implementing those limits would fall to health and safety committees. When associations are involved in the formation of policy, the discretion ingredient in grants of quasi-public status can again be addressed by setting performance criteria—for example, minimum standards for skills, knowledge, courses, and examinations in vocational training programs whose operation is coordinated by labor and business in particular sectors. Even where groups do not enjoy subsidies for their performance of quasi-public duties, they should be regulated in the conduct of those duties. Where they are officially granted quasi-public status, or material state assistance, then performance criteria can be more exacting.

In sum, then, our response to the undesirability objection is that dangers of faction in the area of popular sovereignty could be mitigated by

---

[25] These effects are noted in Cass Sunstein, "Constitutionalism after the New Deal," *Harvard Law Review*, vol. 101 (1987), pp. 480–81: "The movement toward increased congressional control is not without risks of its own [since] . . . undue specificity may produce regulation riddled by factional tradeoffs."

requirements on internal democracy, legislative and judicial oversight, sunset laws that threaten a group with competition for its position, and performance standards. Moreover, we think that similar measures of internal accountability, external oversight, and competition could be deployed to mitigate problems of faction that arise on the other dimensions of democracy (political equality, etc.). But we have not, of course, argued this here, and to that extent the discussion of faction is importantly incomplete. It might, for example, be argued that an associative strategy for equalizing political representation would generate cartels or other concentrations of economic power that would, in turn, present intolerable threats to economic efficiency. We disagree with this objection, and think that some of the comparative evidence discussed in Section II speaks against it. Nevertheless, we think it raises a serious problem and that a fuller discussion of the associative idea would need to show in detail how it could be met.

IV. THE AMERICAN CASE

Thus far we have argued that associative solutions are, in the abstract, attractive ways of advancing democratic ideals, and that the factional potential of such solutions can be tamed by the same strategy of constructive artifice that enlists group contributions. Still, the idea of associative democracy may seem of little relevance to the United States. More than any other economically advanced mass democracy, the United States has a strongly anti-collectivist political culture, a weak state, and a civil society dominated by (relatively disorganized) business interests. The potential for artifice granted, this context poses obvious problems for the associative strategy. At best, it might be thought, the absence of any initial favoring conditions makes the strategy irrelevant. There is simply not enough to get started down the path of democratic associative reform. At worst, it might be feared, pursuit of the strategy under these conditions would be a political nightmare. Giving new license to a congeries of group privilege and particularism, it would exacerbate inequalities and further corrupt and enfeeble the state.

Such concerns have considerable force, and deserve a fuller answer than we can provide here. Briefly, however, while we acknowledge the anti-collectivism of much American political culture, we also see considerable experimentation now going on with associative solutions to policy problems in such areas as regional health and welfare service delivery, local economic development, education and training, and environmental regulation, among many others.

There is, for example, a tradition of delivering many welfare and social services through secondary associations — community organizations, churches, volunteer agencies, and the like. While such organizations often have substantial autonomy in designing the appropriate service mix for the communities they are asked to serve, they are also increasingly inextricably dependent on government fees for such services for their own survival.[26] Much "public" input in local economic development is decided, for good or ill, in "community development corporations," heavily subsidized by government grants, representing different admixtures of independent neighborhood associations and business firms.[27] In education, parent-teacher associations are commonly vested with substantial powers in determining the budget and curriculum of elementary and secondary public schools, and those schools increasingly look to local business interests for support in setting standards on student performance.[28] In training, the largest single training program in the United States, the Job Training Partnership Act (JTPA), is almost wholly administered through "private industry councils" dominated, by statute, by local business interests.[29] In environmental regulation, from the deliberate promotion of bargaining among industry and environmental groups as a prelude to standard setting at the federal level, to the promotion of bargaining between business and community organizations over the appropriate implementation of environmental standards in local neighborhoods and regions, policy is rife with secondary associations exercising de facto public powers.[30]

Some of these efforts display the great strengths of associative governance; others display its many dangers. Our point here is simply that such governance in fact goes on, widely, even in this liberal culture. And its incidence provides a natural basis for more deliberate, and democratic, associative strategies.

[26] For an instructive discussion of the role of nonprofit organizations in welfare-state service delivery, emphasizing the increased dependence of many of these agencies on their ties to government, see Steven Rathgeb Smith and Michael Lipsky, *The Age of Contracting: Nonprofit Agencies and the Welfare State* (Cambridge: Harvard University Press, forthcoming).

[27] A useful (though not impartial) recent survey of local economic development strategies is provided in R. Scott Fosler, *Local Economic Development* (Washington: International City Management Association, 1991).

[28] For an enthusiastic review of some of the emerging linkages between schools and private business associations, see Anthony Carnevale, Leila Gainer, Janice Villet, and Shari Holland, *Training Partnerships: Linking Employers and Providers* (Alexandria: American Society for Training and Development, 1990).

[29] JTPA has been widely criticized as insufficiently accountable to public needs. Among others, see John D. Donahue, *Shortchanging the Workforce: The Job Training Partnership Act and the Overselling of Privatized Training* (Washington: Economic Policy Institute, 1989); United States General Accounting Office (GAO), *Job Training Partnership Act: Inadequate Oversight Leaves Program Vulnerable to Waste, Abuse, and Mismanagement*, GAO/HRD-91-97 (Washington: General Accounting Office, 1991).

[30] Some of the federal experience is reviewed in Charles W. Powers, *The Role of NGOs in Improving the Employment of Science and Technology in Environmental Management* (New York: Carnegie Commission on Science, Technology, and Government, May 1991); the experience of local communities in fostering such environmental bargaining among organized groups is reviewed in Valjean McLenighan, *Sustainable Manufacturing: Saving Jobs, Saving the Environment* (Chicago: Center for Neighborhood Technology, 1990).

Moreover, while we acknowledge the weakness of the American state, we think that at least some sorts of associative reforms can make it stronger. Particularly given a weak state, it is important that group empowerment proceed in a way that is reliably positive-sum with state power. But this merely requires judgment in the choice of associative strategies. It does not generally bar their pursuit. And while we acknowledge, finally, the overwhelming business dominance of the American polity, we think this again simply constrains choice in the groups that are advantaged through the associative strategy. If business is too powerful, then associative resources should be provided to labor or other non-business-dominated groups; the current imbalance is not an argument for abandoning the general idea.

Most generally, we agree that the United States has high levels of inequality, a less-than-competent government, and weak cooperative institutions—that, in brief, it does not work well as a democracy. This, in fact, is the very problem that provides our point of departure. We move, then, to some examples of how an associative strategy might proceed from this point of departure in this distinctive polity. We offer two illustrations of the general look and feel of the associative project: the reform of worker representation and industrial relations in the United States, and the reform of vocational training. In each case we sketch some problems that need to be addressed, indicate the ways that a richer associational setting might help in addressing them, and discuss some measures that might now be taken to promote that setting.

Worker representation

Our goal here—controversial, and surely bitterly contested—would be to improve the organization of American workers. Such improvement would plausibly contribute to the satisfaction of democratic norms in a variety of ways. By extending and deepening the benefits of organized representation to those who are now unorganized or under-organized, it would advance the goal of political equality. It would also have a fair chance of improving distributive equity and economic performance in the United States. At the same time, properly structured worker organization is of particular importance because work is important. The associative framework that determines how it is organized, distributed, and rewarded sets the background and tone for associative action throughout much of the society. So other reforms are more likely to succeed if reforms here succeed.[31]

The system of worker organization in the United States currently suffers from two related problems. First, very few substantive benefits are

---

[31] The force of this claim will emerge in our discussion of the role of associations in vocational training.

provided to workers simply as citizens. We have a low "social" wage. Most benefits are instead provided through individual firms. But benefits are costly and firms compete. So there are obvious incentives to skimp on the provision of benefits. The result is comparatively low and uneven substantive protection for workers.

Second, the system discourages cooperation between employers and employees. Part of the reason for this is the generally low level of worker organization. Genuine cooperation is based on mutual respect, which typically depends on recognition of mutual power. With the disorganization of workers limiting their power, however, employees are commonly incapable of extracting from employers the sorts of institutionalized respect for their interests (e.g., a serious commitment to job security, or consultation in advance of work reorganization) needed to elicit genuine cooperation. The other part of the reason has to do with the structure of union organization. In general, mimicking the decentralized benefit system, unions themselves are highly decentralized. Where they have power, then, they have incentives to free-ride on the interests of others, and to seek maximum reward for their particular labor. Decentralization does permit wildcat cooperation. More commonly, however, it—in conjunction with the low social wage—promotes an economistic job-control unionism unfavorable to cooperation. Altogether, then, an environment featuring a low social wage, low union density, and highly decentralized union organization is dense with incentives to collectively irrational conflict.[32]

This diagnosis suggests four related steps of associative reform of this system: (1) lower the barriers to unionization; (2) encourage alternative forms of self-directed worker organization; (3) raise the social wage; and (4) promote more centralization in wage bargaining, while permitting high levels of decentralization in bargaining over specific work conditions. We consider these in turn.

Even within the current framework of U.S. labor law—which centers on collective bargaining between elected and exclusive worker representatives (unions) and employers—strategies for reducing barriers to worker representation are clear enough. Elections of representatives could be simplified and expedited, bargaining obligations could attach early and survive the arrival of successor employers, the right to use economic force could be enhanced, and, throughout, violations of labor regulation could be remedied with compensatory damages rather than toothless "make whole" remedies. In a more ambitious scheme of reforms, representation

---

[32] For a general review of the U.S. industrial relations system emphasizing these interactions, see Joel Rogers, "Divide and Conquer: 'Further Reflections on the Distinctive Character of American Labor Law,'" *Wisconsin Law Review*, 1990, pp. 1–147; for a recent review of the state of the American labor movement, see the contributions to George Strauss, Daniel G. Gallagher, and Jack Fiorito, eds., *The State of the Unions* (Madison: Industrial Relations Research Association, 1991).

might be awarded upon a simple demonstration of support from a majority of affected workers, rather than the elaborate demonstration elections now required; the individual rights of workplace members of unions without majority status might be enhanced; restraints on the coordination of unions in using economic force could be relaxed; greater attention could be given to the practical requirements of union "security" in maintaining a workplace presence; current restraints on the use of member dues for organizing the unorganized, and for political action, could be relaxed.[33]

Even with such reforms in place, however, most of the economy will remain nonunion, leaving most workers without representation. We would suggest, then, that forms of workplace representation alternative to, though not in direct competition with, unions also be encouraged. This could be achieved directly through a mandate of workplace committees with responsibilities in, for example, occupational health and safety, or training, or areas of concern apart from wages. Alternatively, or as a supplement, government purchasing contracts might be used to enhance worker voice. Eligibility for such contracts could be conditioned on successful employer demonstration of the existence of a works council or some other acceptable form of autonomous employee representation with real powers in the administration of the internal labor market.

The increased levels of worker organization that could be expected to follow on these two changes would mitigate one of the barriers to cooperation noted earlier, namely the weakness of labor organization. With labor stronger, it is possible to imagine a new social contract in the internal labor market, one that would promote cooperation. The terms of the contract are simple enough: labor offers flexibility on internal-labor-market work rules and greater job commitment in exchange for management's commitment to consultation and heightened job security.

To ensure fairness, however, and to promote the stability of associations that contributes to their beneficial effects, a system of multiple worker organizational forms would need an increase in the social wage — our third initiative. For workers, an increased social wage would provide some assurances of fair treatment and security external to the firm. Aside from its direct distributional benefits, this increase would relieve pressures for the internal rigidity and defensiveness associated with job-control unionism. It would make more flexible, productivity-enhancing strategies of work organization more appealing. For employers, the mitigation of job-control consciousness (and the likely reduction of labor costs) among organized workers would remove one powerful incentive to resist worker association in their firms.

---

[33] There are many such statements of possible labor-law reform. A good guide to the issues involved, containing both more and less ambitious recommendations for reform, is provided by Paul Weiler, *Governing the Workplace: The Future of Labor and Employment Law* (Cambridge: Harvard University Press, 1990).

Finally, greater coordination of wage contracts would be needed to overcome a second barrier to cooperation and to reap the full benefits for economic performance. As noted earlier, the American system of contract negotiation is highly decentralized. It is unreasonable to expect the United States to approximate the corporatist peak bargaining of the late 1970s (especially since corporatist systems themselves no longer approximate that). Still, some measures could be undertaken to encourage more encompassing associations than now exist, thus generating an environment better suited to some greater centralization and coordination of wage negotiations (at least on a regional basis).

One step would be to amend the law governing multi-employer bargaining, shifting the presumption away from the voluntariness and instability of such arrangements toward their requirement. In addition, pressures within the union movement for consolidation could be strengthened by selective incentives, for example, in the form of funds for (re)training, conditioned on inter-union cooperation. Government support for business cooperation—for example, consortia pursuing joint research and development strategies—could be conditioned on efforts to consolidate wage policies. Or, following common practice in most systems, "extension laws" on bargaining contracts could be enacted, generalizing their results to nonunion settings.

The effect of this combination of increasing the social wage and promoting more generalization of wage patterns across firms would be to discriminate more sharply between the focus of bargaining within the firm and the focus of bargaining outside it. Within the firm, unions would come to look more like employee-participation schemes, and employee-participation schemes would look more like unions. Worker representation would be secured, but with a particular focus on regulating the internal labor market, and increasing productivity within it, through innovation on issues of job design, work organization, access to training on new firm technology, and the like. Outside the firm, more encompassing organizations, suitable to handling matters affecting workers in general, rather than workers in a particular firm, would be more empowered to pursue that object. They would focus more on securing generalizable wage agreements and the content of the social wage.

Such a system, which relies on associative empowerment and artifice throughout, would likely be a vast improvement on current American industrial relations. It would improve representation, increase productivity, generalize the benefits of cooperation, and better integrate the industrial relations system with state economic and welfare policies.

Vocational training

Our second example of constructive group artifice comes from the area of vocational training. In the United States, as in most other rich countries, intensified international competition and rapid technological change have underscored the need for improvements in workforce skills. To preserve living standards in face of low-wage competition from abroad, labor must be made substantially more productive and firms must become increasingly adept at such "nonprice" aspects of product competition as quality, variety, customization, and service. Success here will require, *inter alia*, that "frontline" production and nonsupervisory workers be equipped with substantially higher and broader skills than they presently possess.

The vocational training problem in the United States consists in the fact that such skills are being provided in insufficient quality and quantity by U.S. schools and firms, and insofar as they are provided, they are directed to college-bound youths and managers. In the public school system, very little occupational training is provided for the "forgotten half" of each high-school cohort that does not go on to college, or the "forgotten three-quarters" of each cohort that does not complete it. And U.S. employers provide their frontline workforce with far less training than do leading foreign competitors. Moreover, the training they do provide is generally narrower than is desirable—for the economy as a whole, for innovative firms drawing from the external labor market, and for individual workers, who typically change employers several times in their working lifetimes.[34] With skills more essential than ever to compensation, the failures of U.S. training have powerfully contributed to the decline in production and nonsupervisory worker wages experienced over the last generation, and to rising inequality in U.S. market incomes.[35]

The problems in the American training system lie on both the "demand" and "supply" sides. We will concentrate here on the supply side, focusing in particular on two central issues.[36]

---

[34] For general reviews of U.S. training problems, making all these points, see U.S. Congress, Office of Technology Assessment, *Worker Training: Competing in the International Economy*, OTA ITE-457 (Washington: Government Printing Office, 1990); and Commission on the Skills of the American Workforce, *America's Choice: High Skills or Low Wages!* (Rochester: National Center on Education and the Economy, 1990).

[35] For a good review of wage trends in the United States, and the more general decline in living standards among nonsupervisory workers, see Lawrence Mishel and David M. Frankel, *The State of Working America*, 1990–91 edition (Armonk: M. E. Sharpe, 1990).

[36] A word of explanation on the focus. Demand by American employers for high and broad frontline workforce skills is extremely weak and uneven. Unless this changes, supply-side innovations geared to improving skill delivery to frontline workers will risk having all the effect of "pushing on a string." Moreover, competitive pressures acting alone cannot be counted on to change the structure of employer demand in the desired way, since employers can choose to respond to those pressures by reducing wages, increasing firm productivity through changes in work organization that "dumb down" most jobs while increasing the human-capital component of a well-paid few, or simply moving away from high-end markets. Most U.S. firms, in fact, have chosen some combination of these "low wage, low skill" competitive strategies. To remedy the demand-side problem, it is essential to foreclose this option. The most obvious way to do this is to build stable floors under wages, and effective linkage between productivity improvements and wage compensation, thus forcing employers to be more attentive to strategies for increasing the productivity of

First, the quality of public-school vocational training is limited by the absence of effective linkages with the economy itself. Most public vocational training in the United States is essentially "stand alone" classroom-based instruction, and while such instruction is certainly important for any training system, it has intrinsic limits.[37] As a general matter, the system will lag behind industry practice in its provision of skills. It will be baffled by the need to make large expenditures on capital equipment, of the sort needed to replicate factories inside schools. And it will have difficulty conveying to students the active knowledge they need to flourish in, and can only acquire from, real-world production situations.

To remedy these problems, denser linkages must be forged between schools and students, on the one side, and employers and their workers, on the other. Through such linkages can flow that which the classroom system now lacks: up-to-date knowledge on industry trends, loans and grants of current equipment on which to train, and, all important, access to actual workplaces, and their principals, for work-based instruction complementary to what goes on in the classroom.

Second, while the quantity of training supplied by government could be expected to increase as a result of the reform of worker representation discussed earlier, the effort by employers must also be substantially increased and improved. Here, the problem is in part that employers are uncertain about the sorts of broad-banded skills that would be appropriate to provide, and in part that they have no confidence that they will capture the returns to training in such skills. Employer training suffers, that is, both from a lack of agreed-upon standards for coordinated training, and from the positive externalities that accompany an open external labor market in which workers are able to move freely among firms, so that one firm's trainee can become another firm's asset. The externalities problem is particularly acute for high and broad skills. Since such skills are, by definition, of use in a wide variety of work settings, their possession increases the potential mobility of workers, enabling one firm to

---

their labor (e.g., skill upgrading). Direct state action can help here, by increasing minimum-wage floors. As regards more specifically associative reform, however—and this is why we do not linger on the demand side—we believe the most important actions are those already outlined in the recommendations just made on improving industrial relations. Deeper and more encompassing worker organizations, especially ones shaped by social interests in improved cooperation, would help create the needed wage floors, wage-productivity linkages, and pressures within firms to upgrade. Moreover, they could be expected to do so in a way that not only raised the aggregate demand for skills and their compensation, but improved the distribution of both. The basic problem on the demand side is that the interests of the bulk of the population, workers, are simply not now centrally in the picture. They are barely represented in the economy, and only very imperfectly represented in the state. The basic solution to under-representation is to improve the conditions of their organization in ways consistent with other democratic norms.

[37] The importance of these limits rises where, as in the United States, the public training system lacks any effective industry-based-training complement.

appropriate the benefits of another firm's training efforts. This is part of the reason that when firms do train, they train narrowly, in job-specific or firm-specific skills.

To remedy the problem of coordination, a mechanism for setting common standards and expectations is necessary. To remedy the externality problem, there are two basic solutions. One is to reduce worker mobility across firms. This permits firms to train workers with the confidence that they recoup any investments made. In effect, this is what is done in Japan. The other solution is to socialize the costs of private-firm training, so that individual employers will not care about worker mobility. This can be done with the assistance of the tax system—for example, in the form of "train or tax" rules, requiring firms either to train or to pay into some general fund. Or it can be done through the private collective organization of employers to a point that they can discipline free riders or, at high levels of joint participation (where close to all relevant competitors or poachers train), become indifferent to them. In effect, this is what is done in successful European training systems, which, like those in the United States, operate with relatively open external labor markets and high rates of inter-firm worker mobility.

As the second, European strategy makes clear, the presence of competent, encompassing, employer and labor associations immensely aids both in addressing the problem of linkage between the worlds of school and work, and in increasing the level and quality of employer-sponsored training.

Facilitating linkage, associations provide the state with timely information on emerging industry trends and practices, new technologies, and skill needs, and with access to the insides of firms. They permit industries to speak with a unified voice to public training providers, to negotiate authoritatively with the state over training curricula, access to firms, requirements on skills certification, rules on the use of equipment, and the like. They permit the state to get closure and enforcement on decisions once made—"If you don't like it, talk to your association" being a far more effective retort to second-guessing firms than "Well, that's just what we decided to do"—while providing monitoring and enforcement capacities to supplement any public training effort. And being broad in their representation, and accountable to members, associations are natural vehicles for developing general standards, of wide applicability, of the sort that protect the training investment made by employees themselves.

Facilitating employer training efforts, industry associations help in part by setting general standards on skills—something no single firm can do. The identification of commonly desired competencies assures workers that acquiring those competencies will improve their position on the external labor market. This leads to increased take-up rates on training, assuring employers of a large pool of workers with high and common skills. And this assurance encourages more proactive industry strategies of upgrading and inter-firm cooperation in implementing those strategies.

But associations also act to facilitate employer training efforts by mitigating the externality problem that discourages those efforts. They require training as a condition of membership, or of receipt of its benefits. They monitor the training that goes on, relieving fears of "suckering." They ease the flow of information about new technology and work practices among members, providing a natural vehicle for voluntary industry benchmarking that creates upward pressures on existing standards. They share training facilities and curricula among themselves, reducing per-capita training costs. More elusive but not less important, they help define and sustain—through means ranging from social gatherings and award dinners to insider gossip and plum subcontracting deals—common norms of "accepted practice." As such norms congeal into obligatory industrial cultures, those who undersupply training come to be seen less as clever businessmen than as social pariahs, to be punished with loss of status and business. This can powerfully discourage even temptations to defection, making the consideration of cooperation more familiar, extending and securing its reach, and lowering monitoring costs. In all these ways, a strong employer association, especially one "kept honest" by a strong union, can provide a powerful boost to the quality and extent of firm training efforts.

How might associative supports be enlisted for a revamped vocational training system in the United States? In general terms, the problems and the instruments at hand to solve them are clear enough. Both labor and employer associations are relatively weak in the United States. Both need to be strengthened, at least in their capacity to discipline their own members, and to deal with one another and with the state effectively, on training matters. Very little public money now goes directly to these purposes, even though the lessons of comparative experience clearly indicate their virtue. Public supports—in the form of direct cash assistance, technical assistance, a greater role in curriculum development, increased legal powers to enforce obligations against their own members—can be provided in exchange for help in carrying out the important public task of training the workforce.

For example, significant improvement in the quality of vocational training will require some recognized occupational standards. But outside a few specialized trades, these do not exist. Joining with public training providers, existing unions and employer associations could be invited, on an industry-by-industry basis, to develop such standards. Their work could be facilitated by the state, in the form of modest financial supports and technical assistance. And it should not be accepted by the state without independent evaluation. But some product should finally be accepted, and enforced as a standard. Such enforcement will naturally be advanced by the primary authors themselves. Employers would look to demonstrated competence, according to these standards, in the awarding of jobs in internal labor markets. Unions would center on them in wage negotiations, or in rules governing job assignments in those markets. But such private actions can also be supplemented through public means. The standard can be made applicable to all federally funded vocational training programs, for example, and adopted as a standard in arbitration and judicial decisions in labor and employment law.[38]

The competency of labor and trade associations to provide training services to members may be explicitly promoted by public policy as well. Public subsidies and technical assistance to such organizations for this purpose, utterly routine in other countries and already tried with some success with a handful of trade and labor organizations in the United States, would be a natural supportive policy. Anti-trust law could be relaxed for joint training activities of member firms;[39] additional amendments may be needed in labor law, to permit union-management cooperation in training activities involving nonunion firms.[40]

Both of the examples just presented involve efforts to improve training by strengthening existing associations. But the formation of new associations around training might be encouraged as well. Industry or regional training consortia composed of firms and unions, for example, could be encouraged through demonstration grant assistance, technical aid, and discounts on public training services provided to their members.[41] These supports would properly be conditioned on those associations providing training services, participating in standard setting, mounting outreach programs to public schools, providing such schools with technical assistance, expanding existing apprenticeship programs (the best, albeit much neglected, example of vocational training in the United States), and otherwise cooperating with public providers, and each other, to move to a more aggressive and inclusive training agenda. The goal again would be to bring more order, and a critical mass, to private training efforts, and to improve effective linkages to schools.

Given the present weakness of associations in the United States, addressing the externality problem probably requires direct government efforts at socializing costs—through unqualified payroll levies or "play or

---

[38] The Department of Labor's Office of Work-Based Learning is already making qualified moves in this direction—"qualified" in that, outside more heavily unionized industries, it remains unclear what, if any, organized voice workers in the industry will have.

[39] Following current practice for joint research and development activities.

[40] Recommendations on how to do this are made in Margaret Hilton, "Shared Training: Learning from Germany," *Monthly Labor Review*, vol. 114, no. 3 (March 1991), pp. 33–37.

[41] An experiment along these lines is now underway in Milwaukee, where several firms (nonunion and unionized), unions, and public training providers have come together around a Wisconsin Manufacturing Training Consortium designed to do just these things. See Joel Rogers and Wolfgang Streeck, "Recommendations for Action" (Madison: Center on Wisconsin Strategy, 1991).

pay" levy structures. The revenues, however, can be used in ways that strengthen future private capacities for self-governance. Funds might, for example, be given to associations for redistribution. The effect would be to create enormous temptations to associations to organize themselves to take a more active role in training, and for firms and unions to join associations—in effect, an inducement to encompassingness of the sort desired. Or, in a "play or pay" scheme, tax relief could be granted to firms that demonstrate that the training they provide conforms with the standards set by industry associations. This would have the same effect of strengthening a collective associative hand in standards, and strengthening associations themselves.

There are many paths to virtue, but this should be enough to make the point. In principle, at least, the associative supports for a more successful vocational training system could be achieved in the United States with fairly standard policy instruments. Those supports would benefit both workers and "better" firms (i.e., those firms interested in upgrading). And, far from engendering further corruption of the state, they would strengthen public capacities to address problems of manifest public concern.

CONCLUSION

The examples just given provide no more than a couple of illustrations of the directions an associative democratic strategy might take in the United States. But they suffice to underscore the sorts of concerns that define that strategy and the considerations relevant to its execution. What we have argued in this essay, and what is displayed in the examples just given, is straightforward enough. To proceed, egalitarian politics must once again be shown to work. To work, it requires associative supports. Those supports can be developed. And developing them, and realizing their contribution to democratic governance, does not require a naive view of associations as free from the threat of faction, or a dangerous view on the surrender of encompassing public authority. Faction can be mitigated through the same artifice that enlists associative contributions, and the strength and competence of public authorities can be enhanced by their enlistment.

More broadly, by assuring greater equality in organized representation among private citizens, and by more effectively recruiting the energies of their organizations into public governance, the aim of the associative strategy is to forge an egalitarian-democratic order without an oppressive state. That is nice work if you can get it—and we have suggested that you can.

Philosophy and Political Science, Massachusetts Institute of Technology
Law, Political Science, and Sociology, University of Wisconsin–Madison

INDEX

313